Consciousness and the Urban Experience

*Studies in the History and Theory of
Capitalist Urbanization 1*

Consciousness and the Urban Experience

DAVID HARVEY

Basil Blackwell

First published in the United Kingdom by
Basil Blackwell Ltd
108 Cowley Road, Oxford OX4 1JF, UK

ACKNOWLEDGMENTS

"Labor, Capital, and Class Struggle around the Built Environment in Advanced Capitalist Societies" was first published in *Politics and Society* 7 (1977), and "Monument and Myth" first appeared in the *Annals. Association of American Geographers* 69, no. 3 (1979). I would like to thank the editors and publishers of these journals for permission to republish these materials here. Figure 1 is reprinted with permission from H. Clout, *Themes in the Historical Geography of France* (Academic Press, 1977) and figure 2 from J. Levron, *Grands travaux. grands architectes du passé* (Editions du Moniteur). Figures 4, 19, 20, 21, and 22 are printed with permission from the Musée Carnavelet and figure 15 by permission of the Louvre. Figure 13 comes from Photo Roger-Viollet; figure 16 from A. Dalotel, A. Faure, and J-C. Freirmuth, *Aux origines de la commune: Le mouvement des réunions publiques à Paris. 1868–70* (Editions Découverte, 1980); figure 17 from J. Rougerie, *Paris libre* (Seuil, 1971); and figure 24 is reproduced, with permission, from the *Collection d'affiches politiques* of Alain Gesgon.

British Library Cataloguing in Publication Data

Harvey, David, *1935 Oct. 31–*
 Consciousness and the urban experience.—
 (Studies in the history and theory of capitalist
 urbanization; 1)
 1. Urbanization   2. Capitalism
 I. Title   II. Series
 307.7'6   HT151
 ISBN 0–631–14574–5

Typeset by Freeman Graphic, Tonbridge
Printed in Great Britain by Page Bros (Norwich) Ltd

for claudia

It was, above all, out of my exploration of huge cities, out of the medley of their interrelations, that this haunting ideal was born.

— *Charles Baudelaire*

Contents

Figures

Tables

Preface

In *The American Scene,* Henry James makes frequent reference to a mythological character called "the restless analyst." I have long been impressed with that. It seems to capture the only kind of intellectual stance possible in the face of a capitalism that reduces all aspects of social, cultural, and political (to say nothing of economic) life to the pure homogeneity and universality of money valuations and then ruthlessly transforms them according to the roving calculus of profit. "Mankind can move mountains," wrote Isaiah Bowman, "but first we launch a bond issue." But there is no necessary security in that. The long swathes of "creative destruction" (a phrase coined, as we shall see, in Second Empire Paris) trailing across the physical and social landscape are hard to ignore. The roving calculus of profit destroys at the same time as it creates. "You sit there in the lurid light of business," says James, contemplating the seemingly solidly implanted buildings of New York, "and you know, without our reminding you, what guarantees, what majestic continuity and heredity *that* represents."

I like to think of these studies on the history and theory of capitalist urbanization, collected together in two companion volumes entitled *Consciousness and the Urban Experience* and *The Urbanization of Capital,* as products of some "restless analyst" of the urban scene. Like James, I view matters from a certain class perspective. But it is a very different class position to which I cleave. For it has been my ambition, ever since the writing of *Social Justice and the City,* to progress toward a definitive Marxian interpretation of the urban process under capitalism. The studies here presented are markings down that path.

I turned to the Marxian categories in the early 1970s, and reaffirm my faith in them here, as the only ones suited to the active construction of rigorous, comprehensive, and scientific understandings of something as complex and rich as the historical geography of the urban process under capitalism. The manner of construction of this science also makes political sense. Rigorous science can never be neutral in human affairs; attempts to put oneself outside of history at best produce rigorous and well-meaning pseudosciences, of which positivism is surely the best example. But Marx also argues that the conscious struggle to create an alternative to capitalism – call it socialism or communism – has to be based on thorough material understandings of how capitalism works and how its workings naturally generate certain states of political and social consciousness. In order to change the world, he seems to say, we have to understand it. But that process cannot be understood one-sidedly. Who, Marx asks, is to educate the educators? Revolutionary understandings of the world cannot be had out of passive contemplation but arise through active struggle. Only through changing the world can we change ourselves. Our task, therefore, is not to understand the world but to change it. But that slogan cannot be read too one-sidedly either. Active reflection on our understandings, critique of bourgeois ideology, the struggle to make Marxian concepts both plain and hegemonic, and the evaluation of our own historical experience of struggle are as important activities as active engagement on the barricades. That is why Marx wrote *Capital*. And that is why I can write these words.

To seek an understanding of capitalist urbanization in Marxian terms is to resort, however, to a framework of understanding that is controversial, incomplete, and in some respects highly problematic. I sought to do something about the incompleteness in *The Limits to Capital*. I there tried to fill in all kinds of "empty boxes" in Marxian theory, such as the circulation of fixed capital and built environment formation; the appropriation of rent; the workings of money, finance, and credit; the production of monetary and financial crises; and the like. I needed to theorize such phenomena if I was ever to construct a comprehensive theory of urbanization. But, curiously, most reviewers passed by (mainly, I suspect, out of pure disciplinary prejudice) what I thought to be the most singular contribution of that work – the integration of the production of space and spatial configurations as an active element within the core of Marxian theorizing. That was the key theoretical innovation that allowed me to shift from thinking about history to historical geography and so to open the way to theorizing about the urban process as an active moment in the historical geography of class struggle and capital accumulation.

I readily confess, of course, that much of my fascination with the spatial dimension of human affairs comes out of my disciplinary background in geography. But if, as Giddens (1981) insists, time-space relations are "constitutive features of social systems," then the question of space is surely too important to be left to geographers exclusively. Social theorists of all stripes and persuasions should take it seriously. Yet there has been a strong and almost overwhelming predisposition to give time and history priority over space and geography. Marx, Weber, Durkheim, and Marshall all have that in common. We consequently lack, as Giddens goes on to observe, the conceptual apparatus "which would make space, and the control of space, integral to social theory." That lack is doubly disturbing. To begin with, the insertion of concepts of space and space relations, of place, locale, and milieu, into any of the various supposedly powerful but spaceless social and theoretic formulations has the awkward habit of paralyzing that theory's central propositions. Microeconomists working with perfect competition find only spatial monopoly and prices that fail to produce equilibrium; macroeconomists find as many economies as central banks and a great deal of guesswork affecting relations between them; sociologists find all sorts of "space-time edges" that disturb otherwise coherent processes of structuration; and Marxists, employing a vocabulary appropriate to universal class relations, find neighborhoods, communities, and nations that partition class struggle and capital accumulation into strange configurations of uneven geographical development. Whenever social theorists actively interrogate the meaning of geographical and spatial categories, either they are forced to so many ad hoc adjustments that their theory splinters into incoherency or they are forced to rework very basic propositions. Small wonder, then, that Saunders (1981, 278), in a recent attempt to save the supposed subdiscipline of urban sociology from such an ugly fate, offers the extraordinary proposition, for which no justification is or ever could be found, that "the problems of space . . . must be severed from concern with specific social processes."

Marxists cannot, unfortunately, claim any superior virtue on this score. One searches the major Marxist journals in vain for serious discussion of spatial concepts and geographical dimensionality. Marx himself is partly to blame for this state of affairs. He certainly gave priority to time over space and was not averse to dismissing the question of geographical variation as an "unnecessary complication." To be sure, as I show in detail in *The Urbanization of Capital* (chap. 2), he sometimes admitted the importance of space and place, but this in no way compensates for theory that is powerful with respect to time but weak with respect to space. Historical materialism appeared to license the study of historical transformations while ignoring how capitalism produces its own geography. This left Lenin and the theorists of imperialism with a huge gap to fill. Unfortunately, they did so by ad hoc adjustments that permitted discussion of the development of capitalism in, say, Russia and India (as if such units made inherent sense) and provoked an alternative rhetoric of exploitation in which centers exploit peripheries, the First World subjugates the Third, and capitalist power blocs compete for domination of space (markets, labor supplies, raw materials, production capacity). But how can we reconcile the idea that people in one place exploit or struggle against those in another place with Marx's view of a capitalist dynamic powered by the exploitation of one class by another? Such ad hoc concessions to spatial questions as Lenin, Luxemburg, and the other theorists of imperialism introduced merely made the theoretical foundations of Marxism-Leninism ambiguous, sparking savage and often destructive disputes over the national question and the right to national self-determination, the significance of the urban-rural contradiction, the prospects for socialism in one country, the appropriate response to urban social movements, the importance of geographical decentralization, and the like. The ad hoc adjustments treated, unfortunately, of capitalism *in* space without considering how space is produced and how the processes of production of space integrate into the capitalist dynamic and its contradictions. Historical materialism has to be upgraded, therefore, to historical-geographical materialism. The historical geography of capitalism has to be the object of our theorizing.

That immediately poses the problem of the proper relation between historical geography (actually experienced) and theory. Much critical ado has been made about the supposed Marxist shortcomings in this regard, chiefly focusing on the enclosure of theory and evidence within such a coherent frame as to preclude "independent" verification. There are various levels of response to that criticism. Firstly, anyone who thinks that there is no problem in the way language of any sort captures experience and represents structures in the external world is flatulently and hypocritically preaching in the wind. The independence of data from theory is always relative. The choice, therefore, is between different modes of approach to a universal problem. There are, secondly, good reasons for preferring one kind of approach to another. The abstract theories of positivism, for example, must first be translated into working models (an exercise that necessarily encloses a representation of theory and data within the same frame) and then tested against data that are supposed to be samples of repetitive and independent events. Such a procedure is perfectly reasonable in relation to certain arenas of enquiry. But it is quite irrelevant to historical geography, which is a unique configuration of highly interdependent events in space and time. Measuring the growth of cities as if there were no trade, capital flow, migration, or cultural and political influence between them makes no sense whatsoever. For that reason, many historians, humanists, and historical geographers prefer to bury their theoretical and political orientations in the ambiguities of common language. Compared to the charming cacophony of that, positivism appears appealingly rigorous.

As a Marxist I am overtly rather than subliminally concerned with rigorous theory building in relation to unique configurations of historical-geographical processes. The theory building does not, however, take place in abstraction but entails a continuous dialogue between experience, action, concept formation, and dialectical theorizing. Since there is considerable and often heated debate within Marxist circles on such matters – including the celebrated polarization between the Althusserian structuralists and historians like E. P. Thompson – I should perhaps explain my own approach more clearly.

The testing of theory depends upon confrontation with experience. But I have never felt comfortable with the idea that there is something called "experience" unmediated by imagination. We always approach the world with some well-honed conceptual apparatus, the capital equipment of our intellect, and interpret the world broadly in those terms. Yet there are moments, events, people, and experiences that impinge upon imagination in unexpected ways, that jolt and jar received ways of thinking and doing, that demand some extra imaginative leap to give them meaning. The "restless analyst" is open to the unpredictable collision of experience and imagination that always lies at the root of new insight. Such creative moments of collision are not entirely accidental either. To be sure, hazard and chance play their part, but one can put oneself in the way of much of that, be an active explorer of urban life and process, open to the innumerable accidents (both good and bad) that can befall any of us. The city, Henri Lefebvre is fond of saying, "is the place of the unexpected"; and he, for one, appreciates and uses it so.

Experience comes in many guises. I wander the streets, play the *flâneur* (though somewhat too purposefully to be truly of that breed), watch people interact, eavesdrop on conversations, read the local newspapers (particularly the gossip pieces and crime reports that we intellectuals are supposed to disdain). Local political action (strike support work, rent control campaigns, the building of a political action center) and international political collaborations give a more collective dimension to experience. And then there is the literature – vast, rambling, diverse, sometimes purely rhetorical and polemical (and no less interesting for that) and at other times represented as dry-as-dust science. The restless analyst has at least to sample all of that, wrestle with the ideas and information advanced, sometimes fight fiercely in intellectual combat with those who advance them. The literature is not purely academic either. Novels, plays, poems, songs, paintings, graffiti, photographs, architectural drawings and plans – all of these give clues, contain potential surprises. I confess my thinking has been as much influenced by Dickens, Balzac, Zola, Gissing, Dreiser, Pynchon, and a host of others, as it has been by urban historians.

But I find myself most deeply impressed by those works, of which I regard Engels's *Condition of the Working Class in England in 1844* as the most brilliant example, that function as both literature and social science, as history and contemporary commentary. It was, I suspect, out of that admiration that I was drawn in the first instance to detailed studies of the Baltimore housing market (reported on in *The Urbanization of Capital*, chap. 4) and later to the study of Paris from the revolution of 1848 to the production of the Commune. Both offered rich mines from which to dig new insights with which to challenge theory. Those studies depended crucially, however, upon the prior existence of some kind of theoretical and conceptual frame upon which data and information could be hung. Engels provided the frame for the Baltimore housing studies, and my own extensions of Marx in *The Limits to Capital* provided the basis for thinking about the transformation of Paris after 1850.

The path between the historical and geographical grounding of experience and the rigors of theory construction is hard to negotiate. I conceive of it as mediated by processes of reflection and speculation. By speculation, I mean the interrogation of the conceptual apparatus through which experience is mediated, the adjustment of conceptual filters and the juggling of perspectives so as to create fresh windows and dimensions to our interpretation of experience. Marx's *Grundrisse* is an excellent example of exactly this process. By reflection, I have in mind the evaluation of experience, a summing up that can point in new directions, pose new problems, and suggest fresh areas for historical and theoretical enquiry. I regard Marx's *Eighteenth Brumaire of Louis Bonaparte* as a model of such activity. Reflection and speculation prepare the way for theory construction at the same time as they define an arena of open and fluid evaluation of theoretical conclusions. If verification has any meaning in the Marxist lexicon, it lies in the open and productive qualities of reflection and speculation in relation to political, class-based action. The studies here presented on "Money, Time, Space, and the City," "Labor, Capital, and Class Struggle around the Built Environment," and "The Urbanization of Consciousness" are meant to combine the qualities of speculation and reflection so as both to inform the more historically grounded studies on Paris (and Baltimore) and to evaluate the more rigorously derived theory presented in *The Urbanization of Capital* and *The Limits to Capital*.

Theory construction, therefore, does not proceed in isolation from reflection, speculation, and historical-geographical experience. But it does proceed rather differently. The tensions within a known conceptual apparatus are used to spin out rigorous lines of argument so as to represent "as in a mirror" (as Marx puts it) the historical and geographical dynamic of a particular mode of production. We reach out dialectically (rather than inward deductively) to probe uncharted seas from a few seemingly secure islands of concepts. Different starting points yield different perspectives on the realities we seek to understand, and what appears as a secure conceptual apparatus from one vantage point turns out to be partial and one-sided from another. But the construction of different theoretical windows helps us map the rich complexity of a mode of production with greater accuracy. Capitalism as viewed from the standpoint of production in the first volume of *Capital* looks very different from capitalism viewed from the standpoint of circulation in the second volume. Bringing the two perspectives together (which Marx never completed) should give us a fuller picture of the structure of a mode of production and its inner contradictions. It is then possible to build upon an understanding of those contradictions and reach out to grasp successive resolutions and internalizations of those tensions within the realms of finance capital, the state apparatus, and the geography of uneven development (cf. *The Limits to Capital*). The validation of such theoretical arguments depends, however, upon successive evaluations of theoretical propositions linked to political action and the reconstruction of historical experience through active and open reflection and speculation. To be sure, there is a constitutive danger of circularity and tautology in all of that. We might see only what we want to see, or reconstruct experience only in theoretically given terms. But that danger exists in all arenas of research and is by no means confined to Marxism. The eternal vigilance of the restless analyst is the only immediate safeguard that we have. In the long run, history and geography have their own ways of negating theoretical perspectives that fail to gain a real material base.

The studies assembled in these two companion works were written against a background of this overwhelming concern to bring theory and historical-geographical experience together in such a way as to illuminate both. Unfortunately, thematic considerations, coupled with the sheer volume of the materials, have dictated a division that reflects, more than it overcomes, the division between historical geography and theory. *The Urbanization of Capital* is biased more toward theorizing, whereas this book contains much more of the history, coupled with some of the more speculative studies. While each book stands on its own, I would at least like to express the hope that they be evaluated as a whole.

The thematic division has, however, another origin. The studies on the urbanization of capital are primarily concerned with how labor, working under capitalist control, creates a "second nature" of built environments with particular kinds of spatial configurations. I am primarily concerned with how capitalism creates a physical landscape of roads, houses, factories, schools, shops, and so forth in its own image and what the contradictions are that arise out of such processes of producing space. This is an easier target for theorizing to the degree that studies on the circulation of capital in general can be broadened and disaggregated to encompass problems of fixed capital formation and circulation and the interventions of finance capital and appropriators of rent. But these processes of urbanization of capital are paralleled by the urbanization of social relations through, for example, the separation of workplace and living place, the reorganization of capitalist systems of production and control, the reorganization of consumption processes to meet capitalism's requirements, the fragmentation of social space in relation to labor market demands, and the like. The urbanization of capital is an objectification in the landscape of that intersection between the productive force of capital investment and the social relations required to reproduce an increasingly urbanized capitalism. But this implies that we should look also at the implications for political consciousness of such processes. The "urbanization of consciousness" has, I therefore submit, to be taken as a real social, cultural, and political phenomenon in its own right. But this topic is far harder to ground theoretically, at least given the theoretical apparatus available to us (in spite of the extraordinary efforts of thinkers like Gramsci and Lukacs). The studies on consciousness and the urban experience are therefore much more speculative and much more heavily reliant upon the detailed interrogation of historical-geographical experience.

But why choose the "urban" as a framework for analysis? It is, after all, but one of several spatial scales on which the production of space and of political consciousness might be examined – neighborhoods, regions, nation-states, and power blocs being others. Indeed, there are many social theorists, including not a few Marxists, who reject the idea of urbanization as a "theoretically specific object of analysis." Examination of the urban process, it is said, can at best yield "real but relatively unimportant insights" into the workings of civil society (Saunders 1981). Even those like Giddens (1981, 147) who take the problem of space somewhat more seriously are prone to argue that "with the advent of capitalism, the city is no longer the dominant time-space container or 'crucible of power'; this role is assumed by the territorially bounded nation state." Only occasional mavericks like Jane Jacobs (1984) insist on privileging the urban as a unit of analysis before all else.

By focusing on urbanization I do not intend that it be considered a theoretically specific object of analysis separate from what capitalism is about. Capital, Marx insists, must be conceived of as a process and not reified as a thing. The study of urbanization is a study of that process as it unfolds through the production of physical and social landscapes and the production of consciousness. The study of urbanization is not the study of a legal, political entity or of a physical artifact. It is concerned with processes of capital circulation; the shifting flows of labor power, commodities, and money capital; the spatial organization of production and the transformation of space relations; movements of information and geopolitical conflicts between territorially-based class alliances; and so on. The fact that cities in the legal sense have lost political power and geopolitical influence or that distinctive urban economies now merge into megalopolitan concentrations is but a part of this urban process. And if that sounds vague and somewhat ambiguous compared to the usual reifications of urban studies, it is deliberately so. I prefer to keep the ambiguity open in order to concentrate on urbanization as a process rather than engaging in secure reifications that conceal rather than reveal the fluid processes at work. That way we can better integrate understandings of the urban process into broader conceptions of the dynamics of capitalism and understand how each is part and parcel of the other.

Personal and intellectual debts are always hard to tabulate. My interest in Paris was stimulated by a Guggenheim Fellowship in 1976–77 and consolidated during a sabbatical from the Johns Hopkins University where "Reds" Wolman (a title that has nothing to do with his politics and everything to do with the color of his hair) helped provide, in his capacity as chairman of the Department of Geography and Environmental Engineering, work conditions of the greatest personal freedom. Carol Ehrlich was a delightful editor to work with at the Johns Hopkins University Press and Alison Richards in the production department at Basil Blackwell did an extraordinary job. Intellectual debts are even harder to record. Much of the time I simply cannot remember who taught me what or from where a particular idea or insight came. I know I have appropriated most of what I know from others. Barbara Koeppel, Ric Pfeffer, Vicente Navarro, Chester Wickwire, and Cliff DuRand made life in Baltimore a very special experience. Among those associated with Hopkins I want to make special mention of Lata Chatterjee, Gene Mumy, Jörn Barnbrock, Amy Kaplan and Erica Schoenberger. I owe, however, an incalculable debt to Dick Walker, Beatriz Nofal, and Neil Smith. I worked so closely with each of them and took so much from all of them that I feel this work is as much theirs as mine.

Consciousness and
the Urban Experience

1

Money, Time, Space, and the City

I am looking to understand the forces that frame the urban process and the urban experience under capitalism. I focus on the themes of money, space, and time because thinking about them helps clear away some of the clutter of detail and lay bare the frames of reference within which urbanization proceeds. That way we can get a better handle on the meaning of the urban experience, find ways to interpret it, and think through viable alternatives. The themes I explore are, on the surface, very abstract. But the abstractions are not of my making. They are embedded in a social process that creates abstract forces that have concrete and personal effects in daily life. The "rationality" of money and the power of the rate of interest, the partitioning of time by the clock and of space according to the cadastral register, are all abstractly conceived features of social life. Yet each in its own way seems to have more power over us than we have over them.

I argue that the very existence of money as a mediator of commodity exchange radically transforms and fixes the meanings of space and time in social life and defines limits and imposes necessities upon the shape and form of urbanization. The particular use of money as capital hardens these connections at the same time as the dynamics of accumulation (accelerating growth, technological revolutions, crises, etc.) render them less and less coherent. This lack of coherence renders the urban process under capitalism a peculiarly open affair, in the sense that confusion, conflict, and struggle are a normal condition and that fixed outcomes cannot be determined in advance. What this seeming openness conceals, however, is an underlying process that precludes liberation from the more repressive aspects of class-domination and all of the urban pathology and restless incoherence that goes with it.

Interior to this general argument I want to construct another, which will, I hope, help us understand the politics of urban protest, the forms of urban power, and the various modes of urban experience. Confusions arise, I shall show, because command over money, command over space, and command over time form independent but interlocking sources of social power, the repressive qualities of which spark innumerable movements of revulsion and revolt. The demands to liberate space from its various forms of domination, to liberate time for free use, and to exist independently of the crass vulgarity of pure money valuations can each be built into social protest movements of enormous breadth and scope. Yet creative use of money, space, and time also lies at the heart of constructive urban experience. It is exactly this dialectic that many of the great urban novelists – some of whose insights I use as raw material – pick up on and weave into their plots and sentiments. The confusion is compounded, however, by the restless and contradictory dynamic of capital circulation and accumulation. Though class struggle then surges to the fore as the principal axis of revulsion and revolt, the other axes do not disappear but take on curiously warped and contorted forms, which in turn undermine the clarity of class struggle and its objectives. Precisely for this reason, urban social movements take on mixed political coloration and can quickly change their spots according to shifting circumstances. The vision of possible alternatives is put up for grabs, and political-economic analysis appears either unduly rigid or just plain dumb in the face of an urban history that is as confused as the multiple forces that shape it. Part of this confusion, I hold, can be rendered tractable by looking carefully at money, capital, space, and time as frameworks binding the political economy of the urban process into particular configurations.

I. MONEY

"It is very difficult to write a novel about money," said Zola (1967, 1236) – "it is cold, glacial, devoid of interest." Money, Simmel (1978) likewise complained, though central to every aspect of our life and culture, is itself devoid of any content "save that of possession" (325); it is "the representation of abstract group forces" (301) which "in every domain of life and in every sense strive to dissolve substance into free-floating processes" (168). "To the extent that money, with its colorlessness and its indifferent quality can become a denominator of all values," Simmel (1971, 330) wrote, "it becomes the frightful leveler – it hollows out the core of things, their specific values and their uniqueness and incomparability in a way which is beyond repair. They all float with the same specific gravity in the constantly moving stream of money."

This was hardly promising raw material for grand literature or even, as Simmel discovered to his cost, good philosophizing. Marx's lengthy enquiries on the subject (including the third chapter of *Capital*) make for dull reading compared with his inspired prose when he confronts exploitation in the labor process. Zola's *L'argent* (as he himself foretold) was uninspired; and Dreiser, who explored themes of distance, desire, and commodification with such dramatic intensity in *Sister Carrie,* came quite unstuck when he tried to construct an epic trilogy on the heartless, undifferentiated world of money and financial manipulation. So even though the truly epic novelists of the nineteenth-century urban scene, like Dickens and Balzac, typically used the circulation of money to tie together their "totalizing vision" (Williams 1960, 28) of city life, they evidently judged it safer to treat money itself as a fact of nature (or at least of human nature) that was as immutable as it was all-encompassing. "Papa! what's money?" asks little Paul of a startled Mr. Dombey, whose stumbling evasions on the subject leave the very junior partner-to-be "still cogitating and looking for an explanation in the fire." Having no answer either, Dickens lets the question dissipate up the chimney (as it were), perhaps to reappear as that "dark and invisible cloud" that he sees hovering over the teeming social life of the city. For money lies not only at the center of Mr. Dombey's concerns. It forms, in the novel as in the social world, the thread of connection that binds men and women, each pursuing their individual courses, "into an effective common life within which all individual lives are eventually held and shaped" (Williams 1960, 28).

The profundity of little Paul's question is matched only by the depth of our inability to provide satisfactory answers. Money is simultaneously everything and nothing, everywhere but nowhere in particular, a means that poses as an end, the profoundest and most complete of all centralizing forces in a society where it facilitates the greatest dispersion, a representation that appears quite divorced from whatever it is supposed to represent. It is a *real* or *concrete abstraction* that exists external to us and exercises real power over us.

The meaning of the phrase "concrete abstraction" deserves elaboration. Money, Marx shows us, arises out of concrete social practices of commodity exchange and the division of labor. The grand diversity of actual labor processes given over to the production of all manner of goods of specific qualities (concrete labor applied to produce use values) gets averaged out and represented in the single abstract magnitude of money (exchange value). Bonds of personal dependency are thereby broken and replaced by "objective dependency relations" between individuals who relate to each other through market prices and money and commodity transactions. "Individuals are now ruled by abstractions," says Marx (1973, 146–68), "whereas earlier they depended on one another." With the growth of the division of labor, money appears more and more as a "power external to and independent of the producers," so what "originally appears as a means to promote production becomes a relation alien (to them)." The "form-giving fire" of the labor process is represented and fetishized as a passive thing – money. Furthermore, "the power which each individual exercises over the activity of others or over social wealth exists in him as the owner of exchange values, of money."

Money becomes the mediator and regulator of all economic relations between individuals; it becomes the abstract and universal measure of social wealth and the concrete means of expression of social power.

Money, Marx (1973, 224–25) goes on to observe, dissolves the community and in so doing "becomes the *real community.*" But what kind of community does money define? What does money represent for it? And how can we locate the meaning of that particular kind of community called "urban" within its frame?

Consider, first, what money represents. "Since labor is motion, time is its natural measure," writes Marx (1973, 205), and from this we see that money is "objectification of general labor time" on the world market (abstract labor). The community of money cannot, therefore, be understood independently of the social meaning of either space or time. I lay aside these crucial interrelations for the moment; they will be taken up later.

The community of money is strongly marked by individualism and certain conceptions of liberty, freedom, and equality backed by laws of private property, rights to appropriation, and freedom of contract. Such personal freedoms and liberties exist, of course, in the midst of an "objective bondage" defined through mutual dependency within the social division of labor and a money economy. But the freedoms are of great social significance: "Since freedom means independence from the will of others, it commences with independence from the will of specific individuals. . . . The inhabitants of a modern metropolis are independent in the positive sense of the word, and even though they require innumerable suppliers, workers and cooperators and would be lost without them, their relationship to them is completely objective and is only embodied in money" (Simmel 1978, 300). The owners of money are free (within constraints) to choose how, when, where, and with whom to use that money to satisfy their needs, wants, and fancies (a fact that the free-market ideologues perpetually dwell upon to the exclusion of all else). The tremendous concern with personal freedoms and the pursuit of liberty (and the anger felt at its frustration) must in Simmel's view, be traced back to the qualities of money economies. Marx likewise attaches bourgeois notions of constitutionality to the inherent qualities of the money form.

There is also something very democratic about money. It is a "great leveler and cynic," says Marx, because it eliminates all other marks of distinction save those contained in its possession. "The existence of the infinite, quantitative grading of money ownership," says Simmel (1978, 391), "permits (social) levels to merge into one another and removes the distinctive formation of aristocratic classes which cannot exist without secure boundaries." The erosion of traditional class distinctions and their replacement by the crass democracy of money was the sort of social transformation that Henry James, for one, viewed with wistful regret. The tendency to eliminate clear class distinctions is reinforced, in Simmel's view, by the rise of a variety of occupations (from the street vendor to the banker) which have no other content than making money. The typical turbulence of the circulation and making of money also incites "the awareness of difference" that underlies the demand for egalitarian reforms, some of which are bound to see the light of day (Simmel 1978, 270, 433).

The style of urban life necessarily reflects such conditions. The breakdown of clear class distinctions is accompanied by rising barriers between individuals. While Simmel will ultimately translate this into a tragic vision of the loneliness of creative individualism (a condition which, unlike Marx, he can see no way to transcend), he nevertheless sees it as "indispensable for the modern form" of urban life: "The pecuniary character of relationships, either openly or concealed in a thousand forms, places an invisible functional distance between people that is an inner protection and neutralization against the overcrowded proximity and friction of our cultural life" (477).

The sense of social structure which Simmel presents is very different from that traditionally associated with Marx. Yet there is nothing here that is actually inconsistent with Marx's theory of money. What is missing, of course, is any consideration of the circulation of capital (as opposed to money) and the class relations implied therein. The processes we have so far described are real enough, but the contrast with the rules of capital circulation is of more than passing interest. It indicates a deep tension between the individualism and equality that the possession of money implies and the class relations experienced in the making of that money.

The objective, measurable, and universal qualities of money call forth other forms of social transformation within the community that money defines. "The idea that life is essentially based on intellect, and that intellect is accepted in practical life as the most valuable of our mental energies," says Simmel (1978, 152), "goes hand in hand with the growth of a money economy." Two aspects of this intellectual activity call for comment. First, the more we deal with abstract symbols of money (like bank notes) rather than with a tangible commodity of intrinsic value (like gold), the more we are forced to resort to abstract and symbolic modes of thought that match the "concrete abstraction" of the money form. "Consider," says Simmel, "the complicated psychological pre-conditions required to cover bank notes by cash reserves" and what this means for the symbolic content of our own thinking. Marx, too, emphasizes how the faith needed to operate on paper money or credit has to have a quasi-religious quality if it is to sustain the complex transactions of a modern money economy. Second, the content of this intellectual activity is deeply affected by the nature of money operations. "The measuring, weighing and calculating exactness of modern times" stands in "a close causal relationship to the money economy," which demands "continuous mathematical operations in our daily transactions." A money economy demands a certain kind of rationalism, based on exact, precise, and rigorous measurement of calculable magnitudes (Godelier 1972). This is the kind of positivist intellectual equipment we necessarily use every time we confront something as simple as a market price.

A money economy, Simmel (1978, 411) concludes, presupposes "a remarkable expansion" and intensification of mental processes to produce "a fundamental re-orientation of culture towards intellectuality." From this derives the growth of independent intellectual activities and professions oriented to exploring the rational calculus of economic life. A material basis is here defined for the rise of powerful vested interests in principles of objective measurement, rational computation, and economic calculation. Such modes of thought can extend over all spheres of social concern. It was, for example, no accident that Sir Isaac Newton was also, for a time, Master of the King's Mint. The kind of materialist and positivist science produced is, however, as great a leveler and cynic as the money form it mimics. All phenomena are brought under a single homogeneous and supposedly universal form of thought. Everything is reduced to a common plane of intellectuality, which functions as the secular religion of the money economy. And such modes of thought have, in turn, to be powerfully protected. For, as Simmel (1978, 172) notes, "Only in a stable and closely organized society that assures mutual protection and provides safeguards against a variety of elemental dangers, both external and psychological, is it possible for such a delicate and easily destroyed material as paper to become [money]."

This sketch, constructed with the aid of Marx and Simmel, of the kind of "community" that money defines is by no means complete. But it does provide a sufficient base out of which to evolve an understanding of other facets of the social process (including, as we shall see, revulsion and revolt against the money calculus) which invest urban life under capitalism with its specific qualities. The first step down that path, however, entails the integration of conceptions of space and time into the argument.

II. TIME

"Economy of time," says Marx (1973, 173), "to this all economy ultimately reduces itself." But what are the qualities of this time to which all economy is to be reduced? We here encounter a paradox. For though money may represent social labor time, the rise of the money form transforms and shapes the meaning of time in important and specific ways. Simmel (1978, 505–6) thus argues that "the modern concept of time – as a value determined by its usefulness and scarcity" became widely accepted only to the degree that market capitalism flourished. Le Goff (1980, 35–36) agrees. The enlargement of the monetary sphere of circulation and the organization of commercial networks over space, he argues, forced the merchant, at least as long ago as the fourteenth century, to construct "a more adequate and predictable measurement of time for the orderly conduct of business." This need was reinforced to the degree that merchants became the organizers of urban-based production. Thus, the "cultivation of urban labor in the fourteenth century" spawned a "fundamental change in the measurement of time which was indeed a change in time itself." Symbolized by clocks and bells that called workers to labor and merchants to market, separated from natural rhythms and divorced from religious significance, "a sort of chronological net in which urban life was caught" was created by merchants and masters. The new definition of time did not pass undisputed by religious authority any more than by the urban laborers called to accept the new temporal discipline. "These evolving mental structures and their material expressions," Le Goff concludes, "were deeply implicated in the mechanisms of class struggle."

But the reach and fineness of mesh of this new chronological net was no greater than the class power that lay behind it. For though bureaucratic and state interests might rally behind it as a convenient framework for social control, the compelling necessity to respect the new definitions of time lay primarily with the merchants and masters who long maintained only a local, and then often by no means dominant, power within the broader society in which they were inserted (Thrift 1981). The issue of time and its proper notation consequently remained, E. P. Thompson assures us, a lively focus of class struggle throughout the birth-throes and even unto the consolidation of urban industrial capitalism. The long historical passage to the domination of this new sense of time was partly a matter of technology, due to the introduction of cheap timepieces (Landes 1983) and of gas and electric lighting to overcome the constraints of the "natural" working day.[1] But more fundamentally it was a question of class relations which forced the use of those technological possibilities along lines dictated by capital circulation. Society became enmeshed in a single and universal chronological net only to the degree that class forces mobilized in both production and exchange came together. And that happened most spectacularly toward the end of the nineteenth century.

The struggle over time in production goes back, both Le Goff and Thompson agree, to at least the medieval period. For his part, Marx notes that the struggle over the length of the working day goes back to the Elizabethan period when the state legislated an increase in the length of the customary working day for laborers freshly released from the land by violent

---

[1] Engels (1971, 336–52) has a most interesting account of the labor struggles waged by carpenters in Manchester after 1844 when gas lighting was introduced as part of a strategy to . increase the length of the working day.

primitive accumulation and consequently prone to be unstable, undisciplined, and itinerant. The incarceration of the unemployed with the mad (which Marx highlights and Foucault erects into a whole book) was but one of many means to bring the labor force to heel. Over several generations, "new labor habits were formed, and a new time-discipline imposed," E. P. Thompson (1967, 90) confirms, forged under the pressure to synchronize both the social and the detail division of labor and to maximize the extraction of the laborer's surplus labor time (the basis of profit). Thus came into being "the familiar landscape of industrial capitalism, with the time-sheet, the timekeeper, the informers and the fines." The battle over minutes and seconds, over the pace and intensity of work schedules, over the working life (and rights of retirement), over the working week and day (with rights to "free time"), over the working year (and rights to paid vacations) has been, and continues to be, royally fought. For the worker learned to fight back within the confines of the newly internalized sense of time: "The first generation of factory workers were taught by their masters the importance of time; the second generation formed their short-time work committees in the ten-hour movement; the third generation struck for overtime or time-and-a-half. They had accepted the categories of their employers and learned to fight back within them. They had learned their lesson, that time is money, only too well" (Thompson 1967, 90).

But even though the new time discipline and its associated work ethic may have been successfully implanted fairly early on in the Manchesters, Mulhouses, and Lowells of the early industrial revolution, it did not so easily take root in the grand metropolis or in rural areas. Time literally sprawls in Dickens's world in a way that mainly reflects the time frame of the merchant capitalist. The High Street clock made it appear "as if Time carried on business there and hung out his sign." The mass of his characters are scarcely tied down to the tight Gradgrind schedule of industrial Coketown. It took revolutions in the realm of circulation rather than in production (as Thompson tends to imply) to impose the universal sense of abstract and objective time we now so commonly accept as basic to our material existence. And in this it was the extraordinary and rapid conquest of space through the advent of the railroad, the telegraph, the telephone, and the radio that finally forced matters (Pred 1973).

It was, after all, only in 1883, Kern (1983, 12) reminds us, that the more than two hundred local times that a traveler encountered on a rail journey from Washington to San Francisco were brought to order and the unprofitable confusion ended that had, for example, the Pennsylvania Railroad system operate on a Philadelphia time that was five minutes different from that of New York. It was only in 1884, also, that the first moves were made toward international agreement on the meridian, time zones, and the beginning of the global day. And it was many years before even the advanced capitalist countries coordinated their clocks.

The tightening of the chronological net around daily life had everything to do with achieving the necessary coordinations for profitable production and exchange over space. Simmel (1971, 328) spelled out the rationale with devastating accuracy. "If all the watches in Berlin suddenly went wrong in different ways even only as much as an hour," he wrote, "its entire economic and commercial life would be derailed for some time." Spatial separation (itself made more and more possible with increasing sophistication of the money economy) "results in making all waiting and breaking of appointments an ill-afforded waste of time." The "technique of metropolitan life," he continued, "is not conceivable without all of its activities and reciprocal relationships being organized and coordinated in the most punctual way into a firm, fixed framework of time which transcends all subjective elements." The tight scheduling of the newly emerging mass transit systems at the end of the nineteenth century, for example, profoundly changed the rhythm and form of urban life (though the idea of fixed time schedules over invariable routes at a fixed price had been around since the first omnibus routes in the 1820s). The coming of the railroad likewise "flaunted agricultural time keeping," for even "the comparatively slow haste of the back-country freight train rumbling from town to town," says Stilgoe (1983, 23), "suffused every structure and space" in the railroad corridors with a new sense of time. The early morning milk train in Thomas Hardy's *Tess* captures that new sense of time and of rural-urban connection across space magnificently.

But there were all kinds of equally significant indirect ways in which the conquest of space after 1840 shifted the whole sense and valuation of time for all social classes. The rise of the journey to work as a phenomenon of urban living was itself connected to the increasing partition of time into "working" and "living" in separate spaces. And there were all manner of secondary effects of such a journey to work upon customary meal times, household labor (and its sexual division), family interactions, leisure activities, and the like. The rise of mass-circulation newspapers, the advent of telegraph and telephone, of radio and television, all contributed to a new sense of simultaneity over space and total uniformity in coordinated and universally uniform time.

Under such conditions the qualities of money could further affect matters. The fact that money can function as a store of value, and hence of social power, that can be held over time allows individuals to choose between present and future satisfactions, and even allows consumption to be moved forward in time through borrowing (Sharp 1981, 163). Individuals are thereby forced to define their own time horizons, their individual "discount rate" or "time preference" as they contemplate whether to expend their social power now or conserve it for later. The social representation of time preference is given by financial institutions, which state time horizons and discount rates for borrowing. Mortgage and interest rates and terms then appear as "concrete abstractions" to which individuals, firms, and even governments have to respond.

The function of money as a store of value also permits the accumulation of social power in individual hands over time. Compared to other forms of social wealth, money power can, as Marx points out, be accumulated without limit – logistical curves of geometrical expansion over time become entirely feasible. Money here counters its democratizing function, since it also counts among its qualities the capacity for a most unequal distribution of a universal form of social power. The question of intergenerational transfer of wealth (or debts) then arises, hence the social significance that Marx and Engels attach to inheritance and the bourgeois form of the family. Even those with limited money resources can find ways, as Hareven (1982) brilliantly demonstrates, to integrate their sense and use of "family time" into the newly emerging demands and schedules of "industrial time."

The shaping of time as a measurable, calculable, and objective magnitude, though deeply resented and resisted by many, had powerful consequences for intellectual modes of thought. The nineteenth and twentieth centuries saw the birth of innumerable professions that had a deep and vested interest in a rigorous definition and measurement of time, since their whole *raison d'être* was to advise on the efficient allocation of what had become a scarce and quantifiable resource. Engineers, chemists, economists, industrial psychologists, to say nothing of the experts in time and motion study, computerization, automation, electronics, and information transfer, all have in common an abstract conception of time that can be used in concrete ways, usually directed toward making money. Small wonder that differential calculus, with its fine analytics of rate of change over measurable time, became the basis for much of modern technical education. Thus economists, while demanding calculus as a prerequisite to the understandings they have to offer, are also quick to point out that "time is a scarce resource that must be spent" and that "a basic problem of human existence" (with respect to which they stand to offer us the friendliest of advice) "is to spend it well, to use it to bring about the greatest return of happiness that can be achieved" (Sharp 1981, 2). The intellectual baggage that goes with the equation "time is money" is evidently of enormous extension and sophistication.

III. SPACE

"Tess . . . started on her way up the dark and crooked lane or street not made for hasty progress; a street laid out before inches of land had value, and when

one-handed clocks sufficiently divided the day" (Thomas Hardy). So begins
E. P. Thompson's (1967) classic piece on time and work-discipline under
industrial capitalism. Yet Thompson makes nothing of the fact that the street
that so impeded Tess's progress was formed "before inches of land had value."
I make the remark because social historians and theorists all too rarely take Le
Goff's (1980, 36) advice to put the simultaneous conquest of time and space
at the center of their concerns. The medieval merchant, Le Goff argues,
discovered the fundamental concept of "the price of time" only in the course
of exploring space. And we have already seen how it was only through the
conquest of space after 1840 that an abstract, objective, and universal sense of
time came to dominate social life and practice.

The priority given to time over space is not in itself misplaced. Indeed, it
mirrors the evolution of social practices in important ways. What is missing,
however, is an appreciation of the practices that underlie the priority. Only in
such a light can we understand those situations in which location, place, and
spatiality reassert themselves as seemingly powerful and autonomous forces in
human affairs. And such situations are legion. They vary from the urban
speculator turning inches of land into value (and personal profit), through the
forces shaping the new regional and international division of labor, to the
geopolitical squabbles that pit city against suburb, region against region, and
one half of the world in sometimes violent conflict with the other. Given the
seriousness of such events, we ignore the question of space at our peril.

Space cannot be considered independently of money because it is the latter,
as Marx (1973, 148) insists, that permits the separation of buying and selling
in both space and time. The breaking of the bonds of personal dependency
through money exchange is here paralleled by the breakdown of local barriers
so that "my product becomes dependent on the state of general commerce and
is torn out of its local, natural and individual boundaries." The world market
ultimately defines the "community" of exchange interactions, and the money
in our pocket represents our objective bond to that community as well as our
social power with respect to it. Here, too, money is the great leveler and
cynic, the great integrator and unifier across the grand diversity of traditional
communities and group interests. Commodity exchange and monetization
challenge, subdue, and ultimately eliminate the absolute qualities of *place* and
substitute relative and contingent definitions of places within the circulation
of goods and money across the surface of the globe. Zola (1980, 452–58)
caught the rural impact of all this with great dramatic intensity in *La terre*. Frank
Norris (1981, 44) saw the same integrations. Watching the prices coming
over the wires that connected them to the world market, the California wheat
ranchers lost their sense of individuality. "The ranch became merely the part
of an enormous whole, a unit in the vast agglomeration of wheat land the
whole world round, feeling the effects of causes thousands of miles distant."
Under the impact of the transport and communications revolution, the world

market and the space it embraced came to be felt as a very real, concrete abstraction in relation to everyone's social practice.

The social effects are legion. To begin with, money "permits agreements over otherwise inaccessible distances, an inclusion of the most diverse persons in the same project, an interaction and therefore a unification of people who, because of their spatial, social, personal and other discrepancies in interests, could not possibly be integrated into any other group formation" (Simmel 1978, 347). By the same token, money creates an enormous capacity to concentrate social power in space, for unlike other use values it can be accumulated at a particular place without restraint. And these immense concentrations of social power can be put to work to realize massive but localized transformations of nature, the construction of built environments, and the like. Yet such concentrations always exist in the midst of the greatest dispersion because the social power that money represents is tied to an immense diversity of activities across the world market.

We here encounter paradoxes with deep implications. The price system, for example, is the most decentralized (socially and spatially) of all socially coordinated decision-making mechanisms, yet it is also a powerful centralizing force that permits the concentration of immense money power in a few hands. Even the notion of distance takes on quite new meanings. Desire, Simmel (69–76) suggests, arises "only at a distance from objects," yet presupposes "a closeness between objects and ourselves in order that the distance should be experienced at all." Money and exchange across the world market turn the metropolis into a veritable bordello of consumer temptation in which money (or the lack of it) becomes itself the measure of distance. This was the theme that Dreiser got at so sensationally in *Sister Carrie*. And it has vital meanings. A whole world of commerce and money exchanges collapses into a confrontation on New York's Fifth Avenue or in Baltimore's Harborplace – between individual desire and a vast array of commodities drawn from all corners of the earth. The nature of political participation is no less dramatically affected. Money, Simmel (1978, 344) notes, permits political participation without personal commitment (people give money more easily than time) as well as participation in far-off causes, often to the neglect of those near at hand. Dickens parodies such a habit through the character of Mrs. Pardiggle in *Bleak House*; she is so obsessed with raising money for the Tookaloopo Indians that she quite neglects her own children.

But what is the nature of this "space" across which and within which such processes operate? The conquest of space first required that it be conceived of as something usable, malleable, and therefore capable of domination through human action. A new chronological net for human exploration and action was created through navigation and map making. Cadastral survey permitted the unambiguous definition of property rights in land. Space thus came to be represented, like time and value, as abstract, objective, homogeneous, and universal in its qualities. What the map makers and surveyors did through mental representations, the merchants and landowners used for their own class purposes, while the absolutist state (with its concern for taxation of land and the definition of its own domain of domination) likewise relished the clear definition of absolute spaces within a fixed spatial net. Builders, engineers, and architects for their part showed how abstract representations of objective space could be combined with exploration of the concrete, malleable properties of materials in space. But these were all just islands of practice, light chorological nets thrown over a totality of social practices in which all manner of other conceptions of place and space – sacred and profane, symbolic, personal, animistic – could continue to function undisturbed. It took something more to consolidate space as universal, homogeneous, objective, and abstract in most social practices. That "something" was the buying and selling of space as a commodity. The effect was then to bring all space under the single measuring rod of money value.

The subsumption of places and spaces under the uniform judgment of Plutus sparked resistance, often violent opposition, from all kinds of quarters. The struggle over the commodification of land and space goes back at least as far and was certainly as long drawn out and fiercely fought as that over the meaning and control of time. Here, too, it was the transport and communications revolution of the nineteenth century that finally consoli-dated the triumph of space as a concrete abstraction with real power in relation to social practices. The independent power of the landlord class was broken, and in the process land became nothing more than a particular kind of financial asset, a form of "fictitious capital" (Harvey 1982, chap. 11). Or, put the other way round, land titles became nothing other than "coined land" (Simmel 1978, 508).

But there is a contradiction in this. The homogeneity of space is achieved through its total "pulverization" into freely alienable parcels of private property, to be bought and traded at will upon the market (Lefebvre 1974, 385). The result is a permanent tension between the *appropriation* and use of space for individual and social purposes and the *domination* of space through private property, the state, and other forms of class and social power (Lefebvre 1974, 471). This tension underlies the further fragmentation of otherwise homogeneous space. For the ease with which both physical and social space could now be shaped – with all that this implies for the annihilation of the absolute qualities of place and of the privileged territoriality of traditional communities sealed off in aristocratic, religious, or royal quarters (among others) – poses a serious challenge to the social order. In whose image and to whose benefit is space to be shaped? Where the land market is dominated by money power, the democracy of money takes charge. Even the largest palace can be bought and converted into office or slum building. The land market sorts spaces to functions on the basis of land price and does so only on the basis of ability to pay, which, though clearly differentiated, is by no means differentiated enough to etch clear class and social distinctions into the social spaces of the city. The response is for each and every stratum in society to use whatever powers of domination it can command (money, political influence, even violence) to try to seal itself off (or seal off others judged undesirable) in fragments of space within which processes of reproduction of social distinctions can be jealously protected.

There was, then, a dramatic transformation in the sense of urban space as the democracy of money increasingly came to dominate the land market in the nineteenth century. As John Goode (1978, 91–107) perceptively notes, "The organization of space in Dickens is based on a tension between obscurity and proximity"; it is a space of accidental encounters in which the exploratory zeal of the merchant class can still hold sway. Characters can freely move across spaces precisely because to do so is not to challenge the prevailing class distinctions. But George Gissing's novels of the late nineteenth century portray a very different London. "The city is no longer the meeting-place of the classes; on the contrary, it is the structured space of separation" that can be "charted, literally mapped out," with "distances which have no contingency" and "zones functioning as class and economic differentials." The "social space of the city, insofar as it is created space," Goode concludes, "is partly organized to keep class relationships to an abstraction – suburbs, ghettoes, thoroughfares are all ways of keeping the possibilities of direct confrontation at bay." The irony, of course, is that at the very historical moment when the potentiality of the city as "a place of encounters" (to use a favorite expression of Lefebvre's) was at its apogee, it became a fragmented terrain held down and together under all manner of forces of class, racial, and sexual domination.

How can this fragmentation be reconciled with the homogeneity of universal and objective space? That question has provoked a variety of theoretical and practical responses. Durkheim (1965), for one, recognized the importance of the fragmentations and represented them as social spaces within the organic solidarity of society as a whole. The urban reformers (like Charles Booth, Octavia Hill, and Jane Addams) and sociologists (particularly of the Chicago School) set out to explore the fragments and to try to identify or impose some sense of "moral order" across them. And there arose a whole host of professionals – engineers, architects, urban planners, and designers – whose entire mission was to rationalize the fragments and impose coherence on the spatial system as a whole (Giedion 1941). These professionals, whose role became more and more marked as progressive urban reformers acquired political power, acquired as deep a vested interest in the concept of homogeneous, abstract, and objective space as their professional confrères did with respect to the concrete abstractions of time and money. Even art, Kern (1983, 144–52) suggests, succumbed in its turn to cubism in a culture that affirmed "the unreality of place" at the same time as it sought to confine forms to a flat surface in homogeneous and abstract space. The consequent tensions between "the world of three dimensions that was their inspiration and the two-dimensionality of painting that was their art" generated canvases that were as fragmented and shattered in their appearance as the urban social landscapes that they often sought to depict.

The growing consensus that space must be, in spite of its evident fragmentations, objective, measurable, and homogeneous (how else could it be ordered for the rational conduct of business?) was accompanied by another emerging consensus toward the end of the nineteenth century. Writers as diverse as Alfred Marshall and Proust concluded that space was a less relevant dimension to human affairs than time. In this, once more, the transport and communications revolution was fundamental. As early as the 1840s, Leo Marx (1964, 194) tells us, Americans were taken with the "extravagant" sentiment that the sublime paths of technological progress were leading inexorably to the "annihilation of space and time" (a phrase apparently borrowed from a couplet of Alexander Pope's: "Ye Gods! annihilate but space and time / And make two lovers happy"). The other Marx (Karl, 1973, 524–44) more soberly reduced this extravagant idea to the annihilation of space *by* time. For though the medieval merchant discovered the price of time through the exploration of space, it was, Marx insisted, labor *time* that defined money, while the *price of time* or *profit* was the fundamental dimension to the capitalist's logic of decision. From this Marx could derive what he saw as a necessary impulsion under capitalism to annihilate the constraints and frictions of space, together with the particularities of place. Revolutions in transport and communications are, therefore, a necessary rather than a contingent aspect of capitalist history.

The consequent victory of time over space and place had its price. It meant acceptance of a way of life in which speed and rush to overcome space was of the essence. Thomas Musil thought he caricatured when, in *The Man without Qualities,* he depicted "a kind of super-American city where everyone rushes about, or stands still, with a stop-watch in his hand. . . . Overhead trains, overground-trains, underground trains, pneumatic express mails carrying consignments of human beings, chains of motor vehicles all racing along horizontally, express lifts vertically pumping crowds from one traffic level to another. . . ." (quoted in Kern 1983, 127) but he was merely describing the kind of organization of flows over space that paralleled Simmel's description of time requirements for the modern metropolis. "Steady uninterrupted flow was becoming the universal American requirement" says Jackson (1972,

238), and engineers and planners raised the science of such flows (of goods, of people, of information, of production processes) to the very pinnacle of their professional expertise (Stilgoe 1983, 26). In this respect the United States quickly established itself as "the most modern form of existence of bourgeois society" (Marx 1973, 104). Gertrude Stein (1974, 93–5) more or less agreed. "The Twentieth Century has become the American Century," she wrote, and "it is something strictly American to conceive a space that is filled always filled with moving." Kerouac's (1955, 25, 111) characters rushing frantically *On The Road* from coast to coast are living embodiments of that spirit: "We were leaving confusion and nonsense behind and performing our one and only noble function of the time, *move*." Such a rush of movement implied, of course, the dissolution of any traditional sense of community. "There was nowhere to go but everywhere," wrote Kerouac, and the sociologists and urban planners belatedly rushed to catch up with concepts like Webber's (1963, 1964) "community without propinquity" situated in "the nonplace urban realm."

The kind of community money defines is, evidently, one in which the organization of space and time, including the precedence of the latter over the former, takes on particular qualities. Money is, in turn, not independent of these qualities, since money represents nothing more than abstract social labor, socially necessary labor time, developed, as Marx (1972, 253) puts it, "in the measure that concrete labor becomes a totality of different modes of labor embracing the world market." The interrelations between money, time, and space form, thus, intersecting nets of very specific qualities that frame the whole of social life as we now know it. But the constraints of that frame do not pass unnoticed or unchallenged. To these challenges we must now turn.

IV. REVULSION AND REVOLT

While the community that money defines through time and space permits all manner of freedoms and liberties, the constraints imposed by the intersecting spatial, chronological, and monetary nets are repressive enough to spark all manner of revulsions and revolts. And from time to time the incoherent pieces of resistance coalesce and well up as some deep-seated demand to construct an alternative society, subject to different rules, outside of and beyond the rational discourse and the disciplines and constraints determined within the community of money. The utopian elements within all such proposals and actions are, it is interesting to note, almost always seeking a different notion of value and different modes of operation in time and space from those that have increasingly come to dominate all aspects of social life.

The cynical leveling of all human activities and experiences to the heartless and colorless qualities of money has always proved hard to accept. "We experience in the nature of money itself something of the essence of prostitution," says Simmel (1978, 377); and Marx (1973, 163) expresses a parallel sentiment. Baudelaire returned again and again to this theme (see chap. 3). From this there arises "a deep yearning to give things a new importance, a deeper meaning, a value of their own" other than the "selling and uprooting of personal values" (Simmel 1978, 404). "Commerce," says Baudelaire (1983b, 65, 88), "is in its very essence satanic." It is "the vilest form of egoism" in which "even honesty is a financial speculation." There are, he goes on to proclaim, "only three beings worthy of respect: the priest, the warrior and the poet. To know, to kill and to create." Simmel (1978, 97) gives that wounded cry a deeper psychological meaning. "Some people consider violent robbery more noble than honest payment, for in exchanging and paying one is subordinated to an objective norm, and the strong and autonomous personality has to efface itself, which is disagreeable." The gangster, the crook, the messianic revolutionary, and even the financial swindler excite as much secret approbation as public condemnation (particularly when their exploits are spectacularly carried off).[2] The ability to live a way of life "that does not have to consider the money value of things" likewise has "an extraordinary aesthetic charm," comments Simmel (1978, 220), and Baudelaire, for one, lived out that aesthetic sense in being simultaneously impoverished poet and exquisite dandy. Sentiments of revulsion and gestures of defiance against the dull rationality of the monetary calculus abound in contemporary life.

Revulsion against the tightening chronological net around all aspects of social life has been no less marked. It took decades before the skilled workers, for example, would surrender their right to "blue Monday," (see Chap. 3, table 9) and in certain occupations, such as mining and construction, absenteeism and intermittent employment are so normal as hardly to call for special comment. And the fight over minutes and moments within the labor process is as eternal as it has been fierce, forcing employers even in recent years to all manner of concessions (flexitime, quality circles, etc.) in order to contain the spirit of revolt in bounds.

[2] The peculiar and deeply paranoid bourgeois fear of the criminal classes in the nineteenth century, a reading of Chevalier (1973) suggests, had much to do with the idea that there was an alternative and subversive underworld that constituted a totally different form of society from that projected by bourgeois culture. "The thieves form a republic with its own manners and customs," wrote Balzac; "they present in the social scene a reflection of those illustrious highwaymen whose courage, character, exploits and eminent qualities will always be admired. Thieves have a language, leaders and police of their own; and in London, where their association is better organized, they have their own syndics, their own parliament and their own deputies" (quoted in Chevalier 1973, 70–71).

There were also many voices within the bourgeoisie, like that of Simmel, who worried about or openly revolted against the rigid discipline of the watch. "We are weighed down, every moment," complained Baudelaire (1983b, 97), "by the conception and sensation of Time." Its seeming scarcity arose, he felt, out of a pace and style of modern life in which "one can only forget Time by making use of it." "It was briefly fashionable," records Benjamin (1973, 54), for Parisians during the 1840s to express their contempt for the discipline of time by taking "turtles for a walk in the arcades." At the end of the nineteenth century in particular, the bourgeois literati sought refuge from the domination of universal and abstract public time through subjective explorations of their own private sense of time (Proust and Joyce spring most easily to mind). Conrad expressed the sense of revolt more directly: he had the anarchist in *The Secret Agent* take on the task of blowing up the Greenwich meridian. But although our thinking about time has never been the same since, this spirit of revolt, which Kern (1983) for one makes much of, was nourished out of a context in which time was becoming more and more rationally and universally defined. What the literati really discovered, of course, was something that had been evident to the working classes for generations: that it takes money to command free time, real as opposed to imaginary release from the rigid discipline of organized public time. In this respect poor Baudelaire lived under a double sufferance: despising money, he lacked the means to put himself outside of the discipline of time. Small wonder that he never ceased to rail against the crassness of bourgeois materialism and elevated the dandy and the flâneur to the status of heroes.

The capacity to appropriate space freely has likewise been held, in both thought and social practice, an important and vital freedom. Freedom to roam the city streets without fear of compromise is not necesarily given by money. Indeed, situations frequently arise where the least privileged in the social order have the greatest liberty in this regard (Cobb 1975, 126). Restriction of the freedom to appropriate space through private property rights and other social forms of domination and control (including that exercised by the state) often provokes all manner of social protest movements (from the reappropriation of central Paris during the Commune by the popular classes expelled therefrom by Haussman's works, to civil rights sit-ins and "take-back-the-night" marches). The demand to liberate space from this or that form of domination and reconstitute it in a new image, or to protect privileged spaces from external threat or internal dissolution, lies at the center of many urban protest movements and community struggles (Lefebvre 1974; Castells 1983). And to the degree that the fragmentation of space which accompanies its homogenization allowed the formation of protected islands outside of direct social control, so opportunities arose for all manner of subversive visions of community and place, and their spatial integument, to take root. Innumerable dissident groups – anarchists like Kropotkin (1968), women of the sort that Hayden (1981) describes, communitarians like the religious and secular groups (the Cabetists, for example) that played such an important role in the settling of America, the alternative life-style movements that created the "communes" of the 1960s, and so forth – all sought to liberate and appropriate their own space for their own purposes. And in so doing they mounted a practical challenge to the supposed homogeneity of abstract, universalized space.

But such social movements must be understood in terms of what they are revolting against. The search for "authentic community" and a "sense of place" became all the more fierce as the community of money and the annihilation of absolute place under the domination of money became more powerfully felt. And the search bore partial fruit. Kinship ties were resurrected by urban dwellers (Hareven 1982), new networks of social contacts forged (Fischer 1982), and whole new communities created that often managed to seal themselves off in protected spaces behind all manner of symbols and signs (from gatehouses and walls to street names and postal codes) to emphasize the special qualities of neighbourhood and place. Urban style and fashion, Simmel (1978) points out, are convenient ways to reintroduce the social distinctions that the democracy of money tends to undermine. And so arose the modern sense of "community" so dear to sociologists, though they took a while to lose that prejudice that sees rurality as the true incarnation of authentic community and the city as merely the site of social breakdown, of pure individualism and social anomie. Gans (1962) thus brought to life in *The Urban Villagers* what had been evident to close observers of the urban scene for many years; that the struggle to create protected places and communities was as fiercely fought in urban areas (Gissing's London, for example) as its evident loss was felt in rural areas (like Hardy's Wessex). Under such conditions, too, the family can take on new meaning and significations, as a "haven in a heartless world" (Lasch 1977), a social center in which considerations of money, time, and space can be treated in a radically different way from those prevailing in public life (Hareven 1982).

The revolt within intellectual circles against the kind of rationality implied within the community of money – a rationality that extended, as we have seen, across conceptions of time and space as well as of value – is as broad as it is historically long. For if Auguste Comte, the father of positivism, anointed the bankers as managers of his utopia (a far from utopian condition, as we seem close to realizing in practice these days), there were many others, from Carlyle and Ruskin, to William Morris and Neitzsche, through Heidegger and Sartre, who saw things quite differently. And if liberals, those "historical representatives of intellectualism and of money transactions," as Simmel (1978, 432) calls them, have been inclined "to condone everything because they understand everything" and to represent it in a kind of passionless and objective scientific discourse, there have been many others, from conservatives to Marxists, prepared to dispute them with a passion liberals have found both disconcerting and distasteful.

More problematic are those social movements that reject rationality and seek solace in mysticism, religion, or some other transcendental or subjective ideology. Religious alternatives or proposals for alternatives to the community of money abound and frequently spark social practices outside of the overwhelming rationalities of modern life. Fascism likewise defines an alternative sense of community to that defined by money, exalts absolute place (the soil, the fatherland), appeals to an entirely different sense of historical time (in which the playing out of myth has great importance), and worships values of a higher order than those embodied in money. Far from being a direct expression of capitalism, fascism as an ideology expresses violent opposition to the rationality implicit in the community of money, and the historical symbols of that community – Jews and intellectuals – are consequently singled out for persecution. Marxists also seek a society in which the value of human life is appraised in ways other than through the market. And while they usually cling to the idea of rational planning as a positive virtue, they have often embraced in practice nationalist definitions of community that are as opposed to their own ideology of internationalism as they are to the universality of money. Indeed, there has been hardly a single dissident cultural, political, or social movement these last two hundred years in the advanced capitalist world that has not had somewhere at its base some kind of striving to transcend the money form and its associated rational conceptions of the proper use of space and time. Most of the vivacity and color of modern life, in fact, arises precisely out of the spirit of revulsion and revolt against the dull, colorless, but seemingly transcendental powers of money in abstract and universal space and time.

Yet all such social movements, no matter how well articulated their aims, run up against a seemingly immovable paradox. For not only does the community of money define them in an oppositional sense, but the movements have to confront the social power of money directly if they are to succeed. Colorless and heartless it may be, but money remains the overwhelming source of social power, and what Marx calls its "dissolving effects" are perpetually at work within the family or within alternative "authentic communities" that social groups struggle to define. Such a tendency is writ large in the history of innumerable organizations, from communes that either founder on money questions or convert into efficient enterprises, religious organizations that become so obsessed with the accumulation of money that they pervert the message they propose, to socialist governments that come to power with noble visions only to find they lack the money to carry out their plans. All manner of oppositional movements have come to grief as they stumble upon the rock of money as the central and universal source of social power.

It takes money, we can conclude, to construct any alternative to the society predicated on the community of money. This is the essential truth that all social movements have to confront; otherwise, it confronts and destroys them. Money may be, as the moralists have it, the root of all evil, yet it appears also as the unique means of doing good. Zola (1967, 224–25) understood that truth very well:

Mme Caroline was struck with the sudden revelation that money was the dung-heap that nurtured the growth of tomorrow's humanity. . . . Without speculation there could be no vibrant and fruitful undertakings any more than there could be children without lust. It took this excess of passion, all this contemptibly wasted and lost life, to ensure the continuation of life. . . . Money, the poisoner and destroyer, was becoming the seed-bed for all forms of social growth. It was the manure needed to sustain the great public works whose execution was bringing the peoples of the globe together and pacifying the earth. She had cursed money, but now she prostrated herself before it in a frightening adulation: it alone could raze a mountain, fill in an arm of the sea, at last render the earth inhabitable to mankind. . . . Everything that was good came out of that which was evil.

Love and money may make the world go around, Zola seems to say, but love of money provides the raw energy at the center of the whirlwind.

V. MONEY, SPACE, AND TIME AS SOURCES OF SOCIAL POWER

That the possession of money confers enormous social powers upon its owners requires no substantial demonstration. Marx (1964b, 167) parodies (though not by much) the seeming magic of its powers thus:

The extent of the power of money is the extent of my power. . . . I am ugly, but I can buy for myself the most beautiful of women. Therefore I am not ugly. . . . I am stupid, but money is the real mind of all things and how then should its possessor be stupid? Besides, he can buy talented people for himself, and is he who has power over the talented not more talented than the talented? Do not I, who thanks to money am capable of all that the human heart longs for, possess all human capacities? Does not my money, therefore, transform all my incapacities into their contrary?

The social power of money has, therefore, ever been the object of desire, lust, and greed. Thus does the concrete abstraction of money acquire its powers relative to and over us.

But what of space and time? Once constituted as concrete abstractions within the community of money, do they not also become sources of social power? Do not those who dominate them also possess strong powers of social control? Such a thesis calls for at least some minimal demonstration. The demonstration will lack point, however, unless we also bear in mind that it is the interconnections between command of money, space, and time as intersecting sources of social power that in the end matter.[3] Money can thus be used to command time (including that of others) and space, while command over time and space can easily be parlayed back into command over money. The property speculator who has the money to wait and who can influence the development of adjacent spaces is in a better situation than someone who lacks powers in any one of these dimensions.

Command over space, as every general and geopolitician knows, is of the utmost strategic significance in any power struggle. The same principle also applies within the world of commodity exchange. Every supermarket manager also knows that command over a strategic space within the overall construction of social space is worth its weight in gold. This value of space lies at the root of land rent. But spatial competition is always monopolistic competition, simply because two functions cannot occupy exactly the same location. Capture of strategic spaces within the overall space can confer much more than its aliquot share of control. The struggle between diverse railroad interests in the nineteenth century provides abundant examples of this principle at work, while Tarbell (1904, 146) pictures Rockefeller "bent over a map and with military precision [planning] the capture of the strategic locations on the map of East Coast oil refineries." Control over strategic land parcels within the urban matrix confers immense power over the whole pattern of development. And although the liberation of space and the annihilation of space by time erode any permanent power that may attach to control of strategic spaces, the monopolistic element is always recreated afresh. Indeed, control over the production of spatial organization then becomes fundamental to the creation of new spatial monopolies. The importance of such monopoly power is precisely that it gives rise to monopoly rent and can thereby be converted into money.

But the created space of society is also, as Lefebvre (1974) insists, the space of social reproduction. Thus, control over the creation of that space also confers a certain power over the processes of social reproduction. We can see

---

[3] These intersections are, I suspect, at the root of Benjamin's (1973) fascination with the figures of the *flâneur*, the dandy, and the gambler in nineteenth-century culture. He comments, for example, "To the phantasmagoria of space, to which the flâneur was addicted, corresponded the phantasmagoria of time, to which the gambler dedicated himself. Gambling transformed time into a narcotic" (174).

this principle at work within the most diverse of social circumstances. The organization of space within the household says much about power and gender relations within the family, for example, while hierarchical structures of authority or privilege can be communicated directly through forms of spatial organization and symbolism. Control over spatial organization and authority over the use of space become crucial means for the reproduction of social power relations. The state, or some other social grouping such as financiers, developers, or landlords, can thus often hide their power to shape social reproduction behind the seeming neutrality of their power to organize space (Lefebvre 1974, 369). Only at certain moments – gross gerrymandering of political boundaries, the dismantling of spaces of opposition by a higher power (the suppression of the Paris Commune or recent attempts to do away with the Greater London Council), corruption within a system of planning permissions – does the nonneutrality of the creation of space become evident. The power to shape space then appears as one of the crucial powers of control over social reproduction. And it is exactly on this basis that those who have the professional and intellectual skills to shape space materially and effectively – engineers, architects, planners, and so on – can themselves acquire a certain power and convert their specialized knowledge into financial benefit.

The relation between command over money and command over time as sources of social power is no less compelling. Those who can afford to wait always have an advantage over those who cannot. The case is at its most obvious during strikes and lockouts when workers (in the absence of any extensive money reserves) can quickly be reduced to starvation while the owners, however much their profits may be singed, continue to dine at full tables. Capitalists can continue to command the surplus labor time of workers in part because they can wait them out during phases of active class struggle. The same principle applies within the bourgeoisie. The merchant who can wait on payment has a power advantage over a producer who cannot, and at moments of crisis well-heeled financiers can dispose of rivals who have to roll over their debts – thus did James Rothschild dispose of the Pereires's Crédit Mobilier in 1867 (see Chap. 3). Differential capacity to command time consolidates the hierarchy of money power within the bourgeoisie.

Similar pressures exist within the work force and in the hidden interiors of family life. If, for example, there is any sense at all to that strange concept of "human capital formation," it is simply that those who can afford to defer present gratification have the opportunity to acquire skills that may form the basis for improved life chances. In effect, workers use time (their own or that of their children) in the hope, sometimes vain, that education will yield a long-run increase in money power. The organization of money and time within the family for this and other purposes is a complex affair; for as Hareven (1982) shows, different trade-offs exist between members of a family (the capacity to mobilize time is not always a matter of money), and different ways for capturing any monetary benefits can also be devised. For while male wage earners may assume that bringing home money gives them the right to command the time of spouse and children, the worktime of women in the home can also be viewed as one of the crucial assets within the family for freeing the time of others to capture monetary benefits in the marketplace (Pahl 1984). Small wonder that the relations between the command of money and time within family life form a crucial zone of gender conflict.

Also, while many within the bourgeoisie fritter away the "free time" given by money wealth in immediate and luxurious self-indulgence (a practice viewed as doubly outrageous when indulged in by workers), there are also those who use the free time so liberated to engage in scientific, artistic, and cultural endeavors that can in turn be parlayed into enormous power in the realms of scientific knowledge, technological understanding, and ideology. Power over research or cultural production time (including the time of others) is a vital power over social reproduction which resides with the wealthy or the state. Many an artist and researcher has tried to revolt against the hegemony of money power over their time. The most successful, of course, have been those who have converted a technical expertise over the efficient disposal of other people's time into the kind of monopoly power that allows them to extract a monopoly price. Herein, to a large degree, lies the significance of the buying and selling of scientific and technical know-how over the proper use of time, space, and money in contemporary society.

Money, time, and space all exist as concrete abstractions framing daily life. Universal, objective, and minutely quantifiable, they each acquire these particular qualities through certain dominant social practices of which commodity exchange and the social division of labor are in the first instance of the greatest importance. Prices, the movements of the clock, rights to clearly marked spaces, form the frameworks within which we operate and to whose signals and significations we perforce respond as powers external to our individual consciousness and will. And no matter how fiercely the spirit of revulsion and revolt may occasionally flare, the tight norms defined by such concrete abstractions are by now so deeply entrenched that they appear almost as facts of nature. To challenge these norms and the concrete abstractions in which they are grounded (to challenge, for example, the tyranny of the public clock or the necessity of the price system) is to challenge the central pinions of our social life.

But the concrete abstractions of money, time, and space are not defined independently of each other. Money, for example, arises out of exchange and the spatial division of labor and represents social labor time. But by the same token the formation of the world market depends crucially upon the rise of an appropriate money form and the spread of the psychological preconditions necessary to its proper use. I insist upon the significance of such interrelations in part because other commentators (ranging from neoclassical economists to time-space geographers) so frequently ignore them. But I also insist that the power relations between individuals, groups, and even whole social classes, and the consequent capacity to find feasible paths of social transformation, are broadly defined through the meshing of monetary, spatial, and chronological nets that define the parameters of social action. For it is hard to go outside of these parameters. Even Conrad's secret agent, who wanted to blow up the Greenwich meridian, might be aghast at the social chaos that would surely now result.

VI. THE CIRCULATION AND ACCUMULATION OF CAPITAL

What happens when we inject the circulation and accumulation of capital into this framework of thought? Capitalists most certainly make use of the social power of money and carefully cultivate command over time and space as sources of social power.[4] But capitalist practices give money, time, and space even more specific (and in some cases restrictive) meanings than they have within the simple community of money. At the same time, these practices create incoherency and contradiction within the intersecting nets of social power.

All money is not capital. But capital is the social power of money used to make more money, most typically through a form of circulation in which money is used to buy commodities (labor power and means of production) which, when combined within a particular labor process, produce a fresh commodity to be sold at a profit. The importance of this form of circulation can be judged by the fact that most of the commodities sustaining daily life under advanced capitalism are produced this way.

Marx lays bare the essential characteristics of such a mode of production and circulation. The perpetual search for profit means "accumulation for accumulation's sake," the perpetual expansion of the value and the physical quantity of output over time. Logistical growth, necessary to maintain stability, is commonly regarded as inevitable and good. But expansion occurs through the exploitation of living labor in production. This presupposes the buying and selling of labor power as a commodity, a class relation between capital and labor, and struggle between them within the labor process as well as in the labor market. This class struggle, when coupled with intercapitalist competition, forces the system to be technologically dynamic. Technological

---

[4] This is one of the profounder and often unrecognized themes worked out in Marx's *Economic and Philosophic Manuscripts*.

change is also seen as inevitable and good. Marx's genius, of course, was to show how and why such a system was necessarily unstable. Technological change tends to remove living labor, the agent of expansion, from production and so undermines the capacity to expand. Periodic crises are, therefore, as inevitable as the twin compulsions toward logistical growth and technological revolution (cf. Harvey 1982, 1985).

Capitalism consequently creates a more and more universal sense of what Hareven (1982) calls "historical time." Cyclical rhythms of prosperity and depression integrate into periodic revolutions in the labor process. From 1848 to 1933, and from then until now, the world has experienced an ever-increasing synchronization of its economic activities. Our experiences, our life chances, and even our conceptual understandings increasingly depend upon where we are situated on the logistical growth curves and their periodic interruptions and descents into confusion and crisis. The temporal net of possibilities appears less and less open and more attached to the lawlike behavior of capitalist development over time.

This history occurs within a geography that is likewise subject to radical transformations. Capitalism, Marx (1973, 407–10) insists, necessarily accelerates spatial integration within the world market, the conquest and "liberation" of space, and the annihilation of space by time. In so doing it accentuates rather than undermines the significance of space. Capitalism has survived, says Lefebvre (1976, 21), "only by occupying space, by producing space." The ability to find a "spatial fix" to its inner contradictions has proven one of its saving graces (cf. Harvey 1982, 1985). While the community of money implies the formation of the world market, therefore, the community of capital requires the geographical deepening and widening of processes of capital accumulation at an accelerating rate.

Although the temporal and spatial rhythms of expansion and contraction are broadly given within the laws of accumulation, there are all manner of cross-cutting tensions that render the historical geography of capitalism an unpredictable and often incoherent affair. If, for example, the fundamental condition of crisis is one of overaccumulation – the existence of excess capital and labor side by side – then such surpluses can be absorbed by temporal displacement (debt-financed long-term investments), spatial expansion (the production of new spaces), or some combination of the two. Which dominates and where cannot be specified in advance. But we can say that the mechanics of urban growth (and indebtedness) and geographical construction (peripherally or within a system of cities) are embedded within such an overall process.

Other tensions exist. Consider, first, the time it takes for capital to complete its circulation from money back to money plus profit. Each labor process has its own turnover time, and increasing fragmentation in the division of labor poses serious problems of coordination under conditions where profit is the sole objective. The problems are overcome through new uses of money. The credit system steps center stage to coordinate devergent turnover times. Furthermore, the acceleration of turnover time yields competitive advantage and so becomes an objective of technological change. This acceleration largely depends, however, on the deployment of fixed capital, which turns over slowly. Again, the technical problems of arranging such forms of investment can be resolved only through appeal to the credit system. The special relation between time and money is put to special use. But a tension arises because the circulation of a part of the capital has to be slowed down in order to accelerate the circulation of the remainder. There is no necessary net gain here. Pressure then arises to accelerate the turnover time of the fixed capital, to write off the value of fixed capital at an accelerating rate (no matter what its physical lifetime), and even to replace it before its economic lifetime is out. Machinery, buildings, and even whole urban infrastructures and life-styles are made prematurely obsolescent; "creative destruction" becomes necessary to the survival of the system. But the capacity to set such processes in motion depends upon conditions within the credit system – the supply and demand for money capital, the rate of money growth, and so on. Cyclical rhythms of investment and disinvestment in machinery and in built environments connect to interest rate movements, inflation, and growth of the money supply, and hence to phases of unemployment and expansion. Time horizons are more and more tightly defined via the credit system. But we also note that the meaning of value and the stability of money as its measure (its devaluation through inflation) also become more elastic in response to changing time horizons. The concrete abstractions of money and time become even more closely intertwined.

Consider, second, how pressures within the circulation of capital lead to the systematic pursuit of the annihilation of space by time. Again, we encounter a contradiction. Space can be overcome only through the production of space, of systems of communication and physical infrastructures embedded in the land. Natural landscapes are replaced by built landscapes shaped through competition to the requirements of acclerating accumulation. The "pulverization" and fragmentation necessary to homogenize space have to take definite forms. Landownership has to be rendered subservient to money power as a higher-order form of property, and land becomes a form of "fictitious capital"; thus, control over the production of space is passed to the interior of the credit system. The uneven development of space then becomes a primary expression of its homogeneity. Immense concentrations of productive force and labor power are assembled in urban areas in the midst of the greatest possible spatial dispersal of commodity flows within a spatially articulated urban hierarchy organized so as to minimize turnover time. This fixed landscape of uneven development then becomes the barrier to be overcome. And overcome it is, but only through the same processes of "creative destruction" which wash away the dead weight of past investments from current concerns. The annihilation of space by time proceeds apace. But it is now the created spaces of capitalism, the spaces of its own social reproduction, that have to be annihilated.

Consider now the social implications of these dual contradictions. Space can be overcome only through the production of a fixed space, and turnover time can be accelerated only by fixing a portion of the total capital in time. The fixed spaces and times can be overcome only through creative self-destruction. We look at the material solidity of a building, a canal, a highway, and behind it we see always the insecurity that lurks within a circulation process of capital, which always asks: how much more time in this relative space? The rush of human beings across space is now matched by an accelerating pace of change in the produced landscapes across which they rush. Processes as diverse as suburbanization, deindustrialization and restructuring, gentrification and urban renewal, through to the total reorganization of the spatial structure of the urban hierarchy, are part and parcel of a general process of continuous reshaping of geographical landscapes to match the quest to accelerate turnover time. The destruction of familiar places and secure spaces of social reproduction provokes many an anguished cry, not only from the poor and impoverished who are left "grieving for a lost home," deprived of even the minor "sources of residential satisfaction in an urban slum" (to appropriate two of Fried's [1963; Fried and Gleicher 1961] more trenchant titles). Zola (1954b, 293–95) records the distress of a businessman of humble origins who discovers his childhood lodgings exposed in the midst of Haussman's demolitions. Henry James (1946) was not to be outdone. Returning to New York after many years of absence, he saw an urban landscape possessed by "the reiterated sacrifice to pecuniary profit" (191) and "in perpetual repudiation of the past" (53). "We are only installments, symbols, stop-gaps," the proud villas seem to say; "we have nothing to do with continuity, responsibility, transmission" (11). There was, James admitted, much about the past that deserved repudiation, "yet there had been an old conscious commemorated life too, and it was this that had become the victim of supersession" (53). The whole American landscape, he complained, sat there "only in the lurid light of business, and you know . . . what guarantees, what majestic continuity and heredity, that represents" (161). Familiar places and secure spaces were being annihilated within the "whirligig of time" – but it was the circulation of capital that was calling the tune.

Out of sentiments such as these many a movement of revulsion and revolt can build against the monstrous figure of the developer, the speculator, the urban renewer, and the highway builder who, like Robert Moses, takes a "meat-axe" to living communities. The evil inherent in such figures has become legendary. They are the centerpieces of what Berman (1982) defines as "the tragedy of development" whose epitome is Goethe's Faust, raging on the hilltop as he contemplates the one small piece of space, occupied by a venerable old couple, that has yet to be integrated into the rationalized and produced space appropriate for modern capitalist forms of development. Zola (1954b, 76–78) recaptures that very same image. Saccard, the archetypal speculator of Second Empire Paris, stands on the butte Montmartre with the "recumbent giant" of Paris at his feet, smiles into space, and "with his hand spread out, open and sharp-edged as a cutlass," cuts through space to symbolize Haussman's wounding slashes through the veins of a living city, wounds that spurt gold and give sustenance "to a hundred thousand navvies and bricklayers." The perpetual reshaping of the geographical landscape of capitalism is a process of violence and pain.

Bourgeois objections to such consequences of capitalism are based on more than Baudelaire's (1983a, 90) lament that "no human heart changes half so fast as a city's face." They record more than nostalgia for the loss of a past, the destruction of the affectivity of "knowable communities" and familiar places (Williams 1973). They go deeper, too, than that anguished culture of modernity which Berman (1982, 15) evokes as a universally shared "mode of vital experience – experience of space and time, of the self and others, of life's possibilities and perils," experience that "promises us adventure, power, joy, growth, transformation of ourselves and the world – and at the same time, that threatens to destroy everything we have, everything we know, everything we are." What is being expressed, rather, is a pervasive fear that the dominant mode of production and social reproduction upon which the perpetuation of bourgeois power rests is itself nothing more than what Marx calls "a self-dissolving contradiction."

It is rather as if the strings within the monetary, temporal, and spatial nets that frame social life are pulled taut in the face of an accumulation process that demands their rapid adaptation and reorganization. Simultaneously tightened and stretched, the nets distort and snap, only to be hastily repaired into a patchwork quilt of new possibilities.

The sensation of disruption and incoherence in the framing of social life, in the true sources of social power, is universally felt but in different ways. For example, the social spaces of reproduction, which appeared so coherent to Gissing and which the Chicago sociologists could conveniently fit into some organic theory of urban form, lose their functional coherence and are transformed under contradictory pressures stemming from changing labor market demand on the one hand and the need to stimulate consumption through the mobilization of fashion and style as artificial marks of social distinction on the other. The obsolescence of "created community" becomes just as important as its firm implantation. The speed-up of labor processes and of the circulation of money, goods, information, and so forth provokes resistance and protest from workers who are nevertheless integrated into the mass expectation of instantaneous satisfaction of their own wants and needs. Control over space likewise loses its coherence. The annihilation of space by time proceeds differentially according to whether it is money, commodities, productive capacity, labor power, information, or technical know-how that is being moved – control within one of these networks of motion can be all too easily by-passed by movement in another (with money and information appearing as superior powers simply by virtue of the speed with which they can be moved). The buying and selling of futures (itself an extraordinary conception requiring psychological and intellectual preconditions that far exceed anything Simmel ever dreamed of) can even invert the realities of economic time so as to make the time incoherencies of a Robbe-Grillet novel appear as a realistic representation. The value of money, once a secure representation of value, gyrates as wildly as the time-space horizons of social action. Not only does inflation render the social power of money suspect, but money itself disintegrates into a cacophony of competing definitions (paper, private debts, coin, gold, state debt, special drawing rights, quantified by mysterious numbers like M1, M2, M3). The circulation of capital explodes the contradictions inherent in the money form and proves far more effective, ironically, than any secret agent at undermining the coherence of money, space, and time as secure frameworks of social power.

These incoherencies create all manner of opportunities for social transformation into which almost any interest group can step with hope of gain. Opportunities for successful class struggle arise for a working class threatened by transformations in labor markets, labor processes, and the spaces of their social reproduction. But the incoherence and the threat to existing power relations coupled with sentimental attachment to the past spark just as many oppositional movements within an increasingly fragmented bourgeoisie. Movements of revulsion and revolt against capitalism, its social basis or particular effects, become as diverse and incoherent as the system they arise in opposition to. That can in turn provoke a demand to impose coherence, to define secure sources and forms of social power. And if capitalism itself appears threatened by its own internal contradictions, then civil society, if it is to remain capitalist, must somehow bring order to the chaos, rout out the incoherencies, and contain the ferments of revulsion and revolt. The openings created for social transformation must be closed off or clearly defined. A higher power, that of the state, must be invoked as a matter of social survival.

State power and authority must be used not only to contain diverse oppositional movements directly but to anchor the frameworks of money, space, and time as sources of social power. State management of the quantity and qualities of money supply is one of its oldest and most venerable of functions. Central bank money now dominates other forms of money within an economy and is as secure as the state power on which it rests. The art of central banking becomes a litmus test of good government, because the state does not possess absolute powers of money creation but has to act as a powerful and secure mediator between the chaotic processes of money creation within its confines and the universal forms of money on the world market. The state manages and secures many of the basic time frames of decision making and coordination. It synchronizes clocks; it regulates the length of the working day, the length of a working life (through compulsory ages of school leaving and retirement), legal holidays and paid vacations, and hours of opening and closing (of commercial establishments and places of entertainment); and it enforces all the other bits and pieces of legislation that define the time frame of much of social life. The state affects the turnover time of capital either indirectly, through taxation procedures defined for amortization and depreciation and the setting of some social rate of time discount, or directly, by taking charge of many long-term investments and so thinking time horizons that the circulation of capital and financial markets cannot afford to contemplate. The state also facilitates planned obsolescence or spreading the costs of creative destruction (compensation for urban renewal or industrial restructuring, or amelioration of the social impacts of changing labor processes, for example). In all of these respects, the state intervenes to set a time frame within which private investment and individual decisions can be made. The state likewise protects rights to the appropriation of space (both private and public). The planning of the location of industry and population, of housing and public facilities, of transport and communications, of land uses, and so on, creates an overall spatial frame to contain and facilitate the innumerable and fragmented decisions that otherwise shape urban development. In all of these respects, the totalitarianism of the liberal capitalist state restrains the disintegrating tendencies of money, time, and space in the face of the contradictions of capital circulation.

To secure these frames of social action, the state needs more than the power, authority, and legitimacy to impose its will. It also must be able to call upon the requisite scientific and technical understandings. This gives added value to the rationality and intellectuality implied in the community of money. The professions that create and guard such knowledge acquire fresh importance, and their leading figures – Keynes, Le Corbusier, Wiener, and Koopmans, for example – enjoy great prestige. Such intellectuals acquire a well-grounded social power to the degree that their knowledge becomes a vital material force, not only with respect to techniques of production, but also with respect to the global framing of social action through control and management of money, space, and time. Those who can monopolize that kind of knowledge are in a powerful social position. It was no accident, therefore, that the tightening of the monetary, spatial, and chronological nets in the latter half of the nineteenth century was accompanied by the rise of distinctive professions, each with its own corner on the knowledge required to give coherence to those nets. The whole thrust of the Progressive movement in America, a movement that had enormous implications for urban and regional management and planning, was to convert power over knowledge into a class power of intellectuals, professionals, and academics over and above the class war between capital and labor. Though it never rose above that war in the manner they imagined, the power of engineers and managers, economists and architects, systems analysts and experts in industrial organization, could not be taken lightly. It became powerfully embedded in key state and corporate functions as planning became the order of the day. Intellectual conflicts over the meanings of money, space, and time had and continue to have very real material effects. The conflict over modernity and design in architecture, for example, is more than a conflict over taste and aesthetics. It deals directly with the question of the proper framing of the urban process in space and time (Giedion 1941).

The ideals of socialism and centralized planning can appear attractive to such a professional class, as the cases of Oskar Lange, Le Corbusier, Hans Blumenthal, and many others abundantly illustrate. Socialism seemed to hold out the possibility of doing everything that the bourgeois state wanted to do but could not. In intellectual circles the debate over socialism was in practice often reduced to debate over the superior organization of productive forces and the superior rationality of state-planned allocations of space and time as opposed to those achieved by market processes in which money power played a dominant role. It took many years of bitter experience and reluctant self-criticism to recognize that the total rationalization of the uses of space and time by some external authority was perhaps even more repressive than chaotic market allocations (cf. Lefebvre 1974; Duclos 1981). Certainly, to the degree that space and time are forms of social power, their control could all too easily degenerate into a replication of forms of class domination that the elimination of money power was supposed to abolish.

VII. THE URBAN PROCESS AND ITS POLITICAL CONFUSIONS

The urban process under capitalism is fraught with the most extraordinary political confusions, the roots of which can partially be exposed by consideration of how urbanization is framed by the intersecting concrete abstractions of money, space, and time and shaped directly by the circulation of money capital in time and space. The tension between the individualism that attaches to the spending of money and the class experience of earning that money splits the social and psychological foundations for political action. The struggle to command time (one's own or that of others) or to put oneself outside of the crass equation of time with money likewise leads to conflicting political perspectives. Those who are forced to give up surplus labor time to others in order to live will themselves engage in all kinds of struggles not only to limit the time taken from them but also to command the time of others (the time of other family members in housework or of those who offer services). And those who have sufficient money power may seek to define and use their own time in idiosyncratic ways. Money becomes the fundamental means to acquire free time. Only the *clochard*, or hobo, avoids that equation. Nevertheless, there is more than passing recognition on the part of even the most idiosyncratic user of free time that proper and efficient social coordination in universal time (in production as well as in exchange and communications) can be a means to liberate free time from the daily chores of production and reproduction. Even the most anarchistic of us like the traffic lights to be linked and the hours of opening and closing to be clearly marked. On the one hand, we recognize that rational social coordinations in universal time are necessary to sustain life in an urbanized world, while on the other we seek individual freedom from all such temporal discipline. The individualism that money imparts to the use of time conflicts with the social rationality required to be able to use that time creatively and well. State planning and regulation (of hours of labor, of opening and closing times, and so forth) appear unmitigated evils from one perspective and saving virtues from the other.

The struggle to command space is likewise plagued by all manner of ambiguities. The freedom to appropriate and move over space at will is highly valued. Money is an important but by no means exclusive means (as any tramp will tell you) of acquiring such freedom. But money is also often used to secure particular spaces against intrusion. The purchase of private property rights secures exclusive rights to dominate a parcel of space. I suspect the reason why car and homeownership make such an attractive combination is because it ensures an individualized ability to command and protect space simultaneously. Those without money power have to define their territorial privileges by other means. The urban gang protects its turf through violence, and low income and minority populations seek to define collective spaces within which they can exercise the strictest social control. Neighborhoods and communities may consequently be organized in ways antagonistic to pure market valuations, though it is surprising how much community action (particularly in more affluent areas) is oriented to purely market ends (from the defense of housing investments to controlled access to life chances within structured labor markets).

But the pulverization of space by private property and its segmentation into controlled social spaces are antagonistic to the ability to appropriate space freely. The inability to stroll a city out of fear of arrest for trespass or of violence because of some transgression of social space is frustrating. Fragmented powers of domination may also inhibit the structuring of urban space for the efficient use of time. Violently defended private and social spaces often render the structure of urban space relatively static and processes of spatial transformation highly conflictual. Even the vast power of money capital (with its penchant for reducing space to a form of fictitious capital) can be frustrated by such monopolies. Rational spatial planning and state control appear to be adequate respfonses to such problems, though such power can be used for radically different class purposes. The use of state power to free up space for capital (through forced expropriation, urban renewal, and the like) is very different from the use of state power to check the extraction of vast money revenues from those who have to appropriate spaces owned by others in order to live. On the other hand, nationalization of the land and abolition of private property rights does not necessarily liberate space for popular appropriation. It can even lead to the erosion of those limited rights to appropriate space given by private property and other mechanisms of securing social space. The prevention of one mode of dominating space merely creates another.

Such tensions obscure political consciousness and render all political programs problematic. Should the struggle to curb money power lead to curbing money uses? Should the struggle to curb the thirst for surplus labor be accompanied by an abandonment of concern for efficient means of producing a surplus product? Can the struggle to liberate space for free appropriation be waged without incurring new and even more damaging forms of domination? Should the struggle to free space and time from some dominant and repressive universal rationality entail abandonment of the search for super-efficient organizations of space and allocations of time to reproduce daily needs with the minimum of effort?

The analysis of money, space, and time in the context of capital accumulation with its dominant class relations reveals much about the dynamics of the urban process, its inner tensions, and the significance of urbanization to capitalism's evolution. It also helps us understand the dilemmas and confusions that the urban experience produces for political and intellectual consciousness. Given the intricate complexity and sheer scale of urbanization under capitalism and the peculiar mix of alienations and opportunities that arises out of the urban experience, the objectives of radical and revolutionary movements are bound to become confused. Political consciousness becomes multidimensional, often contradictory, and certainly fragmented. The history of urban social movements has to be read in exactly such a light. The history of class-based political movements also illustrates how easily these can be torn asunder by exactly such fragmentations. Small wonder that left political movements all too often studiously ignore urban social movements as peripheral froth but in so doing undermine their credibility and their power to undertake a total transformation of capitalism into some alternative mode of production.

Capitalism these last two hundred years has produced, through its dominant form of urbanization, not only a "second nature" of built environments even harder to transform than the virgin nature of frontier regions years ago, but also an urbanized human nature, endowed with a very specific sense of time, space, and money as sources of social power and with sophisticated abilities and strategies to win back from one corner of urban life what may be lost in another. And while it may be true that some are losers everywhere, the vast majority find at least minor compensations somewhere while the rest find solace and hope in the intricacy of the game. Every political movement against the domination of capital must, at some point, confront such confusions. This is also the kind of fragmented and often contradictory political consciousness that permeates our intellectual representations and proposals as to what a genuinely humanizing urban experience might be all about. It is, therefore, imperative that we step back and reflect upon the rationality and social meaning of our conceptions of money, time, and space as frames within which capitalist urbanization and the urban experience unfold. That way, we can more freely seek conceptions that liberate rather than imprison our thinking as to what a noncapitalist but urbanized human future could be all about.

2

Labor, Capital, and Class Struggle around the Built Environment in Advanced Capitalist Societies

In this chapter I shall seek to establish a theoretical framework for understanding a facet of class struggle under advanced capitalism. The conflicts that will be scrutinized are those that relate to the production and use of the built environment, by which I mean the totality of physical structures – houses, roads, factories, offices, sewage systems, parks, cultural institutions, educational facilities, and so on. In general I shall argue that capitalist society must of necessity create a physical landscape – a mass of humanly constructed physical resources – in its own image, broadly appropriate to the purposes of production and reproduction. But I shall also argue that this process of creating space is full of contradictions and tensions and that the class relations in capitalist society inevitably spawn strong cross-currents of conflict.

I shall assume for purposes of analytic convenience that a clear distinction exists between (1) a faction of capital seeking the appropriation of rent either directly (as landlords, property companies, and the like) or indirectly (as financial intermediaries or others who invest in property simply for a rate of return), (2) a faction of capital seeking interest and profit by building new elements in the built environment (the construction interests), (3) capital "in general", which looks upon the built environment as an outlet for surplus capital and as a bundle of use values for enhancing the production and accumulation of capital, and (4) labor, which uses the built environment as a means of consumption and as a means for its own reproduction. I shall also assume that the built environment can be divided conceptually into *fixed capital* items to be used in production (factories, highways, railroads, and so on) and *consumption fund* items to be used in consumption (houses, roads, parks, sidewalks, and the like).[1] Some items, such as roads and sewer

---

[1] This distinction derives from Marx (1967, 2:211; 1973, 681–87).

systems, can function both as fixed capital and as part of the consumption fund, depending on their use.

I shall restrict attention in this chapter to the structure of conflict as it arises in relation to labor's use of the consumption fund rather than its use of fixed capital in the immediate process of production. An analysis of this aspect of class struggle will do much to illuminate, I believe, the vexing questions that surround the relationship between community conflict and community organizing, on the one hand, and industrial conflict and work-based organizing on the other. In short, I hope to be able to shed some light on the position and experience of labor with respect to *living* as well as *working* in the historical development of those countries that are now generally considered to be in the advanced capitalist category. The examples will be taken from the United States and Great Britain. Some preparatory comments on the general theme to be pursued are in order.

The domination of capital over labor is basic to the capitalist mode of production – without it, after all, surplus value could not be extracted and accumulation would disappear. All kinds of consequences flow from this, and the relation between labor and the built environment can be understood only in terms of it. Perhaps the single most important fact is that industrial capitalism, through the reorganization of the work process and the advent of the factory system, forced a separation between place of work and place of reproduction and consumption. The need to reproduce labor power is thus translated into a specific set of production and consumption activities within the household – a domestic economy that requires use values in the form of a built environment if it is to function effectively.

The needs of labor have changed historically, and they will in part be met by work within the household and in part be procured through market exchanges of wages earned against commodities produced. The commodity requirements of labor depend upon the balance between domestic economy products and market purchases as well as upon the environmental, historical, and moral considerations that fix the standard of living of labor (Marx 1967, 1:171). In the commodity realm, labor can, by organization and class struggle, alter the definition of needs to include "reasonable" standards of nutrition, health care, housing, education, recreation, entertainment, and so on. From the standpoint of capital, accumulation requires a constant expansion of the market for commodities, which means the creation of new social wants and needs and the organization of "rational consumption" on the part of labor. This last condition suggests theoretically what is historically observable – that the domestic economy must steadily give way before the expansion of capitalist commodity production. "Accumulation for accumulation's sake, production for production's sake," which jointly drive the capitalist system onward, therefore entail an increasing integration of labor's consumption into the capitalist system of production and exchange of commodities.[2]

The split between the place of work and the place of residence means that the struggle of labor to control the social conditions of its own existence splits into two seemingly independent struggles. The first, located in the workplace, is over the wage rate, which provides the purchasing power for consumption goods, and the conditions of work. The second, fought in the place of residence, is against secondary forms of exploitation and appropriation represented by merchant capital, landed property, and the like. This is a fight over the costs and conditions of existence in the living place. And it is this second kind of struggle that I focus on here, recognizing, of course, that the dichotomy between *living* and *working* is itself an artificial division that the capitalist system imposes.

I. LABOR VERSUS THE APPROPRIATORS OF RENT AND THE CONSTRUCTION INTEREST

Labor needs living space. Land is therefore a condition of living for labor in much the same way that it is a condition of production for capital. The system of private property that excludes labor from land as a condition of production also serves to exclude labor from the land as a condition of living. As Marx puts it, "The monstrous power wielded by landed property, when united hand in hand with industrial capital, enables it to be used against laborers engaged in their wage struggle as a means of practically expelling them from the earth as a dwelling place" (Marx 1967, 3:773). Apart from space as a basic condition of living we are concerned here with housing, transportation (to jobs and facilities), amenities, facilities, and a whole bundle of resources that contribute to the total living environment for labor. Some of these items can be privately appropriated (housing is the most important case), while others have to be used in common (sidewalks) and in some cases, such as the transportation system, even used jointly with capital.

The need for these items pits labor against landed property and the appropriation of rent as well as against the construction interest, which seeks to profit from the production of these commodities. The cost and quality of these items affect the standard of living of labor. Labor, in seeking to protect and enhance its standard of living, engages in a series of running battles in the living place over a variety of issues that relate to the creation, management, and use of the built environment. Examples are not hard to find — community conflict over excessive appropriation of rent by landlords,

---

[2] This condition can be derived directly from Marxian theory by bringing together the analyses presented in Marx (1967, 1:591–640; 2:437–48, 515–16).

over speculation in housing markets, over the siting of "noxious" facilities, over inflation in housing construction costs, over inflation in the costs of servicing a deteriorating urban infrastructure, over congestion, over lack of accessibility of employment opportunities and services, over highway construction and urban renewal, over the "quality of life" and aesthetic issues — the list seems almost endless.

Conflicts that focus on the built environment exhibit certain peculiar characteristics because the monopoly power conferred by private property arrangements not only generates the power to appropriate rent but also yields to the owners command over a "natural monopoly" in space. The fixed and immobile character of the built environment entails the production and use of commodities under conditions of spatial monopolistic competition with strong "neighborhood" or "externality" effects (Harvey 1973, chaps. 2 and 5). Many of the struggles that occur are over externality effects — the value of a particular house is in part determined by the condition of the houses surrounding it, and each owner is therefore very interested in seeing to it that the neighborhood as a whole is well maintained. In bourgeois theory, the appropriation of rent and the trading of titles to properties set price signals for new commodity production in such a way that a "rational" allocation of land to uses can be arrived at through a market process. But because of the pervasive externality effects and the sequential character of both development and occupancy, the price signals suffer from all manner of serious distortions. There are, as a consequence, all kinds of opportunities for both appropriators and the construction faction, for developers, speculators, and even private individuals, to reap windfall profits and monopoly rents. Internecine conflicts within a class and faction are therefore just as common as conflict between classes and factions.

We are primarily concerned here, however, with the structure of the three-way struggle between labor, the appropriators of rent, and the construction faction. Consider, as an example, the direct struggle between laborers and landlords over the cost and quality of housing. Landlords typically use whatever power they have to appropriate as much as they can from the housing stock they own, and they will adjust their strategy to the conditions in such a way that they maximize the rate of return on their capital. If this rate of return is very high, then new capital will likely flow into landlordism, and, if the rate of return is very low, then we will likely witness disinvestment and abandonment. Labor will seek by a variety of strategies — for example, moving to where housing is cheaper or establishing rent controls and housing codes — to limit appropriation and to ensure a reasonable quality of shelter. How such a struggle is resolved depends very much upon the relative economic and political power of the two groups, the circumstances of supply and demand that exist at a particular place and time, and upon the options that each group has available to it.

The struggle becomes three-dimensional when we consider that the ability of appropriators to gain monopoly rents from the old housing is in part limited by the capacity of the construction interest to enter the market and create new housing at a lower cost. The price of old housing is, after all, strongly affected by the costs of production of new housing. If labor can use its political power to gain state subsidies for construction, then this artificially stimulated new development will force the rate of appropriation on existing resources downward. If, however, appropriators can check new development (by, for example, escalating land costs), or if, for some reason, new development is inhibited (planning permission procedures in Britain have typically functioned in this way), then the rate of appropriation can rise. On the other hand, when labor manages to check the rate of appropriation through direct rent controls, then the price of rented housing falls, new development is discouraged, and scarcity is produced. These are the kinds of conflicts and strategies of coalition that we have to expect in such situations.

But the structure of conflict is made more complex by the "natural monopoly" inherent in space. For example, the monopoly power of the landlord is in part modified by the ability of labor to escape entrapment in the immediate environs of the workplace. Appropriation from housing is very sensitive to changes in transportation. The ability to undertake a longer journey to work is in part dependent upon the wage rate (which allows the worker to pay for travel), in part dependent upon the length of the working day (which gives the worker time to travel), and in part dependent upon the cost and availability of transportation. The boom in the construction of working-class suburbs in late nineteenth-century London, for example, can in large degree be explained by the advent of the railways and the provision of cheap "workman's special" fares and a shortening of the working day, which freed at least some of the working class from the need to live within walking distance of the workplace (Kellet 1969, chap. 11). The rate of rental appropriation on the housing close to the centers of employment had to fall as a consequence. The "streetcar" suburbs of American cities and the working-class suburbs of today (based on cheap energy and the automobile) are further examples of this phenomenon (Taylor 1966; Tarr 1973; Ward 1971). By pressing for new and cheap forms of transportation, labor can escape geographical entrapment and thereby reduce the capacity of landlords in advantageous locations to gain monopoly rents. The problems that attach to spatial entrapment are still with us, of course, in the contemporary ghettos of the poor, the aged, the oppressed minorities, and the like. Access is still, for these groups, a major issue.[3]

[3] The McCone Commission Report on the Watts rebellion in Los Angeles in 1964 attributed much of the discontent to the sense of entrapment generated out of lack of access to transportation.

The struggle to fight off the immediate depredations of the landlord and the continuous battle to keep the cost of living down do much to explain the posture adopted by labor with respect to the distribution, quantities, and qualities of all elements in the built environment. Public facilities, recreational opportunities, amenities, transportation access, and so on, are all subjects of contention. But underlying these immediate concerns is a deeper struggle over the very meaning of the built environment as a set of use values for labor.

The producers of the built environment, both past and present, provide labor with a limited set of choices of living conditions. If labor has slender resources with which to exercise an effective demand, then it has to put up with whatever it can get – shoddily built, cramped, and poorly serviced tenement buildings, for example. With increasing effective demand, labor has the potential to choose over a wider range and, as a result, questions about the overall "quality of life" begin to arise. Capital in general, and that faction of it that produces the built environment, seek to define the quality of life for labor in terms of the commodities that they can profitably produce in certain locations. Labor, on the other hand, defines quality of life solely in use value terms and in the process may appeal to some underlying and very fundamental conception of what it is to be human. Production for profit and production for use are often inconsistent with each other. The survival of capitalism therefore requires that capital dominate labor, not simply in the work process, but with respect to the very definition of the quality of life in the consumption sphere. Production, Marx (1973, Introduction) argued, not only produces consumption, it also produces the mode of consumption; and that, of course, is what the consumption fund for labor is all about. For this reason, capital in general cannot afford the outcome of struggles around the built environment to be determined simply by the relative powers of labor, the appropriators of rent, and the construction faction. It must, from time to time, throw its weight into the balance to effect outcomes that are favorable to the reproduction of the capitalist social order. It is to this aspect of matters that we must now turn.

II. THE INTERVENTIONS OF CAPITAL IN STRUGGLES OVER THE BUILT ENVIRONMENT

When capital intervenes in struggles over the built environment, it usually does so through the agency of state power. A cursory examination of the history of the advanced capitalist countries shows that the capitalist class sometimes throws its weight to the side of labor and sometimes to the side of other factions. But history also suggests a certain pattern and underlying rationale for these interventions. We can get at the pattern by assembling the interventions together under four broad headings – private property and homeownership for the working class, the cost of living and the value of labor power, managed collective consumption of workers in the interest of sustained capital accumulation, and a very complex, but very important, topic concerning the relation to nature, the imposition of work discipline, and the like. A discussion of the pattern will help us to identify the underlying rationale, and in this manner we can identify a much deeper meaning in the everyday struggles in which labor engages in the living place.

Private Property and Homeownership for Labor

The struggle that labor wages in the living place against the appropriation of rent is a struggle against the monopoly power of private property. Labor's fight against the principle of private property cannot easily be confined to the housing arena, and "the vexed question of the relation between rent and wages . . . easily slides into that of capital and labor" (Counter Information Services 1973, 11). For this reason the capitalist class as a whole cannot afford to ignore it; it has an interest in keeping the principle of private property sacrosanct. A well-developed struggle between tenants and landlords – with the former calling for public ownership, municipalization, and the like – calls the whole principle into question. Extended individualized homeownership is therefore seen as advantageous to the capitalist class because it promotes the allegiance of at least a segment of the working class to the principle of private property, promotes an ethic of "possessive individualism" (McPherson 1962), and brings about a fragmentation of the working class into "housing classes" of homeowners and tenants (Rex and Moore 1975). This gives the capitalist class a handy ideological lever to use against public ownership and national-ization demands because it is easy to make such proposals sound as if the intent is to take workers' privately owned houses away from them.

The majority of owner-occupants do not own their housing outright, however. They make interest payments on a mortgage. This puts finance capital in a hegemonic position with respect to the functioning of the housing market – a position that it is in no way loath to make use of (Stone 1975; Harvey 1975). The apparent entrance of workers into the petit form of property ownership in housing is, to a large degree, its exact opposite in reality – the entry of money capital into a controlling position within the consumption fund. Finance capital not only controls the disposition and rate of new investment in housing but controls labor as well through chronic debt-encumbrance. A worker mortgaged up to the hilt is, for the most part, a pillar of social stability, and schemes to promote homeownership within the working class have long recognized this basic fact. And in return the worker may build up, very slowly, some equity in the property.

This last consideration has some important ramifications. Workers put their savings into the physical form of a property. Obviously, they will be concerned to preserve the value of those savings and if possible to enhance them. Ownership of housing can also lead to petit landlordism, which has been a traditional and very important means for individual workers to engage in the appropriation of values at the expense of other workers. But more importantly, every homeowner, whether he or she likes it or not, is caught in a struggle over the appropriation of values because of the shifting patterns of external costs and benefits within the built environment. A new road may destroy the value of some housing and enhance the value of others, and the same applies to all manner of new development, redevelopment, accelerated obsolescence, and so on.

The way in which labor relates to these externality effects is crucial, if only because the housing market is in quantitative terms by far the most important market for any one particular element in the built environment. It would be very difficult to understand the political tension between suburbs and central cities in the United States without recognizing the fragmentation that occurs within the working class as one section of it moves into homeownership and becomes deeply concerned to preserve and if possible to enhance the value of its equity. The social tensions omnipresent within the "community structure" of American cities are similarly affected. Home-ownership, in short, invites a faction of the working class to wage its inevitable fight over the appropriation of value in capitalist society in a very different way. It puts them on the side of the principle of private property and frequently leads them to appropriate values at the expense of other factions of the working class. With such a glorious tool to divide and rule at its disposal, it is hardly surprising that capital in general sides with labor in this regard against the landed interest. It is rather as if capital, having relied upon landed property to divorce labor from access to one of the basic conditions of production, preserves the principle of private property intact in the context of class struggle by permitting labor to return to the face of the earth as a partial owner of land and property as a condition of consumption.

The Cost of Living and the Wage Rate

Marx argued that the value of labor power was determined by the value of the commodities required to reproduce that labor power. This neat equivalence disappears in the pricing realm, but nevertheless there is a relation of some sort between wages and the cost of obtaining those commodities essential to the reproduction of the household.[4]

[4] The relation between values and prices in Marxian theory is highly problematic and involves us in the celebrated "transformation problem." To avoid making silly mistakes it is important to bear in mind that the value of labor power is not automatically represented by the wage rate.

An excessive rate of appropriation of rent by landlords will increase the cost of living to labor and generate higher wage demands that, if won, may have the effect of lowering the rate of accumulation of capital. For this reason capital in general may side with labor in the struggle against excessive appropriation and attempt also to lower the costs of production of a basic commodity such as housing. Capitalists may themselves seek to provide cheap housing, as in the "model communities" typical of the early years of the industrial revolution, or they may even side with the demands of labor for cheap, subsidized housing under public ownership, provided that this permits the payment of lower wages. For the same reason the capitalist class may seek to promote, through the agency of the state, the industrialization of building production and the rationalization of production of the built environment through comprehensive land use planning policies, new town construction programs, and the like. Capitalists tend to become interested in such things, however, only when labor is in a position, through its organized collective power, to tie wages to the cost of living.

These considerations apply to all elements in the built environment (and to social services and social expenditures also) that are relevant to the reproduction of labor power. Those that are publicly provided (which means the bulk of them outside of housing and until recently transportation) can be monitored by a cost-conscious municipal government under the watchful eye of the local business community, and, perhaps, in an emergency situation such as that experienced in New York both in the 1930s and the 1970s, even under direct supervision by the institutions of finance capital. In the interests of keeping the costs of reproduction of labor power at a minimum, the capitalist class as a whole may seek collective means to intervene in the processes of investment and appropriation in the built environment. In much the same way that the proletariat frequently sided with the rising industrial bourgeoisie against the landed interest in the early years of capitalism, so we often find capital in general siding with labor in the advanced capitalist societies against excessive appropriation of rent and rising costs of new development. The coalition is not forged altruistically but arises organically out of the relation between the wage rate and the costs of reproduction of labor power.

"Rational," Managed, and Collective Consumption

Workers mediate the circulation of commodities by using their wages to purchase means of consumption produced by capitalists. Any failure on the part of workers to use their purchasing power correctly and rationally from the standpoint of the capitalist production and realization system will disrupt the circulation of commodities. In the early years of capitalist development this problem was not so important because trade with noncapitalist societies could easily take up any slack in effective demand. But with the transition to advanced capitalism, the internal market provided by the wage-labor force becomes of greater and greater significance. Also, as standards of living rise, in the sense that workers have more and more commodities available to them, so the potential for a breakdown from "irrationalities" in consumption increases. The failure to exercise a proper effective demand can be a source of crisis. And it was, of course, Keynes's major contribution to demonstrate to the capitalist class that under certain conditions the way out of a crisis manifest as a falling profit rate was not to cut wages but to increase them and thereby to expand the market.

This presumes, however, that workers are willing to spend their wages "rationally." If we assume, with Adam Smith, that mankind has an infinite and insatiable appetite for "trinkets and baubles," then there is no problem, but Malthus (1951, 321) voiced another worry when he observed that the history of human society "sufficiently demonstrates [that] an efficient taste for luxuries and conveniences, that is, such a taste as will properly stimulate industry, instead of being ready to appear the moment it is required is a plant of slow growth." Production may, as Marx (1973, Introduction) averred, produce consumption and the mode of consumption, but it does not do so automatically, and the manner in which it does so is the locus of continuous struggle and conflict.

Consider, first of all, the relationship between capitalist production and the household economy. In the United States in 1810, for example, "the best figures available to historians show that . . . about two-thirds of the clothing worn . . . was the product of household manufacture," but by 1860 the advent of industrial capitalism in the form of the New England textile industry had changed all that – "household manufactures had been eclipsed by the development of industrial production and a market economy" (Bender 1975, 28–29; Tryon 1917). Step by step, activities traditionally associated with household work are brought within the capitalist market economy – baking, brewing, preserving, cooking, food preparation, washing, cleaning, and even child-rearing and child socialization. And with respect to the built environment, house-building and maintenance become integrated into the market economy. In the United States in the nineteenth century a substantial proportion of the population built their own homes with their own labor and local raw materials. Now almost all units are built through the market system.

The advent of the factory system was a double-edged sword with respect to the household economy. On the one hand it extracted the wage earner(s) from the home. In the early years of industrial capitalism it did so for twelve or fourteen hours a day and, under particularly exploitative conditions, forced the whole household – women and children as well as men – into the wage labor force (in this manner the wages of the *household* could remain stable in the face of a falling wage rate). Of these early years E. P. Thompson (1968,455) writes: "Each stage in industrial differentiation and specialization struck also at the family economy, disturbing customary relations between man and wife, parents and children, and differentiating more sharply between 'work' and 'life.' It was to be a full hundred years before this differentiation was to bring returns, in the form of labour-saving devices, back into the working woman's home."

This "return" of commodities to the household is the other edge of the sword. The factory system produced use values for consumption more cheaply and with less effort than the household. The use values may be in the form of standardized products, but there should at least be more of them and therefore a material basis for a rising standard of living of labor. In the early years of industrial capitalism this did not in general happen. Laborers certainly worked longer hours and probably received less in the way of use values (although the evidence on this latter point is both patchy and controversial, as Thompson 1968, chap. 10, and Hobsbawm 1964, chap. 7, point out). But the rising productivity of labor that occurs with accumulation, the consequent need to establish an internal market, and a century or more of class struggle have changed all of this. Consumer durables and consumption fund items (such as housing) have become very important growth sectors in the economy, and the political conditions and the material basis for a rising standard of living of labor have indeed been achieved.

The experience of labor in substituting work in the factory for work in the household has, therefore, both positive and negative aspects. But such substitutions are not easily achieved because they involve the nature and structure of the family, the role of women in society, culturally entrenched traditions, and the like. The substitutions are themselves a focus of struggle. The rational consumption of commodities in relation to the accumulation of capital implies a certain balance between market purchases and household work. The struggle to substitute the former for the latter is significant because its outcome defines the very meaning of use values and the standard of living for labor in its commodity aspects. The construction of the built environment has to be seen, therefore, in the context of a struggle over a whole way of living and being.

Techniques of persuasion are widely used in advanced capitalist societies to ensure rational consumption. Moral exhortation and philanthropic enterprise are often put to work "to raise the condition of the laborer by an improvement of his mental and moral powers and to make a rational consumer of him" (Marx 1967, 2:516). The church, the press, and the schools can be mobilized on behalf of rational consumption at the same time as they can be vehicles for genuinely autonomous working-class development.

And then, of course, there are always the blandishments of the ad-men and the techniques of Madison Avenue.

It would be idle to pretend that "the standard of living of labor" has been unaffected by these techniques. But, again, we are dealing with a double-edged sword. They may in fact also exert what Marx called a "civilizing influence" on labor and be used by labor to raise itself to a new condition of material and mental well-being that, in turn, provides a new and more solid basis for class struggle (Marx 1973, 409). Conversely, the drive by labor to improve its condition may be perverted by a variety of stratagems into a definition of use values advantageous to accumulation rather than reflective of the real human needs of labor. The human demand for shelter is turned, for example, into a process of accumulation through housing production.

Rational consumption can also be ensured by the collectivization of consumption, primarily, although not solely, through the agency of the state (Preteceille 1975; Castells 1975). Working-class demands for health care, housing, education, and social services of all kinds are usually expressed through political channels, and government arbitrates these demands and seeks to reconcile them with the requirements of accumulation. Many of these demands are met by the collective provision of goods and services, which means that everyone consumes them whether he or she likes it or not. Capitalist systems have moved more and more toward the collectivization of consumption because of the need, clearly understood in Keynesian fiscal policies, to manage consumption in the interests of accumulation. By collectivization, consumer choice is translated from the uncontrolled anarchy of individual action to the seemingly more controllable field of state enterprise. This translation does not occur without a struggle over both the freedom of individual choice (which generates a strong antibureaucratic sentiment) and the definition of the use values involved (national defense versus subsidized housing for the poor, for example).

The built environment has a peculiar and important role in all of this. The bundle of resources that constitute it – streets and sidewalks, drains and sewer systems, parks and playgrounds – contains many elements that are collectively consumed. The public provision of such public goods is a "natural" form of collective consumption that capital can easily colonize through the agency of the state. Also, the sum of individual private decisions creates a public effect because of the pervasive externality effects that in themselves force certain forms of collective consumption through private action – if I fail to keep my yard neat then my neighbors cannot avoid seeing it. The built environment requires collective management and control, and it is therefore almost certain to be a primary field of struggle between capital and labor over what is good for accumulation and what is good for people.

The consumption fund has accounted for an increasing proportion of gross aggregate investment in the built environment since around 1890 in both

Britain and the United States (Kuznets 1961). The housing sector in particular has become a major tool in macroeconomic policy for stabilizing economic growth, particularly in the United States where it has openly been used as a Keynesian regulator (not always, we should add, with success). And there are also strong multiplier effects to be taken into account. Housing construction, for example, requires complementary investments in other aspects of the built environment as well as in a wide range of consumer durables. The multipliers vary a great deal according to design and other considerations, but in all cases they are substantial.

These multipliers assume an added importance when we consider them in relation to the "coercive power" that the built environment can exercise over our daily lives. Its longevity and fixity in space, together with its method of financing and amortization, mean that once we have created it we must use it if the value that it represents is not to be lost. Under the social relations of capitalism, the built environment becomes an artifact of human labor that subsequently returns to dominate daily life. Capital seeks to mobilize it as a coercive force to help sustain accumulation. If our cities are built for driving, for example, then drive we must in order to live "normally" whether we like it or not. The highway lobby in the United States, the automobile, oil, and rubber industries and the construction interests, changed the face of America and used the coercive power of the built environment to ensure rational growth in the consumption of their products (Flink 1975; Leavitt 1970). But labor is not oblivious to such pressures. The configurations of use values that capital urges upon labor may be resisted or transformed to suit labor's purposes and labor's needs – the automobile becomes, for example, a means of escape (we shall consider from what very shortly).

Insofar as capitalism has survived, so we have to conclude that capital dominates labor not only in the place of work but in the living space by defining the standard of living of labor and the quality of life in part through the creation of built environments that conform to the requirements of accumulation and commodity production. To put it this strongly is not to say that labor cannot win on particular issues, not does it imply that there is one and only one definition of use values for labor that fits the need for accumulation. There are innumerable possibilities, but the limits of tolerance of capital are nevertheless clearly defined. For labor to struggle within these limits is one thing; to seek to go beyond them is where the real struggle begins.

The Socialization of Labor and the Relation to Nature

Work and living cannot entirely be divorced from each other. What happens in the workplace cannot be forgotten in the living place. Yet, we have a very poor understanding of the relation between the two (see, however, Vance 1966). The definition of "a use value for labor in the built environment" cannot, therefore, be independent of the work experience. We shall consider two very basic aspects of this in what follows.

We tend to forget that the advent of the factory system required a quite extraordinary adaptation in social life. It transformed the rural peasant and the independent artisan into mere cogs in a system designed to produce surplus value. The laborer became a "thing" – a mere "factor of production" to be used in the production process as the capitalist desired. But the new economic order also required that "men who were non-accumulative, non-acquisitive, accustomed to work for subsistence, not for maximization of income, had to be made obedient to the cash stimulus and obedient in such a way as to react precisely to the stimuli provided." The habituation of the worker to the new mode of production, the inculcation of the work discipline and all that went with it, was and is still no easy matter. Consequently, "the modern industrial proletariat was introduced to its role not so much by attraction or monetary reward, but by compulsion, force, and fear. It was not allowed to grow as in a sunny garden; it was forged, over a fire, by the powerful blows of a hammer" (Pollard 1965, 161, 207). The consequences of this for the manner and forms of subsequent class struggle were legion. And, as Braverman (1974, 139) points out, "The habituation of workers to the capitalist mode of production must be renewed with each generation."

The inculcation of work discipline could in part be accomplished by training, threats, incentives, and cajolery in the workplace. These were effective but not in themselves sufficient. In the early years of industrial capitalism the problems were particularly severe because capitalism had not yet woven the "net of modern capitalist life that finally makes all other modes of living impossible" (Braverman 1974, 151). And so originated the drive on the part of capital to inculcate the working class with the "work ethic" and "bourgeois values" of honesty, reliability, respect for authority, obedience to laws and rules, respect for property and contractual agreements, and the like. The assault on the values of the working class was in part conducted through religious, educational, and philanthropic channels, with the paternalism of the industrialist often thrown into the balance. But there is another component to this that is of particular interest to us here. The early industrialists in particular had to deal with workers both inside the factory and outside of it:

The efforts to reform the whole man were, therefore, particularly marked in factory towns and villages in which the total environment was under the control of a single employer. Here some of the main developments of the industrial revolution were epitomized: these settlements were founded by the industrialist, their whole raison d'être his quest for profit, their politics and laws in his pocket, the quality of their life under his whim, their ultimate aims in his image. . . . Great though the outward difference was between the flogging masters and the model community builders, "from the standpoint of control of labour both types of factory management display a concern with the enforcement of discipline. (Pollard 1965, 115)

This need to socialize labor to a work process through control in the living place is endemic to capitalism, but it is particularly noticeable when new kinds of work processes are introduced. Henry Ford's five-dollar, eight-hour day for assembly-line workers introduced in 1914 was accompanied with much puritanical rhetoric and a "philanthropic" control system that affected nearly every facet of the workers' lives:

A staff of over thirty investigators . . . visited workers' homes gathering information and giving advice on the intimate details of the family budget, diet, living arrangements, recreation, social outlook and morality. . . . The worker who refused to learn English, rejected the advice of the investigator, gambled, drank excessively, or was found guilty of "any malicious practice derogatory to good physical manhood or moral character" was disqualified from the five dollar wage. (Flink 1975, 89)

Gramsci's (1971, 285–318) comments on "Fordism" are perceptive. There arose at that point in the history of capitalist accumulation a "need to elaborate a new type of man suited to the new type of work and productive process." This transformation, Gramsci argued, could only be accomplished by a skillful combination of force and persuasion – the latter including high wages, "various social benefits, extremely subtle ideological propaganda." Ford's puritanical and social control initiatives had the purpose of "preserving, outside of work, a certain psychophysical equilibrium which prevents the physiological collapse of the workers, exhausted by the new method of production." Workers had to spend their money "rationally, to maintain, renew and if possible to increase (their) muscular nervous efficiency." The fierce attack on alcohol and sexual activities was also a part of the comprehensive effort to inculcate "the habits and customs necessary for the new systems of living and working." The events that surrounded the introduction of Fordism are a classic example of the attempt by capital to shape the person in the living place to fit the requirements of the workplace.

Our interest here is, of course, to understand the manner in which industrialists in general, and the community builders in particular, defined the quality of life for their workers and used the built environment as part of a general strategy for inculcating bourgeois values and a "responsible" industrial work discipline. We have already noted a modern version of this in the promotion of working-class homeownership as a means to ensure respect for property rights and social stability – a connection that was recognized early in the nineteenth century in the United States. But we are here concerned with the more direct forms of control of the living space. Bender suggests, for example, that the boardinghouses constructed to house the mill girls of Lowell in the 1820s "served as a functional equivalent of the rural family" and operated as "an effective adaptive mechanism" for the girls being drawn off the New England farms into the factories (1975, 63). This same point was made most effectively in the design and functioning of those institutions concerned to deal with those who could not or would not adapt to the new style of life. As early as Elizabethan times, for example, madness and unemployment were regarded as the same thing, while the advent of industrial capitalism had the effect of defining physical sickness as inability to go to work. Both Pollard, in the British context, and Rothman, in the American, point out the connection between major social institutions – asylums, workhouses, penitentiaries, hospitals, and even schools – and the factory systems, which they closely resembled in layout and in internal disciplinary organization. The rehabilitation of the convict in Jacksonian America, for example, meant the socialization of the convict to something akin to an industrial work discipline (Rothman 1971; cf. also Foucault 1965).

That there is a relationship of some sort between working and living, and that by manipulating the latter a leverage can be exerted on the former, has not escaped the notice of the capitalist class. A persistent theme in the history of the advanced capitalist countries has been to look for those improvements in the living place that will enhance the happiness, docility, and efficiency of labor. In the model communities, this kind of program is quite explicit. George Pullman, in his ill-fated experiment, built the town that bears his name in 1880 in order to

attract and retain a superior type of workingman, who would in turn be "elevated and refined" by the physical setting. This would mean contented employees and a consequent reduction in absenteeism, drinking and shirking on the job. Furthermore, such workers were expected to be less susceptible to the exhortation of "agitators" than the demoralized laborers of the city slums. His town would protect his company from labor unrest and strikes. (Buder 1967, 44)

And, we should add, the whole enterprise was supposed to make 6 percent on the capital invested. The Pullman strike of 1894 was a fitting epitaph to such a dream, demonstrating that direct unified control by the capitalists over the lives of labor in both the workplace and the living place is an explosive issue.

The Pullman strike merely confirmed what had in any case been slowly dawning upon the capitalist producers throughout the nineteenth century. The direct confrontation between capital and labor in the living place exacerbates class tensions and conflict markedly because labor can easily identify the enemy – whether it be in company housing, the company store, company social services, or the workplace itself. It was no accident that some of the fiercest strikes and confrontations – such as Homestead in 1892 and Pullman in 1894 – occurred in company towns. Under such conditions it is advantageous for the capitalist producers to seek out mediating influences that diffuse the target of labor's discontent. The privatization of housing provision, the creation of a separate housing landlord class, the creation of innumerable intermediaries in the retail and wholesale sector, and government provision of social services and public goods all help to accomplish this. These measures also serve to socialize part of the costs of the reproduction of labor power and to facilitate the mobility of labor. For all of these reasons, the industrial capitalists seek to withdraw entirely from any direct involvement in the provision or management of the built environment.

The general proposition that Pullman had in mind, divorced from its paternalism and its tight, unified, and direct control aspects, is still important. The breakdown of the binding links of the old social order was clearly necessary if the new industrial work discipline was to be imposed upon the reluctant peasant or artisan. But this breakdown posed its own problems for social control and threatened the economic and social stability of the new order in a variety of ways. Bourgeois reformers sought to counter such threats and have long argued that proper housing, health care, education, and the like are essential if workers are to become satisfied, virtuous, and solid citizens capable of performing and willing to perform work tasks efficiently and thereby to do their bit to enhance the accumulation of capital.[5] Conversely, the typical industrial city, with its slums and overcrowding, its war of all against all, its signs of "moral degeneration" and vice, its dirt and grime and disease, was regarded as unconducive to the formation of a respectable working-class citizenry. Sometimes the reform strategy rests on a rather simple-minded environmental determinism – the idea that good housing creates good workers periodically appears on the stage of bourgeois reform thought, usually with not very effective consequences. But in its more sophisticated form, bourgeois reform proved capable of tapping and organizing the relation between working and living in a manner that indeed did contribute to the reestablishment of social stability and to the creation of a relatively well-satisfied work force. And in the course of this effort, the reformers defined the meaning of a use value in the built environment for labor in a certain way. Capital seeks to intervene – this time indirectly through bourgeois reform and by means of ideological and political mechan-

---

[5] Much of this material as well as the argument is drawn from R. A. Walker (1976). I am indebted to him for many of the ideas advanced in this chapter. See also Walker 1981.

isms — because to do so serves its own purposes and strengthens its hand in its historic struggle with labor. But as the Pullman strike epitomizes, labor is not always a willing and docile partner in such manipulations.

This brings us to the second aspect of the connection between working and living in capitalist society. Marx's materialist posture led him to regard the relationship to nature as perhaps the most fundamental relation ordering human affairs. This relationship is itself expressed primarily through the work process that transforms the raw materials of nature into use values. The mode of organizing this work process — the mode of production — is therefore the basis upon which Marx builds his investigations. To put it this way is not to engage in a simplistic economic determinism; it merely advances the thesis that the relation to nature is the most fundamental aspect of human affairs. Industrial capitalism, armed with the factory system, organized the work process in a manner that transformed the relation between the worker and nature into a travesty of even its former very limited self. Because the worker was reduced to a "thing," the worker became alienated from his or her product, from the manner of producing it, and, ultimately, from nature itself (Marx 1964b).

That there was something degrading and "unnatural" about such a work process was apparent even to bourgeois consciousness. Indeed, the organization of the factory system appeared just as unnatural to the bourgeoisie as it felt to those who had to live out their daily lives under its regimen. This understanding, as Raymond Williams (1973, 124) points out, was achieved by landed capital well before the industrial revolution:

The clearing of parks as "Arcadian" prospects depended on the completed system of exploitation of the agricultural and genuinely pastoral lands beyond the park boundaries. . . . [These] are related parts of the same process — superficially opposed in taste but only because in the one case the land is being organized for production, where tenants and labourers will work, while in the other case it is being organized for consumption. . . . Indeed it can be said of these eighteenth century arranged landscapes not only, as is just, that this was the high point of agrarian bourgeois art, but that they succeeded in creating in the land below their windows and terraces . . . a rural landscape . . . from which the facts of production had been banished.

With the advent of industrial capitalism the penchant for actively countering in their own consumption sphere what they were organizing for others in the production sphere became even more emphatic for the bourgeoisie. The Romantic poets in Britain — led by Wordsworth and Coleridge — and writers like Emerson and Thoreau in the United States epitomized this reaction to the new industrial order. And the reaction did not remain confined to the realms of the ideologists. It was put into practice in the building of rural estates by the bourgeoisie, the establishment of the country mansion, the flight from the industrial city, and, ultimately, in the design of what Walker (1976) calls "the suburban solution." The attempt to "bring nature back into the city" by writers and designers such as Olmstead and Ebenezer Howard in the nineteenth century, and Ian McHarg and Lewis Mumford in the twentieth, attests to the continuity of this theme in bourgeois thought and practice.[6]

But if the bourgeoisie felt it, the artisan and the displaced peasant experienced the alienation from nature very concretely, and they reacted no less vigorously whenever they could. William Blake, the spokesman for the artisan class, complained bitterly of those "dark satanic mills" and swore with his usual revolutionary fervor that we would "build Jerusalem in England's green and pleasant land." Faced with the brutalizing and degrading routine of the work process in the factory, the workers themselves sought ways to ameliorate it. In part they did so by resorting to the same mystifications as the bourgeoisie, and thus came to share a common romantic image of nature. When asked why the Lowell mill girls wrote so much about the beauties of nature, for example, the editor of their paper responded: "Why is it that the desert-traveller looks forward upon the burning, boundless waste, and sees pictured before his aching eyes, some verdant oasis?" But merely to dream of some romantic, idealized nature in the midst of the desert of the factory was scarcely enough, no matter how much it did to help the laborer through the long and tedious day. Consequently, as Bender (1975, 90) reports: "Residents of Lowell made their periodic and appreciative contact with the natural landscape in a variety of ways. Besides using the cemetery and the public park, they sought nature through flights of fancy, through views from their windows, by walking out of the city (despite the no-trespassing signs . . .), and through summer visits to the country."

The response rested on a mystification, of course, for it reduced "nature" to a leisure-time concept, as something to be "consumed" in the course of restful recuperation from what was in fact a degrading relation to nature in the most fundamental of all human activities – work. But the mystification had bitten deep into the consciousness of all elements in society. To talk now of the relation to nature is to conjure up images of mountains and streams and seas and lakes and trees and green grass, far from the coal-face, the assembly line, and the factory, where the real transformation of nature is continuously being wrought.

But there is a sense which this is a necessary and unavoidable mystification

---

[6] Ebenezer Howard (1955, 127) wrote, for example, of "so laying out a Garden City that, as it grows, the free gifts of Nature – fresh air, sunlight, breathing room and playing room – shall be retained in all needed abundance, and so employing the resources of modern science that Art may supplement Nature, and life may become an abiding joy and delight."

under capitalism. Without it, life would scarcely be bearable. And progressive elements within the bourgeoisie knew this to be as true for their workers as for themselves. Hardly surprisingly, therefore, the bourgeois reformers, often under the guise of moral universals and a romantic imagery, frequently sought to procure for their workers reasonable access to "nature." Olmsted, perhaps the most spectacular of these reformers in nineteenth-century America, saw that "the spontaneous interest of the worker was a more effective stimulus to work than any artificially imposed regimen," and it was a short step from this to proposing parks and sylvan suburbs as an antidote to the usual daily harassments of urban-industrial life (Bender 1975). Turned into practice, in Olmsted's day primarily for the middle classes, but increasingly in modern times for the "respectable" working class, this solution to the problems of urban-industrial life has had a powerful effect upon the physical landscapes of our cities. The counterpoint between nature – represented by pastoral images of the country – and a work process represented by the urban and the industrial is central to the history of the capitalist mode of production. And the counterpoint contains a tension between what Raymond Williams (1973, 294) calls "a necessary materialism and a necessary humanity," adding:

Often we try to resolve it by dividing work and leisure, or society and the individual, or city and country, not only in our minds but in suburbs and garden cities, town houses and country cottages, the week and the weekend. But we then usually find that the . . . captains of the change, have arrived earlier and settled deeper; have made, in fact, a more successful self-division. The country house . . . was one of the first forms of this temporary resolution, and in the nineteenth century as many were built by the new lords of capitalist production as survived, improved, from the old lords. . . . It remains remarkable that so much of this settlement has been physically imitated, down to details of semi-detached villas and styles of leisure and weekends. An immensely productive capitalism, in all its stages, has extended both the resources and the modes which, however unevenly, provide and contain forms of response to its effects.

These "forms of response" serve to define in part the meaning of use values in the built environment for labor. The residents of the contemporary suburbs, whether workers or bourgeois, are no less anxious, for example, to banish "the facts of production" from their purview than were the eighteenth-century landlords because those facts are, for the most part, unbearable. And insofar as workers in conjunction with the capitalists have found ways to do just this they have created an urban landscape and a way of life that is founded on what Williams calls "an effective and imposing mystification" – but a mystification that combines elements of necessity and cruel hoax. Hanging on to some sense of an unalienated relation to nature makes life bearable for the worker if only because it leads to a realistic appraisal of what has been lost and what potentially can be gained. But the romantic mystification of nature conceals rather than reveals the actual source of the sense of loss and alienation that pervades capitalist society. Bourgeois art, literature, urban design, and "designs for urban living" offer certain conditions in the living place as compensation for what can never truly be compensated for in the workplace. Capital, in short, seeks to draw labor into a Faustian bargain: accept a packaged relation to nature in the living place as just and adequate compensation for an alienating and degrading relation to nature in the workplace. And if labor refuses to be drawn in spite of all manner of seductions, blandishments, and a dominant ideology mobilized by the bourgeoisie, then capital must impose it because the landscape of capitalist society must in the final analysis respond to the accumulation needs of capital, rather than to the very real human requirements of labor.

The Interventions of Capital: A Conclusion

Capital seeks to discipline labor as much in the home as in the factory because it is only in terms of an all-embracing domination of labor in every facet of its life that the "work ethic" and the "bourgeois values" necessarily demanded by the capitalist work process can be created and secured. The promotion of homeownership for workers establishes the workers' allegiance to the principle of private property and therefore fits with this general stratagem. Sometimes conflicting with this drive we see that capital also needs to organize the consumption of the workers to ensure that it is cheap and rational from the standpoint of accumulation. The collectivization of consumption tends to take away the sense of individual responsiblity and thereby undercuts the notion of bourgeois individualism is pushed too far. And running as a counterthread in all of this we see the need on the part of capital to promote in the work force a sense of satisfaction and contentment that will lead to spontaneous cooperation and efficiency in the workplace. This condition cannot be cultivated without giving the worker at least the illusion of freedom of choice in the living place and of healthy and satisfying relation to nature in the consumption sphere. Such illusions are pervasive but not always easy to sustain in the face of the realities enforced by the necessities of accumulation for accumulation's sake, production for production's sake. And the conditions in the workplace can never be that easily concealed, no matter how mountainous the mystifications.

Nevertheless, the response of labor to its own condition is constantly subjected to the interventions and mediations of capital. As labor seeks to reorganize its mode of living to compensate for the degradations and disciplines of factory work, so capital seeks to colonize and pervert these efforts for its own purposes, sometimes to be turned cruelly against labor in the course of class struggle. Labor strives to raise its living standards by reducing the cost of living and increasing the use values it can command, but capital constantly seeks to subvert this drive, often through the agency of the state, into a reduction in the value of labor power and into "rational" modes of consumption understood from the standpoint of accumulation. As labor seeks relief from a degrading relation to nature in the workplace, so capital seeks to parlay that into a mystified relation to nature in the consumption sphere. As labor seeks more control over the collective conditions of its existence, so capital seeks to establish collectivized forms of consumption and individual homeownership. The power of capital is omnipresent in the very definition of "a use value in the built environment for labor."

Conflicts in the living place are, we can conclude, mere reflections of the underlying tension between capital and labor. Appropriators and the construction faction mediate the forms of conflict – they stand between capital and labor and thereby shield the real source of tension from view. The surface appearance of conflicts around the built environment – the struggles against the landlord or against urban renewal – conceals a hidden essence that is nothing more than the struggle between capital and labor.

Capital may be omnipresent in such struggles, but it is neither omniscient nor omnipotent. The dynamics of accumulation require periodic rationalizations through crises that affect the working class in the form of bouts of widespread unemployment. At such moments the plans to coopt labor by the provision of "healthful and satisfying" living environments, by a contented relation to nature in the living place, go awry. In using the built environment as a coercive tool over consumption, capital ultimately coerces itself because it sets the conditions for the realization of values quite literally in a sea of concrete. And once committed, capital cannot go back. Pullman discovered this elemental fact in his ill-fated model town. When conditions of overaccumulation became apparent in the economy at large it became necessary to lay off workers, but Pullman could not do so because the profits to be had from the town were contingent upon full employment in the factory. The solution for the individual capitalist is to withdraw from the production of consumption fund items for the workers he or she employs. But the problem remains for the capitalist system as a whole. As problems of overaccumulation arise in capitalist societies – and arise they must – so the most well-laid plans of the capitalist fall by the wayside and the mechanisms for mystification, cooptation, disciplining labor, and inculcating the work ethic and bourgeois virtues begin to crumble. And it is at just such times that labor recognizes that the bargain that it has struck with capital is no bargain at all but founded on an idealized mystification. The promises of capital are seen to be just that and incapable of fulfillment. And it also becomes evident that the needs of labor for use values in the built environment are incapable of being met by the captains of the system who promise so much but who can deliver so little.

III. CLASS CONSCIOUSNESS, COMMUNITY CONSCIOUSNESS, AND COMPETITION

The phrase "the standard of living of labor" plainly cannot be understood outside of the context of actual class struggles fought over a long period in particular places around the organization of both working and living. This continuously shifting standard defines the needs of labor with respect to use values — consumption fund itsems — in the built environment. Individual workers have different needs, of course, according to their position in the labor force, their familial situation, and their individual requirements. At the same time, the processes of wage rate determination in the workplace yield different quantities of exchange value to workers in different occupational categories. The social power that this money represents can be used to procure control over certain use values in the built environment. The way this money is used affects the appropriation of rent and the functioning of the price signals that induce the flow of capital into the production of new consumption fund items. We can envisage three general situations.

Consider, first, a situation in which each worker seeks independently to command for his or her own private use the best bundle of resources in the best location. We envisage a competitive war of all against all, a society in which the ethic of "possessive individualism" has taken root in the consciousness of workers in a very fundamental way. If the use values available in the built environment are limited, which is usually the case, then individuals make use of their market power and bid for scarce resources in the most advantageous locations. At its most elemental level this competition is for survival chances, for each worker knows that the ability to survive is dependent upon the ability to secure access to a particular bundle of resources in a reasonably healthy location. There is also competition to acquire "market capacity" — that bundle of attitudes, understandings, and skills that permits the worker to sell his or her labor power at a higher wage rate than the average (Giddens 1973, 103). Symbols of status, prestige, rank, and importance (even self-respect) may also be acquired by procuring command over particular resources in prestigious locations. These symbols may be useful in that they help a worker gain an easier entry into a particularly privileged stratum within the wage-labor force. And finally we can note that if the relation to nature in the workplace is felt to be as degrading as it truly is, then there is a positive incentive to seek a location far enough away that the "facts of production" are in no way represented in the landscape. In other words, workers may compete to get as far as possible away from the workplace (the automobile proves particularly useful for this purpose).

The competitive situation that we have here outlined is in most respects identical to that assumed in neoclassical models of land use determination in urban areas (Alonso 1964; Mills 1972). Individual households, such models assume, attempt to maximize their utility by competing with each other for particular bundles of goods in particular locations subject to a budget constraint. If it is assumed that the two most important "goods" being competed for are locations with lower aggregate transportation costs and housing space, then it can be shown with relative ease that individuals will distribute themselves in space according to (1) the distribution of employment opportunities, usually assumed to be collected together in one central location, and (2) the relative marginal propensities to consume transportation services and living space in the context of the overall budget constraint. Competitive bidding under these conditions will generate a differential rent surface that, in the case of a single employment center, declines with distance from the center at the same time as it distributes individuals by income in space. In this case the ability to appropriate differential rent is entirely created by competitive behavior within the working class. Also, if new development is typically distributed in response to the pricing signals set by such differential rents, then it is easy to show that a spatial structure to the built environment will be created that reflects, to a large degree, social and wage stratifications within the labor force.

The second situation that we wish to consider is one in which collective action in space – community action – is important. The pervasive externality effects and the collective use of many items in the built environment mean that it is in the self-interest of individuals to pursue modest levels of collective action (Olson 1965). Workers who are homeowners know that the value of the savings tied up in the house depends on the actions of others. It is in their common interest to collectively curb "deviant" behaviors, bar "noxious" facilities, and ensure high standards of public service. This collectivization of action may go well beyond that required out of pure individual self-interest. A consciousness of place; "community consciousness," may emerge as a powerful force that spawns competition between communities for scarce public investment funds, and the like. Community competititon becomes the order of the day.

This process relates to the appropriation of rent in an interesting way. Community control enables those in control to erect barriers to investment in the built environment. The barriers may be selective – the exclusion of low-income housing, for example – or more or less across the board, a ban on all forms of future growth. Actions of this sort have been common in suburban jurisdictions in the United States in recent years. The cartel powers of local government are in effect being mobilized to control investment through a variety of legal and planning devices. Homeowners may use these controls to maintain or enhance the value of their properties. Developers may seek to use such controls for rather different purposes. But "community consciousness" typically creates small legal "islands" within which monopoly rents are appropriatable, often by one faction of labor at the expense of another faction. This latter situation gives rise to internecine conflicts within the working class along parochialist community-based lines. The spatial structure of the city is very different under these conditions compared to the product of individual competition.

The third kind of situation we can envisage is that of a fully class-conscious proletariat struggling against all forms of exploitation, whether they be in the workplace or in the living place. Workers do not use their social power as individuals to seek individual solutions; they do not compete with each other for survival chances, for ability to acquire market capacity, for symbols of status and prestige. They fight collectively to improve the lot of all workers everywhere and eschew those parochialist forms of community action that typically lead one faction of labor to benefit at the expense of another (usually the poor and underprivileged).

Under such conditions the appropriation of rent cannot be attributed to the competitive behavior of individual workers or of whole communities. It has to be interpreted, rather, as something forced upon labor in the course of class struggle. A differential rent surface may arise in an urban area, but it does so not because labor automatically engages in competitive bidding but because the class power of the appropriators is used to extract a rent to the maximum possible, given that resources are scarce and that they exist in a relative space. Because we witness a consequent social stratification (according to income) in space, and a development process that exacerbates this social ordering, we cannot infer that this is simply a reflection of individual workers expressing their "subjective utilities" through a market. Indeed, it may express the exact opposite – the power of the appropriators to force certain choices on workers no matter what the individual worker may think or believe. The power to appropriate rent is a class relation, and we have to understand it that way if we are to understand how residential differentiation emerges within cities and the degree to which this phenomenon is the outcome of free or forced choices.

The three situations we have examined – competitive individualism, community action, and class struggle – are points on a continuum of possibilities. We cannot automatically assume labor to be at any particular point on this continuum. This is something to be discovered by concrete investigations of particular situations. The United States, for example, appears to be strongly dominated by competitive individualism and community consciousness compared to the more class-conscious working class in Europe. From the standpoint of capital, individual and community competition is advantageous because it then seems as if the appropriation of rent results from labor's own actions rather than from the actions of the appropriators themselves. The overt forms of conflict around the built environment depend, therefore, upon the outcome of a deeper and often hidden ideological struggle for the consciousness of those doing the struggling. This deeper struggle between individual, community, and class alignments and consciousness provies the context in which daily struggles over everyday issues occur.

IV. A CONCLUSION

The capitalist mode of production forces a separation between working and living at the same time as it reintegrates them in complex ways. The superficial appearance of conflict in contemporary urban-industrial society suggests that there is indeed a dichotomy between struggles in the workplace and in the living place and that each kind of struggle is fought according to different principles and rules. Struggles around the consumption fund for labor, which have been the focus of attention in this paper, seemingly arise out of the inevitable tensions between appropriators seeking rent, builders seeking profit, financiers seeking interest, and labor seeking to counter the secondary forms of exploitation that occur in the living place. All of this seems self-evident enough.

But the manner and form of such everyday overt conflicts are a reflection of a much deeper tension with less easily identifiable manifestations – a struggle over the definition and meaning of use values, of the standard of living of labor, of the quality of life, of consciousness, and even of human nature itself. From this standpoint, the overt struggles between landlord-appropriators, builders, and labor, which we began by examining, are to be seen as mediated manifestations of the deep underlying conflict between capital and labor. Capital seeks definitions, seeks to impose meanings conducive to the productivity of labor and to the consumption of the commodities that capitalists can profitably produce. Like Dickens's *Dombey and Son,* capital deals "in hides but never in hearts." But labor seeks its own meanings, partly derived out of a rapidly fading memory of artisan and peasant life, but also out of the ineluctable imperative to learn what it is to be human. "Human nature" has, then, no universal meaning but is being perpetually recast in the fires of restless struggle. And even though capital may dominate and impose upon us a predominantly *capitalist* sense of human nature, the resistances are always there, and the internal tensions within the capitalist order – between private appropriation and socialized production. between individualism and social interdependency – are so dramatic that we, each of us, internalize a veritable maelstrom of hopes and fears into our present conduct. The human nature that results, with all of its complex ambiguities of desire, need, creativity, estrangement, selfishness, and sheer human concern, forms the very stuff out of which the overt struggles of daily life are woven. The manner in which these struggles are fought likewise depends upon a deeper determination of consciousness – individual, community, or class-based as the case may be – of those who do the struggling. From this standpoint it must surely be plain that the separation between working and living is at best a superficial estrangement, an apparent breaking asunder of what can never be kept apart. And it is at this deeper level, too, that we can more clearly see the underlying unity between work-based and "community"-based conflicts. They are not mere mirror images of each other, but distorted representations, mediated by many intervening forces and circumstances, which mystify and render opaque the fundamental underlying class antagonism upon which the capitalist mode of production is founded. And it is, of course, the task of science to render clear through analysis what is mystified and opaque in daily life.

3

Paris, 1850–1870

Paris is indeed an ocean. Sound it: you will never touch bottom. Survey it,
report on it! However scrupulous your survey and reports, however numerous
and persistent the explorers of this sea may be, there will always remain virgin
places, undiscovered caverns, flowers, pearls, monsters – there will always be
something extraordinary, missed by the literary diver.

                                                                    – *Balzac*

If everything were as it seems on the surface, there would be no need
for science.

                                                                    – *Marx*

Paris in 1850 was a city seething with social, economic, and political
problems and possibilities. Some saw it as a sick city, wracked by political
torments, torn apart by class struggles, sinking beneath its own weight of
decadence, corruption, crime, and cholera. Others saw it as a city of
opportunity for private ambition or social progress. If the right keys to the
mystery of the city's possibilities were found, the whole of Western
civilization stood to be transformed. The city had, after all, grown rapidly in
population, from 786,000 in 1831 to more than a million in 1846 (table 1).
Its industry had undergone a remarkable growth, and it had even enhanced
its traditional centralized role as the national hub of communications,
finance, commerce, culture, and, of course, state administration. With such a
dynamic past, how could it not have a dynamic future?

But in 1850 the city was evidently trapped within a double strait jacket,
each of which appeared to reinforce the other. It was, first of all, caught in the

I have acknowledged the detailed sources in the text, but I want to pay special tribute here to
that extraordinary labor of love by Jeanne Gaillard, *Paris, la ville, 1852–1870,* without which
much of what I have done here would have been impossible. Unfortunately, T. J. Clark's *The
Painting of Modern Life* (Alfred Knopf: New York, 1985) was published just as this was going to
press. There are some striking contrasts and parallels between his treatment of class relations
and representations in Haussman's Paris and mine.

Table 1. The Population of Paris, 1831–1876

Year	Old Paris	Communes Annexed in 1860	Paris after 1860	% Change
1831	785,866	75,574	861,436	
1836	899,313	103,320	1,002,633	16.39
1841	936,261	124,564	1,059,825	5.70
1846	1,053,897	173,083	1,226,980	15.77
1851	1,053,261	223,802	1,277,064	4.08
1856	1,174,346	364,257	1,538,613	20.48
1861			1,696,141	10.24
1866			1,825,274	7.61
1872			1,851,792	1.45
1876			1,988,800	7.40

aftermath of the deepest and most widespread capitalist crisis yet experienced. This was a full-fledged crisis of overaccumulation, in which massive surpluses of capital and labor power lay side by side with apparently no way open to reunite them in profitable union. The city had seen many an economic crisis before, usually triggered by natural calamity of war. But this one was different. It could not easily be attributed to God or nature, for capitalism had matured by 1847–48 to a sufficient degree that even the blindest bourgeois apologist could see that financial conditions, reckless speculation, and overproduction had something to do with the human tragedy that swept out of Britain in 1847 and quickly engulfed the whole of what was then the capitalist world. In 1848, reform of capitalism or its revolutionary overthrow stared everyone starkly in the face.

That Paris took the revolutionary path was not entirely fortuitous. And it was more than just that famed revolutionary tradition that had the citizens of Paris put political interpretations on the least sign of economic difficulty, take to the streets, erect barricades, and proclaim their rights as the rights of man. For the other strait jacket that held the city down was a veritable eighteenth-century structure of social practices and infrastructures dominating manufacturing, finance, commerce, government, and labor relations, to say nothing of the almost medieval frame of physical infrastructures within which all these activities and practices were confined.

In these years Paris looked around and was unable to recognize itself. Another, larger city had overflowed into the unaltered framework of streets, mansions, houses and passageways, piling man on man and trade on trade, filling every nook and corner, making over the older dwellings of the nobility and gentry into workshops and lodging houses, erecting factories and stockpiles in gardens and courts where carriages had been moldering quietly away, packing the suddenly shrunken streets and the now overpopulated gothic graveyards, resurrecting and overloading the forgotten sewers, spreading litter and stench into the adjacent countryside. (Chevalier 1973, 45)

While there was nothing unique about the accompanying human misery, degradation, disease, crime, and prostitution – common enough features within the industrialism of the time – this ancient infrastructure was hardly compatible with the increasingly sophisticted and efficient capitalist organization of production emerging in the new manufacturing towns not only in Britain – France's main commercial rival – but also in Belgium, Germany, Austria, and even in certain other regions of France. For though Paris had enhanced its position in the international division of labor after the revolution of 1830, it had done so less through outright revolution in its system of production than through piecemeal adaptation of old methods. A growing detail and social division of labor, backed by the special qualities of its output and the volume of its internal market, had been the basis of its dynamism. To the degree that it had not moved to meet the new and rather exacting requirements of capital accumulation, its agony during the crisis of 1847–48 was double and more prolonged, its path to recovery strewn with all manner of particular obstacles, compounded by a political and cultural evolution that created nothing but doubt, confusion, and fear.

Different segments of society saw the crisis quite differently. The craft workers, for example, armed with corporatist traditions, saw de-skilling, loss of independence, fragmentation of tasks, and technological change, increasingly imposed by capitalist control of production and distribution, as the core of the problem. The February Revolution, in which they played such a key role, was for them an occasion to put the question of labor and the right to work squarely on the political agenda. The social republic was as important to them as the political republic. In this they had a strange assortment of bourgeois allies, running all the way from small masters and shopkeepers, who felt equally threatened by the new systems of production and distribution, to romantic poets and writers like Lamartine, Hugo, and George Sand, who believed in the nobility of work and labor within the relatively safe confines of a romanticized artisan tradition. Though the romantics were quickly deceived when they encountered real workers on the barricades, the growth of socialist sentiment of some sort (varying from Fourier and Proudhon through the Saint-Simonians and Cabetists to the Christian socialism of Leroux and the republican socialism of Louis Blanc) connected powerfully with increasing craft worker consciousness to generate a ferment of utopian plans and expectations during the 1840s (Corcoran 1983; Bartier et al. 1981).

Such socialist sentiment plainly alarmed the bourgeoisie. Fear of the "reds" compounded their confusion as to how to represent, explain, and react to the political-economic crisis. Some saw archaic structures and practices of government and finance as the root of the problem and sought to modernize the French state, liberate the flows of capital, and give greater impetus to the economy. Progressive elements in Paris had also long sought strong state interventions to rationalize and renew plainly failing physical infrastructures. But their efforts were stymied by other factions of the bourgeoisie trapped either in a kind of fiscal conservatism which guaranteed total paralysis at a time of severe economic depression, or by traditional rights to property ownership (largely absentee and rural) which seemed to offer hope of personal salvation in the midst of national ruin. To the degree that many of the landowners fled the city in 1848 and took their purchasing power with them, they helped plunge Parisian industry, commerce, and property markets even deeper into the mire of depression.

The confused series of events that brought "that cretin" (the phrase is due to that impeccable bourgeois, Adolphe Thiers, rather than to Marx) Louis Napoleon Bonaparte to power, first as president of the Republic (elected by universal suffrage) in December 1848 and four years later as emperor, need not detain us unduly, since there are abundant and quite brilliant accounts elsewhere, beginning, of course, with Marx's *Class Struggles in France, 1848–1850* and the *Eighteenth Brumaire* (cf. Agulhon 1983; Dautry 1977). Suffice it to remark that the questions of work and of a socialist response to the crisis were swept off the immediate political agenda in the savage repression of the June Days, when Parisian workers took to the streets to protest the closure of the National Workshops (the Second Republic's response to the demand for the right to work). But subsequent elections indicated that democratic socialist sentiment was alive and well. Worse still, it appeared in rural areas, reminding France that the roots of its revolutionary as well as its reactionary tradition lay very much in the countryside. It was partly in the face of this threat that the bourgeoisie capitulated so easily to the authoritarianism of Empire.

The other threat was of the social destruction and devaluation attendant upon overaccumulation. Caught up in internecine struggles, no single faction of the bourgeoisie had the authority or legitimacy to impose its will. To the degree that Louis Napoleon appeared a compromise who each faction thought could be controlled, he was put in a position where he could play off popular will, factionalism, and traditional loyalties to the Napoleonic legend (particularly in the army) and so consolidate a very personal power. This left him to face up to the whole complex of problems of reform and modernization, control of the labor movement and its pretensions, revival of the economy, and how to exit from the profound economic, political, and cultural malaise in which France languished between 1848 and 1851.

The eighteen years of the Second Empire were nowhere near as "cretinous" or "farcical" as Thiers and Marx (from opposite ends of the political spectrum) had predicted. They were a deadly serious experiment with a form of national socialism – an authoritarian state with police powers and a populist base. It collapsed, like most other experiments of its ilk, in the midst of dissension and war, but its tenure was marked by the imposition of intense labor discipline and the liberation of capital circulation from its preceding constraints. But it was not evident then (any more than now) exactly which new social practices, institutional frames and structures, or social investments would work. The Second Empire was, then, a phase of striving for adjustment to a burgeoning and demanding capitalism in which diverse economic and political interests consciously sought this or that advantage or this or that solution only to find themselves all too frequently caught in the unintended consequences of their own actions.

It was in such a context that the emperor and his advisers sought to liberate Paris – its life, culture, and economy – from constraints that bound it so tightly to an ancient past. While certain immediate needs were clear, such as improved access to the central market of Les Halles, slum clearance around the city center, and improved traffic circulation between the rail stations and into the city center, there were a whole host of other questions which were much more problematical. There were problems of ends and means; the proper role of the state in relation to private interests and the circulation of capital; the degree of state intervention in labor markets, in industrial and commercial activity, in housing and social welfare provision; and the like. There was, above all, the political problem of how to get the Parisian economy back on its feet without sparking the solid resistance of a still powerful haute bourgeoisie, feeding the insecurities of a middle class always under threat of marginalization in spite of its seemingly solid implantation, and pushing the workers to outright revolt. From this standpoint we have to see the emperor as ultimately the prisoner of the class forces he began by seeming to outwit with such abandon and disdain. That he was able to get so far and do so much merely testifies to the tremendous upset generated out of the heat of 1848, an upset that affected not only economy and polity but traditional ways of representing the world and acting upon those representations. Here, too, Parisian life in the period 1848–51 was in total turmoil, a turmoil that affected painting (this was, after all, the period of Courbet's great breakthrough into an art world that could not comprehend what he was about), letters, science, and management as well as industry, commerce, and labor relations. Only after all the tumult had quieted could the solid resistance to the authoritarianism of Empire begin.

Paris in 1870 was fundamentally changed from its condition in 1850. And the changes were far-reaching and deeply rooted, though not enough to prevent that other great event in Parisian history, the Paris Commune. But while there were continuities between the revolutions of 1848 and 1871, there was much that separated them. The eighteen years of Empire had bitten as deep into the consciousness of Parisians as Haussman's works had cut open and reconstructed the physical fabric of the city.

How is the story of this massive transformation to be told? A simple and direct narrative of historico-geographical change might suffice. But how are we to build that narrative without a proper understanding of the inner workings and relations of urban economy, polity, society, and culture? Yet to dissect the totality into isolated fragments is also to lose contact with the complex interrelations that intertwine to produce the simple narrative of historico-geographical change that must surely be our goal. I shall take a middle course by trying to understand the historico-geographical transformation of Paris during the Second Empire in terms of a series of intersecting and interlocking themes, none of which can properly be understood without the others. The problem, then, is to present the interlocks and interrelations without lapsing into tedious repetitions. I must here put a certain burden upon the reader, who must try to keep the themes in perspective as part of a totality of interrelations that constitutes the driving force of social transformation in a given place over a certain time.

The themes collect together under certain headings. I begin with space relations, in part because I think it important to put the question of the materiality of space relations in the very forefront of analysis, if only because it is so often relegated to the position of afterthought. I do not mean by so positioning it to privilege it in the overall analysis, but if some privilege attaches to position (which is invariably the case), then why not accord space relations that privilege, if only for a change? The following three themes – finance capital, the propertied interest, and the state – link together as part of a theory of distribution (the splitting of surplus value into interest, rent, and taxes). Putting considerations of distribution before those of production might appear a little odd, but there is, as Marx himself commented, an initial "production-determining distribution," which has great significance for understanding the workings of any mode of production. In this case, the positioning largely follows from the fact that the new space relations (both external and internal) were created out of a coalition of the state, finance capital, and the landed interest and that each had to go through a painful adjustment to the other to do what had to be done in the way of urban transformation. The state is, of course, more than just a facet of distribution (though without taxes it would not get very far), so other aspects of state action, legitimacy, and authority are taken up here as well as in later sections where appropriate.

Production and labor processes are the focus of concern in section 5. We see here how shifts in technique, organization, and location were tied to changing space relations (the rise of a new international division of labor and the interior reorganization of Paris) as well as to credit, rent costs, and state policies (thus illustrating how distribution and production interlock within an urban context). But producers also need labor as a prime productive force. This brings us to consider the Parisian labor market (sec. 6), with all of its multiple facets of population growth, immigration, wage rate determination, mobilization of an industrial reserve, levels of skill, and attitudes toward work and labor organization.

The participation of women in the labor force was important and controversial. To the degree that they occupied a bridge position between the labor market and the reproduction of labor power in the home, their position in Parisian society as a whole deserves explicit consideration (sec. 7). This provides a sociological context for considering the reproduction of labor power (sec. 8). That process was partially located outside of Paris in the provinces and not at all well integrated into the overall system of production and distribution, and the consequences became only too apparent during the Commune. This leads us to reflect (sec. 9) on the realities and conceptions of community and class in a society where both were undergoing radical transformation.

Questions of science and sentiment (sec. 10) and of rhetoric and representation (sec. 11) are then taken up to try to uncover what people knew, how they knew it, and how they put their ideas to work socially, economically, and politically. I am here looking to reconstruct ideologies and states of consciousness, at least as far as these were articulated and are recoverable for present consideration. This puts us in a better position to understand what I call, in the final section (12), the "geopolitics of an urban historical geography," which, while no substitute for the historical-geographical narrative we seek, at least points more directly at that target.

I envisage, then, a spiral of themes which, starting with the comparative statics of spatial relations, moves through distribution (credit, rent, taxes), production and labor markets, reproduction, and consciousness formation to set the space in motion as a real historical geography of a living city. The general theory that lies behind the analysis of production and distribution dynamics in space is given in *The Limits to Capital*. More detailed aspects can be found in *The Urbanization of Capital*.

I. THE ORGANIZATION OF SPACE RELATIONS

The more production comes to rest on exchange value, hence on exchange, the more important do the physical conditions of exchange – the means of communication and transport – become for the costs of circulation. . . . While capital must on one side strive to tear down every spatial barrier . . . and conquer the whole earth for its market, it strives on the other side to annihilate this space with time.

– *Marx*

The integration of the national space of France had long been on the agenda. But by 1850, "The implantation of the structures and methods of modern large scale capitalism rendered the conquest and rational organization of space, its better adaptation to new needs, imperative" (Leon 1976, 241). The amelioration of the interior space of Paris had been sporadically debated throughout the July Monarchy. By 1850, that, too, had become imperative.

Louis Napoleon was prepared to act on both counts. On October 9, 1852, he signaled the forthcoming declaration of an Empire dedicated to peaceful works. "We have immense uncultivated lands to clear, roads to open, harbors to excavate, rivers to make navigable, canals to finish, our railway network to complete" (Girard 1952, 111). On June 23, 1853, Baron Haussman took office as prefect of the Department of the Seine. On that day the emperor handed him a map of Paris on which he had sketched in the new pattern of roads he wanted built (Haussman 1890, 2:53).

The difference this time was that there was a nascent social system bursting to undertake the work and turn long-held hopes and visions into living reality. The surpluses of capital and labor power, so crushingly evident in 1848, were to be absorbed through a program of massive long-term investment in the built environment. Within a year of the declaration of Empire, more than a thousand were at work on the construction site of the Tuileries; untold thousands were back at work building the railroads; and the mines and forges, desolate as late as 1851, were racing to meet the burgeoning demand. What was, perhaps, the first great crisis of capitalism was overcome, it seemed, through the long-term application of capital to the reorganization of space relations.

The achievements appeared remarkable and the effects even more so. The railway network expanded from a few strands here and there (1931 kilometers, to be exact) in 1850 to an intricate web of some 17,400 kilometers in 1870 (fig. 1). The volume of traffic expanded twice as fast as industrial output at the same time as it shifted to the rail system and away from other modes of transport (table 2). Although the imperial roads languished, the feeder roads to the rail system were increasingly used and improved. The telegraph system went from nothing in 1856 to 23,000 kilometers ten years later when it could be used not only for governmental purposes but also to coordinate markets and financial decisions. Only with respect to ports and maritime trade did the emperor not live up to his promises, but this was more than offset by the surge of surplus French capital abroad. About a third of the disposable capital went mainly to open up space in other lands (Plessis 1973, 110). French-financed railroads spread their tentacles down into the Iberian and Italian peninsulas and across central Europe into Russia and the Ottoman Empire. French finance built the Suez Canal, opened in 1869. The transport and communications system that was to be the foundation of a new world

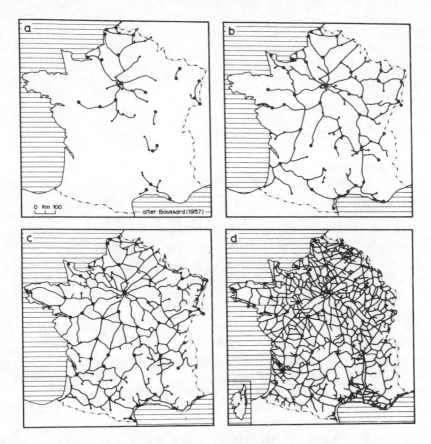

*Fig. 1.   The changing rail network of France, (a) 1850, (b) 1860, (c) 1870, (d) 1890.
(Reproduced, with permission, from H. D. Clout, Themes in the Historical
Geography of France, Academic Press, 1977.)*

market and a new international division of labor was broadly laid out between 1850 and 1870.

Whether or not all this would have happened, no matter what the regime, is debatable. This was, after all, the era of massive investment in transport and communications throughout the whole of what was then the advanced capitalist world, and France's performance, following the initial burst of energy after 1852, barely kept pace with and in some cases lagged behind that of the other major powers. In a few instances, such as the Suez Canal, the government could reasonably claim that its guiding vision and material help was essential to their completion. And there is general agreement that the particular mix of financial reforms and governmental policies, loosely derived

Table 2. Internal Transport by Mode and Volume, 1852–1869

| Year | Commodities (thousands of km/tons) | | | | | Passengers (thousands of passenger kms) | | |
	Road	Canal & Navigable Waterway	Coastal Shipping	Rail	Total	Road	Rail	Total
1852	2.6	1.7	1.3	0.6	6.2	1.36	0.99	2.35
1869	2.8	2.0	0.8	6.2	11.8	1.46	4.10	5.56

Source: Plessis (1973), 116.

from the Saint-Simonian orientation of the emperor and some of his close advisers, had a great deal to do with the spectacular boom of the period immediately after 1852. That there were limits to such a process of absorbing surpluses of capital and labor soon became apparent. The problem, of course, was that "productive" employment under capitalism has always meant profitable employment. Once the choicer and more lucrative segments of the railroad network were completed by 1855, followed by Haussman's first network of roads in 1856, the state had to find increasingly sophisticated ways to keep the work in progress. And by the mid-1860s, the whole process ran up against the realities of capitalist finance. For this was, make no mistake, a project undertaken not simply at the behest of an all-powerful emperor but organized through the association of capitals. As such, it was subject to the powerful but contradictory logic of capital accumulation.

The new space relations had powerful effects on Parisian economy, politics, and culture. The orientation of the new transport investments reemphasized the tendency toward centralization of administration, finance, economy, and population in Paris. Such a result was seen as a virtue by many. "Paris is centralization itself," proclaimed the emperor with pride; "it is the head and heart of France," elaborated Haussman (1890, 2:202). But there was more to this centralization than mere politics. Even the decision to put Paris at the hub of the new rail network for political and strategic reasons made perfect economic sense to the degree that Paris was both the principal market and the principal manufacturing center in the nation. Agglomeration economies naturally drew new transport investments and new forms of economic activity toward it. But within the continuity of this centralization and agglomeration there were all kinds of other shifts generated by the reduction of spatial barriers and the annihilation of space by time.

To begin with, Parisian industry and commerce were opened up to interregional and international competition. But they also gained easier access to export markets. The position of Parisian industry and commerce therefore changed appreciably in relation to a shifting international division of labor. The costs of assembly of raw materials in Paris also fell (the price of coal fell while the pit-head price in Pas-de-Calais was rising) to make many of the inputs upon which Parisian industry relied correspondingly cheaper. The increased regularity, volume, and speed of flow of goods into the factories and out into the city markets reduced the turnover time of capital and opened up the possibility for big business operations in both production and distribution. The revolution in retailing – the rise of the big department stores – and the shifting power relations between merchants and producers was in part a product of the new space relations (Miller 1981, 37). The Parisian food market was likewise relieved of close dependency upon local and often hazardous supplies and increasingly drew upon provincial and foreign sources, provoking "a veritable revolution in consumption" (Rougerie 1968a, 96). The vegetable gardens, orchards, and animal husbandry that had once flourished in the city had largely disappeared by 1870 (Retel 1977). The bourgeoisie could then look forward to fresh vegetables from Algeria and the Midi, while even the poor could supplement their diets with potatoes from the west and turnips from the east. And it was not only goods that moved. Tourists flooded in from all over the world (adding to the effective demand), shoppers poured in from the suburbs, and the Parisian labor market spread its tentacles into ever remoter regions in order to satisfy a burgeoning demand for labor power.

The flows of information via the telegraph and the rise of a mass daily press also changed the context of space and time in which daily life was lived (see Chap. 1). It raised the old issue of the proper balance between centralization and decentralization of political power in new ways (Greenberg 1971). It challenged the meaning of community in a world where interests seemed to have less and less clear-cut geographical boundaries. And this was not only a question for the bourgeoisie. The new internationalism of the workers' movement sat uneasily with that struggle for local autonomy which gave the Commune much of its specific political coloration. In all of these respects, the changing space relations were a fundamental aspect of the shifting political economy of Parisian life.

The transformation of external space relations also put intense pressure on the thrust to rationalize the interior space of Paris itself. Haussman's exploits in this regard have, of course, become one of the great legends of urban planning (Giedion 1941). Backed by the emperor and armed with the means to absorb surpluses of capital and labor in a vast program of public works, he reorganized the spatial frame of social and economic life in the capital. The investments covered not only a new network of roads but water supply,

sewers, parks, monuments and symbolic spaces, schools, churches, administrative buildings, housing, hotels, commercial premises, and the like.

Part of what was special about it all was the conception of urban space
employed. Instead of "collections of partial plans of public thoroughfares
considered without ties or connections," Haussman (1890, 2:34) sought a
"general plan which was nevertheless detailed enough to properly coordinate
diverse local circumstances." Urban space was seen and treated as a totality in
which different quarters of the city and different functions had to be brought
into relation to each other to form a working whole. This conception, already
implicit in the sketch that the emperor passed to Haussman, was step by step
imposed upon the interior space of Paris as the public works took tangible
shape (fig. 2).

Haussman's passion for exact spatial coordination was symbolized by the
triangulation that produced the first accurate cadastral and topographical map
of the city in 1853. His concern for the totality of the urban space was best
represented by his fierce struggle, successful in 1860, to annex the suburbs
where unruly development threatened the rational evolution of a spatial order
within the agglomeration that was Paris. He also built a sophisticated
hierarchical form of administration – with himself, naturally, positioned at
the top – through which the complex totality of Paris could be better
controlled by an organized decentralization and delegation of power and
responsibility to the arrondissements (where he built many of the *mairies* to
symbolize such a presence to the populace). And he fought, in the end not so
successfully, to counter the privatism and parochialism of individual and local
interests with legislation and rhetoric focused on the public interest for a
rational and orderly evolution of space relations in the city.

But whatever else he and the emperor may have had in mind – the creation
of a Western capital to rival imperial Rome, the expulsion of "dangerous
classes" and insalubrious housing and industry from the city center – one of
the clearest effects of their efforts was to improve the capacity for the
circulation of goods and people within the city's confines. The flows between
the newly established rail stations, between center and periphery, between
left and right banks, into and out of central markets like Les Halles, to and
from places of recreation (Bois de Boulogne by day, the *grands boulevards* by
night), between industry and commerce (to the new department stores), were
all facilitated by the construction of some ninety miles of spacious boulevards
which reduced the cost, time, and (usually) aggravation of movement
remarkably. The new road system had the added advantage that it neatly
surrounded the traditional hearths of revolutionary ferment and would permit
the free circulation of forces of order if needed. It also contributed to the free
circulation of air into insalubrious neighborhoods, while the free play of
sunlight by day and of newly installed gas lighting by night underscored the

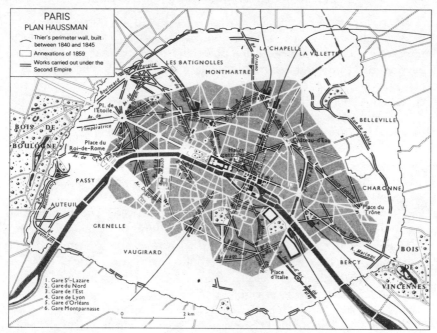

Fig. 2. The transformation of Paris: Road building and annexation, 1850–1870.
(Reproduced, with permission, from J. Levron, Grands Travaux, Grands Architectes du
Passé, *Editions du Moniteur, Paris, 1979.)*

transition to a more extroverted form of urbanism. And, in an extraordinary engineering achievement, a marvel to this day, the flows of water and sewage were revolutionized (Pinkney 1958).

It was ruthlessly done and took time, money, technical skill, and incredible administrative ability. Yet the dramatic transformation of the interior space of Paris was by no means all due to Haussman. The realignment of traffic movement from the principal axis of the Seine to multiple railheads was less a consequence than a compelling condition for that work. Haussman himself recognized that it was a "necessity of the first order" to put the rail stations, now the principal points of entry into Paris, "into a direct relation with the heart of the city by way of large thoroughfares" (Girard 1952, 118). The Petite Ceinture railroad, which ringed Paris and gave such dynamism to suburban growth, owed little to Haussman either. And, as we shall see, there were all manner of shifts in the operation of land and property markets, in industrial location and labor processes, in marketing and distribution systems, in population distribution and family formation, to which Haussman was adjusting rather than leading.

The reshaping of the interior space of Paris was, therefore, a response to processes already in motion. But it also became a framework around which those very same processes – of industrial and commercial development, of housing investment and residential segregation, and so on – could cluster and play out their own trajectories and so define the historical geography of the city. To his credit, Haussman well understood his limited role. For though he had authoritarian powers and frequent delusions of grandeur, he also recognized that he had to liberate more than just the flows of goods and people from their medieval constraints if Paris was to be transformed. The force he had to mobilize, and it was in the end the force that mastered him, was the circulation of capital. But this, too, was a compelling condition present at the very birth of Empire. The surpluses of capital and labor power absolutely had to be absorbed if the Empire was to survive. The absorption of such surpluses via the public works that so transformed the interior space of Paris entailed the free circulation of capital through the construction of a particular spatial configuration of the built environment. Freed from its feudal constraints, capital could then freely move to reorganize the interior space of Paris according to principles that were uniquely its own. Haussman wanted to make Paris a capital worthy of France, even of Western civilization. In the end he simply helped make it a city in which the circulation of capital became the real imperial power. How that came about and with what consequences must now be taken up in detail. That the shaping of space has to be seen as an active rather than a passive moment in the urban process that unfolded is, however, undeniable. The actual organization of space is a first-order material fact with which all historical materialist analysis must come to grips.

II. MONEY, CREDIT, AND FINANCE

> The credit system accelerates the material development of the productive forces and the establishment of the world market.
>
> – *Marx*

On the morning of December 2, 1851, Emile Pereire hurried to the house of James Rothschild to reassure the bedridden banker that all had gone smoothly with the coup d'état. The story of their subsequent break and awesome struggle, which lasted until the Pereire brothers' downfall a year before James died in 1868, is one of the legends of high finance (Autin 1984; Bouvier 1967; and Zola's *L'argent*). Behind it lay two quite different conceptions of the role of money and finance in economic development. The *haute banque* of the Rothschilds was a family affair, private and confidential, working with opulent friends without publicity and deeply conservative in its approach to money, a conservatism expressed through attachment to gold as the real money form, the true measure of value. And that attachment had served Rothschild well. He remained, as a worker publication of 1848 complained, "strong in the face of young republics" and a "power independent of old dynasties." "You are more than a man of state. You are the symbol of credit." The Pereires, for their part, tried to change the meaning of that symbol. They had long seen the credit system as the nerve center of economic development and social change. Amidst a welter of publicity, they sought to democratize savings by mobilizing them into an elaborate hierarchy of credit institutions capable of undertaking projects of long duration. The "association of capital" was their theme, and grand, unashamed speculation in future development was their practice. The conflict between the Rothschilds and the Pereires was, in the final analysis, a personalized version of a deep tension within capitalism between the financial superstructure and its monetary base (Harvey 1982, chap. 10). And if, in 1867, those who controlled hard money managed to bring down the credit empire of the Pereires, it was a pyrrhic victory, for by then a new financial system consistent with the requirements and contradictions of modern capitalism had come into being.

The problem in 1851 was to absorb the surpluses of capital and labor power. The Parisian bourgeoisie universally recognized the economic roots of the crisis through which they had just passed but were deeply divided as to what to do about it (Tudesq 1956). The government took the Saint-Simonian path and sought by a mix of direct governmental interventions, credit creation, and reform of financial structures to facilitate the conversion of surplus capital and labor into new physical infrastructures as the basis for economic revival. It was a politics of mild inflation and stimulated expansion (a sort of primitive Keynesianism) lubricated by the strong inflow of gold from California and Australia. The *hautes banques* and their clients were deeply suspicious; and the government, distrustful of their Orleanist political sympathies, turned to those administrators like Persigny, the Pereires, and Haussman who accepted the idea that universal credit was the way to economic progress and social reconciliation. In so doing they abandoned what Marx (1967, 3:592; 1973, 156) called the "catholicism" of the monetary base and turned their bank into "the papacy of production."

The story of financial reform under the Second Empire is complicated in its details (Dupont-Ferrier 1925; Levy-Leboyer 1976). But the Pereires' Crédit Mobilier was undoubtedly the controversial centerpiece. Initially formed to get railroad construction and all ancillary industries back in business, it was an investment bank that held shares in companies and helped them assemble the necessary finance for large-scale undertakings. It could also sell debt to the general public at a rate of return guaranteed by the earnings of the companies controlled. It thus acted as an intermediary between innumerable small savers hitherto denied such opportunities for placement (the Pereires made much of the supposed "democratization" of credit) and a wide range of industrial enterprises. They even hoped to turn it into a universal holding company that, through assembly of funds and mergers, would bring all economic activity (including that of the government) under common control. There were many, including those in government, who were suspicious of what amounted to a planned evolution of what we now know as "state-monopoly capitalism." And although they were ultimately to fail, the victim of an aroused conservative opposition and their own overextended speculation (a fate that Rothschild had predicted in his letter to the emperor and had helped seal), their opponents were forced to adopt the new methods. Rothschild hit back with the same form of organization as early as 1856, and by the end of the Second Empire a whole host of new financial intermediaries (such as the Crédit Lyonnaise, founded in 1863) had emerged that were to dominate French financial life from then until now.

In itself, as the Pereires recognized, the Crédit Mobilier would not be effective without a wide range of other institutions integrated into or subordinated to it. The Bank of France (a private but state-regulated institution) increasingly took on the role of a national central bank. It was much too fiscally conservative for the Pereires' taste. It took the tasks of preserving the quality of money very seriously, even at the price of tightening credit and raising the discount rate to levels that the Pereires regarded as harmful to economic growth (Autin 1984; Plessis 1982). The Bank of France turned out to be the major center of financial opposition to the Pereires' ideas. It dealt almost exclusively in short-term commercial paper, discounting commercial bills of exchange. The Crédit Foncier, a new institution finally stitched together on December 10, 1852 (shortly after the Crédit Mobilier), was to bring rationality and order to the land and property mortgage market. Founded under the Pereires' influence, it was to be an important ally in their concerns. Other organizations, such as the Comptoir d'Escompte de Paris (founded in 1848) and the Crédit Industriel et Commerciale (1859), dealt in special kinds of credit. And within their own empire, the Pereires, with government blessing, spawned a wide range of hierarchically-ordered institutions, such as the Compagnie Immobilière. At its height the Crédit Mobilier integrated twenty French-based and fourteen foreign-based companies into its extraordinarily powerful organization.

The effects of all this on the transformation of Paris were enormous. Indeed, without some reorganization of finance the transformation simply could not have progressed at the pace it did. It was not just that the city had to borrow (a topic I take up later), but Haussman's projects depended upon

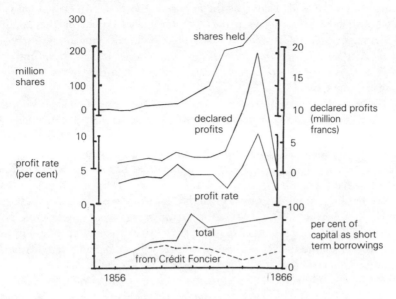

Fig. 3.   The operations of the Pereires' Compagnie Immobilière, 1856–1866.
(After M. Lescure, 1980.)

the existence of companies that had the financial power to develop, build, own, and manage the spaces he opened up. Thus did the Pereires become "in many respects and in many places the secular arm of the prefect" (Autin 1984, 186). The Compagnie Immobilière de Paris emerged in 1858 out of the organization of the Pereires created in 1854 to take on the first of Haussman's big projects, the completion of the rue de Rivoli and the Hôtel du Louvre. The company went on to build along the Champs-Elysées and the boulevard Malesherbes and around the Opera and the parc Monceau. It increasingly relied on speculative operations as a source of profit. In 1856–57 it drew three-quarters of its income from rents received on housing and industrial plants and only a quarter from the buying and selling of land and property. By 1864 the proportions were exactly the reverse (Lescure 1980, 19). The company could also easily augment its capital via the Crédit Mobilier (which held half its shares) and bolster its profits by a leveraging operation based on a cosy relationship with the Crédit Foncier (borrowing half of its capital from the latter at 5.75 percent on a project that returned 8.7 percent yielded the company 11.83 percent, Pereire explained to astonished shareholders). The company increasingly shifted to short-term financing (fig. 3), which made it vulnerable to movements in the interest rate dictated by the Bank of France (which explains the Pereires' obsession with cheap credit). It also contracted building work out to enterprises financed by the Crédit Mobilier (so provoking considerable concentration in the building industry – see Lescure 1980, 66; see also table 4), and it sold or rented the buildings to management companies or commercial groups in which the Crédit Mobilier often had a like stake.

The Pereires were masters at creating vertically integrated financial systems that could be put to work to build railroads; to launch all manner of transportation, industrial, and commercial enterprises; and to create massive investments in the built environment. "I want to write my ideas on the landscape itself," wrote Emile Pereire – and indeed he and his brother did. But they were not alone. Even Rothschild stooped so low as to parlay his property holdings around his own Gare du Nord into a profitable real estate venture, and many a builder, contractor, architect, or owner sought profit by the same route. And while this was not, as we shall see, the only system of land development in Paris, it was *the* means for engineering the "Haussmanization" of Paris.

But this was only the tip of a veritable iceberg of effects on the economy and life of Paris. Money, finance, and speculation became such a grand obsession with the Parisian bourgeoisie ("business is other people's money," cracked Alexandre Dumas the younger), that the *bourse* seemed to become the center of corruption as well as of reckless speculation that gobbled up many a landed fortune. Its nefarious influence over daily life was immortalized afterwards in Zola's *L'argent* and *La curée* (fig. 4). It was through such means that immense centralization of financial power also became possible. The top six families held 158 out of 920 seats on company boards registered in Paris in the mid-1860s – the Pereires held 44 and the Rothschilds 32 (Plessis 1982, 81) – provoking complaints about the immense power of a new "feudality of finance" (Duchêne 1869). This power was felt internationally (the Pereires threatened, said their detractors, to substitute a new international paper money under their control for gold) as well as in all realms of urban organization – the Pereires merged the gas companies into a single regulated monopoly, bringing industrial and street lighting to much of Paris; founded (again by merger) the Compagnie des Omnibus de Paris, so increasing the number of passengers moved from 36 million in 1855 to 110 million by 1860; financed one of the first department stores (the Louvre, in a building they had trouble renting out); and tried to monopolize the dock and entrepôt trade (Autin 1984, 249–56).

The reorganization of the credit system had far-reaching effects upon Parisian industry and commerce, the labor process, and the mode of consumption. Everyone, after all, depended on credit. The only question was who was to make it available to whom and on what terms. Workers bedeviled by seasonal unemployment lived by it; small masters and shopkeepers needed

Fig. 4. The Stock Exchange, lithograph by Alphonse Chigot, 1857. (Musée Carnavelet.)

it to deal with the seasonality of demand – the chain was endless. Indebtedness was a chronic problem in all classes and arenas of activity. But the credit system of the 1840s was as arbitrary and capricious as it was insecure (only land and property gave true security). Proposals for reform of the credit system abounded in 1848. Artisans, small masters, and craft workers sought some kind of mutual credit system under local and democratic control. Proudhon's experiment with a People's Bank offering free credit under the banner "Merchants of money, your reign is over!" collapsed with his arrest in 1849 (Hyams 1979, 154–71). But the idea never died. When workers began to organize in the 1860s, it was to questions of mutual credit that they increasingly turned. Their Crédit au Travail, started in 1863, foundered in 1868, hopelessly insolvent with "loans outstanding to forty-eight cooperatives, of which eighteen were bankrupt and only nine could pay" (Kelso 1936, 102). Indifference on the part of government and, more surprisingly, on the part of fellow workers was blamed. Consumer cooperatives ran into similar problems, many families preferring the antagonistic relation and default on debts to local shopkeepers to the economic burden of cooperation in the face of periodic unemployment and lagging real incomes. The municipal pawnshop of Mont-de-Piété continued to be the last resort for the mass of the Parisian populace. The dream of free credit appeared more and more remote. "It entailed," said a member of the *Workers' Commission of 1867* (126), "the reversal of the entire system of private property on which merchants, landlords, government, etc. lived."

The credit system was rationalized, expanded, and democratized through the association of capitals, but at the expense of often uncontrolled speculation and the growing absorption of all savings into a centralized and hierarchically organized system that left those at the bottom even more vulnerable to the arbitrary and capricious whims of those who had some money power. Yet it took a revolution in the credit system to produce the revolution in space relations. Within Paris that process depended, however, upon a much tighter integration of finance capital and landed property. To the manner of this integration we now turn.

III. RENT AND THE PROPERTIED INTEREST

It is the ground-rent, and not the house, which forms the actual object of
building speculation in rapidly growing cities.

– *Marx*

Between 1848 and 1852, the Parisian property market underwent its severest and most prolonged depression of the century. In some bourgeois quarters, where the depression hit hardest, vacancy rates stood as high as one-sixth, rents fell by half, and property prices (if sales were possible at all) were severely depressed (Daumard 1965, 23–35; fig. 5). The Second Empire reversed all that. It proved the golden age in a century noted for relatively secure and high rates of return and appreciation on Parisian property. But it was also an era in which the social meaning and orientation of property ownership in the city changed radically. Parisian property was more and more appreciated as a pure financial asset, as a form of fictitious capital whose exchange value, integrated into the general circulation of capital, entirely dominates use value. There was a world of difference, as Zola himself recognized, between the massive speculation of his antihero Saccard (*La curée*) and the minor dabblings described in Balzac's *Cousin Bette.*

Speculation on the Parisian property market had, of course, a long and not so respectable history. When Louis Philippe's prime minister, Guizot, issued his famous invitation, *"enrichissez-vous,"* the Parisian bourgeoisie responded with an incredible speculative binge that lasted well into the 1840s. They did so in part because property was one of the few secure forms of investment open to them. It was remunerative simply because housing provision lagged behind growth of population. The number of houses in the city increased

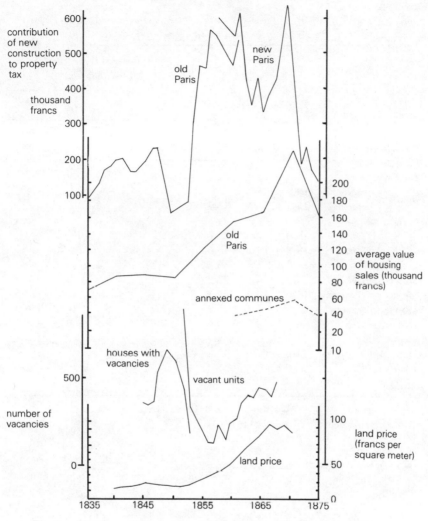

Fig. 5.　New construction, housing and land values, and vacancy rates in Paris, 1835–1875. (After A. Daumard, 1965, and J. Gaillard, 1977.)

from 26,801 in 1817 to 30,770 in 1851, while population rose from 713,966 to 1,053,897 (Sutcliffe 1970, 115). The rate of return on worker housing stood at 7 percent in the 1820s and probably continued at that level at the price of undermaintenance and overcrowding in those insalubrious quarters so graphically described in the novels of Balzac and Eugène Sue. In

Table 3. Role of Property in Personal Wealth and the Distribution of Parisian Property Ownership by Socioeconomic Category, 1840–1880

| | % of Parisian Fortunes Held as Property, 1847 | | | % of Parisian Property Held by Social Group | | | |
| | | | | 1840 | 1880 | | |
Socioeconomic Category	in Paris	ex-Paris	Total	%	Total %	Center %	Periphery %
Landowner[a]	39.8	21.3	61.1	8.9	53.9	49.1	59.3
Merchants[b] active	16.0	5.3	21.3	14.2	14.5	17.7	11.0
retired	23.5	20.5	43.7				
Company					3.5	5.9	0.9
Shopkeeper[c] active	18.0	7.0	25.0	48.8	13.6	9.6	18.1
retired	38.8	2.2	41.0				
Functionary	13.0	33.4	46.4	4.3	2.2	3.1	0.7
State employee	10.7	16.5	27.2	4.0	0.6	1.0	0.2
Diverse employees	14.0	10.2	24.2	2.3	2.7	2.8	2.6
Liberal professions[d]	37.5	7.3	44.8	17.2	8.1	10.1	6.0
Diverse[e]	8.7	0.9	9.6	0.3	0.8	0.5	1.1
Homeworker	15.8	2.3	18.1				
Day worker	15.6	1.6	17.2				
Domestic	2.8	5.3	8.1				
Total	27.4	17.3	44.7				

Source: Daumard (1965), 237, 241, and Daumard (1973), 216.
[a] Includes those who listed this as their position.
[b] Includes industrialists as well as wholesalers and merchants.
[c] Includes artisans.
[d] Doctors, lawyers, teachers, etc.
[e] Probably includes the homeworkers, day workers, and domestics in property ownership columns.

bourgeois quarters the return was closer to 5 percent (rarely less), since tenants were harder to come by and more exacting (Daumard 1965, 137). This nevertheless compared very favorably with the 3 percent or so to be had on state debt.

Thanks to Daumard's (1965) meticulous studies, we can discern the main lines of change that followed. Parisian property, while a favored means of storing wealth within all segments of the bourgeoisie, was dominated in the 1840s by shopkeepers and artisans (one-half), with liberal professions and commercial interests holding another third. By 1880, the pattern had changed completely. Shopkeepers and artisans had dropped to 13.6 percent and liberal professions to 8.1 percent, being supplanted by a class of people who identified themselves solely as landowners (53.9 percent). Only commercial interests (particularly when joined with the new category of "companies") maintained their position (table 3). And only in the periphery did shopkeepers retain a significant presence, having a quarter of the sales there in 1870 but falling to 18.1 percent in 1880. Commerce, companies, and liberal professions had a disproportionate share of center city property, though they were nowhere near as dominant as the property owners. The lower middle class and petite bourgeoisie, therefore, were steadily excluded from property ownership (particularly in central locations) and replaced by a haute bourgeoisie of landlords and commercial interests. Such a change is consistent with important shifts in commercial, financial, and manufacturing structure (see sec. 5) that saw the subordination of artisans and small-scale producers and shopkeepers to the hegemony of grand commerce and finance. There is also evidence that all social groups were increasingly willing to engage in the buying and selling of property as a speculative activity.

Ownership began and remained highly dispersed. In 1846, Daumard calculates, the average owner controlled only two properties, and although some of these may have been individually large, the majority were not. There was, and continued to be, considerable variation from quarter to quarter. If there was any pattern to it all in 1850, Gaillard (1977, 85–120) suggests, the "progressive" large-scale propertied interests were Right Bank rather than Left, central rather than peripheral. The tendency toward concentration of ownership, which Daumard detects in some central areas on the Right Bank, was merely a perpetuation of a pattern already evident in 1850 and earlier. Indeed, the prior manner of appropriation of space in Paris had a key role to play in the subsequent reorganization of that space. The form and style of landownership on the Left Bank (large-scale aristocratic owners intermingled with artisans and shopkeepers) kept it deeply resistant to Haussman's works, with results that can still be discerned today. The large-scale commercial interests collected in the Right Bank's center were not only amenable to change but had actively promoted it and planned for it under the July Monarchy.

In Paris, the urban based propertied interests constituted a powerful political force under the July Monarchy and were considered Orleanist in their political sympathies. Their social attitudes and power left an indelible mark upon the Parisian landscape of 1850. They typically undertook few improvements except those dictated by personal whim or the search for status. The capital they engaged was mainly seen as securing revenue or, in the case of shopkeepers, a use value, rather than as the productive circulation of capital via the construction of the built environment. Speculative as opposed to custom building was relatively restricted, haphazard, and small in scale, and was largely peripheral. Insufficient to meet popular needs, it was supplemented by the formation of shantytown slums such as the infamous Petite Pologne. The housing stock was expensive and by and large in bad condition. The owners also tended to resist public improvements, partly because of the myopic spatial perspective that typically attaches to small-scale ownership, partly because the uneven distribution of benefits among dispersed owners militated against any easy consensus for change, and partly out of their mortal fear of higher taxes and diminished revenues. That Parisian physical infrastructures were deteriorating in relation to burgeoning needs was evident enough, however, to spark a plethora of plans for change under the July Monarchy. But little was done, largely because of the attitudes and political power of the property owners. This was the condition that absolutely had to change if Paris was to be modernized.

The circumstances under which Haussman came to Paris were propitious in a number of respects. The emperor was not particularly indebted to a class openly Orleanist in its political sympathies. It was, moreover, a class that had been put very much on the political defensive. Years of accumulated hate for grasping and negligent landlords – popularly caricatured as M. Vautour – spilled out in the workers' movement of 1848. And even after the June Days and the remarkable electoral triumph of the "party of order" in 1849, a social democratic socialism deeply antagonistic to landlordism (waving Proudhon's slogan, "property is theft") was all too much in evidence, particularly in Paris. To these political troubles was added the chronic depression in the Parisian property market. Much weakened, therefore, the propertied interest was willing to accept almost anything that would guarantee the perpetuation of its rights and a resurgence of the market.

The Empire obliged on both counts. It suppressed the left without compunction and laid the foundation for a spectacular recovery in the Parisian property market. By 1855, the vacancy rate had fallen to an all-time low, property prices were rising rapidly (see fig. 5), and Louis Lazare, who had his fingers on a great deal of detailed information, was complaining of rates of return of 12 percent or more. Daumard's (1965, 228) carefully reconstructed figures for housing built along the new boulevards in selected central city locations indicate solid rates of return throughout the whole Second Empire period:

Rate of return (%)	> 5	5–5.9	6–6.9	7–7.9	8–8.9	< 9
Number of cases (%)	4.6	6.8	32.7	36.7	13.8	5.2

There is little reason to suspect that rates of return on old housing were much less (Daumard 1965, 168). The owners could simply dictate terms to tenants. Parisian property, in short, became a secure and high-yielding investment protected from the fluctuations that typified the stock market. A material foundation was here laid for a political rapprochement between Parisian property owners and Empire (Gaillard 1977, 136). Unbeholden at the beginning, the Empire increasingly looked to them as a base of support in a capital where opposition sentiment dominated as early as 1857.

Yet Haussman's relations with the propertied interest were often troubled and at best ambivalent. This helps explain why the latter's support for Empire was less enthusiastic than might have been expected. To begin with, Haussman's conception of urban space was radically different from that of typically myopic and dispersed owners. While very much in favor of private property in general, Haussman was not, therefore, solicitous of anyone's private property rights in particular. He was prepared to ride roughshod over particularist opposition, and that was bound to stir resentment. Furthermore, it was hard to bring equal benefits to so many dispersed owners. Toward the end of the Empire, Gaillard (1977, 110–12) notes, there were many complaints from property owners who felt left out of the grand speculative feast accompanying the public works. Haussman also had to battle the fiscal conservatism of owners which kept them from investing productively in the transformation of urban space or from approving of public action with such an aim. If Paris was to be transformed, then capital had to be mobilized, not only into buying and selling, but also into demolition, reconstruction, and long-term management of the urban space according to collectivist principles that were quite alien to the privatism of traditional property owners. It was, in short, the capitalist form of private property in land which Haussman encouraged, and in so doing he collided head-on with more traditional and deeply entrenched attitudes and practices.

Haussman (1890, 2:51–52) well anticipated the resistance he might encounter. He promptly demolished the two main channels of landowner influence over renewal decisions. The planning commission was reduced to just him, and the municipal council, appointed rather than elected, was easily coopted. He nevertheless found it prudent to still the property owners' fears of higher taxes by devising creative methods of debt financing which rested on expansion of the tax base rather than on any increase in the rate of taxation. He also came armed with strong powers of expropriation "for reasons of public interest" and of condemnation for "insalubrity" bequeathed to him out of the social legislation of the Second Republic. He was prepared to use both in ways their initiators had hardly envisaged. With the propertied interest in any case demoralized, Haussman struck hard and fast at the core of the problem with scarcely any opposition.

That the property owners subsequenty staged a successful counterattack through the judiciary and the Conseil d'Etat (both of which they came to dominate) is a well-known story. In 1858, they regained the right to betterment values, which Haussman had previously retained (with much financial benefit) for the city. They gained increasingly favorable compensation judgments for land taken and via a maze of decrees and legal judgments managed to turn the tables entirely on Haussman by the early 1860s (Pinkney 1958, 185–87; Sutcliffe 1970, 40–41; Gaillard 1977, 27–30). Haussman (1890, 2:310, 371) was later to claim that this "victory of privatism over public interests" and the rising costs of compensation coupled with loss of revenues consequent upon these judgments lay at the root of the fiscal problems that beset the city in the 1860s. Daumard's (1965, 215) data certainly show that owners received compensation well above market value after 1858. If the property owners consolidated their alliance with the Empire, therefore, they did so partly at Haussman's expense. And although it would be stretching matters somewhat to argue that they had a direct role in his downfall, enough of them were sufficiently discontented to raise no protest when he fell.

There were deeper processes at work, however, which deserve finer scrutiny. They illustrate the conflicts that arise, not only when purely and partially capitalistic practices with respect to the use of property collide, but also when the tensions inherent in the capitalistic form of rationality rise to the surface. Haussman set out to master such tensions. It was no reflection on his genius that they ended up mastering him. It was his genius to see with such clarity that new practices of property ownership had to be mobilized if Paris was to be transformed and modernized.

The Circulation of Capital in the Built Environment

The mobilization of capital flow to transform the built environment of Paris during the Second Empire was a spectacular affair. "Capital rushed like air into a vacuum," wrote Halbwachs (1928), but it was mainly capital of a certain sort which rushed in, that of the associated capitalists mobilized via the new system of financing (see sec. 2). Haussman's strategy was two-pronged. If he could not find development companies willing or resourceful enough to undertake the massive projects he had in mind, he used the power of the state to mobilize the financing and undertake the brunt of the work (Massa-Gille 1973, chap. 5). The city could then recapture the betterment values derived from its own investments, thereby becoming, as critics complained, the biggest speculator of all. Private landowners stood by aghast as benefits they felt legitimately belonged to them poured into the city's coffers. It was on this basis that they mobilized their successful legal counterattack of 1858. But Haussman's second and preferred strategy was, in the end, even more powerful and compelling. It was, he argued, "best to leave to speculation stimulated by competition" the task of "recognizing the people's real needs and satisfying them" (quoted in Sutcliffe 1970, 117). To this end he forged an alliance between the city and a coterie of financial and real estate interests (builders, developers, architects, etc.) assembled under the umbrella power of "associated," or "finance," capital. It was, therefore, a well-organized form of monopolistic competition which he had in mind. And it had to be this way, because the city subsidized the works through donations of land rather than money. To draw the benefits, companies had to be large enough to orchestrate their own externality effects and be able to wait (sometimes several years) for the rise in land value to materialize.

The renewal put large concessions in the hands of a few capitalists who had privileged access to the state (including funds from the newly founded Crédit Foncier) and behind whom stood a phalanx of financiers (like the Pereires) who had a plethora of other interests, including insurance, construction, and building management companies. It was associated, or finance, capital applied to land development, an innovation born out of the particular structures of Empire and opposed to traditional forms of landownership and use. But the very nature of their operations restricted them to meeting the demand for housing and commercial premises from the affluent classes or large-scale commerce. Largely active in the center and west, they played a crucial role in the formation of the predominantly bourgeois quarters that adorned Haussman's new boulevards. But their permanent impact upon landownership (as opposed to short-term buying and selling, which, as we saw in the case of the Pereires, increasingly dominated their operations) was relatively weak, property companies holding less than 6 percent of central city properties in 1880 (see table 3). This was, nevertheless, the system that aroused the jealousy, fear, and ire of the conventional propertied interests (Gaillard 1977, 121–27). And although some private owners, small-scale builders, architects, and the like evidently participated to some degree in the renewal, they found it increasingly difficult to do so (Daumard 1965, 267).

The provision of middle- and low-income housing, however, lay entirely outside this sytem of development. There sprang up beside it, therefore, a radically different system of land and housing development in the "relatively impoverished" hands of small-scale owners. "Tardily nourished by expropri-ation and modestly irrigated with credit from the Crédit Foncier," they nevertheless had considerable opportunity to speculate in housing construc-tion, particularly on the northern and eastern peripheries, which formed a veritable urban frontier where low land prices allowed even those with modest savings (lawyers, merchants, shopkeepers, artisans, and even workers) to parlay processes of demographic growth and rising demand for low-income

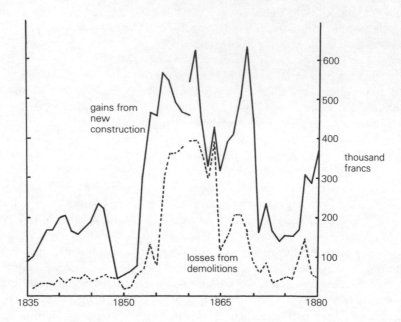

Fig. 6.   Increase in property tax base through new construction (solid line) *versus decrease in property tax base through demolitions* (broken line) *in Paris, 1835–1880. (After A. Daumard, 1965.)*

housing into a little personal gain (Gaillard 1977, 127–44). In the course of the Second Empire, some of these developers built up a very substantial business, mainly in the peripheral arrondissements and entirely outside the system of land development which dominated in the center (Lameyre 1958, 152). They were, nevertheless, stimulated to accumulate capital through investment in the built environment by the example set by the central city renewal. Their generally favorable response to the annexation of the suburbs in 1860 rested on their hope, vain as it turned out, that incorporation within the city would both enhance land values and bring them the rich benefits of expropriation and privileged access to credit. Their sense of having been deceived when such benefits did not materialize led them to become leading critics of Haussman's politics toward the end of the 1860s (Gaillard 1977, 104–15).

There was, however, a remarkable surge in housing construction, which, after an initial phase when demolitions exceeded new units (fig. 6), added substantially to the city's housing stock, more than keeping pace with population growth for the first time in the century during the 1860s when housing units expanded by 27 percent and population by only 11 percent

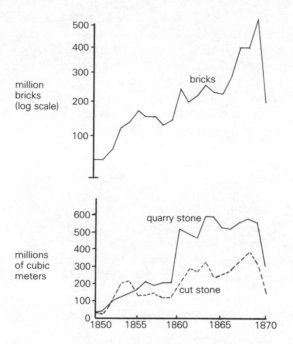

Fig. 7. Volume of construction materials (bricks and stone) entering Paris, 1850–1870. (After J. Gaillard, 1977.)

(Girard 1981, 186). But within this remarkable overall performance there were some equally remarkable divergencies. Paris, Gaillard (1977, 82) notes, was divided into two types of development and construction, "each with its own geographical domain, its own clientele, and its own rhythms." Small-scale, largely brick construction of low-income housing on the periphery (Belleville, Batignolles, and similar areas), active in the 1850s, exploded in the 1860s under the pressure of family formation out of the preceding immigration wave coupled with population displacement from the center. The number of bricks entering the city (a good index of this sort of activity) expanded continually until 1870. Speculative activity of this sort served the mass of the population and drew its profits out of already low worker incomes (sec. 8). In contrast, the flow of stone to adorn the facades of Haussman's new boulevards (fig. 7) fluctuated more closely with the number of expropriations and the supply of credit. After an initial surge up until 1854, competition for funds (mainly from railroad building) and high interest rates checked growth until 1859, while the financial troubles of 1864 and 1867–68 led to rapid contractions in this kind of construction (Sutcliffe 1970, 118). and it is also noticeable how the overall pace of growth in this sector slackened in the

1860s as the demand for high-income housing reached a saturation point.

The mass of the Parisian housing market oriented to working-class needs marched to an entirely different drummer than that which Haussman sponsored around the urban renewal. The glamour of the latter has led to undue emphasis upon it, although special attention is warranted to the degree that it represented a radical and innovative departure from traditional forms of land development. What is interesting, however, is the way in which the increasing liberty of circulation of capital in the production of built environments spilled over and outward to the small-scale urban developers of the periphery. From this standpoint Haussman's integration of the suburbs into the urban frame had, both administratively and spatially, a crucial role to play in facilitating the growth of systems of land development which had languished in preceding periods. And to this system the working class appeared to have no effective answer. A few feeble attempts to mount cooperative endeavors collapsed ignominiously. In this sense the divergencies within the Parisian development process were held together by a common underpinning, that of the circulation of capital.

Rent and the Sorting of Land to Uses

Large- and small-scale developers also had this in common: they increasingly sought to profit from rising land and property values rather than investing in rents as a steady source of income. The separation between developer and ultimate owner had important impacts upon the level and pattern of land rents and property prices, which in turn generated a different land-use rationale within the city. We here encounter another major transformation worked through during the Second Empire. Land and property rents and prices increasingly functioned to allocate land to uses according to a distinctively capitalistic logic.

That Parisian land and property values more than doubled during the Second Empire is common wisdom (see fig. 5). The details are harder to reconstruct and indicate a geographical pattern and a rhythm of temporal change of such intricate complexity as to defy easy description (Girard 1981, 173–75; Sutcliffe 1970, 158; Gaillard 1977, 67–139; Daumard 1965). Land prices on the inner streets could be half those along the new boulevards and could vary even more strongly from quarter to quarter. It was precisely across such steep land value gradients that the large-scale developers could operate so successfully, since the new road system created marvelous opportunities to capture rising location rents. The Pereires, for example, paid Fr 430 per square meter at the mid-point of boulevard Malesherbes to help open the way to land they had purchased around the parc Monceau (about a kilometer away) for Fr 50 and land a bit beyond that, which they had purchased earlier for less than Fr 10 (Autin 1984, 186). As soon as the renewal passed through, land prices shot up. Lameyre (1958, 140–42) records land along the boulevard Sebastopol that went for Fr 25 in 1850 selling for Fr 1,000 per square meter in 1857, and Gaillard (1977, 92) notes how land values increased tenfold in two years on certain areas of the Left Bank after the 1867 Exposition. With geographical gradients and temporal shifts of this order, it is small wonder that speculation in the Parisian land market was an active business. But as the speculation proceeded, the intricate pattern of local peaks and troughs that had once characterized the Parisian rent surface began to be ironed out, leaving a more systematic map of land values in its place (Halbwachs 1909). In this way the systematization of space relations implicit in the new road system carried over into a more systematic organization of land values and uses.

The pattern that emerged showed, as might be expected, a strong gradation from center to periphery (where land could still be had for between Fr 15 and Fr 30 per square meter in 1870) and a tremendous distinction between the bourgeois west and a working-class east, separated by a high-rent commercial center that distinguished a dynamic Right Bank from a rather more lethargic Left. Within this regional structure of land values some sharp gradients continued to exist, but they now tended to represent distinctions of use. For example, land prices fell from Fr 1,000 per square meter around Les Halles to Fr 600 at the rue Saint-Denis to between Fr 150 and Fr 250 per kilometer further east in solidly working-class quarters. And then there were the usual (by modern standards) distinctions betwen prime sites at key intersections, along the new boulevards, or within the burgeoning commercial complexes and the lower values on back streets and in residential areas.

This rental sorting of land to uses – a process pushed by land speculation – becomes even more evident when we consider geographical and temporal shifts in property values. The extent of the property boom is indicated by a rise in the total value of parisian property from 2.5 billion to 6 billion francs between 1852 and 1870, with the increased value of already existing property accounting for 1.5 billion of the increase. The average sale price of houses in old Paris tripled during the same period (see fig. 5). Again, there is much intricate variation to be considered. But we can also detect some generalizing processes at work behind the overall rise and increasing geographical segregation in property rents and values.

Haussman treated it all as a matter of demand and supply, arguing that housing rents would have gone up much faster if he had not opened up access to fresh land at the periphery for development. His critics replied that the demolitions restricted supply and that the renewal sparked the immigration wave that so stimulated demand. While there is an element of truth to both positions, matters were somewhat more complicated. To begin with, construction costs were falling with improved efficiency in the building industry, while there was also, as discussed earlier, a strong surplus of housing construction relative to population, particularly in the 1860s. Rising land costs, though a vital source of gain to developers and builders, were not in themselves sufficient to account for rising rents and property values. A more cogent explanation lies in Gaillard's account of the "*embourgeoisement*" (or "gentrification," as we might now call it) of much of the Parisian housing market.

Haussman's policies and access to credit privileged high-value housing construction. Falling construction costs, coupled with interior designs that economized on use of space, also put this kind of housing within reach of that segment of the middle class whose incomes were rising. The value of Parisian housing stock increased accordingly. There is also considerable evidence of overproduction of high-value housing, relative even to rising effective demand. The Pereires, for example, found it hard to dispose of all their properties on the boulevard Malesherbes in the 1860s – a foretaste of their distress to come. But the logic of this kind of "growth machine," once set in motion, is hard to stop. And part of that logic is to seek protection for both the property values created and the clientele served through increasing spatial segregation. The Second Empire witnessed, therefore, not only the progressive gentrification of the renewed city center but also the rapid creation of exclusive bourgeois quarters toward the west.

Contrast this with that "relatively impoverished" system of housing provision for the lower classes, which lacked the privileges accorded high-value construction. Falling costs were more than offset by rising land prices, since it was hard for worker families already crowded into one room to economize much further on space. Furthermore, as we shall see, family formation in the 1860s out of the largely celibate immigration wave of the 1850s changed the nature of the housing demand (sec. 6). Demolition and gentrification in the center restricted low-income supply there and forced low-income demand into other spaces (such as the Left Bank boarding houses, which saw a rapid increase in rents as a consequence) or into new zones of building on the periphery. And although there was a considerable building boom there, there is little evidence of overproduction. Rising property values in the working-class sector of the housing market are better explained by the nature of the speculative building process and the increasing proportion of disposable income which most workers were forced to spend on housing (sec. 8). There was also increasing spatial segregation, but largely by default, since it proved hard to attract bourgeois property owners or tenants into areas where the land development process was more and more oriented to low-income speculative housing. The east-west distinction (which had the *average* property values on the west side exceed that of any quarter on the east) consolidated out of this dual and class-oriented system of housing provision.

The speculative process also entailed heightened competition between different types of users. Financial and commercial uses raised rents between the Bourse and the Chaussée d'Antin to the point where all other uses were precluded, thus imparting a strong dynamic to the northwest center, which was lacking elsewhere (Sutcliffe 1970). Property development on the Left Bank, which lacked such a commercial center and which in any case absorbed a disproportionate number of educational and religious institutions, therefore had a very different dynamic. Though rents rose (from nearly Fr 500 per year in 1860 to over Fr 800 in 1864 for a furnished room near Odean) under the pressure of demand from displaced central city workers and a rising student population, the pace of renewal was leisurely, and speculation was restrained by the peculiar qualities of landownership structure and the absence of strong competition for the use of land from finance, commerce, or industry (Gaillard 1977, 85–100). Industry, for its part, also had to cope with the shifting surface of property values, holding on close to the center only at the price of a drastic reorganization of its labor process or out of access advantages, which made the payment of high rents feasible and desirable. Those industries closely tied to central city markets tended, therefore, to agglomerate toward the inner northeast in the midst of craft worker quarters where rents, though much higher than on the periphery, were also much lower than in the commercial and financial inner northwest or the bourgeois residential west. Otherwise industry was forced to seek out cheaper land on the periphery or land of special qualities (nodal points within the communication system, for example) for which it was worth paying a premium rent.

The reorganization, stimulated by the rise of a new credit system, of land and property markets along more purely capitalistic lines (with, to be sure, some strong centers of traditionalist resistance, as on the Left Bank) had important effects. It increasingly bound the organization of the interior space of Paris to price competition between different users for control of space. Industrial, commercial, governmental, and residential uses all competed with each other, as did industries of different sorts and housing of different qualities. That Paris was more spatially segregated in 1870 than in 1850 was only to be expected, given the manner in which flows of capital were unleashed to the tasks of restructuring the built environment and its spatial configuration. The new condition of land use competition organized through land and property speculation forced all manner of adaptations upon users. Much of the worker population was dispersed to the periphery (with longer journeys to work) or doubled up in overcrowded, high-rent locations closer to the center. Industry likewise faced the choice of changing its labor process or suburbanizing.

The absorption of labor and capital surpluses through the reconstruction of Paris had all manner of negative effects, such as increasing displacement and segregation, longer journeys to work, and rising rents and overcrowding, that many at the time regarded as downright pathological. Where contemporaries like Louis Lazare went wrong, however, was in attributing all such pathological effects to the evil genius of Haussman. In this, of course, critics were engaging in that traditional French practice (by no means yet extinct) of attributing any or all signs of pathology to the defective policies and politics of a supposedly all-powerful state. Exactly how powerful that state was in general, and how powerful Haussman in particular, requires, therefore, careful consideration.

IV. THE STATE

> But it is precisely with the maintenance of that extensive state machine in its numerous ramifications that the material interests of the French bourgeoisie are interwoven in the closest fashion.
>
> – *Marx*

The French state at mid-century was in search of a modernization of its structures and practices that would accord with contemporary needs. This was as true for Paris as it was for the nation. Louis Napoleon came to power on the wreckage of an attempt to define those needs from the standpoint of workers and a radicalized bourgeoisie. As the only candidate who seemed capable of imposing order on the "reds," he swept to victory as president of the Republic. As the only person who seemed capable of maintaining that order, he received massive support for constituting the Empire. Yet the emperor was desperately in need of a stable class alliance that would support him (rather than see him as the best of bad worlds) and in need of a political model that would assure effective control and administration. The model he began with (and was gradually forced to abandon in the 1860s) was of a hierarchically-ordered but popularly-based authoritarianism. The image he used was of a vast national army led by a popular leader and in which each person would have his or her place in a project of national development for the benefit of all. Strong discipline imposed by the meritocracy at the top was to be matched by expressions of popular will from the bottom.

It is tempting to interpret the gyrations of personnel and policies under the Second Empire as the arbitrary vacillations of an opportunistic dreamer surrounded by venal and grasping advisers. I shall follow Gramsci (1971, 219–23) and Zeldin (1958, 1963), who, from opposite ends of the political spectrum, view the Empire as an important transition in French government and politics that, for all its tentativeness, helped bring the institutions of the nation into closer concordance with the modern requirements and contradictions of capitalism. In what follows I shall focus on how this political transition took place in Paris and what the consequences were for the historical geography of the city.

State Intervention in the Circulation of Capital

The idea of "state productive expenditures" derives from the Saint-Simonian doctrine to which the emperor and some of his key advisers, including Haussman, loosely subscribed. Debt-financed expenditures, the argument goes, require no additional taxation and are no added burden on the treasury, provided that the expenditures are "productive" and promote that growth of economic activity which, at a stable tax rate, expands government revenues sufficiently to cover interest and amortization costs. State-financed public works of the sort that the emperor asked Haussman to execute could, in principle at least, help absorb surpluses of capital and labor power and ensure their perpetual full employment at no extra cost to the taxpayer.

The main tax base upon which Haussman could rely was the *octroi* – a tax on commodities entering Paris. Haussman was prepared to subsidize and deficit-finance any amount of development in Paris, provided it increased this tax revenue. He would, for example, virtually give land away to developers but by tightly regulating building style and materials ensure an expansion of tax receipts. From this, incidentally, derives Haussman's strong partiality for expensive housing for the rich.

The story of Haussman's slippery financing has been too well told to bear detailed repetition (Pinkney 1958; Massa-Gille 1973; Sutcliffe 1970). By 1870 his works had cost some 2.5 billion francs, of which half were financed out of budget surpluses, state subsidies, and resale of lands. He borrowed 60 million by direct public subscription (an innovation) in 1855 and sought another 130 million in 1860, which was finally disposed of only in 1862 when the Pereires' Crédit Mobilier took one-fifth. The loan of 270 million authorized after severe debate in 1865 was disposed of only with the active help of the Crédit Mobilier. Haussman needed another 600 million, and the prospects of obtaining another loan were poor. So he began to tap the Public Works Fund, which was meant as a floating debt, independent of the city budget, designed to smooth out the receipts and expenditures attached to public works that took a long time to complete. The construction costs were normally paid by the builder, who was then paid by the city in as many as eight annual installments (including interest) after the project was complete. Since the builder had to raise the capital, this was in effect a short-term loan to the city. In 1863, some of the builders ran into difficulty and demanded immediate payment on a partially finished project. The city turned to the Crédit Foncier, which, at the emperor's urging, lent the money on security of a letter from the city to the builder stating the expected completion date of the project and the schedule of payment. Haussman was, in effect, borrowing money from the Crédit Foncier via the intermediary of the builders. And it could all be hidden in the Public Works Fund, which was not open to public scrutiny. By 1868, Haussman had raised nearly half a billion francs this way.

Given Haussman's association with the Pereires and the Crédit Foncier, it is hardly surprising that his misdeeds were first revealed in 1865 by Leon Say, protégé of the Rothschilds. This gave grand ammunition to those opposed to Empire (Jules Ferry's *Comptes fantastiques d'Haussman* hit the presses to great effect in 1868). A fiscally conservative, unimaginative, and politically motivated bourgeoisie undoubtedly played a key role in Haussman's dismissal. But there was a much deeper problem here, stemming from the form of state involvement in the circulation of capital. Between 1853 and 1870 "the City's debt had risen from 163 million francs to 2,500 millions, and in 1870 debt charges made up 44.14 percent of the City's budget." City finances thus became incredibly vulnerable to all the shocks, tribulations, and uncertainties that attach to the circulation of interest-bearing capital. Far from controlling the future of Paris, let alone being able to stabilize the economy, Haussman "was himself dominated by the machine he and his imperial master had created." He was, Sutcliffe (1970), 42) concludes, fortunate that national political issues forced him out of power, because an overstretched municipal financial structure "could not have survived the repercussions of the international depression of the 1870s." Here, as in other times and places (New York in the 1970s springs immediately to mind), a state apparatus that set out to solve the grand problems of overaccumulation, through deficit-financing its own expenditures, in the end fell victim to the slippery contradictions embodied in the circulation of interest-bearing money capital. Indeed, there is a sense in which the fate of Haussman mimics that of the Pereires. In this respect, at least, the emperor and his advisers modernized the state into the pervasive contradictions of contemporary capitalist finance.

The Management of Labor Power

"I would rather face an hostile army of 200,000," said the emperor, "than the threat of insurrection founded on unemployment" (Thomas n.d., 65). To the degree that the 1848 revolution had been made and unmade in Paris, so the question of full employment in the capital was a pressing issue. The quickening pace of public works partially solved the problem. "No longer did bands of insurgents roam the streets but teams of masons, carpenters and other artisans going to work; if paving stones were pulled up it was not to build barricades but to open the way for water and gas pipes; houses were no longer threatened by arson or fire but by the rich indemnity of expropriation" (quoted in Pinkney 1958, 178). By the mid-1860s more than a fifth of the working population of Paris was employed in construction. This extraordinary achievement was vulnerable on two counts. First, as Nassau Senior put it, "A week's interruption of the building trade would terrify the government." Second, the seemingly endless merry-go-round of "productive expenditures" put such a heavy burden of debt on future labor that it condemned much of the population to perpetual economic growth and "forced work in perpetuity" (cf. Harvey 1982, 266–70). When the public works lagged, as they did for both political and economic reasons after 1868, falling tax receipts and unemployment in the construction trades became a very serious issue. That this had a radicalizing effect on workers who, contrary to bourgeois opinion, were by no means as opposed to Haussman as was generally thought, is suggested by the disproportionate number of construction workers who participated in the Commune (Rougerie 1965, 129–34).

Not all labor power surpluses could be so absorbed. Furthermore, there proved to be vast labor power reserves throughout France that flooded into Paris, particularly in the 1850s, partly in response to the employment opportunities created by the public works. So although the indigency rate (an approximate indicator of the labor surplus) dropped from one in every 16.1 inhabitants to one in 18.4 between 1853 and 1862, the absolute number of indigents at no point declined, while the rate itself rose again to one in 16.9 in 1869 (Gaillard 1977, 224–30).

Haussman's policy toward this massive industrial reserve army underwent an interesting evolution. Eighteenth-century traditions of city charity as a right, of the city's duty to feed the poor (even from the provinces), were gradually abandoned. Haussman substituted a more modern neo-Malthusian policy. Indeed, given the pressures on the city budget, the size of the welfare problem, and the shifting forms of financing, he had no choice. He argued that the city best fulfilled its duty by providing jobs, not welfare, and that if it looked after job creation it might reasonably diminish its obligation to provide welfare. If the jobs were provided and poverty continued to exist it was, he hinted, the fault of the poor themselves, who consequently forfeited their right to state support. The state apparatus conceived of its responsibilities toward the poor, the sick, and the aged in a very different way in 1870 than in 1848. This change of administrative attitude toward welfare, medical care, schooling, and the like contributed, Gaillard (1977, 331–34) suggests, to that sense of loss of rights and of community that lay at the root of the social upheavals from 1868 to 1871. That such neo-Malthusian policies should have provoked such popular response is not surprising. Certainly, the

Commune sought to reestablish these rights, and even Haussman, seeking to shore up support for an ailing regime, found himself having to pay increasing attention to welfare questions as unemployment increased and the Empire struggled to live up to its own propaganda that it provided welfare from the cradle to the grave (Kulstein 1969, 100).

Haussman adopted similar principles with respect to the price of provisions. When prices rose unduly, social protest usually provoked a hurried state subsidy. But Haussman believed in a free market. If price fluctuations tied to variable harvests caused difficulty, then the answer lay in a revolving fund into which bakers or butchers paid when supply prices were low and from which they withdrew when supply prices were high. The burden on the city budget was negligible, and price stability was achieved. Haussman thus pioneered commodity price-stabilization schemes of the sort that became common in the 1930s. But he preferred to do without them and abandoned all such schemes as free-market liberalism came to the center of government policy after 1860. By that time the elimination of spatial barriers and better distribution within the city were, in any case, bringing greater security to the city's food supply.

While no simple guiding principles were established in the administration of the city's immensely complicated social welfare machinery, Haussman's instincts led him, as Gaillard's (1977, 269–331) detailed studies abundantly illustrate, in two quite modern directions at first sight somewhat inconsistent with the centralized authoritarianism of Empire. First, he sought to privatize welfare functions wherever he could (as in the case of education, where he conceived of the state's role as confined to the schooling of indigents only). Second, he sought a controlled decentralization in order to emphasize local responsibility and initiative. The dispersal of the social welfare burden from Paris to the provinces and the decentralization of responsibility for health care, education, and care of the poor into the arrondissements fitted into an administrative schema which, while in no way abandoning hierarchy, connected the expectation of service to local ability to pay.

Surveillance and Control

The Second Empire was an authoritarian police state, and its penchant for surveillance and control stretched far and wide. Apart from direct police action, informers, spies, and legal harassment, the imperial authorities sought to control the flow of information, mobilized extraordinary propaganda efforts (see Kulstein 1969), and used political power and favors to coopt and control friend and foe alike. "The supreme glory of Napoleon III," wrote Baudelaire (1983b, 73) "will have been to prove that anybody can govern a great nation as soon as they have got control of the telegraph and the national press."

The system worked well in rural France (Zeldin 1958) but was harder to impose on the cities. Paris posed severe problems, in part because of its revolutionary tradition and in part because of its sheer size and labyrinthine qualities. While Haussman and the prefect of police (often at loggerheads over jurisdictional questions) were the main pinions of surveillance and control, various governmental departments (Interior, Justice, etc.) were also involved. And laws were shaped with this end in mind. Censorship of the press had been reimposed under the Second Republic – "all republican journals were forbidden," St. John (1854, 25) noted ironically, "and those only allowed that represented the Orleanist, Legitimist, or Bonapartist factions." The Empire, in its press laws, simply tightened what the "party of order" had already imposed. Even the street singers and entertainers, viewed as peddlars of songs and scenes of socialism and subversion by the authorities, had to be licensed and their songs officially stamped and approved by the prefect under a law of 1853 (Clark 1973a, 121). The political content of popular culture was hounded off the streets, as were many of the street entertainers themselves (Rifkin 1979).

The police (who the workers always referred to as spies) were far more dedicated to collecting information and filing reports on the least hint of political opposition than they were to controlling criminal activity. While they managed to instill considerable fear, they do not appear to have been very effective at their work, in spite of a major administrative reorganization in 1854 (Payne 1966). The fear arose from the vast network of potential informers. "The police are organized in the workshops as they are in the cities," wrote Proudhon; "no more trust among workers, no more communication. The walls have ears" (quoted in Thomas n.d., 174). Lodging houses were kept under strict surveillance, their records of comings and goings regularly inspected, and the concierge often coopted into the police network of informers (St. John 1854, 34). And when the emperor struck down the workers' right to association, coalition, and assembly (together with the right to strike) in 1852, he replaced it with a system of *conseils de prud'hommes* (councils of workers and employers to resolve disputes within a trade) and mutual benefit associations for workers. To prevent both from becoming hotbeds of socialism, the emperor appointed the administrative officers (usually on the advice of the prefect of police), who furnished regular reports. A similar system of control was established when the right to hold public meetings was finally conceded in 1868 – "assessors" with power to monitor and close down unduly "political" meetings were appointed and obliged to file extensive reports (Dalotel, Faure, and Freirmuth 1980). The propaganda system, as Kulstein (1969) shows, was no less elaborate. Controlled flows of news and information through an official and semiofficial press, all manner of official pronouncements, and administrative actions (for many of which the prefect was responsible) sought to convince the popular classes of the merits of those at the top (of the emperor and empress in particular). It was rather as if charitable works and officially sponsored galas, expositions, and fêtes were expected to make up for loss of individual freedom.

Such a system had its limits. It is hard to maintain surveillance and control in an economy where the circulation of capital is given free rein, where competition and technical progress race along side by side, sparking all manner of cultural movements and adaptations. The dilemmas of press censorship illustrate the problem. The Parisian press grew from a circulation of one hundred fifty thousand in 1852 to more than a million in 1870 (Bellet 1967). Though dominated entirely by new money interests, these were diverse enough to create controversies that were bound to touch on government policies. When Say attacked Haussman's finances in the name of fiscal prudence, he was eroding the emperor's authority. Republican opponents like Ferry (1868) could opportunistically follow suit. And censorship could not easily be confined to politics; it dealt with public morality too. Most of the songs rejected by the authorities were bawdy rather than political (Rifkin 1979), and the government got into all kinds of tangles in its prosecutions of Baudelaire, Flaubert, and others for public indecency. The effect was to erode the class alliance that should have been the real foundation of the emperor's power. The political system was, in short, ill adapted to a burgeoning capitalism. Since the empire was founded on a capitalist path to social progress, the shift toward liberal Empire was, as Zeldin (1958, 1963) insists, present at its very foundation.

The same difficulties arose with attempts to control the popular classes. Propaganda as to the emperor's merits had to rest on something other than his charity. The formula of "fêtes and bread" did well enough on the fêtes, in which the working classes took genuine delight (Corbon 1863, 93; Duveau 1946), but did less well on the bread. Falling real wages in the 1860s made a mockery of claims to social progress and made the fêtes look like ghastly extravaganzas mounted at working-class expense. How, then, could the emperor live up to his own rhetoric that he was not a mere tool of the bourgeoisie? His tactic was to try to coopt Paris workers by conceding the right to strike (1864) and the rights of public assembly and association (1868). He even promoted collective forms of action. Thus did the French branch of the International issue from a government-sponsored visit of workers to the London Exposition of 1862 (provoking the natural suspicion that it was a mere tool of Empire). And though popular culture had been lulled by years of repression into a surface state of somnolence (Rifkin 1979), an underground current of political rhetoric quickly surfaced as soon as the opening came in 1868.

The urban transformation also had ambivalent effects on the power to watch and control. The dens and rookeries and narrow, easily barricaded streets were swept away and replaced by more easily controlled boulevards. But an uprooted population, dispersed from the center, augmented by a flood of immigrants, milled around in new areas like Belleville, which became their exclusive preserve. The workers became less of an organized threat, but they became harder to monitor. The tactics and geography of class struggle therefore underwent a radical change.

Shaping the Spaces of Social Reproduction

"In the space of power, power does not appear as such," writes Lefebvre (1974, 370); "it hides under the organization of space." Haussman clearly understood that his power to shape space was also a power to influence the processes of societal reproduction.

His evident desire to rid Paris of its industrial base and working class and so transform it, presumably, into a nonrevolutionary bastion of support for the bourgeois order was far too large a task to complete in a generation (indeed, it has finally been realized only in the last twenty years). Yet he harassed heavy industry, dirty industry, and even light industry to the point where the deindustrialization of the city center was an accomplished fact by 1870. And much of the working class was forced out with it though by no means as far as he wished (figs. 8 and 9). The city center was given over to monumental representations of imperial power and administration, finance and commerce, and the growing services that spring up around a burgeoning tourist trade. The new boulevards not only provided opportunities for military control, but they also permitted (when lit with gas lighting and properly patrolled) free circulation of the bourgeoisie within the commercial and entertainment quarters. The transition toward an "extroverted" form of urbanism, with all of its social and cultural effects (see Benjamin 1973), was assured (it was not so much that consumption increased, which it did, but that its conspicuous qualities became more apparent for all to see). And the growing residential segregation not only protected the bourgeoisie from the real or imagined dangers of those dangerous and criminal classes (Chevalier 1973) but also increasingly shaped the city into relatively secure spaces of reproduction of the different social classes. To these ends Haussman showed a remarkable ability to orchestrate diverse social processes, using regulatory and planning powers and mastering the geography of externality effects, to reshape the geography of the city.

The effects were not always those Haussman had in mind, in part because the collective processes he sought to orchestrate took matters in a quite different direction (this was true for industrial production, as we shall later see). But his project was also political from the very start (Gaillard 1977, 6) and automatically sparked political counterprojects, not simply within the

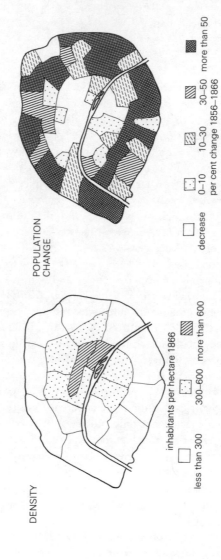

DENSITY

inhabitants per hectare 1866

less than 300   300–600   more than 600

POPULATION
CHANGE

decrease   0–10   10–30   30–50   more than 50

per cent change 1856–1866

Fig. 8.   Population density in 1866 and population change, 1856–1866. (After L. Girard, 1981, and E. Canfora-Argandoña and R.-H. Guerrand, 1976.)

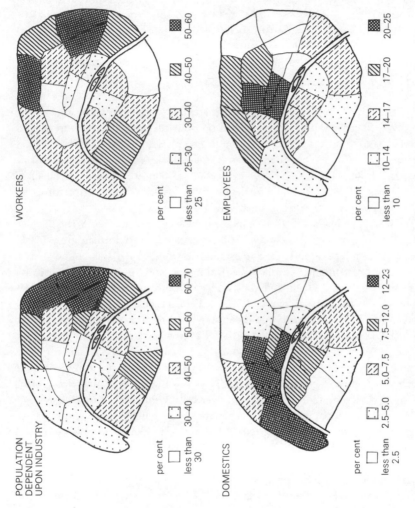

Fig. 9. *Distribution of industrially dependent population, workers, employees, and domestics in Paris by arrondissements in 1872. (After L. Chevalier, 1950.)*

WORKERS

per cent

less than 25 25–30 30–40 40–50 50–60

POPULATION
DEPENDENT
UPON INDUSTRY

per cent

less than 30 30–40 40–50 50–60 60–70

EMPLOYEES

per cent

less than 10 10–14 14–17 17–20 20–25

DOMESTICS

per cent

less than 2.5 2.5–5.0 5.0–7.5 7.5–12.0 12–23

working class, but among different factions of the bourgeoisie. Thus Chevalier (the emperor's favorite economist) argued against ridding the city of industry, since this would undermine stable employment and threaten social peace. Louis Lazare (1869) used the influential *Revue municipale* not only to execrate the speculations of the Pereires but also to castigate Haussman's works for the way they emphasized the social and geographical divisions between "the old Paris, the Paris of Luxury" and "the new Paris, that of Poverty" – a sure provocation to social revolt. Haussman (and the emperor) had to seek a coalition of interests in the midst of such warring voices.

The Search for a Class Alliance

It was the duty of any prefect to cultivate and consolidate political support for the government in power. Since he had no political party behind him and no natural class alliance to which he could appeal, Napoleon III had to find a deeper social basis for his power than a mere family name and support from the army (Marx 1963a). Haussman needed to conjure up some such class alliance out of a politically hostile city and so give better grounding to imperial power and, by extension, his own.

The drama of his fall tends to conceal how successful he was at this, under conditions of shifting class configurations (shaped by rapid urban growth and capital accumulation) and stressful modernization, which was bound to stir up "blind discontent, implacable jealousies and political animosities" (Haussman 1890, 2:viii). Nonetheless, as kingpin in an incredible "growth machine" (Molotch 1976), he had all kinds of largesse to distribute, around which all manner of interests could congregate. The trouble, of course, is that when the trough runs dry the interests feed elsewhere. Furthermore, as Marx (1963, 90) often noted, the bourgeois is "always inclined to sacrifice the general interest of his class for this or that private motive" – a judgment with which Haussman tacitly concurs by complaining in his *Memoires* (1890, 2:371) of the "prevalence of privatism over public interest." In the absence of a powerful political party or any other means for cultivating expressions of support from some dominant class alliance, Haussman always remained vulnerable to quick betrayal out of narrow material interests. His slippery financing, from this standpoint, has to be seen as a desperate move to keep the trough full in order to preserve his power.

Haussman's relation with the landlord class was always difficult, since he took a grander view of spatial structure than that defined by narrow property rights. And the landlord class was itself fragmented, as we saw in section 3, into feudal and modern, large and small, central and peripheral. But Gaillard (1977, 136) is probably right in sensing "the progressive tightening of the alliance between the Empire and the Parisian property owners." This, however, had as much to do with the transition in the meaning of property ownership as it did with any fundamental adaptation on the part of government. In any case, property owners of any sort are probably the most likely of all to betray class interests for narrow private gain. Haussman's alliance with the Pereires was, while it lasted, extremely powerful, but here, too, finance capital was in transition. The downfall of the Pereires and the growing ascendancy of fiscal conservatism in financial circles undermined in the late 1860s what had been a solid pillar of his support. It was, recall, a protégé of Rothschild's who first attacked Haussman's methods of financing. At the same time, Haussman's relations with the industrial interests went from bad to worse, so that by the end of Empire they were solidly against him. Here he definitely reaped what he himself had sown in his struggle to rid the city of industry. And commercial interests, though much favored by what Haussman did, were typically pragmatic, taking what they could but not being enthusiastically supportive in return. Most interesting of all is Haussman's relation to the workers. These forever earned his wrath and denigration (see his *Memoires*, 2:200) by voting solidly republican as early as 1857. And he rarely made attempts to cultivate any populist base. Yet surprisingly little worker agitation was directed at him in the troubled years of 1868–70, and his dismissal was greeted with dismay and demonstrations in the construction trades. As the grand provider of jobs, he had evidently earned the loyalty of at least part of the working class. And if there were problems with high rents, workers well understood that it was landlords and not Haussman who pocketed the money.

There were deeper sources of discontent that made it peculiarly hard to maintain a stable class alliance within the city. The transformation itself sparked widespread nostalgia and regret (common to aristocrat and worker alike) at the passing of "old Paris" and contributed to that widespread sense of loss of community which Gaillard (1977, 331–32) makes so much of. Old ways and structures were upset, but nothing clearly emerged to replace them. And here the failure to establish an elected form of municipal government for the city surely hurt. For Haussman (1890, 2:197–202) steadfastly refused to see Paris as a community in the ordinary sense but treated it as a capital city within which all manner of diverse, shifting, and "nomadic" interests and individuals came and went so as to preclude the formation of any solid or permanent sense of community. It was therefore vital that Paris be administered for and by the nation, and to this end he promoted and defended the organic law of 1855, which put all real powers of administration into the hands of an appointed prefect rather than elected officials. Haussman may have been right about the transitoriness of the Parisian community. But the denial of popular sovereignty in the capital was a burning issue that pulled many workers and bourgeois into support of the Commune (Greenberg

1971). From this standpoint, Haussman's failure to sustain a permanent class alliance had less to do with what he did than with how he did it. But then the authoritarian style of his administration had everything to do with the circumstances that gave rise to the coup d'état in the first place. So it stood to reason that he could not long survive the transition to liberal Empire.

The towering figure of Haussman dominates the state apparatus of Paris throughout the Second Empire. To say that he merely rode out the storm of social forces unleashed through the rapid accumulation of capital is by no means to diminish his stature, because he rode out the storm with consummate artistry and orchestrated its turbulent power with remarkable skill and vision for some sixteen years. It was, however, a storm he neither created nor tamed, but a deep turbulence in the evolution of French economy, politics, and culture, that in the end threw him as mercilessly to the dogs as he threw medieval Paris to the *démolisseurs*. In the process the city achieved a visage of capitalist modernity which has lasted to this day.

V. ABSTRACT AND CONCRETE LABOR

Abstract wealth, value, money, hence *abstract labor* develop in the measure that concrete labor becomes a totality of different modes of labor embracing the world market.

– *Marx*

The question of work lay at the heart of the Parisian workers' movement of 1848. Though they did not make the revolution on their own, their force and power was indispensable to the overthrow of the July Monarchy. Led by skilled workers from the craft tradition – a superior class, which Corbon (1863) put at 40 percent of the work force – these workers, confident in their skills, possessed of an unshakeable faith in the nobility of work, and believing that labor was the source of all wealth, sought a new kind of industrial order which would temper the insecurity of work, alleviate their relative penury, and stave off growing trends toward de-skilling and increasing exploitation (Sewell 1980, 158–61). They sought a *social* republic that would support their efforts to reorganize work and the social relations of production so as to set the stage for social progress for decades to come.

In uneasy alliance with bourgeois republicans who put the political ahead of the social revolution, the workers pushed their ideas on the right to work (at their own trade and not just any makeshift job), the creation of new employment opportunities (the National Workshops), and the right to association into the forefront of the provisional government's program. They obtained an informal "workers' parliament" (the Luxembourg Commission),

Table 4. *Employment Structure of Paris: Chamber of Commerce Surveys, 1847 and 1860*

	1847 (Old City)			1860 (New City)		
Occupation	Firms	Workers	Workers per Firm	Firms	Workers	Workers per Firm
Textile & clothing	38,305	162,710	4.2	49,875	145,260	2.9
Furniture	7,499	42,843	5.7	10,638	46,375	4.4
Metals & engineering	7,459	55,543	7.4	9,742	68,629	7.0
Graphic arts	2,691	19,132	7.1	3,018	21,600	7.2
Food	2,551	7,551	3.0	2,255	12,767	5.7
Construction	2,012	25,898	12.9	2,676	50,079	18.7
Precision inst.	1,569	5,509	3.5	2,120	7,808	3.7
Chemicals	1,534	9,988	6.5	2,712	14,335	5.3
Transport equipment	530	6,456	12.2	638	7,642	12.0

Source: Daumas and Payen (1976).

which, though thrown to them as a sop set about not only discussing but also resolving various practical aspects of the organization of labor. These were the first steps toward "a state-aided system of producers' associations" with a workers' parliament as the central organizing force (Gossez 1967; Sewell 1980). If the workers were "savages," a "vile multitude," mere criminal and "dangerous classes," as the bourgeoisie was wont to depict them, then 1848 showed all too clearly the kind of danger they posed and the kind of savagery they had in mind (Chevalier 1973). The workers were, Victor Hugo proudly proclaimed, "the savages of civilization."

This setting is important because it has much to say about the subsequent development of the labor process and industrial organization in Paris. The crushing of the workers' movement in the June Days, the dispersal of the National Workshops, and the disbanding of the Luxembourg Commission in no way ended matters. They still possessed political means of expression and were free to build their own organizations. By October 1851 "there were no fewer than 190 socialist-inspired workers' associations in Paris" (Agulhon 1983, 115). It was, most historians agree, fear of this "red" revival that led the bourgeoisie to rally behind a coup d'état that immediately set about to suppress all independent forms of worker organization and expression. This opened the way to new paths of industrial development in which the association of capitals was to prevail over the association of laborers. But the manufacturers still had to deal with the power of craft labor in labor markets and in the workshop. The evolution of Parisian industry during the Second Empire therefore took a very special path.

Table 5. Economically Dependent Population in Paris: Census of 1866

Occupation	Owners	Employees + Workers	Families	Total	%
Textile and clothing	26,633	182,466	103,964	313,063	25.3
Building	5,673	79,827	71,747	157,247	12.7
Arts and graphics[a]	11,897	73,519	60,449	145,865	11.8
Metals	4,994	42,659	50,053	98,906	8.0
Wood and furniture	5,282	27,882	33,093	66,257	5.3
Transport	9,728	35,022	48,938	93,688	7.6
Commerce	51,017	78,009	101,818	230,840	18.6
Diverse[b]	10,794	50,789	58,435	120,018	9.7
Unclassified	2,073	4,608	5,417	12,098	1.0
Total	128,091	575,981	533,914	1,237,987	(100.0)

Source: Rougerie (1971), 10. (N.B. The total population of Paris in 1866 stood at 1,825,274 – see table 1.)
[a] Includes printing, *articles de Paris*, precision instruments, and work with precious metals.
[b] Includes leather, ceramics, chemicals.

Paris at mid-century was by far the most important and diversified manufacturing center in the nation. And in spite of its image as a grand center of conspicuous consumption, it in fact remained a working-class city, heavily dependent upon the growth of production. In 1866, for example, 58 percent of its 1.8 million people depended upon industry, whereas only 13 percent depended upon commerce (Chevalier 1950, 75). But there were some very special features of its industrial structure and organization (tables 4, 5, and 6). In 1847, more than half the manufacturing firms had fewer than 2 employees, only 11 percent employed more than 10, and no more than 425 qualified for the title of "*grands enterprises*" (more than 500 workers). It was difficult in many cases to distinguish between owners and workers; and since the craft workers had in any case evolved hierarchical forms of command, there was little basis within the small enterprises for strong class antagonisms (a condition that prevailed throughout the Second Empire and led a whole wing of the workers' movement, particularly that influenced by Proudhon, to disapprove of strikes, push for association, and confine their opposition to financiers, monopolists, landlords, and the authoritarian state). It was also very difficult to distinguish commerce from manufacturing, since the atelier in the back was often united with the boutique on the street front.

These conditions varied somewhat from industry to industry, as well as with location. Apart from food and provisions (in which the distinction between industry and commerce was particularly hard to define), the textile

Table 6. *Business Volume of Parisian Industry, 1847–1848*
(Old Paris) and 1860 (New Paris) (billions of francs)

Business	1847–48	1860
Food and beverages	226.9	1,087.9
Clothing	241.0	454.5
Articles de Paris	128.7	334.7
Building	145.4	315.3
Furniture	137.1	200.0
Chemical and ceramic	74.6	193.6
Precious metals	134.8	183.4
Heavy metals	103.6	163.9
Fabrics and thread	105.8	120.0
Leather and skins	41.8	100.9
Printing	51.2	94.2
Coach building	52.4	93.9

Source: Gaillard (1977), 376.

and clothing trades, together with furniture and metal working, dominated, cut across by all manner of *"articles de Paris"* for which the city had become and would remain justly famous. Most of the classic sectors for capitalist industrial development were, therefore, absent from the capital; and even textiles, which had been important, were by 1847 mostly dispersed to the provinces, leaving the clothing industry behind in Paris. Plainly, most of Parisian industry was oriented to serving its own market. Only in the metal working and engineering sectors could any semblance of a "modern" form of capitalistic industrial structure be discerned.

This vast economic enterprise could not easily be transformed. Yet it underwent significant evolution in terms of industrial mix, technology, organization, and location. It surged out of the depression of 1848–50 with a surprising élan that first infected light industry and then, after 1853, spread to the building trades and heavy engineering and metal working. During the 1860s the pace of growth slowed, particularly in the large-scale industries, and became more selective as to sector and location.

The *Enquêtes* of 1847–48, 1860, and 1872 (well worked over by historians such as Daumas and Payen 1976; Chevalier 1950; Gaillard 1977; and Retel 1977) allow a reconstruction of the general path of industrial evolution. The *Enquête* of 1860 lists 101,000 firms employing 416,000 workers – an increase of 11 percent over 1847, with most of the net gain due to annexation of the suburbs, since comparable data for old Paris indicate a loss of 19,000 workers. But the number of firms increased by 30 percent, indicating a surprising expansion of small firms. By 1860 the number of firms employing fewer than 2 workers had risen to 62 percent (from 50 percent in 1847–48), and the number employing more than 10 workers had fallen from 11 to 7 percent. This increasing fragmentation was observable in many sectors and was particularly marked in old Paris. In the clothing trades, for example, the number of enterprises increased by 10 percent, while workers employed declined by 20 percent. The figures for the chemical industry were even more startling – 45 percent more firms and 5 percent fewer workers. Machine building, the largest-scale industry in 1847–48, with an average of 63 employees per firm, had fragmented to an average of 24 workers by 1860. Everything points, then, to the vigorous growth of many very small firms and an increasing fragmentation of industrial structure, a process that continued until the end of the Empire and beyond (Gaillard 1977; Daumas and Payen 1976). Furthermore, this growth and fragmentation of small firms could be seen both close to the center and in peripheral locations.

The strong absolute growth of large firms between 1847–48 and 1860 (the number remained virtually unchanged from 1860 to 1872) was accompanied by a strong peripheral movement toward suburban locations (fig. 10). But even here the movement was not uniform. Large-scale printing retained its central location as the major industry on the Left Bank, while metal working moved only as far as the inner northern and eastern peripheries. Large-scale chemical operations, however, tended to move much farther out (fig. 11).

The case of the chemical industry is interesting to the degree that it captures much of the complex movement at work in Parisian industry during this period. On the one hand, large-scale and often dirty enterprises were either forced out or else voluntarily sought out peripheral locations at favored points within the transport network where land was relatively cheap. On the other hand, product innovation meant the proliferation of small firms making specialized products like porcelain, pharmaceuticals, and artificial jewelry, while other industries mainly in the *articles de Paris* category generated specialized demands for small quantities of paints, dyes, and the like, which could best be met by small-scale production. Within many industries there was a similar dual movement that saw a growth of some large firms in suburban locations and an increasing fragmentation and specialization of economic activity particularly close to the center. "The advance of the factory system," notes Girard (1981, 215), "coincided with the fragmentation of production, an increasing role of outwork at home paid by the piece."

That this form of highly specialized development had much to do with the superior skills of those "superior" workers was fairly evident. That the small scale and the turn to outwork, paid by the piece, were concessions to the strong predilection of craft workers to conserve their own autonomy,

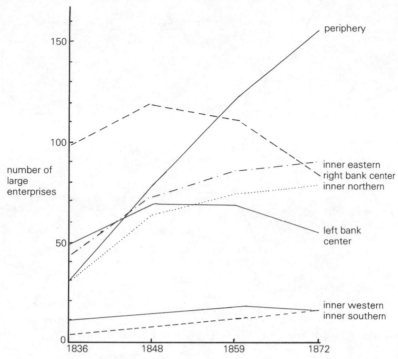

Fig. 10.   Number of large enterprises in different sectors of Paris according to the surveys of 1836, 1848, 1859, and 1872. (After M. Daumas and J. Payen, 1976.)

independence, and control over the labor process also cannot be doubted. Yet there was a major transformation of social relations which the raw statistics tend to hide. For what in effect happened, Gaillard (1977) convincingly argues, is that there was an increasingly sophisticated detail division of specialized labor in which the products of individuals, small firms, and outworkers and piece-workers were integrated into a highly efficient production system. Individual laborers and small firms were increasingly locked into a network of commercial and production relations which weighed heavily upon them (Gaillard 1977, 390) and within which a much-hated and oppressive system of foremen, overseers, subcontractors (outlawed under the social legislation of 1848), and other go-betweens could become all too firmly implanted (Duveau 1946, 252–69). So though the craft workers continued to be important, their position underwent a notable degradation. The extreme division of labor helped achieve an unparalleled quality and technical perfection, but it yielded neither higher wages nor increasing liberty to the

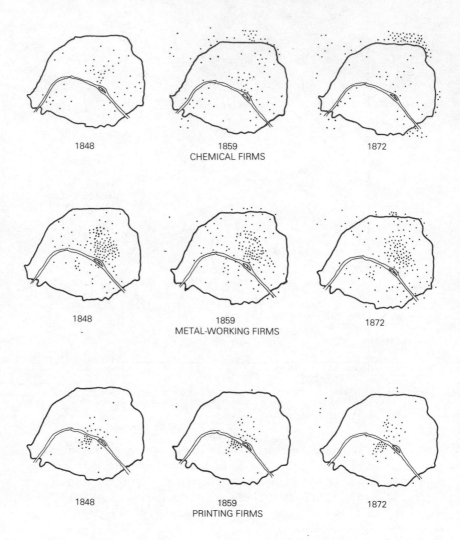

Fig. 11. The location of large-scale chemical, metal working, and printing firms in Paris according to the enquiries of 1848, 1859, and 1872. (After J. Retel, 1977.)

worker (Girard 1981, 216). It meant, rather, the gradual subsumption of formerly independent craft workers and owners under the formal domination of a tightly controlled commercial and industrial organization. Behind this general evolution, however, lay a variety of forces that deserve deeper scrutiny.

Changing Space Relations, External Competition, and Export Markets

The reduction of spatial barriers opened up the extensive and valuable Parisian market to provincial and foreign competition (a process further encouraged after the move toward free trade in 1860). But it also meant that Parisian industry had access to geographically more dispersed raw materials and food supplies to feed its laborers and meet its demand for intermediate products at lower cost. Given industry's powerful base in the Parisian market, this meant that Paris could just as easily compete in the provinces and abroad as it could be competed with.

Paris in fact expanded its share of a growing French export trade from around 11 percent in 1848 to 16 percent by the early 1960s (Gaillard 1977, 380). As might be expected, the luxury consumer goods in which Paris specialized were well represented in this vast export surge. But more than half the locomotives and railway equipment and a fifth of the steam engines produced in Paris followed French capital abroad, while even some of the food industry (such as sugar refining) could find a place in provincial markets. The Parisian industrial interest, unlike some of its provincial counterparts, was by no means opposed to free trade, since Parisian manufacturing was evidently capable of dominating provincial and international markets in certain lines of production.

But its advantageous position in relation to this new international division of labor carried some penalties. Parisian industry was more and more exposed to the vagaries of foreign markets. The general expansion of world trade in the period was an enormous boon, of course, but industrialists had to be able to adapt quickly to whims of foreign taste, the sudden imposition of tariff barriers, the rise of foreign manufacturing (that had the ugly habit of copying French designs and producing them more cheaply though with inferior quality), and the interruptions of war (of which the American Civil War had particularly dire effects, since America was a major export market). Parisian industry also had to adapt to the peculiar flow requirements of foreign trade. Gaillard (1977, 391) thus notes how the growth of the American trade increased problems of seasonal unemployment. The arrival of raw cotton from America in autumn put money into the hands of American buyers, who spent it as fast as they could in order to get their products back to the United States by spring. Three months of intense activity could be followed by nine months of "dead season." The *Enquête* of 1860 showed that more than one-third of Parisian firms had a dead season, with more than two-thirds of those producing *articles de Paris* and more than half in the furniture, clothing, and jewelry trades experiencing a dead season of between four and six months (Chevalier 1950, 96). I shall take up the problems this posed for the organization of production and labor markets shortly.

Foreign and provincial competition not only challenged Parisian industry in international and provincial markets, but it also looked with a hungry eye at the enormous and expanding consumer and intermediate goods market that Paris offered. External competition became increasingly fierce in the 1860s (Gaillard 1977, 443). At first, the challenge came from mass-produced goods, where, with cheaper labor and easier access to raw materials, provincial and foreign producers had a distinct cost advantage, which falling freight rates made ever more evident. Shoe production thus dispersed into the provinces, to Pas-de-Calais, l'Oise, and similar places. But where mass production went, luxury goods could all too easily follow. The exact process whereby this occurred can best be illustrated by examining the new relations emerging in Paris between industry and commerce.

Industry in Relation to Finance and Commerce

The relative power of industrial, financial, and commercial interests shifted markedly during the Second Empire in Paris. While certain large enterprises remained immune, the mass of small-scale industry was increasingly subjected to the external discipline imposed by financiers and merchants. The latter became, in effect, the agents that ensured the transformation of concrete labor to abstract requirements.

The rise of a new credit system favored the creation of large-scale production and service enterprises in several different ways. Direct financing of factory production using modern forms of technology and industrial organization became feasible. In this, the Pereires pioneered the way but were quickly followed by a whole gamut of financial institutions. But the indirect effects were just as profound. The changing scale of public works and construction (at home and abroad) and the formation of a mass market for many products (signaled by the rise of the department store, itself a child of the credit system) favored large-scale industry. The absorption of small savings within the new credit structures tended also to dry up small, local, and familiar sources of credit to small businesses without putting anything in their place. The net effect was to redistribute credit availability and put it more and more out of direct reach of small producers and artisans.

The new credit system was not, therefore, welcomed by most industrialists, who saw the financiers, all too correctly in the case of the Pereires, as instruments of control and merger (Gaillard 1977, 387). The class relation between producers and money capitalists was typically one of distrust. Indeed, the downfall of the Pereires probably had as much to do with the power of commercial and industrial interests within the Bank of France as it did with the much-vaunted personal antagonism of Rothschild. The lengthy polemics waged against the excessive monopoly power of the financiers toward the end of the Second Empire (see Duchêne 1869) earned the plaudits of artisans and small businesses and partly explains the growing bourgeois opposition to the economic policies of the Empire.

Yet the small-scale producers and artisans, faced as they often were with lengthy dead seasons and all manner of settlement dates, had a desperate need for short-term credit. The Bank of France provided discount facilities on commercial paper but served only a very few customers (Plessis 1982). Only toward the end of the period did other financial institutions arise to begin to fill this gap. What existed in their stead was an informal and parallel financing system based either on kinship ties or on small-scale credits offered between different buyers and sellers – a system that spread down even into the lower levels of the working class, who simply could not have survived if they had not been able to buy "on time." And it was out of such a system that a newly consolidating merchant class came to exercise an increasing degree of control over the organization and growth of Parisian industry.

Commerce had always had a special place in the Parisian economy, of course. But at mid-century the distinctions between manufacturing and merchanting were so confused that the expression of a distinctive merchant interest lay with various kinds of specialized traders (in wine, for example). Commerce was, for the most part, very definitely the servant of industry. The Second Empire, Gaillard (1977) shows us, was marked by a growing separation of production from merchanting and a gradual reversal of power relations to the point where much of Parisian industry was increasingly forced to dance to the tune that commerce dictated. The transformation was gradual rather than traumatic, for the most part. Owners simply preferred to keep the boutique and give up the atelier. But they did not give up a direct relation to the producers. They typically became the hub of a network of subcontracting, production on command or by the piece, and of outwork. In this way an increasingly autonomous merchant class became the agent for the formal subsumption of artisan and craft labor under the rule of merchants' capital (cf. Marx 1976). although Parisian industry retained a kind of artisanal structure, the social position of the artisan underwent a substantial and in some cases quite traumatic transformation from relative independence to relative subservience within an increasingly sophisticated, well-organized, and externally controlled detail and social division of labor (cf. Marx 1967, 1:342).

The remarkable degree of fragmentation of tasks and specialization in Parisian industry gave it much of its competitive power and reputation for quality in both local and international markets. And the Second Empire saw increasing refinements in this form of organization. Artificial flower making, which already tended to be specialized as to type of flower in different workshops in 1848, was by the end of the Empire organized into a whole system of workshops producing parts of particular flowers. Maxime du Camp

(1875, 6:235) complained of the "infinite division of labor" that called for the coordination of nine different skills to produce a simple knife. That such a system could work at all was entirely due to the efficient organizing skills of the merchant entrepreneurs who supplied the raw materials, organized the detail division of labor among numerous scattered workshops or through piecework at home, supervised quality of product and timing of flows, and absorbed the finally assembled product into well-defined markets.

Yet these very same agents who reorganized Parisian industry to ward off foreign competition also brought foreign and provincial competition right into the heart of the Parisian market. Under competitive pressure to maximize profits, the Parisian merchants were by no means loath to search out all manner of different supply sources from the provinces and even from abroad, extending their network of commands and outwork well outside of Paris wherever they found costs (particularly that of labor) cheaper. They thus stimulated external competition as much as they organized to repel it and in some cases actively organized the geographical dispersal of some phases of production to the provinces. Foreign and provincial merchants, for their part, once an itinerant or seassonal presence in the city, tended to settle permanently and, making use of international and provincial contacts, organized an increasingly competitive flow of goods into the Parisian market (Gaillard 1977, 378). Examples even exist, as in the hat and glove trade, of the separation of production (which went to the provinces) from design and marketing, which remained in the capital (Gaillard 1977, 446).

There were other developments in merchanting that had a strong impact upon various aspects of Parisian industry. The rise of the large department stores meant the formation of ready-to-wear or -use mass markets. Demand shifted to whatever could be mass produced profitably, irrespective of its use value or qualities. Mass marketing did not necessarily mean mass factory production, but it did imply the organization of small workshop production along different lines. Worker complaints as to the declining concern for quality of product and the de-skilling of work in the craft tradition had much to do with the spectacular growth of this kind of trade as large department stores like the Bon Marché (founded in 1852 and with a turnover of seven million francs by 1869), the Louvre (1855), and Printemps (1865) (Duveau 1946, 215; Gaillard 1977) became centerpieces of Parisian commerce.

By the 1860s, a hierarchically structured credit system was increasingly becoming the powerful nerve center for industrial development, but it had not yet extended down to the small enterprise. The merchants, well served when need be by both new and old credit structures, stepped in to become the organizing force for much small industry. The increasing autonomy of this merchant class during the Second Empire was signaled by the formation of distinctive merchant quarters, around the Chaussée d'Antin in the northwest center and to a lesser degree around Mail et Sentier and in the northeast center (rue Paradis, then as now, was the thriving center for glass and porcelain ware). It was from here that local, provincial, and international production for the Parisian market and for export was increasingly organized. These quarters also offered special kinds of white-collar employment opportunities, which left an imprint on the division of social space in the city (see fig. 9). And, Gaillard (1977) notes, there arose in these quarters special traditions in relation to politics, education, religion, and the like that led merchants to participate very little in either the formation or the repression of the Commune. Nevertheless, the increasing autonomy of the merchant class and the rise of new financial power spun a complex web of control around much of Parisian industry, while the merchants' concern for profit and their geographical range of operation led them toward a restructuring of Parisian industry to meet the conditions of a new international division of labor. The small-scale producers, once proud and independent craft workers and artisans, were increasingly imprisoned within a network of debts and obligations, of specific commands and controlled supplies; were forced into the position of detail laborers within an overall system of production whose evolution appeared to escape their control. It was within such a system that the processes of de-skilling and domination, which had been evident before 1848, could continue to work their way through the system of production. That the workers recognized the nature of the problem is all too clear. The Workers' Commission of 1867 debated the problems at length and put the question of social credit and the liberty of work in the forefront of its social agenda. But by then there had been nearly twenty years in which the association of capital had dominated the noble vision of the association of labor.

Industry, the State, and Private Property

Haussman, as we have seen, had no compunction about expelling noxious or unwanted industry (like tanning and some chemicals) from the city center by direct clearance or use of the laws on insalubrity (Daumas and Payen 1976, 147). He also sought by all manner of indirect means (taxation, annexation of the suburbs, orientation of city services) to push most industry, save that of luxury goods and *articles de Paris,* out of the city center. His anti-industry policies derived in part from the desire to create an "imperial capital" fit for the whole of Western civilization, but just as important was his concern to rid Paris of the political power of the working class by getting rid of its opportunities for employment (Zeldin 1958, 76). In this he was only partially successful. Though the deindustrialization of the very center was an accomplished fact by 1870 (Daumas and Payen 1976, 135), the improvements in communications and in urban infrastructures (gas, water, sewage, etc.) made Paris a very attractive location. Haussman to some degree counteracted with the one hand what he sought to do with the other. But his failure to attend to the needs of industry and his patent favoring of residential development (as, for example, in the design of the third network of roads) earned him increasing opposition from industrial interests, which had, in any case, been powerful enough to thwart some of the emperor's plans for relocation. And to the degree that provincial and international competition picked up in the 1860s at the same time that Haussman's campaign against industry intensified, so the difficulties of Parisian industry were more and more laid at his door, and a lively opposition to Empire provoked.

Rent, however, was an important cost that Parisian industry had to bear. The shifts in the rent surface associated with Haussman's works had a strong effect upon industrial organization and location. The rapidly rising rents in the new financial and commercial quarters (Bourse, Chaussée d'Antin) and in the high-quality residential quarters toward the west and northwest either forced existing industry out or else acted (on the western periphery, for example) as a barrier to the implantation of new industry. Rising rents in the center either pushed industry out toward the suburbs or forced it to cluster or intensify its use of space in locations of particular advantage. Metal working, for example, dispersed a relatively short distance toward the northeast, where it found good communications and access to superior quality labor supply (see fig. 11).

The higher slopes of the rent surface, however, proved very fertile locations (Haussman compared them to the vineyards on Mount Vesuvius that improve in fertility with closeness to the top). This was particularly true for those industries for which immediate access to the luxury consumer goods market (or to industries that supplies such markets) was of vital importance. The attractions of a central location were enhanced by the centralization of commerce in the large department stores, the central hotels that served a growing tourist trade, and the central provisions market of Les Halles, which drew all manner of people to it. The public works and urban investments created an additional market of seemingly endless demand (including that for lavish furniture and decoration), much of it concentrated close to the city center. Many industries had a strong incentive to cling to central locations – pharmaceuticals, toiletries, paints, metal working (particularly of the ornamental sort), carpentry, and woodworking, as well as the manufacturers of modish clothing and *articles de Paris*. But the high rents had to be paid. And here the adaptation that saw the growth of outwork paid by the piece made a great deal of sense, because the workers then bore either the high cost of rent themselves (working at home in overcrowded quarters) or the cost of inaccessibility to the center. The merchants, for their part, could save on rental costs while making sure production was organized into a configuration that flowed neatly into the high points of demand. The independent ateliers that did remain were caught in a cost squeeze that either forced them into the arms of the merchants or pushed them to a fierce reorganization of their own detail division of labor and a reduction of labor costs. Rising rents in the city center exacted a serious toll on industry and the laborers and in so doing played a key role in the industrial restructuring of Paris under the Second Empire.

Productivity, Efficiency, and Technology

There is a general myth, of which historians are only now beginning to disabuse us (e.g. Hershberg 1981), that large-scale industry drives out small because of the superior efficiency achieved through economies of scale. The persistence of small-scale industry in Paris during the Second Empire appears to refute the myth, for there is no doubt that the small workshops survived precisely because of their superior productivity and efficiency. Yet it is dangerous to push the refutation too far. The industries in which economies of scale could easily be realized (such as textiles and, later on, some aspects of clothing) dispersed to the provinces, and large-scale engineering either suburbanized or went elsewhere. And the small-scale industry that was left behind and that exhibited such vigorous growth achieved economies of scale not through fusion of enterprises but by the organization of interindustrial linkages and the agglomeration of innumerable specialized tasks. It was not size of firm that mattered but geographical concentration of innumerable producers under the organizing power of merchants and other entrepreneurs. And it was, in effect, the total economies of scale achieved by this kind of industry within the Paris region that formed the basis for its competitive advantage in the new international division of labor.

There is another myth, harder to dispel, that small industry and production by artisans is less innovative when it comes to new products or new labor processes. Corbon (1863) strongly denied that idea, detecting a very lively interest in new product lines, new techniques, and the applications of science among the "superior" workers and artisans, though he did go on to remark that they tended to admire the application of everything new anywhere but in their own trade. But too much success was to be had from product innovation (particularly in the luxury goods sector) for small owners to let the opportunities pass them by. And new technologies rapidly proliferated. Even steam engines, of feeble horsepower to be sure, were organized into patterns of collective use among the ateliers (Gaillard 1977, 438). And the clothing industry adopted the sewing machine, leather working used power cutting knives, cabinet makers used mechanical cutters, and manufacturers of *articles de Paris* were fairly possessed of a rush to innovate when it came to dyeing, coloring, special preparations, artificial jewelry, and the like. Building and construction also saw major innovations (such as the use of mechanical elevators). The picture that emerges is one of lively innovation and rapid adoption of new labor processes. The objections of the craft workers were not to the new techniques but, to judge from the Workers' Commission of 1867 and the writings of workers like Varlin (Foulon 1934; Lejeune 1977), to the manner in which these techniques were forced on them as part of a process of standardization of product, de-skilling, and wage reduction. Here, too, the increasing integration of specialized detail division of labor under the command of merchants and entrepreneurs lent special qualities to the transformation of the labor process. The evident technological vigor of small industry in paris was not necessarily the kind of vigor the workers appreciated.

The Experience of Laboring

So what was it like, working in Parisian industry during the Second Empire? It is hard to construct any composite picture from such a diversity of laboring experience. Anecdotes abound, and some bear repeating because they probably capture the flavor of the work experience for many.

A recent immigrant from Lorraine in 1865 rents, with his wife and two children, two minuscule rooms in Belleville toward the periphery of Paris. He leaves every morning at five o'clock armed with a crust of bread and walks four miles to the center, where he works fourteen hours a day in a button factory. After the rent is paid, his regular wage leaves him Fr 1 a day (bread costs Fr 0.37 a kilo), so he brings home piecework for his wife, who works long hours at home for almost nothing. "To live, for a laborer, is not to die," was the saying of the time (Lepidis and Jacomin 1975, 230).

It was descriptions of this sort that Zola used to such dramatic effect in *L'assommoir*. Coupeau and Gervaise visit Lorilleux and his wife in the tiny, messy, stiflingly hot workroom that attaches to their living quarters. The couple are working together drawing gold wire, making column chain. "There is small link, heavy chain, watch chain and twisted rope chain," explains Coupeau, but Lorilleux (who calculates he has spun eight thousand meters since he was twelve and hopes someday "to get from Paris to Versailles") only makes column chain. "The employers supplied the gold in wire form and already in the right alloy, and the workers began by drawing it through the draw plate to get it to the right gauge, taking care to reheat it five or six times during the operation to prevent it from breaking." This work, though it needs great strength, is done by the wife, since it also requires a steady hand and Lorilleux has terrible spasms of coughing. Lorilleux demonstrates how the wire is twisted, cut, and soldered into tiny links, an operation "performed with unbroken regularity, link succeeding link so rapidly that the chain gradually lengthened before Gervaise's eyes without her quite seeing how it was done" (70–71). The irony of the production of such specialized components of luxury goods in such dismal and impoverished circumstances was not lost on Zola. And it was only through the tight supervision of the organizers of production that such a system could prevail. But Gervaise later encounters a very different kind of production process when she visits Goujet, the metal worker, after a frightening journey through the industrial segment of northeast Paris. Goujet shows her how he makes hexagonal rivets out of white-hot metal, gently tapping out three hundred twenty-millimeter rivets a day, using a five-pound hammer. But that craft is under challenge, for the boss is installing a new plant:

The steam engine was in one corner, concealed behind a low brick wall. . . . He raised his voice to shout explanations, then went on to the machines; mechanical shears which devoured bars of iron, taking off a length with each bite and passing them out behind one by one; bolt and rivet machines, lofty and complicated, making a bolt-head in one turn of their powerful screws; trimming machines with cast-iron flywheels and an iron ball that struck the air furiously with each piece the machine trimmed; the thread-cutters worked by women, threading the bolts and nuts, their wheels going clickety-click and shining with oil. . . . The machine was turning out forty-four-millimetre rivets with the ease of an unruffled giant. . . . In twelve hours this blasted plant could turn out hundreds of kilogrammes of them. Goujet was not a vindictive man, but at certain moments he would gladly . . . smash up all this iron work in his resentment because its arms were stronger than his. It upset him, even though he appreciated that flesh could not fight against iron. The day would come, of course, when the machines would kill the manual worker; already their day's earnings had dropped from twelve francs to nine, and there was talk of still more cuts to come. There was nothing funny about these great plants that turned out rivets and bolts just like sausages. . . . He turned to Gervaise, who was keeping very close to him, and said with a sad smile, . . . "maybe sometime it will work for universal happiness." (176–77)

Thus were the abstract forces of capitalism brought to bear on the concrete experience of laboring under the Second Empire.

VI. THE BUYING AND SELLING OF LABOR POWER

[Capital] can spring into life, only when the owner of the means of production and subsistence meets in the market with a free laborer selling his labor-power. And this one historical condition comprises a world's history.

– Marx

The growth of industry and commerce coupled with the expansion of construction in Paris put strong pressure on labor markets during the Second

Empire. Where was the supply to come from? How and under what conditions were workers prepared to surrender rights over their labor power to others? And how did the quantities and qualities of labor power offered in Paris affect the form and geographical distribution of economic activity?

In 1848 Paris had an enormous surplus of labor power. To those thrown out of employment by the collapse of Parisian industry and trade were added a flood of provincial workers seeking the traditional protections of Paris in times of trouble. The numbers enrolled in the National Workshops rose from 14,000 to over 117,000 between March and June 1848 (McKay 1933, 159). The repression of the June Days led many to flee the city, but unemployment remained a key problem in both the city and the nation. The labor surpluses in Paris were partially absorbed during the recovery of 1849–50, but it took the dramatic upsurge of economic activity after 1852 to turn a labor surplus with falling wages into labor scarcity and rising nominal wage rates – though the increases were largely offset by inflation (Rougerie 1968a) – until the 1860s. The response to this scarcity was a massive immigration wave into the city during the 1850s, followed by increasing absorption of that other segment of the industrial reserve army – women – when nominal wage rates stagnated and real wage rates fell during the 1860s. Thus were the quantitative needs of Parisian industry and commerce broadly satisfied.

The qualities of the labor supply are harder to dissect (cf. Hanagan 1982). Paris had already lost most of its real artisans – workers in control of their own labor process and working independently for market exchange. Cottereau (1980, 70) puts them at no more than 5 percent of the economically active population in 1847. But there were few machine operators either. The mass of the work force was divided between craft workers, who were fully initiated (usually by apprenticeship) into all aspects of a trade, skilled workers, whose skills were confined to specialized tasks within the detail division of labor; and unskilled workers, often itinerant day laborers, grading into the indigent and criminal classes variously referred to as "dangerous classes" or "lumpen-proletariat." Literate and numerate workers could also find employment in the burgeoning white collar occupations spawned by the revolutions in banking, and commerce and by the rise of tourism.

The craft workers, as Sewell (1980) convincingly documents, had evolved powerful methods of informal control over labor markets during the preceding half-century. They possessed hidden forms of corporatist organiz-ation and were capable of negotiating collectively with owners over rates for the job, conditions of work, and length of employment. Labor markets were often centralized and under collective control, employers hiring from a central assembly point or in a particular locale where workers could exchange information and exert maximum pressure on employers and other workers to respect collective norms. This power did not guarantee steady or secure employment. The ups and downs of trade were felt more as periodic, seasonal, and occasionally prolonged unemployment (the last usually triggering political protest and social unrest) rather than as variations in wage rates. This system of control had the added advantage of easy integration of migrant craft workers into the urban labor market (a relic of the *tour de France* of the *compagnonnage* system).

It is hard to get any exact estimate of the proportion of Parisian workers operating in labor markets of this kind, but it was plainly substantial. And the craft workers by their example and their political leadership undeniably set the tone for the Parisian labor market in the 1840s and were at the heart of the workers' movement of 1848. They were the group with whom the association of capitals had to do battle.

The Second Empire saw a diminishing control over labor markets by craft workers (Chevalier 1950; Gaillard 1977). It also saw redefinitions of skills of the sort Marx describes so well in *Capital* as production moves through the increasing detail and social division of labor to machine and factory production. In some industries, craft skills were eliminated and replaced by specialized skills within a detail division of labor. In others, machine operators replaced craft workers. Some of the specialized skills that arose out of transformations of the labor process were monopolizable, but others were relatively easy to reproduce. Here, too, the tendency was toward de-skilling and the use of easily reproducible skills in lower-quality mass production systems (either factories or integrated workshops). The boundary between skilled and unskilled became more blurred as it became easier, given changes in techniques and organization, to introduce unskilled migrants or women into the workshops. Traditional labor market controls also tended to break down as the Parisian labor market exploded in size and dispersed in space. The centralized hiring points, still a matter of comment in the *Enquête* of 1847–48 (see Retel 1977, 199–207) had all but disappeared by 1870. And most commentators agreed that the labor market had become characterized by a much more pervasive competitive individualism in 1870 than had existed in 1848.

Yet the craft workers continued to exercise extraordinary power and influence. They remained, according to Denis Poulot's (1980) vivid descriptions of life and customs in the Parisian workshops of 1870, self-confident to the point of arrogance, opinionated, boisterous, and incurably independent to the point of indiscipline (see table 9). They suffered (according to Poulot, an employer) from the incurable belief which Varlin, one of their members, put this way: "Most workers have nothing to learn from owners who are not skilled in their profession and who are only exploiters" (Workers' Commission of 1867, 99). They continued to exercise collective pressure on labor markets, largely by staying put in their traditional quarters (even in the face of urban renewal and rising rents). Industries that needed their skills had to go to them (which accounts in part for the persistence of industry close to the center and toward the northeast). Indeed, part of the whole pattern of locational shift and innovation in Parisian industry during the Second Empire must be interpreted as a response to the power of such workers, who could only be by-passed through de-skilling and industrial reorganization. And, of course, this group provided much of the political leadership for the workers' movement. It was from the craft worker quarters that much of the explosive political force of the Commune emanated.

The continued presence of such power and influence is all the more remarkable given the intense repression of the workers' movement after 1852. Denied all rights of association, combination, unionization, public assembly, or of going on strike, they were also faced with a battery of laws covering such matters as the *livret* (a kind of work record book, which each worker was supposed to have), jurisdictional disputes (in the event of any conflict of opinion between employer and worker, said the law, that of the employer must prevail), and worker participation in the *conseils de prud'hommes* (trade councils) which always kept them in a minority (Thomas n.d.). They were also faced with a surveillance system that was all too ready to cry conspiracy at the least hint of informal or open discussion. Workers, however, had long been conditioned to this kind of repression and knew only too well how to organize covertly within it (Sewell 1980; Hanagan 1980). But in Paris they had another power. Their skills and abilities were indispensable for much of Parisian industry. For this reason legislation on the *livret* remained largely a dead letter among the craft workers (Duveau 1946, 234).

It was, in the end, transitions in the labor process which did more to undermine their power than any amount of political repression. As the conditions of abstract labor shifted, so the concrete labor that the craft workers had to offer became less significant. But even here the craft workers had abundant opportunities to parlay their power into new configurations. To the degree that the boundary between master and worker was often highly porous, so upward mobility (by marriage or straight succession) was possible, though less so than in earlier times. The hierarchical organization of their own labor system also gave them opportunities to insert themselves as supervisors, foremen, and subcontractors within the detail and social division of labor. And their renowned skill, education, and adaptability allowed them to colonize new trades and monopolizable skills as these opened up. In so doing, they lost their status as craft workers and became the core of an "aristocracy of labor" which was to be the basis of trade union socialism after 1871. The evidence that this transition was already under way is best represented in the evolution of the French branch of the International after 1864, as it moved from expressing the mutualist ideology emanating from

Table 7. *Annual Incomes and Wage Rates by Occupation in Paris, 1847–1871*

Occupation (Males)	Duveau's Estimates, 1860			Average Hourly Rates		
	Annual Wage	Hourly Rate	Dead Season (Months)	1847	1860	1871
Mechanic	1,500	5.00–6.50	3	4.50	4.50	5.00
Carpenter	1,350	5.50–6.00	4	5.00	5.00	6.00
Mason	1,150	4.50–5.50	4	4.00	5.00	5.00
Hatter	1,150	4.00–5.00	3	4.00	5.00	6.50
Jeweler				4.00	5.00	6.00
Bronze worker	1,050	4.00–5.00	4	4.50	5.00	7.00
Locksmith				4.00	4.50	4.50
Printer				4.00	5.00	5.00
Tailor	1,000	4.00–5.00	4	3.50	4.50	5.00
Joiner				3.50	4.00	5.00
Painter	980	4.50–5.00	5	3.50	4.50	6.00
Cobbler	950	3.00–3.50	2½	3.00	3.00	3.50
Bakery worker	900	4.00–5.00	irregular	4.25	5.00	6.60
Team worker	850	2.00–2.50				
Ebonist	700	3.00–4.00	4	3.50	4.50	5.00
Day laborer				2.50	3.00	3.25
Navvy				2.75	3.00	4.00
Women						
Laundress	685	2.00–2.25				
Fashion	640	2.25–3.50				
Flower maker	420	1.50–2.25	3–6			
Mechanic	387	1.50–2.25				
Custom tailor	340	1.00–2.25				

Sources: Duveau (1946), 320–28 (cols. 1–3), and Rougerie (1968a), tables 4 and 6 (cols. 4–6).
Simon (1861), 286–87, gives dead season estimates for women's employment.

the craft tradition to the revolutionary trade union consciousness of an industrial proletariat (Rougerie 1968b).

The pattern of skills and trades underwent a substantial structural revolution between 1848 and 1870. New trades came into being (electrician, for example), while others died out (Haussman's public works all but eliminated the trade of water carrier, for example). Machine skills came to both factory and workshop – the sewing machine revolutionized the clothing trades, with particularly bad effects (Duveau 1946, 288) – and replaced older crafts. Shop assistants, bank clerks, managers, hotel employees, and bureaucrats also became much more conspicuous in the 1860s as specialized white collar occupations arose in banking, commerce, tourism, and government. Here lay the seeds for an upwardly mobile petit bourgeoisie that was soon to match the declining shopkeepers in wealth and power. And it was into this flux that provincial immigrants and women were inserted and craft workers transformed to create radically new structures within the labor market.

Wage Rates and Worker Incomes

All sources agree that wage rates rose by some 20 percent or more during the Second Empire and that the increases were widely spread across different occupations (table 7), including those dominated by women (Duveau 1946, 327). The wage rates, which remained fairly standardized, though less so at the end of the Empire than at its beginning, are much easier to tabulate than are worker incomes because of unstable employment and the notorious dead season. Duveau (1946, 320–28) draws upon numerous contemporary monographs to get rough estimates of the dead season and annual worker incomes. The latter varied from Fr 700 to Fr 1,500 for men and Fr 345 to Fr 685 for women, depending upon occupation. To the degree that these figures refer to conditions at roughly mid-point of the Empire they presumably under-estimate annual incomes toward the end of the period (though the wage rates patiently assembled by Rougerie (1968a) correspond more closely to those of Duveau for 1871 than they do for earlier dates).

The movement of real wages is very different. Rougerie (1968a, 84) concludes that the rise in the cost of living almost offset the rise in nominal wages and that if the cost of workers' necessities is used as a standard then the rise in nominal wage rates would be more than offset. The latter calculation is particularly tricky, since, as Rougerie himself points out and Gaillard (1977, 245–46) emphasizes, the Second Empire also saw revolutions in consumption habits that affected workers as well as the bourgeoisie. However this may be, all sources agree that prices rose during the Second Empire, fundamentally affecting the workers' standard of living. Thomas (n.d., 179) gives the following estimates of annual living costs (in Francs) for a family of four:

Years	Housing	Food, Heating, etc.	Total
1855–53	121	931	1,051
1854–62	170	1,052	1,222
1864–73	220	1,075	1,295

These costs, spearheaded by rent increases that were a never-ending source of complaint (see sec. 3 and 8), increased by 20 percent. When we compare these costs with Duveau's estimates of annual incomes (see table 7), we see that only mechanics and carpenters averaged enough to support a family of four. All other groups needed a supplementary source of income, that of the woman, if basic family needs were to be met. This condition was universal enough to command widespread comment and concern before the Workers' Commission of 1867. The budgets there drawn up (excluding the more fanciful ones) indicated annual needs of between Fr 1,670 and Fr 2,000 for a family of four, although a carpenter in that year with 337 days' work (a most unusual occurrence) could get only Fr 1,470. The single male, who could meet his basic needs for Fr 700 or so, was, under such circumstances, ill advised to form a family unless with a woman who worked. Women, however, simply could not survive alone on the wages they received (see sec. 7). This disparity was to have enormous social effects upon working-class life.

There were, however, some shifts in timing and pattern within this overall picture of movement in the nominal and real wage. Duveau (1946, 320), for example, detects an increasing polarization within the working class between a small but growing group of privileged workers whose incomes more than kept pace with the cost of living (and who might even aspire to property ownership) and the increasing mass of workers in the "unhappy" category who simply could not make ends meet no matter how hard they tried. Such a trend is hard to confirm. But contemporary accounts, such as Poulot's (1980), certainly give the impression that at least some workers were sufficiently well off either to accumulate some small savings or to choose freely not to work on Mondays and to spend lavishly at the cabarets.

How hard it was to make ends meet depended, however, on the conjuncture. Conditions appear to have been very difficult before 1857. Bad harvests and the inflationary effects of deficit financing and inflows of gold from California and Australia combined to generate strong price rises in the face of stagnating wages. Conditions improved rapidly thereafter as labor shortages forced wages up and improved transport brought prices down. The rough equilibrium between wage movements and cost of living shifts that appears to have prevailed in the early sixties came unstuck after 1866 when financial difficulties (the collapse of the Crédit Mobilier) and the cessation of the public works combined with fiercer external competition to make life extremely hard indeed for much of the Paris working class. This general picture (confirmed by Rougerie 1968a; Duveau 1946; and Thomas n.d.) undoubtedly contained innumerable nuances depending upon occupation, sex, and location. Some of the forces shaping these nuances deserve deeper scrutiny.

Temporal and Spatial Fragmentation in the Labor Market

In Paris, as elsewhere (cf. Thompson 1967), the struggle for command over the laborer's time was royally fought. Legislation of March 1848 to restrict the Parisian workday to ten hours had been rolled back to twelve by September and then so riddled with exceptions that on this score the worker had almost no protection. Duveau (1946, 236–48) puts the average workday at eleven hours for much of the Second Empire but notes tremendous variation between craft workers (who still often took "Saint Monday" off) and those who worked fourteen-hour days in some of the small sweatshops. But the biggest problem of all was insecurity of employment, for which Second Empire Paris was notorious. The dead season in some sectors was so long that even craft workers producing high-quality products for high wages during one part of the year were forced to supplement their incomes by participating in mass production at low wages for the rest of the year. It is very hard, therefore, to translate standard rates for a job into any sense of worker incomes. Furthermore, there existed a fluid conduit for the translation of craft workers for one part of the year into mere skilled laborers for the other part. And if, as Chevalier (1950, 96) shows, the problem of the dead season tended to diminish in aggregate, there were many contemporary observers like Fribourg (1872) who saw its increase in certain trades as a major problem in the closing years of the Second Empire. The instability of employment in certain crafts may well, if Fribourg is right, have made regular factory employment more attractive, even at lower wages and with diminished control over the labor process. Certainly, one of the attractions of Paris to prospective employers was the availability of highly qualified labor power at low cost during the dead season.

The Parisian labor market also became more fragmented geographically. The growth and dispersal of population, housing, and employment was accompanied by an increasing separation of working and living. Lazare (1869, 1870) makes much of the increasing journey to work (mostly on foot and over long distances) as a growing burden on workers, particularly recent immigrants forced to settle on the periphery. Tartaret (Workers' Commission of 1867, 240) complained that many workers now had to walk three hours a day to get to work and back. Cheaper transport systems oriented to workers' needs or a shorter working day to compensate for increased travel time emerged as issues (Duveau 1946, 363). The craft workers who clung to central locations had few complaints on this score, however, and focused their wrath on high rents instead. The increasing dispersal and fragmentation of the labor market had a variety of effects. Cochin (1864, 83) worried that the emergence of new employment centers, each with its own tradition, style, and ties, would turn Paris into a city of inhabitants, not citizens. Certainly, wage differentials between one part of the city and another (between center and suburb, particularly) became more marked. But geographical fragmentation also increased the sense of separation of workers and owners who often used to live under the same roof, accelerated the breakup of the apprenticeship system (Gaillard 1977, 417), and made the informal systems of labor market control harder to maintain. Though some, like the carpenters, kept their corporatist traditions intact until after the Commune, other trades witnessed a severe erosion of their collective power simply because of geographical spread and fragmentation.

The Parisian labor market had never been totally centralized, of course, and French workers had a well-earned reputation for individualism, as Poulot's *Le sublime* so well illustrates. But something more was needed than corporatist tradition to cope with the new geographical patterns and the rising individualism. The shift within the Paris branch of the International from mutualism toward revolutionary trade unionism can be read as exactly such an adaptation.

Immigration

The rapid increase in population from just under 1.3 million in 1851 to nearly two million on the eve of the siege of Paris in 1870 (see table 1) was largely fueled by a massive immigration wave of between 400,000 and 450,000 people (Chevalier 1950; Pinkney 1958, 152). Much of the labor reserve in Paris came from the provinces. Its movement was in part to be attributed to depressed rural conditions in the 1850s – provoked in part by changing space relations, which destroyed some rural industries, broke down local self-sufficiency, and generated a slow modernization process in French agriculture (Price 1983; Weber 1976). When this was put up against the tremendous boom in employment opportunities created by the public works in Paris and the revival of Parisian industry, it is not hard to understand the fundamental impulsion behind the immigration. The Parisian labor market had for many years spread its tentacles out into the provinces, mainly to the north but in some special cases, such as the celebrated migrations of stonemasons from the Creuse (Nadaud 1895), deep into rural France. But the coming of the railroads shifted the field of influence of the Parisian labor market outward (Chevalier 1950) to give it even greater geographical coherence and range. Furthermore, the diversity and size of the Parisian labor market made it an attractive destination, no matter what the differences in wage rate. When rural conditions improved in the 1860s and Parisian wages stagnated, immigration continued, though at a slower rate than the vast flood of the 1850s.

The integration of immigrants into the Parisian labor market was a complex affair. Chevalier (1950, 233) shows there was little relation between the skills the immigrants possessed and the jobs they took up in Paris. Many were unskilled, at least in the jobs that Paris offered, and had to find their own paths to job opportunities. The continuing shortages of skilled labor provided an incentive toward technical and organizational change in Parisian industry, even in the face of the vast immigration wave. And the immigrants proved, for the most part, adept at adopting the new skills opened up. There were, to be sure, certain exceptions. The traditional seasonal migrations of skilled construction workers became a more and more permanent affair, with the stonemasons' lodging houses still operating as employment exchanges and receiving points for new immigrants (Pinkney 1958, 157–61; Pinkney 1953). Privileged paths of integration also existed for those of particular regional origins (from Auvergne or even Germans in the Faubourg Saint-Antoine). Gaillard (1977, 405) also finds examples of Parisian industries experiencing shortages of skilled labor and recruiting it directly – wood and metal workers from Alsace, for example. But with the exception of the construction trades, much in demand because of the public works and therefore in the forefront of the immigration wave, it seems that the immigrants did not possess the qualities needed to sustain traditional forms of labor but were quick to form the new qualities required for new labor processes.

This mass influx of largely unskilled but adaptable immigrants created all kinds of opportunities for Parisian industry. There were many dirty jobs to be had – the white lead works were a notorious enough death trap that the workers were shunned on the street – and the growth of mass production opened up many semiskilled jobs for which the new immigrants could be relatively easily trained. And to the degree that most of these immigrants found housing on the periphery, so they increased the attraction of suburban locations for certain newer industries. The mass of the unskilled immigrants therefore underwent a very different socialization process into the ways of industrial capitalism from that achieved through the transformation of craft workers. Thus arose a formidable social division within the Parisian labor market, one that was to have pronounced political effects signaled by the low participation of suburban industrial workers in the events of the Commune (Rougerie 1965).

The Employment of Women

The employment of women – that other great reservoir of surplus labor – underwent some most peculiar gyrations after 1848. Women accounted for 41.2 percent of the work force (not including domestics) in 1947–48, declined to 31 percent in 1860, and went back up to 41.3 percent by 1872 (Duveau 1946, 284–95; Gaillard 1977, 406–11). The declining participation in the 1850s is partly a statistical aberration, since the industrial mix in the suburbs annexed in 1860 was more oriented to male employment. But there was still a very real relative decline explained by the heavy predominance of males in the immigration wave that hit Paris in the 1850s and the deindustrialization and depopulation of the city center that had been the main bastion of women's jobs. Rising male salaries may also have diminished the incentive for married women to engage in what was in any case poorly paid work – women's rates were less than half those of men for comparable work, according to Duveau (1946, 323). And the young single women who did immigrate probably entered as domestic servants brought in from the country estates of the nobility, meaning that most of them ended up on the western, nonindustrial side of the city (see fig. 9). The east-west division of Paris therefore took the demographic form of a male east and a female west.

The general reversal of women's participation after 1860 had equally cogent explanations. The increasing competitive pressure on Parisian industry, particularly with respect to labor costs, made the employment of lower-paid women not only attractive but imperative in certain sectors. And in the face of declining immigration, that vast captive labor reserve of women which had been dispersed to the periphery during the 1850s must have been eyed hungrily by many an employer. Women's wage rates, already low, were a third less in the suburbs compared to the center (Duveau 1946, 327). Not only did their employment exert a downward pressure on wage rates, but they could be used directly to confront the power of craft workers in certain trades. The use of women to break one of the first major (illegal) strikes in the printing workshops in 1862 made a deep impression upon employers and workers alike (Thomas n.d., 200). And although men, partly as a consequence, typically inveighed against the employment of women, they were increasingly forced to recognize in the 1860s that the male wage was insufficient to support a family. To the degree that the immigrants of the 1850s formed families in the 1860s, so the employment of women became more and more of a sheer economic necessity.

Within these general trends, of course, there were innumerable nuances, depending upon technological and organizational changes and product innovations that opened up some occupations (particularly machine tending of the sort that Zola describes) and eliminated others. Considerable debate also arose over the education and position of women and the organization of their labor (Simon 1861; Leroy-Beaulieu 1868). On the one hand, the Parisian convents became centers of tightly organized, low-paid, and highly competitive women's labor – a fact that created considerable resentment in male workers and fueled the anticlerical sentiment that was to flourish under the Commune. On the other hand, small groups of socialist feminists tried, in the late 1860s, to revive the experiments of 1848 with women's cooperatives for production and consumption (Vanier 1960, 109; Dalotel 1981). This brings us, however, to broader questions on the position of women which deserve consideration in their own right.

VII. THE CONDITION OF WOMEN

The change in an historical epoch can always be determined by women's progress towards freedom.

– *Marx*

"The worst destiny for a woman," wrote Michelet (1981, 65) in *La femme* (published in 1859), "is to live alone." He here used what was a distressing fact of life in Second Empire Paris as a basis for moral judgment. He cites the disproportionate number of young women whose bodies were never reclaimed from the public hospitals (a fact Gaillard 1977, 222–24, confirms) as grisly support for his thesis on the inevitable fate of a woman who lived outside the protections of the family.

Legally considered a minor under the Code Napoleon, it was almost impossible for a woman to make her own way in life, economically or socially, without some kind of protection from father, husband, kin, lover, pimp, institutions (like convents and schools), or employer (Thomas 1966). That such "protection" was open to all manner of abuse (social, economic, sexual) was all too evident, though there were many men who took their paternalistic responsibilities seriously, while women found innumerable ways, individually and sometimes collectively, to carve out special positions for themselves within the overall constraints that hemmed them in.

Consider, first, the possibility of some reasonable economic independence through gainful employment. Women's wages (see table 7) were for the most part insufficient to meet even basic needs. Simon's (1861) study depicts a woman working at home for twelve hours a day with the shortest possible dead season and receiving, at generous estimate, an annual income of Fr 500. After deducting the basic costs of rent and clothing, she is left with fifty-nine centimes a day for food – enough for some bread and milk. And this presumes she remains healthy, able to work at full capacity. Employment in the workshops or in retailing (street vending and food preparation, for example) offered equally dismal prospects (Thomas 1966, chap. 1). A highly skilled seamstress or bookbinder could occasionally aspire to economic independence. And the new department stores (so graphically described in Zola's *Au bonheur des dames*) offered a new kind of opportunity for attractive and well-turned-out women, closely chaperoned within a paternalistic system of control (Miller 1981). These opportunities expanded after an 1869 strike of commerce workers, which led employers to rely more heavily on more "docile" women's labor (McBride 1977–78). The irony of all this, of course, is that Parisian industry and commerce relied heavily on women's labor power, which had to be reproduced, for the most part, in conjunction with that of the male within the frame of some household unit.

Domestic employment, by far the most important occupation for women in the city (111, 496 in 1861), had special characteristics (McBride 1976). It offered adequate food, problematic shelter, and less intense conditions of labor. But the hours were long (often fifteen to eighteen hours a day on call all week) and conditions of living strictly regulated (domestics, like all women, were viewed legally as minors and subject to strict supervision). Though they might often change employers, they could never escape the condition of virtual enslavement to the employer's whims. And that sometimes meant sexual whims (tales of domestics required to take care of the sexual needs of sons who might otherwise fulfill them under less controlled conditions abounded). Since unwanted pregnancy was cause for instant dismissal, that meant abortion or prostitution. "Fallen" domestics accounted for most of the prostitutes and most of the illegitimate births and probably made up the majority of the unclaimed bodies which Michelet cited. Yet the position of domestic, if the dangers could be avoided, was not unattractive, given the alternatives. Money wages, though low, could be put by (domestics were the largest group of small savers), and some kind of training and even education procured, and faithful domestics could expect a pension or legacy in old age. Domestic service was also a reasonably protected path for the socialization of young rural women into the dangers of urban life (they concentrated in the safer bourgeois quarters of the west – see fig. 9). While it was hard to marry and even harder to have children and stay in service, a prudent young domestic who put something by as a dowry and had learned skills of household management was not a bad marriage prospect for the shopkeeper or artisan. Most domestics were, therefore, rather young (40 percent were under twenty-five years of age).

Educated women, for their part, could aspire to be governesses, companions, and schoolteachers, occupations again giving little liberty of action and for which the remuneration was generally poor – four thousand schoolmistresses earned less than Fr 400 a year (Thomas 1966, 15; see also Michel 1981). Only women of independent means (those who married under the system called *le régime dotal* retained certain rights and protection of property brought as dowry into marriage [Green 1965, 95]) could void the economic basis for social domination by the institutions and customs of a male-dominated society. To be a well-endowed widow was a privilege that many might hope for but that few attained. Married women who separated, like George Sand, could regain control over their property only after a legal struggle that usually rested on extorting concessions from a husband who had the legal power to put his wife in jail for up to three years if she left without his agreement.

So what, then, could a single woman do, living on bread and a little milk and working twelve hours a day? There were, most agreed, two basic options: lapse into prostitution or establish a liaison (formal or informal) with a man. Prostitution was extremely widespread – thirty-four thousand women in Paris in the 1850s, according to figures cited by Zeldin (1973, 1:307) – and treated with the usual total hypocrisy by the bourgeoisie (Corbin 1978). It was associated with a wide range of other activities from the lower-class dance halls to the higher-class opera and theater and merged into the profession of "mistress." For the woman, the temptations were enormous, though the probability of parlaying good looks into a share of a banker's fortune (like Zola's *Nana*) was very low. Besides, there was too much competition at the top, since the high points of courtesan and bourgeois life were already well occupied (did the marquis of Hertford really pay a million francs for one night with that exquisite beauty and sometime mistress of Napoleon III, the countess of Castiglione?). Most prostitution was out of desperation and sheer hunger (more like Gervaise's stumbling on the boulevards after three days without food in *L'assommoir* than the spectacular rise and fall of her daughter *Nana*). Prostitution was quite simply as extensive and ghastly as the poverty that bred it. Only an occasional *madame* was talented enough to turn it into a reasonable business, and even then it was hard to keep the pimps at bay. But for a woman living on bread and a little milk, the offer of a good evening out or a cheap jewel was more than a little tempting. And for married women with families in the direst straits, it was too often the only option. Poulot (1980) even worried that working class women (including wives) were taking to the streets in a spirit of class vengeance and class war.

Compared to this, any kind of reasonably secure liaison with a man of means must have appeared like true economic emancipation. In a large city like Paris, where a certain anonymity could easily be preserved, all kinds of liaisons were possible, none of them without their dangers. It was customary, for example, for the large numbers of students from the provinces to take mistresses, thus giving rise to the curious profession of "grisette." One close English observer of student life, while falling over backwards not to condone the condition, ended up conveying a certain admiration for such women. They looked after their students faithfully and well, even managed the budget, in return for relief from dull and ill-remunerated employment. While they might, like the ill-fated Fantine in Hugo's *Les misérables,* be left totally in the lurch when the student returned to provincial responsibilities, and while marriage was out of the question, they sometimes received support for children and perhaps some sort of payoff (being set up with a shop being a favorite) in return for their faithful service. St. John (1854, 233–308) even went so far as to regret the replacement of "grisettes" by "lorettes," who used their powers of seduction for pure and shorter-term monetary gain (though even that appeared an appropriate response to a legal system that seemed to have been constructed solely for "the protection of men of pleasure"). Given the open flauntings of mistresses (it was a sign of affluence in the middle class to be able to support one) and the innumerable intersections between the bourgeoisie and the demimonde of the cafés and boulevards, the theaters and the opera, the possibilities and temptations were infinite. Even Haussman had a fairly open and longstanding liaison with an actress who thrived on his protection.

"In order to have enough to live on," said Paule Minck, women "take a lover and cynically admit it" (Dalotel 1981, 134). The trouble was that the woman had an economic need for the man, whereas for the man a wife and children were economic liabilities, unless the woman worked. Out of that inequality all kinds of relations arose. Within the working class of Paris, concubinage was as common as marriage. The latter typically arose out of longstanding family connections, often reaching back into the province of origin (Duveau 1946, 419–30). Concubinage sometimes meant temporary liaisons, but many were relatively permanent, marriages in all but name. The problem was that, economically powerless entering a relationship and legally powerless to get out of marriage, women were exposed to all manner of exploitation by the dominant males. Either their income was indispensable (in which case women were thrown into the workshops, where sexual harassment and violent abuse was, according to the Workers' Commission of 1867 (217), all too common), or their labor power was absorbed as assistants and helpers in home production, commerce, or subcontracting. They might be taken in and given protection but then put to work (their labor power was cheaper than that of an apprentice under such conditions) and abandoned if they became pregnant (Duveau 1946, 426). And they might be expected to manage the household as well (Thomas 1966, 6). They had no real recourse if abandoned for another woman or for the companionship of the cabaret or the wine house. Imprisonment within failed relationships was a severe enough problem that most women speakers at the public meetings after 1868 emphasized the right to divorce and free union (Dalotel, Faure, and Freirmuth 1980).

Yet there were, clearly, many affective relationships established between men and women, within or without marriage, and often under the most impoverished of economic circumstances. Most men spoke warmly of the values of family life before the Workers' Commission of 1867, and Poulot

(1980) observed as many such supportive relationships among his workers as more casual liaisons and contested marriages. Le Play (1983, 9; 1878, 5:427–30) shows that women often controlled the household budget, even allocating the man his lunch money. This practice, which employers sought to enhance by giving take-home pay slips, led Poulot to characterize the "good wife" as one who knew how to economize and manage household expenditures while encouraging sober and industrious habits on the part of her mate. Cottereau (1980, 25–27) suggests employers sought an alliance with the wives in their struggle to control their workers (which also explains employer interest in the education of women). But he concludes that such a strategy rarely worked and that solidarity between husband and wife in the face of employer exploitation was quite general.

The "good wife" had a number of important roles. Hellerstein (1976) suggests, for example, that increasing constraints on women's access to public life, the separation of home and workplace, and the growing disorder and chaos of urban life revolutionized the role of bourgeois women in nineteenth-century Paris. Women became not only managers and governors of the household (a role eschewed by their aristocratic forebears) but took on the role of creators of order, particularly a spatial and temporal order, within the interior space of the household. The latter became more and more strictly their preserve; they managed the servants, kept the accounts, and imposed a strict discipline on the inner organization of the household. The discipline was simultaneously an expression of capitalist-rationality and a kind of structured and controlled response to the perceived disorder and uncontrolled passions that reigned not only in the streets but also in the marketplace (McBride 1976, 21–22). This outer space of excessive stimulation and passion was supposed to be closed to them. "A contained woman, contained in a corset, contained in a house, was an orderly woman." Some women tried to stay close to the worlds of work and power (and the *Salons* of Second Empire Paris were as renowned, if not more so, than their predecessors), but that was not the path of "the good wife" who, like Olivia Haussman, simply ruled competently over the household. It was within this interior space that a kind of "domestic feminism" could arise, a center of considerable women's power.

Within the household the woman also acquired an extremely important role as educator – this in spite of Proudhon's influential protest that the education of children ought to be under the authority of the father. The education of women in turn became the focus of intense public debate and concern. The church saw its almost exclusive grip on the education of girls as essential to the perpetuation of its moral influence, while bourgeois re-formers, like Jules Simon and Victor Duruy, thought that social progress depended crucially upon more liberal and thorough education of women of all social classes. The respect accorded the mother was quite extraordinary. Le

Play (1983, 9) notes, for example, that respect for the mother was a key element in the carpenters' corporation's ritual. And the *mère terrible* lurks in the background of almost every piece of poetry and fiction. If the various manuals of the time are anything to go by, it also seems that the role of sexual partner was not to be neglected, although as Zeldin (1973, 1:293–303) comments, the incidence of painful gynecological diseases (afflicting perhaps as much as 80 percent of Parisian women) was so great as to be a serious barrier to a regular sexual partnership. Venereal diseases also took a terrible toll in life and pain.

These roles, in spite of contemporary bourgeois opinion (which modern historians such as Tilly and Scott 1978 tend to replicate), appear to have carried over into even the lowest strata of working-class life (Berlanstein 1979–80). Of course, they had to be much modified by the fact that the working-class wife (or equivalent) was expected, besides taking care of the household, to supplement the family income as seamstress or outworker, or more often by retailing food, taking in laundry, or acting as the man's assistant in the atelier or the shop (Le Play 1983, 149, 274). Better-off workers could hope to set their wives up as corner grocers, wine sellers, laundresses, and so forth. But women appear to have had considerable control over household management and accounts, education, health care, and even family limitation. In those roles they appear to have been trusted and often highly valued companions.

The issue of family limitation opens up the thorny problem of abortion. Domestics, mistresses, actresses, all had strong incentives to terminate unwanted pregnancies. So, too, did working-class women whose contribution to the family income was at stake and who often appear to have had the tacit approval of men who saw "little sense in breeding their own competition" (Corbon 1863, 65). The Parisian birthrate was extremely low, compared to the national average. Later observers considered that abortion was already a large-scale business by the 1850s, and the widespread knowledge of all kinds of methods of self-inducing abortion (some folkloric and others more powerful, even dangerous) later in the century surely had its roots in earlier times (McLaren 1978). But here, too, women appear to have exercised a certain amount of control over their own bodies, consistent with the thesis of a domestic rather than a strongly public and political feminism.

Conventional family structures, whether legally sanctified or not, survived and allowed women all the possibilities and limitations inherent in such a situation. Many marriages within the bourgeoisie were pure business ventures, a habit that spread down to shopkeepers and petite commercants with particularly vicious effects. But working-class relationships appear to have been far more supportive than bourgeois opinion (like that of Zola) allowed. Thomas (1966) shows that most women who participated in the Siege and the Commune, far from being enraged, bestial furies (see sec. 11), were simply being supportive of their men in very traditional ways. And to the degree that an alternative feminist politics was evident in the women's clubs and associations then set up, it was oriented toward establishing an economic basis for the emancipation of women through the collective organization of production and consumption (Moses 1984). The rank and file of the women involved in the Commune were the seamstresses, dressmakers, finishers, cutters, washerwomen, trimmers, and artificial flower makers (the domestics hardly participated at all), who had had long experience (since most of them were over forty years of age) of the economic basis of their own domination and who, like men, saw collectivist and cooperative politics as their answer.

But if a single theme stands out during the Second Empire, it is that of increasing women's control over the interior space of the household, coupled with the increasing commodification of women in public life. One has only to read Balzac to realize that this was not entirely new, any more than land or financial speculation was new. But, as in these other cases, the Second Empire saw a quantum leap onto a different plane of practices. Both the monetization and commodification of sexual relations and personal liaisons in all classes and the increasing significance of women within the domestic economy of the household as well as in the labor market betokened a sea change in the role of women in society. But it was a sea change blocked by traditional structures of male domination and economic organization. Yet within the increasing monetization of social relations (see Chap. 1) a guerrilla war was unfolding, a war in which domestics learned how to use and even swindle their employers; prostitutes to short-change their clients; lorettes to replace grisettes; wives or comanions to put tighter clamps on the circulation of revenues; and working women to take up the challenge of new kinds of factory work and service roles and to explore alternative forms of organization which could form an economic basis for their future emancipation. It was as if women learned that if they were a valued commodity with a money value, then they could use the democracy of money as a tool toward their own liberation.

VIII. THE REPRODUCTION OF LABOR POWER

> Variable capital is therefore only a particular historical form of . . . the labor-fund which the laborer requires for maintenance of himself and his family, and which, whatever the system of social production, he himself must produce and reproduce.
>
> *– Marx*

The reproduction of labor power, for which women then, as now, bore heavy responsibility, has two aspects. There is first the question of food, sleep, shelter, and relaxation sufficient to return the laborer refreshed enough to be able to work the next day. There are then the longer-term needs, which attach to raising the next generation of workers through having, raising, and educating children.

It is probably fair to say that on the average the resources available to the mass of male workers were barely sufficient for daily needs and quite insufficient for long-term needs of child-rearing. This general judgment – which, to be sure, needs much nuancing – is consistent with many of the basic facts of Parisian demography during the Second Empire. In 1866, for example, only a third of the total population could claim Paris as their place of birth. Even in the 1860s, past the peak of the great immigration wave, as Chevalier (1950, 50) calculates, natural population growth was nine thousand a year, compared to an annual immigration of eighteen thousand. The long-term reproduction of labor power appears to have been very much a provincial affair Paris met its demand for labor as Marx (1967, 1:269) put it, "by the constant absorption of primitive and physically uncorrupted elements from the country." The links with the provinces were more intricate, however, than the bare facts of immigration. Children were often sent back to the provinces to be raised, and even the working class engaged in that common French practice of putting their children out to rural wet nurses, which, given the high death rate, was more akin to organized infanticide than to the reproduction of labor power (Fay-Sallois 1980). Paris was, in any case, full of single males (60 percent of males between 21 and 36 in 1850). Marriages, if contracted at all, occurred relatively late (29.5 years for men in 1853, rising to nearly 32 years in 1861), and the average number of children per household stood at 2.40 compared to 3.23 in the provinces, with an illegitimacy rate of 28 percent compared to 8 percent elsewhere. Furthermore, the natural population growth there was almost entirely due to the young age structure of the population, itself a function of immigration (Chevalier 1950, 46–52; Girard 1981, 136).

The demographic picture did shift somewhat toward the end of the Second Empire. Household formation picked up in the 1860s and shifted outward to the suburbs, leaving the center single and older in age structure. The chronic slum poverty of the center, which affected mainly new immigrants and the old, was now matched by the suburbanization of family poverty affecting the young (Gaillard 1977, 225; fig. 12). The changing age structure triggered by the vast immigration wave of mainly young unmarried people in the 1850s worked its way through the demographics of the city, quarter by quarter.

The idea that those who drew so freely on this labor power had some sort of responsibility or self-interest in its reproduction dawned slowly on the bourgeoisie. And even those, like the emperor, who saw that bourgeois failure in this regard had had something to do with the events of 1848 were unable to define a basis, let alone a consensus, for intervention. Bourgeois reformers were nevertheless much preoccupied with the question. Fecund

POPULATION IN
LODGING ROOMS
1876

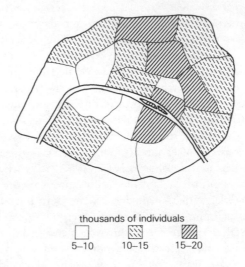

thousands of individuals

5–10   10–15   15–20

INDIGENCE 1869

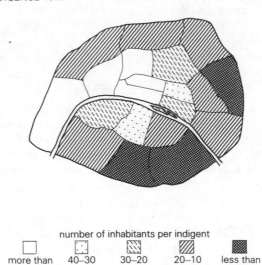

number of inhabitants per indigent

more than   40–30   30–20   20–10   less than
40   10

Fig. 12.   *The total population living in lodging rooms in 1876 and the indigence rate in Paris, 1869. (After J. Gaillard, 1977.)*

with ideas, though short on their application, their enquiries and polemics yielded much information and many ideas that, after the trauma of the Commune, became the basis for social reform under the Third Republic. How and why the configuration of class forces stymied their efforts in the fields of housing, nutrition, education, health care, and social welfare deserves careful reconstruction.

Housing

The Second Empire witnessed, as we saw in section 3, a radical transformation in the system of housing provision. Bourgeois housing was largely captured by the new system of finance, land development, and construction, with the effect of increasing residential segregation within the city. A parallel system of small-time speculative building to meet the demand for working-class housing also sprang up on open land on the periphery. But though the system of housing provision changed, worker incomes remained relatively low, putting fairly strict upper limits on the housing they could afford. A relatively well-off family with stable employment and two people working might make Fr 2,000 a year in 1868 and be able to afford not much more than Fr 350 a year rent. How much and what quality of housing could be provided for Fr 350 or less? Under the best of conditions, the answer was not much; and under the worst, where land and construction were expensive and landlords aggressively sought their 8 percent or more, housing conditions were nothing short of dreadful.

Rapidly rising rents placed an increasing burden on the working population. As early as 1855 Leon Say signaled 20 to 30 percent rises all over the city, so that a single room could not be had for much less than Fr 150 (Guerrand 1966, 85). Corbon (1863, 181) puts rents on working-class housing in 1862 70 percent higher than pre-1848, and Thomas (n.d., 179) has housing costs increasing by 50 percent in each decade of the Empire. The statistical series assembled by Flaus (1949) indicates a lower figure of between 50 and 62 percent for the whole period, with rents less than Fr 100 increasing by only 19.5 percent. But as Gaillard (1977, 129–31) points out, there were few rents less than Fr 100 to be had; the rent of a single room for registered indigents averaged between Fr 100 and Fr 200 in 1866. A report on the rents paid by these forty thousand or so indigent families put the average at Fr 113 in 1856, rising to Fr 141 in 1866 even after the annexation of the suburbs had brought the cheaper suburban housing into the sample (Guerrand 1966, 95). There is a strong consensus that rising rents outpaced workers' nominal incomes, particularly during the 1860s.

The increases were consistent with the general rise in property values (see fig. 5) and affected all social classes. Those living on fixed incomes or even off the stagnent rents of rural estates and who could afford to pay no more than Fr 700 or so had a particularly hard time of it. Innumerable cases of hardship and of forced relocation could be found within this segment of the bourgeoisie (Lameyre 1958, 174). But for those who participated in the economic gains of the Second Empire, the rising rents posed no problem. For the more than half-million people who lived by their labor in the city, it was an entirely different story.

Workers could adapt to this situation in a number of ways. There is evidence, largely anecdotal, that they spent an increasing proportion of their budget on housing. Audiganne (1854, 2:379) indicates that workers were spending as much as one-seventh of their income on housing in 1860 compared to one-tenth in former times, and Poulot (1980, 146) puts the figure as high as 30 percent ten years later. They could also save on space. For a family already confined to one room (and that was true for two-thirds of the indigents surveyed in 1866) doubling up came hard, but it was not impossible and far from uncommon for the poorer families. It was easier for single people, and many lodging houses (see fig. 12) did indeed take on the aspect of barracks, with multiple beds per room for low-paid single workers. It was also possible to seek out lower-cost accommodations on the periphery, thus often trading off a long journey to work on foot for a lower rent. But the pressures were such that the rents on speculative housing on the periphery, though lower, were by no means that much lower, particularly given the strong penchant that suburban builders and property owners had for getting their cut of the Parisian property boom by profiteering at the worker's expense. The last resort was to populate one of the innumerable shantytowns that sprang up, sometimes temporarily, on vacant lots on the periphery or even close to the center.

The paucity of worker incomes relative to rents left its indelible stamp upon the city's housing situation. And it was partly out of this history that Engels (1935) fashioned his famous argument that the bourgeoisie has only one way of solving the housing question: by moving it around. There is no better illustration of that thesis than Paris under the Second Empire. Gaillard's (1977, 209) descriptions, taken from the reports of the Health Commissioners, of the temporary shantytowns that arose right next door to the new construction sites in the city center, and to which everyone turned a blind eye, are simply horrifying. The proliferation and overcrowding of lodging houses close to the center; the construction of poorly ventilated, cramped, and poorly serviced dwelling houses that became almost instant slums; and the celebrated "additions," which in some cases transformed the interior courts behind Haussman's splended facades into highly profitable working-class slums, were all a direct concession to the fact that worker incomes were insufficient to afford decent housing (Commission des Logements Insalubres de Paris 1866). Far from ridding the city of slums, Haussman's works, insofar as they assisted the general rise in rents at a time of stagnant worker incomes, accelerated the process of slum formation, even in the heart of the city itself. On a simple traverse from the city center to the fortifications, Louis Lazare counted no fewer than 269 alleys, courtyards, dwelling houses, and shantytowns constructed without any municipal control whatsoever. Though much of the housing for impoverished families was to be found in the suburban semicircle running around the east of the city, with particular concentrations in the southeast and northeast, there was intense overcrowding of single workers in the lodging houses close to the city center (see fig. 12), and there were patches of poor housing even within the interstices of the predominantly bourgeois west.

Such a dismal housing situation could not but have had social effects. It presumably accentuated what was already a strong barrier to family formation, and both Simon and Poulot attributed what they saw as the instability and promiscuity of working-class life to high rents and inadequate housing (thus avoiding, in Poulot's case, the implication that perhaps the low wages he paid had something to do with it). There was considerable evidence also to connect inadequate and insalubrious housing to the persistent though declining threat of epidemics of cholera and typhoid. Sheer lack of space also forced much social life onto the streets, a tendency exacerbated by the general lack of cooking facilities. This forced eating and drinking into the cafés and cabarets, which consequently became collective centers of political agitation and consciousness formation.

With bourgeois reformers deeply aware of and nervous about such a condition and an emperor who recognized that the consolidation of working-class support through the "extinction of pauperism" (to cite a tract the emperor had written in 1844) was important to his rule, it is surprising that so little in the way of tangible reform was accomplished. Laws on insalubrity, passed under the Second Republic at the urging of a Catholic reformist, were either used selectively by Haussman for his own purposes or remained a dead letter – less than 18 percent of the total housing stock was inspected in eighteen years (Guerrand 1966, 105). The plan to build a series of *cités ouvrières* (large-scale working-class housing that drew some inspiration from Fourier's ideas for collective working-class housing, the *phalanstère*) was launched in 1849, with Louis Napoleon subscribing some of the funds, but quickly ground to a halt in the face of virulent conservative opposition, which saw *cités ouvrières* as breeding grounds for socialist consciousness and as potential hearths of revolution. The workers, however, viewed them more as prisons, since the gates were locked at 10 o'clock and life was strictly regimented within. Proposals for individualized housing, more acceptable to the conservative right and the Proudhonists of the left, generated many designs (there was even a competition at the Paris Exposition of 1867) but little action, since the proposal to subsidize the provision of low-income housing had generated only sixty-three units by 1870, and the one co-operative society (to which the emperor again generously subscribed) had built no more than forty-one units by that same date (Guerrand 1966).

The failure of action in spite of the emperor's evident interest (he gave personal financial support to both collectivist and individualized initiatives, inspired articles and government programs, and was responsible for the translation of English tracts on the problem) was partly a matter of confused ideologies. Fourier, with his collectivist model, and Proudhon, who came out very strongly in favor of individual homeownership for workers, split the left. Proudhon's influence was so strong that no challenge was mounted to property ownership under the Commune when resentment against landlords was at its height (Guerrand 1966, 199). With such a wide consensus stretching from Le Play on the Catholic right to Proudhon on the socialist left, the only real option was to take care of the housing problem within the framework of private property. But homeownership for the workers was not feasible except with government subsidy. And at that point the government ran up against the powerful class interest of landlords, to whom it was increasingly beholden as a basis for its political power (sec. 3), and a general attachment to freedom of the market, which, for someone like Haussman, was a cardinal principle of action. Powerful class forces compounded ideological confusion to stymie any action on the housing problem over and beyond the slum clearance that Haussman masterminded. It was only after the Commune, when the reformers saw that the pitiful slums and inner courtyards were better breeding grounds for revolutionary action than any *cité ouvrière* could ever have been, that housing reform began to have any teeth.

Nutrition

The "revolution in consumption" facilitated by falling transport costs of agricultural products and by economies of scale and efficiency within the Parisian distribution system did not entirely pass the worker by, even though it also meant an increased "stratification of diet and taste" across the social classes (Gaillard 1977, 243). Bread, meat, and wine formed the basis of a distinctive working-class diet (quite different from that in the provinces) and was increasingly supplemented and diversified by fresh vegetables and dairy products. Meat was rarely eaten by itself, of course, but was incorporated in soups and stews, which formed the heart of the main meal. To the degree that diversity and security of food supply improved, there is evidence that standards of nutrition improved at the same time as the cost of living rose. That Paris was still vulnerable to harvest failure became all too evident in

1868–69, when there was a repeat of the very difficult phase of high prices of 1853–55. It then became evident, too, that restricted working-class incomes made it difficult for the mass of the population, as opposed to the bourgeoisie, to take advantage of the more diversified food base (Gaillard 1977, 233–67; Duveau 1946, 328–43).

The system of food distribution had some important characteristics. The large lodging-house population and the lack of interior cooking facilities for many families (63 percent of indigents had only a fireplace for food preparation) forced much food consumption and preparation onto the streets and into the restaurants and cafés. The periodicity of worker incomes (during the dead season in particular) meant that much food was purchased on credit. Yet the food typically entered the highly centralized markets (Les Halles) or abattoirs (La Vilette) or wine depots (Bercy) in bulk. The breakdown of bulk via a whole system of retailers, street vendors, and the like also rested on credit. At the same time it opened up innumerable possibilities for petite-entrepreneurial activity, often organized by women, though here as in other aspects of life under the ultimate control of men.

This intricate system of intermediation had interesting social consequences. Workers evidently viewed it ambivalently. On the one hand, it provided many opportunities for supplementary employment (particularly of women), and even a chance of upward mobility into the petit-bourgeois world of the shopkeeper. On the other hand, the intermediaries made what were often close to life-and-death decisions as to when and when not to extend credit and were often viewed as petty exploiters. It was to circumvent this that the workers' movement began to build a substantial consumer cooperative movement in the 1860s, and many of these had a considerable success. Nathalie Lemel joined with the indefatigable Varlin to found La Marmite, a food cooperative to which workers could subscribe Fr 50 annually and then have rights to cheap, well-prepared food on a daily basis at much lower cost than in the restaurants. By 1870 there were three branches doing a very busy trade (Foulon 1934, 56–67).

Lemel and Varlin had dual objectives. Not only did they seek to take care of the needs of those who had no place to cook for themselves, but they also saw the cooperatives as centers of political organization and collective action. In this they were simply confirming the slowly dawning fears of bourgeois reformers – that the mass of the population of Paris, deprived of the facilities and comforts necessary to a stable family life, were being forced onto the streets and into places where they could all too easily fall prey to political agitation and ideologies of collective action. That the cabarets, cafés, and wine merchants provided the premises for the elaboration of scathing criticism of the social order and plans for its reorganization was all too evident to Poulot. That they were hearths for the formation and articulation of working-class consciousness and culture became all too apparent as political agitation mounted after 1867. The emphasis that bourgeois republicans like Jules Simon put upon the virtues of stable family life (in a decent house with adequate cooking facilities) was in part a response to the dangers that lurked when food, drink, and politics became part of a collective working-class culture.

Education

The social reformers of the Second Republic had envisaged a system of free, secular, and compulsory state primary education for both sexes. What they got, after the victory of the "party of order," was the Falloux Law of 1850, which promoted a dual system of education – one religious and the other provided by the state – while bringing all teaching under the supervision of local boards in which the traditional power of the university was now matched by that of the church and other elected and appointed officials. It is generally conceded that the law brought few benefits and many liabilities. Coupled with niggardly state educational budgets, it contributed to the dismal record of educational achievement during the Second Empire (Anderson 1970, 1975).

Problems in part arose because educational policy lay at the mercy of church-state relations. Anxious to rally Catholics to his cause, the emperor not only supported the Falloux Law but was reluctant to undermine its spirit until 1863 when, already at loggerheads with the pope over his Italian policy, he appointed Duruy, a liberal free-thinker and reformer, as minister of education. Duruy struggled against great odds and with only limited success to give a greater dynamism to the state sector and so undermine the power of the church. His moves toward free and compulsory primary education and toward state education for girls were often vitiated by legislative tampering and meagre educational budgets. But there were all kinds of other conflicts. Apart from the interminable philosophical and theological debates (religion versus materialism, for example), there was no clear consensus within the bourgeoisie as to the objectives of education. Some saw it as a means of social control which should therefore inculcate respect for authority, the family, and traditional religious values – a total antidote to socialist ideology, which some teachers had been rash enough to promote in the heady days of 1848. Even traditionally anticlerical republicans were content to see a hefty dose of religion in education if it could protect bourgeois values (hence the support many of them gave to the Falloux Law). The trouble was that the religious values promoted within the church were, for the most part, of an extra-ordinarily conservative and backward variety. As late as the 1830s the church had preached against interest and credit, and by the 1850s it was little enamored of materialist science. The church's backwardness in such matters in part accounts for the violent anticlericalism of many of the students (particularly medical students) who made up the core of the Blanquist revolutionary movement (Hutton 1981).

Others, however, saw education as a way to bring the mass of the population into the spirit of modern times by inculcating ideals of free scientific enquiry and of materialist science and rationality appropriate to a world of scientific progress and universal suffrage. The problem was how to do it. Some, like Proudhon, were deeply antagonistic to state-controlled education (it should always remain under the control of the father, said Proudhon), while others feared that without centralized state control there would be nothing to stop the spread of subversive propaganda. Duruy struggled for responsible and progressive education and was simultaneously appreciated and vilified on all sides. Given such confusions, it is not surprising that the net outcome was meager progress for educational provision and equally meager progress in educational content. Yet, as Auspitz (1982) argues, the debate in the 1860s over the role of education was to have a lasting influence on French political life. Progressive Catholics and republicans alike were, in education as in housing and other facets of social welfare, striving to define a philosophy and practice that would give mass education a new meaning in bourgeois society. The debate was vital, even if the achievements before 1870 were minimal.

To the degree that Paris drew its labor power from the four corners of France, the general failure to improve education had a serious impact upon the quality of labor power to be had there. The general decline in illiteracy throughout France was helpful, of course, but it still left around 20 percent of Parisians in that category by 1872; and even many of those who could read and write had only the most rudimentary form of education, leaving them with marginal abilities when it came to any kind of skill demanding formal schooling. There was little in the educational system of Paris to offset this dismal national picture. The government initially sided with those who saw education simply as a means of control. State and religious schools developed equally side by side (Gaillard 1977, 281). Haussman's budget allocations to education were parsimonious in the extreme when compared with his lavish expenditures on public works. He looked to religious and private schools to meet the needs of new immigrants and the newly forming suburban communities and did his best to limit free schooling to the children of indigents, so payment to attend state schools was commonly demanded. Teachers' pay, around Fr 1,500 a year, was barely sufficient to make ends meet for a single person and certainly insufficient to raise a family. For purely budgetary reasons Haussman (and quite a few taxpayers also) preferred to leave schooling to the private sector, particularly to the religious institutions, where teachers' pay was even lower (around Fr 800).

This picture began to change only after 1868, when Duruy finally forced through the principle of free public education and Gréard set about reforming educational provision in Paris (Girard 1981, 288). But by then Haussman's laissez-faire and privatist strategy had shaped a very distinctive map of educational provision in the city. The annexed suburbs of 1860 formed what can only be described as an educational wasteland of few and inadequate public schools and weak religious or private development, since this was hardly an area of affluent parents who could afford to pay. Haussman's neglect of schooling here is best evidenced by the fact that he spent only four million francs on new schools in the annexed zone between 1860 and 1864, compared to forty-eight million for the new *mairies,* sixty-nine million for new roads, and five and one-half million for new churches (Gaillard 1977, 270). The rate of school attendance was low and illiteracy higher than the city average. Here were to be found those "ragged schools" in which were assembled "children of all ages who had nothing in common save their same degree of ignorance" (Gréard, quoted in Girard 1981, 289). Here was the space of social reproduction of an impoverished and educationally marginalized working class. In the bourgeois quarters of the west, Haussman's system worked, since the public schools were used free by the poor quite separately from the private and religious schooling preferred by the bourgeoisie. In some of the central quarters populated by craft workers, petit bourgeois, and commerce, the public schools were seen as a common vehicle for educating all children in technical and practical skills, which the Catholic schools found it difficult to impart. Thus was the increasing social segregation of space in the city reflected in the map of educational provision (Gaillard 1977, 288–89).

The qualities of this educational system also varied greatly. While there were progressive Catholic schools (and the church put special emphasis upon its efforts in education in Paris), the state sector usually had an advantage in science and other modern subjects. However, the tight surveillance of teachers made possible by the supervisory boards set up in 1850 kept the whole of the educational system biased toward control and religious indoctrination rather than enlightened materialism. But to the degree that the Catholic schools preached intolerance as well as respect for traditional values they became less and less popular with the liberal bourgeoisie, many of whom turned to the Protestant schools instead. The education of girls was left, until Duruy's reforms of the late 1860s, almost exclusively in the hands of the church. Interestingly enough, it was here that the question of the proper balance between moral teachings and vocational skills became most explicit as the issue of women's role (sec. 7) came to the fore.

The failures of the formal educational system to produce a labor force equipped with modern technical skills would not have been so serious were it not for a breakdown of other more traditional modes of skill formation. The apprenticeship system, already in serious trouble by 1848, went into a generalized crisis in the Second Empire (Gaillard 1977, 416–23). In some trades, given the pressures of competition and fragmentation of tasks (sec. 5), apprenticeship degenerated into cheap child labor and nothing else. The geographical dispersal of the labor market and the increasing separation of work and residence created a further strain within a system that had always been open to abuse unless subject to close surveillance and control by all parties involved. The system seems to have survived reasonably well in only a few trades, such as jewelry. Furthermore, even some of the traditional provincial centers of skill formation for the Parisian labor market were more and more cut off as seasonal migrations gave way to permanent settlement. There therefore arose, on the part of both employers and the working class, a demand for a school system that could replace the apprenticeship system through vocational training and skill formation in educational institutions. The few private institutions that formed in the 1860s realized some success, thus pioneering the way for educational reform after the Commune. But it was mainly the children of the petite bourgeoisie or well-off workers who could afford the time or money to attend them. The same limitation affected the popular adult education courses that were established in central city areas in the 1860s.

The rudiments of working-class education then, as now, were imparted in the home, where, according to most bourgeois observers and in spite of Proudhon's injunctions, the woman usually played the main role. Simon's strong interest in the education of women in part derived from what he saw as the need to improve the quality (moral as well as technical) of the education that mothers could impart. Thereafter, children's education ran up against the conflict "the more they earn the less they learn" – a vital problem for households close to the margin of existence. Much of the uneducated working class proved hostile to compulsory education and the apprenticeship system for this very simple reason. A different attitude prevailed among craft workers, who venerated the apprenticeship system and bewailed its degeneration. It was from this sector of the working class that the demand for free, compulsory, and vocationally oriented education was most strongly voiced. And they were prepared in this respect to take matters into their own hands. There was no lack in Paris of dissident free-thinkers and students anxious, as the Blanquists were, to offer education for political reasons or, more frequently, for small sums of cash. Varlin, for example, both educated himself and learned principles of moral and political economy from a part-time teacher (Foulon 1934, 20–26). Herein, as the more savvy members of the bourgeoisie like Poulot realized, lay a serious threat – the autodidacts among the craft workers, with their free-thinking and critical spirit, might lead the mass of uneducated laborers in political revolt. That the free-thinking students who formed the core of the Blanquist revolutionary movement, who joined the International, or who adhered to the popular radical press could take on similar radicalizing roles also became all too apparent in the numerous public meetings to which many an uneducated worker was drawn after 1868 (Dalotel, Faure, and Freirmuth 1980). And it was, after all, in the educational wasteland of the periphery that the anarchist Louise Michel (1981) began her extraordinary and turbulent career as a teacher. From this standpoint, the bourgeoisie was to reap the harvest of its own failure in the field of educational reform and investment – a lesson it was to take to heart after the Commune as education became the cornerstone of its effort to stabilize the Third Republic.

The Policing of the Family

What really went on in the heart of the family, whether legally constituted or not, is for the most part shrouded in mystery. How effective the kinship system was in integrating immigrants into Parisian life and culture and in providing some kind of social security is likewise open to debate. The occasional biographies and autobiographies (such as those of Nadaud, Varlin, Louise Michel, and Edouard Moreau) indicate the tremendous importance of family (or free union) and kin within the social networks of Parisian life. Yet we are dealing here not only with politically active people but with educated craft workers or petit bourgeois professionals or shopkeepers whose social condition, as we have seen, was quite different from that of the mass of uneducated immigrants. Many of the latter, however, drew their mates from their province of origin and presumably imported into Paris as many systems of family and kin relations as existed in provincial France (Duveau 1946; Le Play 1983). For the first generation of such immigrants, the Parisian melting pot probably had little meaning, and, through the formation of distinctive colonies from Brittany, Creuse, Auvergne, and Alsace, they could even preserve provincial cultures within the overall frame of Parisian life. Yet there are many indications also of a too rapid melting into the alienation and anomie of large-scale urban culture. The unclaimed bodies from the hospitals, the high rates of children apprehended for vagabondage, the orphans and abandoned children, all point to the breakdown of traditional security systems embedded in the family and kinship organization in the face of insecurity of employment, wretched living conditions, and all the other pathologies and temptations (drink, prostitution) of Parisian life.

Within the family and kinship systems that did survive, it appears that the older woman acquired a certain prestige based upon her capacities as mother, nurse, and educator, as the manager of the reproduction of labor power within the home (sec. 7). This was a role that many men clearly valued, that bourgeois reformers sought to encourage as a pillar of social stability, and that the church sought to colonize through the education of girls as purveyors of religious values and morality. Such a role was doubly important because one of the key values which women were expected to inculcate was respect for the authority of the father within the home and of church or state outside. That such an ideology was hegemonic is suggested by the fact that the farthest most radical feminists went was to claim mutual respect within free union. For it was, as we saw in section 7, almost impossible for a woman to survive, economically or socially, outside of a liaison with a man.

Even though women may have controlled the purse strings, there was all too often too little in the purse to provide for the proper reproduction of labor power. The dead season meant terrible seasonal strains on income, and rent payment dates (customarily three or six months in advance) put a similar strain on expenditures. It was hard for families to stay together under such material conditions without some other forms of support. The numbers with savings in the Caisses d'Epargne (set up in 1818 and then consolidated in 1837 to promote working-class thrift) expanded enormously, but the average amount put by fell to around Fr 250 per depositor by 1870 – enough for a rainy day or two but not much more. The other resource – to farm out needy children to kin – was probably equally limited insofar as most kin were in the same financial boat (see, however, Berlanstein 1979–80). Where the kinship system was probably most effective, however, was in tracking down employment opportunities for those in immediate need. Outside of this, the family had to look to state or charitable support.

Paris had traditionally been the welfare capital of France, with a tradition of religious and state charity as a right to which all indigents could appeal. This system, under attack by conservative republicans in the Second Republic, was steadily dismantled by Haussman, whose neo-Malthusian attitudes to the welfare question we have already noted (sec. 4). The idea, of course, was to reduce the fiscal burden and to force welfare provision back within the framework of family responsibilities – a strategy that would have made more sense if families had had the financial resources to meet the burden. As it was, hospitals and medical care could not be so easily displaced, and the poverty problem was such as to keep support for indigents a major item in the city budget. Haussman's strategy of decentralization and localization of responsibility for welfare provision simply kept pace, in the end, with the rapid suburbanization of family and child poverty. The only other strategy was to look to the formation of mutual benefit societies and other forms of mutual aid within the working class. The government took several steps to encourage such organizations but was terrified that they might become centers of secret political mobilization – which, of course, they did. Their considerable growth and their attempted surveillance and control by the government forms an interesting chapter in the struggle for political rights and economic security. Women found it hard to gain access to such societies, nor could they independently draw upon their benefits – a limitation that in part undermined the fundamental aim of support to the family. But the government's insistence on strict surveillance and control also limited the development of the societies in important ways. Here, as with the surveillance system that attached to welfare for indigents, the authoritarian state was stepping crudely down a road toward the policing of the family which was to be trodden with much greater sophistication by subsequent generations of bourgeois reformers.

IX. COMMUNITY AND CLASS

The Commune was therefore to serve as a lever for uprooting the economical
foundations upon which rests the existence of classes, and therefore
of class rule.

– Marx

Individuals evolve allegiances broader than those given by the individualism of money and loyalty to family and kin. Class and community define two such broader social configurations. There is a tendency in modern times to see these as mutually exclusive categories that give rise to antagonistic forms of consciousness and political action (cf. Chap. 1). This plainly was not so in Paris under the Second Empire. That many felt at home with the idea that there was a community of class as well as a class of community was not an ideological aberration; it had a real material base. What was perhaps more surprising was the way many evidently felt not only that community and class provided compatible categories and identities but that their synthesis was the ideal toward which any progressive civil society must strive. The idea of association – so fundamental within the workers' movement and in the practices of finance capital – either ignored or unified the distinction. Yet it was also true that the conceptions and realities of both community and class underwent a very rapid evolution as the Second Empire progressed. Haussman's works and the transformation of the Parisian land and property market upset traditional notions of community as much as they upset the sociospatial structure, and transformations in financial structures and labor processes had no less an impact upon the material basis of class relations. It is only in terms of such confusions that the extraordinary alliance of forces which produced the Paris Commune – the greatest class-based communal uprising in capitalist history – can be fully appreciated.

Class

Daumard's (1965, 1973) reconstruction of the fortunes left by Parisians in 1847 yields a vivid picture of the distribution of wealth by socioeconomic

Table 8. *Inherited Wealth by Socioprofessional Categories, 1847*

Category	Index of Average Value of Wealth per Recorded Death	% Leaving No Wealth	% of Recorded Deaths	% of Total Wealth
Business (commerce, finance, etc.)	7,623	26.3	1.0	13.8
Land and property owners	7,177	8.6	3.7	54.0
High functionaries	7,091	13.0	0.6	8.0
Liberal professions and managers	1,469	39.4	2.0	5.6
Middle functionaries	887	16.9	1.7	3.2
Rentiers and pensioners	709	38.2	5.7	8.3
Shopkeepers	467	35.7	6.1	5.8
State & private employees	71	52.8	2.7	0.4
Home workers	61	48.5	1.8	0.2
Clergy	15	75.9	0.4	0.1
Domestics	13	81.6	6.9	0.2
Without attribution (& Diverse)	4	79.2	29.1	0.1
Workers	2	92.8	30.2	0.2
Manual laborers	1	80.5	8.1	0.0
All categories	503	72.6	100.0	100.0

Source: Daumard (1973), 196–201. (N.B. I have combined certain minor categories from differently constructed tables without, I think, violating the overall picture.)

category (table 8). Four major groupings stand out. At the top sat a haute bourgeoisie of business (merchants, bankers, directors, and a few large-scale industrialists), landed gentry, and high state functionaries. Accounting for only 5 percent of the sample population, they had 75.8 percent of the inherited wealth. The lower classes (constituting the last four categories) made up three-quarters of the population but collectively accounted for 0.6 percent of the wealth. Between lay an upper middle class of civil servants, lawyers, professionals, and upper management combined with pensioners and those living off interest. Shopkeepers, once the backbone of the middle class, were, as we have already noted, on the way down the social scale (with almost the same proportion of the population, their share of wealth fell from 13.7 percent in 1820 to 5.8 percent by 1847). But they still were a notch above the lower middle class of employees and lower-level managers (mainly white collar) and the self-employed (mainly craft workers and artisans). The disparities of wealth within this class structure were enormous.

We can look at this class structure another way. To begin with, "the old contrast between town and country, the rivalry between capital and landed property" (Marx 1972, 47) is very much in evidence. The disproportionate presence of rural gentry and state functionaries is directly connected with the centralized role of Paris in national life. The peasant class is not actively seen, but its presence is everywhere felt, not only as the reserve of labor power upon which Paris could draw, but also as the source of the taxes that supported government and the unearned incomes that the property owners spent so liberally. When we add in pensioners and rentiers (living off interest), we find nearly a tenth of the population, controlling more than 70 percent of the wealth, living off unearned incomes. Here lay much of the enormous effective demand that Parisian industry was so well placed to satisfy. The dominance of the "idle rich" or "consuming classes" had tremendous implications for Parisian life, economy, and politics, as did the overblown role of state functionaries. We find only a fifth of the haute bourgeoisie engaged in economically gainful activities. This had a great effect on the comportment of the bourgeoisie, its social attitudes, and its internal divisions.

The internal divisions within the mass of the lower class (74.3 percent in Daumard's 1847 sample) are harder to discern. The differences between craft, skilled, unskilled, casual, and domestic laborers (see secs. 5 and 6) were obviously relevant, though Poulot (1980) later preferred distinctions based on attitudes toward work and work skill and discipline (table 9). Contemporaries often dwelt (with considerable fear) on that most contentious of all social divisions: between the laboring and "dangerous" classes. Before 1848, much of the bourgeoisie lumped them together (Chevalier 1973). The workers' movement of 1848 defined a different reality without totally dispelling the illusion (sec. 11). But it left open how to classify the miscellaneous mass of street vendors, ragpickers and scavengers, street musicians and jugglers, errand boys and pickpockets, occasional laborers at home or in the workshop. For Haussman (1890, 2:200) these were the "true nomads" of Paris, floating from job to job and slum to slum, bereft of any municipal sentiment or loyalties. For Thiers they constituted the "vile multitude" who saw the erection of barricades and the overthrow of government as pure theater and festival. Marx was hardly more charitable. The "whole indefinite, dis-integrated mass" of "vagabonds, discharged soldiers, discharged jailbirds, escaped galley slaves, swindlers, mountebanks, *lazzaroni*, pickpockets, trick-sters, gamblers, *maquereaux*, brothel keepers, porters, *literati*, organ grinders, ragpickers, knife grinders, tinkers, beggers," – "scum, offal, refuse of all classes" – made up a lumpenproletariat, an important support for Napoleon's coup d'état. Corbon (1863, 34–48) tried to take some of the drama out of the contrasts. The "useless class" accounted for only a fifth of the lower classes, and many of them, like the ragpickers, were so impoverished as to be both passive and "inoffensive" (except for the sight of their poverty); they were not socialized to regular labor, produced and consumed almost nothing, and lacked intelligence, ambition, or concern for public affairs. The "vicious" group among them might be shiftless and perverse, but again had to be distinguished from the minority of truly offensive "dangerous classes" made so much of in the novels of Hugo, Sue, and Balzac and given such political prominence by analysts as diverse as Thiers and Marx. Then, as now, the question of how to define "marginality" or the "informal sector" and its economic and political role was contentious and confusing. Given the insecurity of employment, the boundary between the "street people" and the workers must have been highly porous. The large number of women trapped in poverty and forced to make a living off the street also gave a strong gender component to the actual constitution of this lowest layer in the population (and, as we shall see in section 11, compounded sexual fears with fear of revolution within the bourgeoisie). The street people – living off rather than in the city – were, however, a vital force in Parisian economy, life, and culture.

The boundary between these lower classes and the socioeconomic groups that lay above them was also confused and rendered porous by social and economic insecurity. Hugo (1976, 15) remarked, for example, on "that indeterminate layer of society, sandwiched between the middle and lower classes, which consists of riff-raff who have risen in the world and more cultivated persons who have sunk, and which combines the worst qualities of both, having neither the generosity of the worker nor the respectable honesty of the bourgeois." Many shopkeepers (whose aggregate position, we have seen, was in strong decline) were close to this margin of survival. Locked in a network of debt, they were forced to cheat, scrimp, and cut corners in order not to lose the little they had built up out of a lifetime of hard work. Ruthlessly exploitative of the people they served, they could also latch onto revolution in the hope for economic improvement. Many of the workshop owners were in a similar position. There were few large-scale factories (425 with more than five hundred workers in 1848 – see sec. 5) so the material conditions for the direct confrontation between capital and labor in production were not powerfully present. The distinction between workers and masters in the small-scale workshops that dominated Parisian industry was often ill-defined, and they worked closely enough together for bonds of sympathy and cooperation often to be as strong as daily antagonisms (Sewell 1980, 259). Both resented the new mass production techniques and the "confection" system and felt as oppressed by the power of high finance and commerce as they were angry at and envious of the idle rich, who in return, as Poulot complained, looked upon those who worked with their hands for a living with equal measures of disgust and disdain. An often radical petite bourgeoisie of small masters, threatened by new production processes and indebtedness, was much more important for Parisian political life than any class of capitalist industrialists.

Table 9. A Reconstitution of Poulot's Typology of Parisian Workers, 1870
(after Cottereau 1980)

	True Workers	*Workers*	*Mixed Workers*
Work habits and skills	Skilled workers, not always as capable as the "sublimes" — they agree to everything the owner demands in order to win promotion. They work nights and Sundays willingly and never absent themselves on Mondays. They cannot be diverted from their duties by comrades, friends, or family	No more than reasonably skilled, but willing to work nights and Sundays and never absent themselves on Mondays. They are motivated solely by monetary gain	Least skilled and incapable of supervising anyone. They simply follow the flow of the rest and will take Mondays off with them sometimes
Drink and society	Of an "exemplary sobriety." They never get drunk and control their bad humor or sadness by keeping it to themselves. They seek consolation in work. They refuse the camaraderie of the workshop and are often rejected by their workmates for that reason	They get "pickled" occasionally, but usually at home on Sundays. They rarely drink with workmates because their women would not permit it	They get drunk most often at home but also with workmates and celebrate paydays, Monday mornings, and collective events
Life before marriage	They prefer professional prostitutes rather than seduction and marry without practicing concubinage	They sleep around with laundresses, domestic servants, etc. and thereby avoid the cost of rent or having to live in with the masters. When they marry they often desert their mistresses and look for a good housekeeper from their native region	They are either celibate in rooming houses or marry a shrewish wife . . . or pass to "sublimism"
Economic condition	They are the most well off, have savings and participate in mutual benefit societies from which they try to exclude the "sublimes." Their wives are often concierges or small-scale retailers	They sometimes have some surplus money to pay off their debts. Their wives are often concierges or small-scale retailers	They have permanent difficulties making ends meet
Family life	They act as heads of households, regard their women as inferior by nature. They put strong barriers between their family and work life	The wife usually manages the household and often controls the friendships and behaviors of the husband	The wife is a rough policewoman feared by her mate. She has a tight hold on the purse strings and is the main barrier between the worker and "sublimism"
Politics	True democrats, they are against both the Empire and socialism. They share Proudhon's views on "just aspirations to ownership" and look to association between capital and labor. They read the republican opposition journals, rarely attend political meetings, and disapprove of utopian schemes and worker demagoguery. They defend the Republic and are scorned by socialists	They do not really understand socialist rhetoric and reject the more advanced ideas. They like to go to public meetings where they can be persuaded by the demagogues	They follow the ideas of the "sons of God" and read what they recommend. They go often to the public meetings and defer entirely to the ideas of the leaders

Simple "Sublimes"	True Sublimes	"Son of God" and Sublime of Sublimes
Skilled workers, capable of directing a team, but often see "ripping off" the boss as a duty. Will quit work rather than submit to strict discipline and therefore move a lot from master to master. Always take Mondays off and refuse Sunday and nightwork	Elite workers of exceptional skill and indispensable to the point where they can openly defy their bosses without fear of reprisal. Often earn a living working only 3½ days a week	The most able to direct production teams with great personal influence over others. They organize collective resistance to the bosses and dictate rhythms of work. The sublime of sublimes never submits to workshop discipline, works at home, but is the "prophet of resistance" within the work force
Lose at least one day every two weeks through drinking and are often drunk on Saturdays and Mondays, but spend Sunday with their families	Truly alcoholics. Unable to function in or out of the workplace without *eau-de-vie*	Get drunk only on feast days and with friends and family. They love to drink and discuss politics and can get drunk more on the politics than the drink
They are either celibate, living in rooming houses, or in concubinage. They marry to make sure they have children to look after them in old age	They guard their freedom jealously and live alone or in free union. They marry only to have children to care for them in old age	Play "Don Juan" until their late 30s and seduce with ease the wives and daughters of workers on their team. Marry late and to ensure children to care for them in old age, but often live in free union. Wives usually also work
In permanent economic difficulty and live from day to day. Frequently in debt, they make a virtue out of not paying off debts. The wives are usually workers also	Always in economic difficulty and lack the resources to support a family, even though the companion usually works too	Not in so great difficulty but make a point of principle not to pay off debts to retailers or landlords
If the wife has "bourgeois" attitudes there is a lot of conflict. If she does not work she has to resort to welfare to survive. Wives who work tend to share the men's attitudes toward bosses and work and express their solidarity openly	If the wife is not also a sublime, there is a permanent conflict with a lot of violent and drunken beatings and brawling. If the wife is a sublime, there is common understanding in the midst of many rows. The wife will "take to the streets" and is proud to so support children at the expense of the exploiters	The woman companion asserts more and more control as the man grows older and loses vigor
They reflect on socialism every payday and consider themselves exploited by bosses and landlords who are considered thieves. They sometimes go to public meetings, but nearly always with a "son of God"	They rarely talk politics, never read or go to public meetings, but listen very attentively to the commentaries of the "sons of God"	Read the press daily and offer profound commentary on politics to which others listen with respect. They dream of solutions to the social problem, are against Proudhon, and animate the workers' movement. Prepared for martyrdom. The sublime of sublimes is more reflective, a "man of principle" who acts as prophet and guru to the workers' movement. Prepared to do battle against the Republic, they are the most respected orators at meetings

The bourgeoisie also registered some confusions. *"La bohème"* was more than a dissipated group of youthful students, posturing and impoverished. It really comprised an assortment of dissident bourgeois, often individualistic in the extreme, seeking identities as writers, journalists, painters, artists of all kinds, who often made a virtue of their failure and mocked the rigidities of bourgeois life and culture. Courbet's café companions often bore more resemblance to Poulot's "sublime" workers than they did to any other layer of the bourgeoisie. And a large number of students (mostly of provincial origin and usually living on a meager allowance) added to the confusions of class. Skeptical, ambitious, contemptuous of tradition and even of bourgeois culture, they helped make Paris "a vast laboratory of ideas" (Zeldin 1973, 1:481) and the foyer of utopian schemes and ideologies. Relatively impoverished, they were forced into some kind of contact with the street people and some workers and knew only too well the rapacity of the shopkeeper and the loan shark. They formed the core of many a revolutionary conspiracy (the Blanquists, for example), were active in the International, and were likely to launch their own spontaneous movements of protest into the streets of the Left Bank. And they often merged with the disgruntled layers of *la bohème*. A strong dissident movement within the bourgeoisie, which sometimes encompassed relatively well-off lawyers and professionals as well as successful writers and artists, had its roots in these layers of the population.

This class structure underwent a certain transformation during the Second Empire. While data are lacking to make exact comparisons, most observers agree that if there was any change at all in the lopsided distribution of wealth, it was toward greater rather than less inequality. Important shifts occurred within the class fragments, however. Business activities (banking, commerce, limited companies) became relatively more important within the haute bourgeoisie, drawing to their side not only those state functionaries (like Haussman) bitten with the Saint-Simonian vision but also a segment of the propertied class which found diversification into stocks and shares and Parisian property more remunerative than relatively stagnant rural rents. But if traditional landed property became rather less prominent, divisions between finance, commerce, and industry became more so, while rivalries among fractions (such as that between the Rothschilds and the Pereires) assumed greater importance. The haute bourgeoisie was no less divided in 1870 than it was in 1848, but the divisions were along different lines.

There were similar important mutations within the working class. Transformations in the labor process and in industrial structure had their effects. The consolidation of large-scale industry in certain sectors such as printing, engineering, and even commerce (the large department stores) set the stage for more direct confrontation between labor and capital in the workplace, signaled by the printers' strike of 1862 and the commerce workers' strike of 1869. The reorganization and de-skilling of craft work also exacerbated the sense of external domination either by the small masters or by the innumerable intermediaries who controlled the highly fragmented production system (Corbon 1863, 83). Strikes by tailors and bronze workers in 1867 and by tanners and woodworkers in 1869 symbolized the growth of a sense of confrontation between capital and labor, even in trades where outwork and small-scale production were the rule. The prospects for craft workers to become small masters seem to have diminished as the latter were either proletarianized or forced to separate themselves out as a distinctive layer of bosses with all that this entailed.

But if Paris had a rather more conventional sort of proletariat in 1870 than it did in 1848, the working classes were still highly differentiated. "The crucible in which workers were forged was subtle," says Duveau (1946, 218); "the city created a unity out of working class life, but its traditions were as multiple as they were nuanced." And nothing was done to assuage the condition of that dead weight of an industrial reserve army and of the underemployed. Living close to the margin of existence, their numbers augmented by migration, they merged into a massive informal sector whose prospects looked increasingly dismal as Haussman shifted the state apparatus toward a more neo-Malthusian stance with respect to welfare provision. But with nearly a million people living at or below the poverty level (according to Haussman's own estimates), there were limits to how far even he could afford to go. A surge of unemployment in 1867 thus provoked the emperor into opening an extensive network of soup kitchens to feed the hungry (Kulstein 1969).

The internal composition of the middle classes also shifted. While the liberal professions, managers, and civil servants participated in the fruits of economic progress, the rentiers and pensioners had a harder time of it as rising living costs and rents in Paris eroded some of their wealth (unless, of course, they switched to more speculative investments, in which case, if Zola's *L'argent* is anywhere near accurate, they were as likely to lose their fortunes to the stock-exchange wolves as to augment their stagnant rural rents). The shopkeepers, if their diminishing hold on Parisian property is anything to go by, continued their descent into the lower middle class or even lower, except for those who found new ways of selling (like the grand department stores and the specialized boutiques, which catered to the upper classes and the flood of tourists). At the same time, the boom in banking and finance created a whole host of intermediate white collar occupations, some of which were relatively well paid.

The class structure of Paris was in full mutation during the Second Empire. By 1870 the lineaments of old patterns of class relations – traditional landowners, craft workers and artisans, shopkeepers and government employees – could still be easily discerned. But another kind of class structure was now being more firmly impressed upon it, itself confused between the state-monopoly capitalism practiced by much of the new haute bourgeoisie and the growing subsumption of all labor (craft and skilled) under capitalist relations of production and exchange in the still vast fields of small-scale Parisian industry and commerce. Economic power was shifting within these frames. The financiers consolidated their power over industry and commerce, at least in Paris, while a small group of workers began to acquire the status of a privileged aristocracy of labor within a mass of growing impoverishment. Such shifts produced abundant tensions, all of which crystallized in the fierce class struggles fought out in Paris between 1868 and 1871.

Community

Then, as now, the ideals and realities of community were hard to sort out. As far as Paris was concerned, Haussman (1890, 2:200) would have nothing to do with the ideal, and if the reality existed he was blind to it. The Parisian population was simply a "floating and agitated ocean" of immigrants, nomads, and fortune- and pleasure-seekers of all types (not only workers but also students, lawyers, merchants, etc.) who could not possibly acquire any stable or loyal sense of community. Paris was simply the national capital, "centralization itself," and had to be treated as such. Haussman was not alone in this view. Many in the haute bourgeoisie, from Thiers to Rothschild, thought of Paris only as "the geographical key to a national power struggle" whose internal agitations and propensity for revolution disqualified it for consideration as a genuine community of any standing (Greenberg 1971, 80). Yet many who fought and died in the siege of Paris and in the Paris Commune did so out of some fierce sense of loyalty to the city. Like Courbet, they defended their participation in the Commune with the simple argument that Paris was their homeland and that their community deserved at least that modicum of freedom accorded to others (Rougerie 1965, 75). And it would be hard to read the *Paris Guide of 1867,* the collective work of some 125 of the city's most prestigious authors, without succumbing to the powerful imagery of a city to which many confessed a passionate and abiding loyalty. But the *Guide* also tells us how many Parisians conceived of community on a smaller scale of neighborhoods, *quartiers,* and even the new arrondissements created only seven years before. That kind of loyalty was also important. During the Commune, many preferred to defend their quarters rather than the city walls, thus giving the forces of reaction surprisingly easy access to the city.

"Community" means different things to different people. It is hard not to impose meanings and so do violence to the ways in which people felt and acted. Haussman's judgments, for example, were based on a comparison with a rural image of community. He knew all too well that the "community of money" prevailed in Paris, rather than the tight network of interpersonal relations that characterized much of rural life. Yet while Haussman denied the possibility of community of one sort, he strove to implant another, founded in the glory of Empire and oozing with symbols of authority, benevolence, power, and progress, to which he hoped the "nomads" of Paris would rally. He used the public works (their monumentalism in particular); the universal expositions; the grand galas, fêtes, and fireworks; the pomp and circumstance of royal visits and court life; and all the trappings of what became known as the *fête imperiale* to construct a sense of community compatible with authoritarian rule, free-market capitalism, and the new international order. Haussman tried, in short, to sell a new and more modern conception of community in which the power of money was celebrated as spectacle and display on the *grands boulevards,* in the *grands magasins,* in the cafés and at the races, and above all in those spectacular "celebrations of the commodity fetish," the *expositions universelles* (Benjamin 1973). No matter that some found it hollow and superficial, a construction to be revolted against during the Commune, as Gaillard (1977, 231) asserts. It was a remarkable attempt, and much of the population evidently bought it, not only for the Second Empire but also well beyond. In his decentralization of functions within the arrondissements and in the symbolism with which he invested them (the new *mairies,* for example), he also tried to forge local loyalties, albeit within a hierarchical system of control. Again, he was surprisingly successful. Loyalties to the new arrondissements built quickly and have lasted as a powerful force to this day. They were vital during the Commune, perhaps since the arrondissements were the units of National Guard enrollment, and the latter, perhaps not by accident, turned out to be the great agent of direct, local democracy. Haussman's impositions from above became the means of expression of grass-roots democracy from below.

That sentiment of direct, local democracy had deep historical roots. It was expressed in the Parisian sections of 1789 and in the political clubs of 1848, as well as in the manner of organizing public meetings after 1868. There was strong continuity in this political culture, which saw local community and democracy as integral to each other. That ideology carried over to the economic sphere, where Proudhon's ideas on mutualism, cooperation, feder-ation, and free association had a great deal of credibility. But Proudhon emerged as such an influential thinker precisely because he articulated that sense of community through economic organization which appealed so strongly to Parisian craft workers and small owners. And Paris had long been divided into distinctive *quartiers,* urban villages, each with its own distinctive qualities of population, forms of economic activity, and even styles of life. The flood of immigrants often had their distinctive "receiving areas" within the city based upon their place of origin or their trade, while the "nomads" of Paris seem often to have used their kinship networks as guides to the city's labyrinths.

There is a thesis, held in rather different versions by writers as diverse as Lefebvre (1974) and Gaillard (1977), that Haussman's transformations, land speculation, and imperial rule disrupted the traditional sense of community and failed to put anything solid in its place. Others, such as Greenberg (1971), argue that the administration's refusal of any measure of self-governance that would give political expression to the sense of community was the major thorn in Parisians' side. The Commune can then be interpreted as an attempt by an alliance of classes to recapture the sense of community that had been lost, to reappropriate the central city space from which they had been expelled, and to reassert their rights as citizens of Paris.

The thesis is not implausible, but it needs considerable nuancing to make it stick. It is, for example, fanciful to argue that the notion of community had been more stable and solidly implanted in 1848. There was sufficient disarray then in evidence for the thesis of Haussman's disruptions to be easily dismissed as a romanticized retrospective reconstruction. What is clearer is that the realities and ideologies of the construction of community underwent a dramatic transformation in Second Empire Paris. And the same processes that were transforming class relations were having equally powerful impacts upon community. The community of money (see Chap. 1) was simply dissolving and overpowering all other bonds of social solidarity.

Haussman's urbanization was conceived on a new and grander spatial scale. He simultaneously linked communities that had formerly been isolated from each other. At the same time, this linking allowed such communities specialized roles within the urban matrix. Spatial specialization in social reproduction became more significant, just as did spatial specialization in production and service provision. True, Haussman's programs also wiped out some communities (Ile de la Cité, for example), punched gaping holes through others, and sponsored much gentrification, dislocation, and removal (see fig. 13). This provoked a great deal of nostalgia for a lost past on the part of all social classes, whether directly affected or not. Nadar, a photographer, confessed it made him feel a stranger in what should have been his own country. "They have destroyed everything, even memory," he lamented (*Paris Guide of 1867,* 170). But however great the sense of loss or the "grieving for a lost home" (Fried 1963) on the part of the many displaced, collective memories in practice were surprisingly short and human adjustment rather rapid. Chevalier (1973, 300) notes how memories and images of the old Ile de la Cité were eradicated almost instantaneously after its destruction. The loss of community, which many bourgeois observers lamented, probably was generated primarily by the breakdown of traditional systems of social control consequent upon rapid population growth, increased residential segregation, and the failure of social provision (everything from churches to schools) to keep up with the rapid reorganization of the space of social reproduction. Haussman's neo-Malthusianism with regard to social welfare plus the insistence upon authoritarian rule rather than municipal self-government undoubtedly exacerbated the dangers. The problem was not that Belleville was not a community but that it became the sort of community which the bourgeoisie feared, which the police could not penetrate, which the government could not regulate, where the popular classes, with all their unruly passions and political resentments, held the upper hand. This is what truly lay behind the prefect of police's complaint of 1855:

The circumstances which compel workers to move out of the center of Paris have generally, it is pointed out, had a deplorable effect on their behavior and morality. In the old days they used to live on the upper floors of buildings whose lower floors were occupied by the families of businessmen and other fairly well-to-do persons. A species of solidarity grew up among the tenants of a single building. Neighbors helped each other in small ways. When sick or unemployed, the workers might find a great deal of help, while on the other hand, a sort of human respect imbued working class habits with a certain regularity. Having moved north of the Saint Martin canal or even beyond the barrières, the workers now live where there are no bourgeois families and are thus deprived of their assistance at the same time as they are emancipated from the curb on them previously exercised by neighbors of this kind. (quoted in Chevalier 1973, 198–99)

The growth and transformation of industry, commerce, and finance; immigration and suburbanization; the breakdown of controls in the labor market and the apprenticeship system; the transformation of land and property markets; growing spatial segregation and specialization of *quartiers* (of commerce, craft work, working-class reproduction, etc.); reorganization of housing, social welfare provision, and education – all of these taken together under the overwhelming power of the money calculus promoted vital shifts in the meaning and experience of community. Whatever the sense of community had been in 1848, it was radically changed, but no less coherent or viable (as the Commune was to prove), in 1870. Let us probe these differences a little more deeply.

The Community of Class and the Class of Community

The workers' movement of June 1848 was crushed by a National Guard drawn from over three hundred provincial centers. The bourgeoisie who moved within the commercial orbit of Paris had the advantage of "much better communications over long distances than the working class, which possessed strong local solidarity but little capacity for regional or national action" (Margadant 1982, 106). The bourgeoisie used its far-flung spatial network of commercial contacts to preserve its economic and political power.

Behind this incident lies a problem and a principle of some importance. Does "community" entail a territorial coherence – and if so, how are boundaries fixed? Or can "community" mean simply a community of interest without regard to particular spatial boundaries? What we see, in effect, is the bourgeoisie defining a community of class interest sprawled over space. This was, for example, the secret of Rothschild's success (with his far-flung family network of correspondents in the different national capitals). But armed with the lessons of 1848 and following their class interests, the haute bourgeoisie in business and administration (such as Pereire, Thiers, and Haussman) increasingly thought and acted along such lines. Thiers mobilized to repress the Commune in exactly the same way as had been done in 1848. The bourgeoisie had discovered that it could use its superior command over space to crush class movements of no matter how intense local solidarity (a principle of even greater significance today, as the international bankers confront a socialist Nicaragua, and as they undermined a socialist Chile).

The workers were also pressed to redefine community in terms of class and space. Their movement of 1848 had been marked by xenophobia against foreign workers coupled with intense sympathy for oppressed peoples everywhere. The new space relations and changing international division of labor prompted writers like Corbon (1863, 102) to argue that the labor question now had no local solution but had to be looked at from a European perspective, at least. The problem was then to make this internationalist perspective compatible with the mutualist and corporatist sentiments that infused the working-class tradition. The tradition of *compagnonnage* and the *tour de France* provided some kind of basis for thinking about new kinds of worker organization which could command space in a fashion comparable to the bourgeoisie. This was the problem the International faced up to. The effect was to create an enormous and uncontrollable panic within the ranks of the bourgeoisie, precisely because the International set out to define a community of class "across all provinces, industrial centers and states" (Reybaud 1869) and so match the power the bourgeoisie had found so effective in 1848. In practice the bourgeoisie trembled without good reason. The relative weakness of the International's connections, coupled with the powerful residue of a highly localized mutualism, became all too apparent in the War of 1870 and the Commune. In contrast, the creation of the city-wide Fédération des Chambres Syndicales Ouvrières in 1869 – an umbrella organization (under Varlin's leadership) for the newly legalized trade unions – helped build a worker perspective on labor questions on a scale consistent with Haussman's urbanization. This kind of organization synthesized powerful traditions of localized mutualism and direct democracy into city-wide strategies of class struggle over the labor process and conditions of employment. This was to be part of that volatile mix that gave the Commune so much of its force.

The space over which community was defined altered as the scale of urbanization changed and spatial barriers were reduced. But it also shifted in response to new class configurations and struggles in which the participants learned that control over space and spatial networks was a source of social power (see Chap. 1). At this point the evolutions of class and community intersected to create new and intriguing possibilities and configurations.

The new communities of class were paralled by new forms of the class of community. The social space of Paris had always been segregated. The glitter and affluence of the center had long contrasted with the dreary impoverishment of the suburbs (Copping 1858, 5); the predominantly bourgeois west, with the working-class east; the progressive Right Bank, with the traditionalist though student-ridden Left. Within this overall pattern there had been considerable spatial mixing. Dismal slums intermingled with opulent town houses; craft workers and artisans mingled with aristocratic residences on the Left Bank and in the Marais; and the celebrated vertical segregation (rich bourgeois on the second floor above the boutique and worker families in the garret) did bring some social contact between the classes. Masters and employees in industry and commerce had also traditionally lived close to each other.

While it would be untrue to say that Haussman created spatial segregation in the city, his works coupled with the land-use sorting effect of rent in the context of changed land and property markets did definitely produce a greater degree of spatial segregation, much of it based on class distinctions. Slum removal and building speculation consolidated bourgeois quarters to the west, while the separate system of land development in the northern and eastern peripheries (sec. 3) produced tracts of low-income housing unrelieved by any intermingling with the upper classes. Land-use competition also consolidated the business and financial quarters, while industrial and commercial activities also tended toward a tighter spatial clustering in selected areas of the center – printing on the Left Bank, metal working on the inner northeast, leather and skins around Arts et Métiers, ready-to-wear clothing just off the *grands boulevards*. And each type of employment quarter often gave social shape to the surrounding residential quarters – the concentrations of white collar employees (see fig. 9) to the north of the business center, the craft workers to the northeast center, the printers and bookbinders (a very militant group) on the Left Bank. Zones and wedges, centers and peripheries, and even the fine mesh of quarters were much more clearly class-determined or occupationally defined in 1870 than they had been in 1848. Though this had much to do with the spatial scale of the process that Haussman unleashed, it was also a reflection of fundamental transformations of the labor process, the industrial structure, and class relations. The consolidation of commercial and financial power, the rising affluence of certain segments of the haute and middle bourgeoisie, the growing separation of workers and masters, and increasing specialization in the division of labor were all registered in the production of new communities of class. Old patterns could still be discerned – the intermingling on the Left Bank was as confused as ever – but it was now overlaid with a fiercer and more definite structuring of the spaces of social reproduction. Spatial organization and the sense of community that went with it were caught up the processes of reproduction of class configurations. The social landscape of Paris was transformed accordingly.

X. SCIENCE AND SENTIMENT, MODERNITY AND TRADITION

Upon the different forms of property, upon the social conditions of existence,
rises an entire superstructure of distinct and peculiarly formed sentiments,
illusions, modes of thought and views of life.

– Marx

To try to peer inside consciousness is ever a perilous exercise. Yet something has to be said about the hopes and dreams, the fears and imaginings that inspired people to action. But how to reconstruct the thoughts and feelings of Parisians of more than a century ago? To be sure, there is a vast literary record (popular and erudite), which, when complemented by cartoons, paintings, sculpture, architecture, engineering, and the like, tells us how at least some people felt, thought, and acted. Yet many left no such tangible mark. The mass of the population remains mute. It takes a careful study of language, words, gestures, popular songs, theater, and mass publications (with titles like *La science pour tous, Le Roger Bontemps, La semaine des enfants*) to get even a fragmentary sense of popular thought and culture (Rifkin 1979).

The Second Empire had the reputation of being an age of positivism. Yet, by modern standards, it was a curious kind of positivism, beset by doubt, ambiguity, and tension. Thinkers were "attempting in differing ways and to differing extents to reconcile aspirations and convictions that [were] incompatible" (Charlton 1959, 2). What was true for the intelligentsia, the artists, and the academicians was also profoundly true for the craft workers. The latter have an impassioned concern for progress, only to resist its applications in the labor process: "Hence the worker who reads, writes, has the spirit of a poet, who has great material and spiritual aspirations, the devotee of progress, becomes, in fact, a reactionary, retrograde and obscurantist, when it comes to his own trade" (Corbon 1863, 83). For the craft workers, of course, their art was their science and their de-skilling was no sign of progress, as leaders like Varlin were ceaselessly to complain.

Since Paris was the hearth of intellectual ferment, not only for the cream of the country's intelligentsia, but also for the "organic intellectuals" of the working class, it experienced these tensions and ambiguities with double force. There were also innumerable intersections in which the sense of increasing prostitution of the craft worker to the money power of capitalism was mirrored by the submission of the skills of writer and artist to the dictates of the market. Here was the unity of experience that put *la bohème* on the side of craft workers in revolution.

Most were struck by the virtues of science. The achievements of medicine had particular importance. Not only were the medical students often in the avant-garde in the political and scientific movements of the 1860s, but the imagery of the cool dissection of something as personal as the human body became a paradigm of what science was all about. That imagery was important. Science was not so much a method as an attitude given to the struggle to demystify things, to penetrate and dissect their inner essence. Such an attitude even underlay the powerful movement toward "art for art's sake." Not only scientists but writers, poets, economists, artists, historians, and philosophers could all aspire to science. "It was free of conventional morality and of any didactive motive; it was 'pure' in the sense they wished their art to be 'pure,' [and] its objectivity and impartiality resembled their determination to avoid sentimentality and an open display of personal feeling" (Charlton 1959, 10). It was every writer's ambition, as Sainte-Beuve wrote in praise of *Madame Bovary,* to wield "the pen as others wield the scalpel." Flaubert (1982, 25), the son of a doctor, was fascinated by the dissection of cadavers all his life. "It's a strange thing, the way I'm attracted by medical studies," he wrote, but "that's the way the intellectual wind is blowing nowadays." Delacroix (1980, 96) was moved to observe that "science, as demonstrated by a man like Chopin is art itself . . . *pure reason embellished by genius.*" Many artists saw themselves as no different from Pasteur, who was then penetrating the mysteries of how fermentation took place in what they saw as an exactly analogous spirit.

Others, sensing the widening gap, sought to close it. "The time is not far off," wrote Baudelaire, "when it will be understood that any literature which refuses to march fraternally between science and philosophy is a homicidal, suicidal literature" (cited in Klein 1967, 86). Hugo (1976, 1047) agreed. "It is through science that we shall realize that sublime vision of poets; social beauty. . . . At the stage which civilization has reached, the exact is a necessary element in what is splendid, and artistic feeling is not only served but completed by the scientific approach; the dream must know how to calculate." Craft workers like Varlin would surely have agreed; that was, after all, why they set out to educate themselves (Foulon 1934). The historian Michelet (1981, 350) was even more programmatic. He sought "the poetry of truth, purity itself, [that] which penetrates the real to find its essence . . . and so breaks the foolish barrier which separates the literature of liberty from that of science."

Confusions and ambiguities arose because few were ready to separate science from sentiment. While a scientific posture helped liberate thinkers from the traps of romanticism, utopianism, and, above all, from the mysticism of received religion, it did not absolve them from considering the directions of social progress and the relation to tradition. "A little science takes you away from religion; a lot brings you back to it," said Flaubert (1976, 325). Auguste Comte led the way. The founder of an abstract, systematic, and theoretical positivism in the 1820s converted to a more humanistic strain of thought in the 1840s. From 1849 until his death in 1856, tract after tract dedicated to the foundation of positivist churches of humanity issued forth from his house close by the place Sorbonne. Nor did those concerned with constructing a science of society want to separate fact entirely from value. Prior to 1848, social science had been divided between the grand systematizers like Comte, Saint Simon, and Fourier, whose abstractions and speculations might inspire although they had little to do with the social relations of the time, and the empiricists, who confined themselves to moving but Malthusian descriptions of the awful pathologies and depravities to which the poor were exposed and the dangerous classes prone. Neither tactic yielded incisive social science. It took Proudhon to make the connection between capitalism, pauperism, and crime (Chevalier 1973, 269). The medical students who later formed the core of the Blanquist movement likewise used their materialist scalpels to great effect in the dissection of society and its ills. But other, less encouraging trends could also be observed. Le Play combined positivism with empiricism to construct a new kind of social science used exclusively to support the cause of Catholicism, while the political economists were no less assiduous in shaping a social science to political ends.

These confused cross-currents are hard to understand without reference to the complex evolution of class relations and alliances which produced 1848, the conservative Republic, and the Empire. In the revolution of 1848, progressive social democrats were joined on the barricades by a motley assortment of *la bohème* (Courbet and Baudelaire, for example), romantics (Lamartine, George Sand), utopian socialists (Cabet, Blanc) and Jacobins (Blanqui, Delescluze), as well as by an equally motley assortment of craft workers, students, street people, prostitutes, and other representatives of the dangerous classes. The bitter days of June shattered that alliance in all manner of ways. Whatever their actual role may have been, the powerful ideological stamp that the romantics and the socialist utopians put upon the rhetoric of 1848 was totally discredited with the June repression. The poet Lamartine, initially one of the most popular heroes of the revolution, received fewer than eighteen thousand votes out of the more than seven million cast for president in December 1848. The people had evidently decided, "We've had enough poetry," and "poets cannot cope" (Flaubert 1964, 359; Fortescue 1983). Like many others, Proudhon found the demagoguery and rhetoric vapid and utopian, totally lacking in realism or practicality. Yet romanticism and utopianism had been the first line of defense against the subordination of all modes of thought to religion. Some other means of defense and protest had to be found. Zeldin (1963, 39) puts the transformation this way:

Utopianism was now, generally speaking, displaced by positivism; the mystic belief in the virtue of the people and hopes for a spiritual regeneration gave way to a more guarded pessimism about mankind. Men began to look on the world in a different way, for splendid illusions had been shattered before their eyes, and their very style of talking and writing changed.

Herein lies the significance of Courbet's sudden breakthrough into realism (called "socialist" by many) in art, Baudelaire's fierce and uncompromising embrace of a modernity given a much more tragic dimension by the violence of 1848, and Proudhon's initial confusion followed by total rejection of utopian schemes. Courbet, Baudelaire, and Proudhon could, and did, make common cause (Clark 1973a, 1973b; and Rubin 1980). Their disillusionment with romanticism and utopianism was typical of a social response to 1848 that looked to realism and practical science as means to liberate human sentiments. They may have remained romantics at heart, but they were romantics armed with scalpels, ready to shelter from the authoritarianism of religion and Empire behind the shield of positivism and detached science. The respectable bourgeoisie drew a similar sort of conclusion, though for quite different reasons. Professional schools should be organized, wrote one, "to train competent workers, foremen, managers of factories" for the "combats of production" instead of producing "unemployed *bacheliers* embittered by their impotence, born petititoners of every public office, disturbing the state by their pretensions" (Gildea 1983, 321).

It would seem that the Empire, with its concerns for industrial and social progress, would have welcomed this turn to realism and science, would have encouraged and coopted it. And on the surface it did just that, through promotion of universal expositions dedicated to lauding new technologies, the establishment of worker commissions to examine the fruits and applications of technological change, and the like. Yet the Second Empire did nothing to reverse and, until 1864, even exacerbated what most commentators agree was a serious decline of French science from its pinnacle early in the century into relative mediocrity by the end (Fox and Weisz 1980; Weisz 1983). Little was done to support research – Pasteur, for example, had a hard time obtaining funds (Williams 1965) – while government policies (denying students free speech on political questions, for example) often threw the universities into such turmoil that student protests were forced into the streets or into underground conspiracies like the Blanquist. Science and positivism, free-thought and materialism, became forms of protest against the mysticism of religion and the censorious authoritarianism of Empire.

The contradictions in imperial policy also have to be understood in terms of the shaky class alliance upon which Louis Napoleon had to rest his power. It was, indeed, his genius and misfortune that he sought the implantation of modernity in the name of tradition, that he used the authoritarianism of Empire to champion the freedoms and liberties of private capital accumulation. He could occupy such an odd niche in history precisely because the instability of class relations in 1848 gave him the chance to rally the disillusioned and fearful of all classes around a legend that promised stability, security, and, perhaps, national glory. Yet he knew he had to move forward. "March at the head of the ideas of your century," he wrote, "and those ideas follow and support you. March behind them and they drag you after them. March against them, and they overthrow you" (cited in Zeldin 1958, 101). The problem, however, was that Napoleon had to seek support from a Catholic church that was reactionary and uncultured at the base and led by a pope who totally rejected reconciliation with "progress, liberalism and modern civilization" (Green 1965, chap. 3). To be sure, there were progressive Catholics, unloved by Rome, who, like Montalembert, supported the coup d'état but later so deplored the alliance with Empire that they were hauled before the public prosecutor. But the net effect, at least until the breakdown of the alliance with Catholicism in the 1860s, was to surrender much of education to those who thought of it solely as a means to social control rather than as the cutting edge of social progress (sec. 8). That, combined with censorship, transformed the free-thought movement in the universities into the cutting edge of criticism of Empire.

The Empire also was vulnerable because it straddled uncomfortably the break between modernity and tradition. It sought social and technological progress and therefore had to confront in thought as well as in action the power of traditional classes and conceptions (religion, monarchical authority, and artisanal pride). The Empire was also founded on legend; but the legend could not bear too close inspection. There were two principal embarrassments: the manner of the First Empire's emergence from the First Republic and its ultimate collapse. The censors sought to impose a tactful silence on such matters, banning popular performances and plays (even one by Alexander Dumas) that referred to them (Rifkin 1979). Victor Hugo, thundering against the iniquities of Napoleon *le petit* from the safety of exile, took up the cudgels. He inserted a brilliant but, from the standpoint of plot, quite gratuitous description of the defeat at Waterloo into *Les miserables* (302–18), editorializing as he did so that for Napoleon I to have won at Waterloo "would have been counter to the tide of the nineteenth century," that it would have been "fatal to civilization" to have "so large a world contained within the mind of a single man," and that "a great man had to disappear in order that a great century might be born." *Les miserables* was "in everyone's hands" in the Paris of 1862, and Hugo's message was surely not lost on his readers (Tchernoff 1906, 517).

This kind of exploration of tradition was not new. The grapplings of historians and writers like Michelet and Lamartine with the meaning of the French Revolution had played a major role in the politics of the 1840s. Republicans used history and tradition after 1851 to make political points. They were as much concerned to invent tradition as to represent it. This is not to accuse them of distortion, but of reading the historical record in such a way as to mobilize tradition to a particular political purpose. It was almost as if the dead weight of tradition were such that social progress had to depend on its evocation, even when it did not weigh "like a nightmare on the brain of the living," as Marx puts it in the *Eighteenth Brumaire* (15). In this respect, artists, poets, novelists, and historians made common cause. Many of Manet's paintings of the Second Empire period, for example, portray modern life through the overt recreation of classical themes (he took the controversial *Olympia* of 1863 directly from Titian's *Venus d'Urbino*). He did so, Fried (1969) suggests, in a way that echoed Michelet's political and republican tracts of 1846–48 while answering Baudelaire's (1981) plea for an art that represented the heroism of modern life.

The experience of craft workers was no different. Their resistance had forced much of Parisian industry to all manner of adaptations (sec. 5). They had defended their work and their life-style fiercely and had used corporatist tactics to do so (sec. 11). When the emperor invited them to inspect the virtues of technological progress, they responded with a defense of craft traditions. Yet their power was being eroded and sometimes swamped by competition and technological change within the new international division of labor. This posed enormous problems for the "organic intellectuals" of the working-class movement as well as for revolutionary socialists who sought a path to the future but had to do so on the basis of fiercely held ideological traditions (stemming, in the Blanquist case, from the French Revolution). And the mass in-migration of often unskilled workers (sec. 6) clinging to bastardized rural traditions and parochialist perspectives did not help matters, though the coup d'état had revealed strong patterns of rural revolutionary consciousness and resistance, thus reimporting to Paris a revolutionary sentiment, which Paris had so often prided itself as exporting to a backward countryside. The problem, however, was that the new material circumstances and class relations in Parisian industry and commerce required a line of political analysis and action for which there was no tradition. The International, which began rooted in mutualist and corporatist traditions, had to invent a new tradition to deal with the class struggles of 1868–71 (sec. 11). It was, sadly, more successful after the martyrdom of many of its members in 1871 than before. Consciousness is as much rooted in the past and its interpretations as in the present. Flaubert (1979b, 134) caught the dilemma only too well: "To accomplish something lasting, one must have a solid foundation. The thought of the future torments us, and the past is holding us back. That is why the present is slipping from our grasp."

That apostle of modernity, Baudelaire, faced this dilemma all his life, careening from side to side with the same incoherence as he slid from one side of the barricades to the other (Klein 1967; Clark 1973a). He signaled rejection of tradition in his *Salon of 1846*, urging artists to explore the "epic qualities of modern life," for "our age is no less rich than ancient times in sublime themes." Parisian life is "rich in poetic and wonderful subjects," such as "scenes of high life and of the thousands of uprooted lives that haunt the underworld of a great city, criminals and prostitutes." "The marvelous envelops and saturates us like the atmosphere; but we fail to see it." Yet he dedicated his work to the bourgeoisie, invoking an almost Saint-Simonian vision of their heroism: "You have entered into partnership, formed companies, issued loans, to realize the idea of the future in all its diverse forms." Every Saint-Simonian, it was said, combined the qualities of visionary poet and astute businessman. Baudelaire, himself in struggle against tradition and the "aristocrats of thought," proposed an alliance with those seeking to overthrow traditional class power. Both could nourish the other until "supreme harmony is ours." (Baudelaire 1981, 104–7).

The seeds of dissolution of that alliance were already present in Baudelaire's first representation. How, after all, could artists depict the heroism in those "uprooted lives" in ways not offensive to bourgeois taste? And from what perspective? Baudelaire would be torn for the rest of his life between the stances of *flâneur* and dandy, a disengaged and cynical voyeur, and man of the people who enters into the life of his subjects with passion. In 1846 that tension was only implicit; but 1848 changed all that. He fought on the side of the insurgents in February and June and perhaps also in May. He was horrified by the betrayal by the bourgeoisie but also by the empty rhetoric of romanticism and utopianism. He took Proudhon as hero for a while, then linked up with Courbet, attracted by the realism of both men. He later wrote, "1848 was charming only through an excess of the ridiculous." He also learned the truth of the Maoist adage, "You cannot make an omelet without breaking eggs." He recorded his "wild excitement" and his "natural" and "legitimate" "pleasure in destruction." But he could not stand the product. Compared to that, even return to the secure power of tradition appeared preferable. In between the high points of revolution he helped edit reactionary newspapers, later writing, "There is no form of rational and assured government save an aristocracy." After his "fury" at the coup d'état, he tried to withdraw from politics into pessimism and cynicism, only to confess his addiction when the pulse of revolution began to throb. And there is more than a hint of Blanquist sentiment in the lines "The Revolution and the Cult of Reason confirm the doctrine of sacrifice" (Baudelaire 1983b, 56–74; Klein 1967; Clark 1973a).

There is, then, a contradiction in Baudelaire's sense of modernity after the bittersweet experience of "creative destruction" on the barricades of 1848. Tradition has to be overthrown, with violence if necessary, in order to grapple with the present and create the future. But the loss of tradition wrenches away the sheet anchors of our understanding and leaves us drifting, powerless. The aim of the artist, he wrote in 1860, is "to extract from fashion the poetry that resides in its historical envelope," to understand modernity as "the transient, the fleeting, the contingent" as against the other half of art, "the eternal and immovable." The fear, he says, in a passage that echoes Flaubert's dilemma, is "of not going fast enough, of letting the spectre escape before the synthesis has been extracted and taken possession of" (Baudelaire 1981, 402–8). But all that rush leaves behind a great deal of human wreckage. "The thousand uprooted lives" cannot be ignored. There is an eloquent and beautiful evocation of that in the story of "The Old Clown" in *Paris Spleen* (25–27). Paris there becomes a vast theater, a gaudy evocation of the *fête impériale*. "Everywhere joy, money-making, debauchery; everywhere the assurance of tomorrow's daily bread; everywhere frenetic outbursts of vitality." But among the jugglers and clowns, the "dust, shouts, joy, tumult," Baudelaire sees "a pitiful old clown, bent, decrepit, the ruin of a man" in a cabin "more miserable than that of the lowest savage." The absoluteness of his misery is "made all the more horrible by being tricked out in comic rags." The clown "was mute and motionless. He had given up, he had abdicated. His fate was sealed." The author feels "the terrible hand of hysteria" gripping his throat, and "rebellious tears that would not fall" blur his sight. He wants to leave money, but the motion of the crowd (often a symbol of progress for Baudelaire) sweeps him away. Looking back, he says to himself, "I have just seen the prototype of the old writer who has been the brilliant entertainer of the generation he has outlived, the old poet without friends, without family, without children, degraded by poverty and the ingratitude of the public, and to whose booth the fickle world no longer cares to come." Would the craft worker who, as Corbon put it, has "the spirit of a poet" feel any less?

The prose poem "Loss of a Halo" calls for similar commentary (Benjamin 1973, 152–54; Wohlfarth 1970; Berman 1982). Baudelaire (1947, 94) records a conversation between a poet and a friend who surprise each other in some place of ill repute. The poet explains that, terrified of horses and vehicles, he hurried across the boulevard, "splashing through the mud, in the midst of seething chaos, with death galloping at me from every side." A sudden move caused his halo to slip off his head and fall into "the mire of the macadam." Too frightened to pick it up, he leaves it there but finds he enjoys its loss because he can now "go about incognito, be as low as I please and indulge in debauch like ordinary mortals." Besides, he takes a certain delight in the thought that "some bad poet" might pick it up and put it on.

Much has been said about "Loss of a Halo." Wohlfarth (1970) records the "shock of recognition" in the image when juxtaposed with the *Communist Manifesto*: "The bourgeoisie has stripped of its halo every occupation hitherto honored and looked up to with reverent awe." Capitalism "has converted the physician, the lawyer, the priest, the poet, the man of science, into its paid wage laborers." The poem signifies, to Wohlfarth, "the writer's plight amidst the blind, cut-throat *laissez-faire* of the capitalistic city: the traffic reduces the poet in his traditional guise to obsolescence and confronts him with the alternative of saving his skin or his halo." What better way to summarize the dilemma of the craft workers in the revolution of 1848? Berman (1982, 155–64) takes interpretation in another direction. He focuses on the traffic:

The archetypal modern man, as we see him here, is a pedestrian thrown into the maelstrom of modern city traffic, a man alone contending against an agglomeration of mass and energy that is heavy, fast and lethal. The burgeoning street and boulevard traffic knows no spatial or temporal bounds, spills over into every urban space, imposes its tempo on everybody's time, transforms the whole modern environment into "moving chaos." . . . This makes the boulevard a perfect symbol of capitalism's inner contradictions: rationality in each individual capitalist unit leading to anarchic rationality in the social system that brings all these units together.

But those who are willing to throw themselves into this maelstrom, to lose their halo, acquire a new kind of power and freedom. Baudelaire, says Berman, "wants works of art that will be born in the midst of the traffic, that will spring from its anarchic energy . . . so that 'Loss of a Halo' turns out to be a declaration of something gained." Only a bad poet will try to pick up the halo of tradition and put it on. And behind that experience Berman sees

Haussman, that archetype of the capitalist developer, the archangel of creative destruction. The poem is itself a creative product of the transformation of Paris.

Wohlfarth sees it differently. It is no accident that the poet ends up in a place of ill repute. Here "Baudelaire foresees the increasing commercialization of bourgeois society as a cold orgy of self-prostitution." That image also echoes Marx on the degradation of labor under capitalism, as well as his thoughts on the penetration of money relations into social life: "Universal prostitution appears as a necessary phase in the development of the social character of personal talents, capacities, abilities, activities" (1973, 163). Baudelaire's fascination with the prostitute – simultaneously commodity and person through whom money seems to flow in the very act of sex – and the dissolution of any other sense of community save that defined by the circulation of money (see Chap. 1) is beautifully captured in his "Crépuscule du soir":

> Against the lamplight, whose shivering is the wind's,
> Prostitution spreads its light and life in the streets:
> Like an anthill opening its issue it penetrates
> Mysteriously everywhere by its own occult route;
> Like an enemy mining the foundations of a fort,
> Or a worm in an apple, eating what all should eat,
> It circulates securely in the city's clogged heart.
> (translated by David Paul, cited in Benjamin 1973, 57)

The city itself has become prostituted to the circulation of money and capital. Or, as Wohlfarth concludes, the place of ill repute is the city itself, an old whore to whom the poet "like old lecher to old mistress goes," as the Epilogue to *Paris Spleen* puts it. Having dubbed the city "brothel and hospital, prison, purgatory, hell," Baudelaire declares: "Infamous City, I adore you."

How do representations of Paris fit into such complex molds? Haussman was not above the struggle between modernity and tradition, science and sentiment. Subsequently lauded or condemned as the apostle of modernity in urban planning, he could do what he did in part because of his deep claims upon tradition. "If Voltaire could enjoy the spectacle of Paris today, surpassing as it does all his wishes," he wrote in his *Memoires* (533), "he would not understand why . . . Parisians, his sons, the heirs of his fine spirit, have attackd it, criticized it and fettered it." He appealed directly to the tradition of Enlightenment rationality and even more particularly to the expressed desire of writers as diverse as Voltaire, Diderot, Rousseau, and Saint-Simon, and even to socialists like Louis Blanc and Fourier, to impose rationality and order upon the chaotic anarchy of a recalcitrant city. The Haussmanization of Paris, suggests Vidler (1978), carried the "techniques of rationalist analysis and the formal instruments of the *ancien régime,* as refurbished by the First Empire and its institutions, to their logical extreme." It was, I suspect, in part because of these roots in tradition that Haussman's works gained the acceptance they did. Several authors in the *Paris Guide of 1867* praised the works in exactly these terms.

But Paris had also long been dubbed by many a sick city. Haussman could also appear in the guise of surgeon:

After the prolonged pathology, the drawn-out agony of the patient, the body of Paris, was to be delivered of its illnesses, its cancers, and epidemics once and for all by the total act of surgery. "Cutting" and "piercing" were the adjectives used to describe the operation; where the terrain was particularly obstructed a "disembowelling" had to be performed in order that arteries be reconstituted and flows reinstated. The metaphors were repeated again and again by the pathologists, the surgeons, and even by their critics, becoming so firmly embedded in the unconscious analogies of urban planning that from that time the metaphor and the scientific nature of the action were confused and fused. (Vidler 1978, 91)

The metaphors of "hygienic science" and "surgery" were powerful and appealing, given the imagery of the time. Zola recaptures them to great effect in *La curée.* Fortunately, Haussman had more than such metaphors to guide him. He also saw the city dispassionately as an artifact that could be understood and shaped according to natural scientific principles and techniques. The towers from which the triangulation of Paris proceeded symbolized a new spatial perspective on the city as a whole, as did his attachment to the geometry of the straight line and the accuracy of leveling to engineer the flows of water and sewage. The science he put to work was exact, brilliant, and demanding; "the dream" of Voltaire and Diderot had learned to calculate. But there was ample room for sentiment – from elaborate street furnishings (benches, gas lights, kiosks) and monuments and fountains (like that in the place Saint-Michel) to the widespread planting of trees along the boulevards and the construction of gothic grottoes in the parks, everything reimported romance into the details of a grand design that spelled out the twin ideals of Enlightenment rationality and imperial authority. The modernity that Haussman created was powerfully rooted in tradition. Even the necessity of creative destruction had its precedents in the revolutionary spirit (fig. 13). Wrote About in the *Paris Guide of 1867* (33), "Like the great destroyers of the eighteenth century who made a *tabula rasa* of the human spirit, I applaud and admire this creative destruction." While Haussman would never evoke it, the creative destruction of the barricades of 1848 helped pave his way. Baudelaire, who knew only too well the "natural

Fig. 13.   The creative destruction of Paris: The rebuilding of the Place Saint Germain and the clearance of the Ile de la Cité. (Photo Roger Viollet and Musée Carnavelet.)

pleasure in destruction," could not and did not protest the transformation of Paris. His celebrated line "Alas, a city's face changes faster than the heart of a mortal" is directed more at our incapacity to come to terms with the present than at the process of transformation.

The tension that Haussman could never resolve, of course, was transforming Paris into the city of capital under the aegis of imperial authority. That project was bound to provoke political and sentimental responses. He delivered up the city to the capitalists, speculators, and moneychangers. He gave it over to an orgy of self-prostitution. There were those among his critics who felt they had been excluded from the orgy, and those who thought the whole process distasteful and obscene. It is in such a context that Baudelaire's images of the city as a whore take on their particular meaning. The Second Empire was a moment of transition in the imagery of Paris. The city had long been depicted as a woman. Balzac saw her as mysterious, capricious, and often venal, but also as natural, slovenly, and unpredictable, particularly in revolution. The image in Zola is very different. She is now a fallen and brutalized woman, "disemboweled and bleeding," the "prey of speculation, the victim of all-consuming greed" (Vidler 1978, 91). Could so brutalized a woman do anything other than rise up in revolution? Here the imagery of gender and of Paris formed a strange connection, one that boded ill, as we shall see (sec. 11), for both women and the city in 1871.

XI. RHETORIC AND REPRESENTATION

> It is always necessary to distinguish between the material transformation of the
> economic conditions of production, which can be determined with the
> precision of natural science, and the legal, political, religious, artistic or
> philosophic – in short, ideological forms in which men become conscious of
> conflict and fight it out.
>
> *– Marx*

How did people view each other, represent themselves and others to themselves and others? How did they picture the contours of Parisian society, comprehend their social position and the radical transformations then in progress? And how were these representations transposed, used, and shaped in the rhetoric of political discourse? These are easy and important questions to pose but tough ones to answer.

Once again, the experience of 1848 provides a benchmark against which much that followed has to be understood. "Order" and "disorder" were code words, but behind them lay some unforgettable experiences. Tocqueville's are illustrative. On May 15, when the National Assembly was invaded by the political clubs, a man appeared at the rostrum

whom I never saw save on that day, but whose memory has always filled me with disgust and horror. His cheeks were pale and faded, his lips white; he looked ill, evil, foul, with a dirty pallor and the appearance of a mouldering corpse; no linen as far as one could see, an old black frock-coat thrown about spindly and emaciated limbs; he might have lived in a sewer and have just emerged from it. I was told that this was Blanqui. (cited in Clark 1973a, 16)

Or again, on June 24, Tocqueville encounters an old woman in the street with a vegetable cart that impedes his path. He orders her "sharply" to make room

Instead of doing so, she left her cart and rushed at me with such sudden frenzy that I had trouble defending myself. I shuddered at the frightful and hideous expression on her face, which reflected demagogic passions and the fury of civil war. . . . It is as though these great public emotions create a burning atmosphere in which private feelings seethe and boil. (cited in Hertz 1983, 36)

   The bourgeoisie feared not only the collapse of public order but the horror of uncaged emotions, unbridled passions, the explosion of evil from the subterranean Paris of sewers and filth. The fear of disorder was inordinate. No wonder that the "party of order" took such a Draconian path to repression, creating first a Republic without republicans and then caving in to Empire as the only hope. But the Empire was anything but orderly. So who or what was to blame for it? Workers pointed (if they were permitted to speak their mind at all) to the anarchy of free-market capitalism, with its periodic bouts of speculation, market collapse, and unemployment; its unbridled greed and money passion; its undermining of job security, skills, and worker dignity; and its fierce waging of class war. The bourgeoisie blamed irresponsible and feckless government, subversives, bohemians, free-thinkers, socialists, and utopians who might incite that "vile multitude" to riot and revolution at the slightest provocation. Both sides might rally to the defense of the established order, but the "order" they had in mind varied from craft workers defending their skills to landlords and bankers defending their different kinds of property. An English visitor was surprised to find, for example, that the "society" his hosts proclaimed as so threatened referred exclusively to the fashionable circles in which they moved (St. John 1854, 91). The same words evidently carried very different meanings; the challenge is to interpret those meanings correctly.
   That task is made more problematic by the existence of political repression and censorship. All manner of hidden and allegorical meanings, of veiled references and subtle innuendoes, entered into political discourse and appear to have been widely understood. Catholicism had left a legacy of appreciation for symbolism and allegory which could be put to political use (including by the church once it moved into opposition to Empire). Corporatist traditions within the labor force and the Masonic movement (with all their rituals of initiation) provided all kinds of codes and languages. And the rewriting of history, particularly of the revolutionary period (see sec. 10), was used to shape popular imagery. The censors were alive to such problems – they rejected a simple song that mentioned a bonnet, presumably because it might be taken

as a reference to the republican cap of liberty (Rifkin 1979). But what could the authorities do when critics of Empire turned funerals, fêtes, and other public events into occasions for spontaneous mass demonstrations? The problem was not simply that twenty-five thousand workers could turn up at twenty-four hours' notice for the funeral of a republican leader's wife, but that any burial with its tradition of graveside discourse could turn into a mass political meeting.

The means of representation and communication were also multiplying rapidly. The explosion in newspaper circulation was accompanied by political diversification and the rise of skilled editors who knew how to skirt the censor. Others preferred to confront, make their point, and be closed down in a blaze of glory. By the late 1860s, newspapers and journals were opening up by the month (Tchernoff 1906, 506–26). When an influential newspaper like *Le Rappel* was controlled by no less fierce a critic than the exiled Victor Hugo, the government was surely in trouble. The penny press also exploded as the popular taste for education, romance, and travel came together with a commercial apparatus capable of exploiting it. Much of the material was innocuous enough to appear as pabulum for the masses. But some of it, like the pamphlets on French history, had strong political overtones. By 1860, this penny literature was more numerous and popular than the daily press (Copping 1858, 80). Worse still, all such publications relied heavily on illustrations. Drawings and cartoons – those of Daumier being by far the most famous – were extraordinary vehicles for political satire and polemic. Nor could Courbet's gallant thrust of 1848–51 to create an art of and for the people be easily forgotten (Clark 1973a). The *Salons* continued to be political events to which the popular classes were drawn as much as the bourgeoisie (who sought to raise the entry price one day a week so as not to have to rub shoulders with a riffraff of smelly and sweaty workers). And while the government could ban performances of Victor Hugo's plays, they could not stop *Les misérables* from being in almost everyone's hands almost immediately after it was published in 1862. And herein lay another problem. The improved transport and communications systems and the flood of foreign visitors (a tenfold increase of visitors from England between 1855 and 1863, according to Green [1965, 76]), made the flow of foreign news and commentary much greater at the same time as it increased the capacity to smuggle in any number of political tracts produced by those in exile. The emperor's decision to offer amnesty to the exiles in 1859 hinged not so much on magnanimity as on the simple idea that it was easier to keep them under surveillance in France than it was abroad. Realizing that only too well, Proudhon for awhile and Hugo for the rest of the Empire preferred to remain outside.

It is invidious, perhaps, to select out of the swirl and confusions of images, representations, and political rhetoric any dominant themes. Yet there are some that stand out, that cry out for further explication. Within each we shall see manifested that overriding concern for the tension between order and disorder as well as between modernity and tradition.

Two Cities, Two Peoples

Four o'clock. The other Paris awakes, the Paris of work. The two cities hardly know each other, the one that rises at midday and the one that beds down at eight. They rarely look each other in the eye and then – all too often – only on the sad and somber days of revolution. They live far from each other; they speak a different language. There is no love lost between them; they are two peoples. (*Paris Guide of 1867*, 30)

No matter how intricate the class structure and the division of social space in actuality, the simplistic image of Paris as a city divided into two classes and two spaces erupts again and again in representations of the time. It was an image with a long history. Before 1848, the "other Paris" was seen in terms of "dangerous classes," whose utter destitution inspired sometimes pity but more often horror, disgust, and loathing. Terms like "savage" and "barbarian" and epithets like "animal" gave racial coloration to bourgeois imagery, justifying the murderous violence with which the bourgeoisie often approached workers and the impoverished (Chevalier 1973, 360–61). "Equality asserted itself triumphantly," wrote Flaubert (1964, 334) of 1848; "an equality of brute beasts, a common level of bloody atrocities; for the fanaticism of the rich counterbalanced the frenzy of the poor, the aristocracy shared the fury of the rabble, and the cotton nightcap was just as savage as the red bonnet."

Though 1848 may have proved there were differences between the laboring and dangerous classes, it had also promised, then denied, real political power to the workers. Power shifted, relatively permanently as it turned out, to the bourgeois side of the barricades. Thereafter, many in the bourgeoisie felt free to tar all those who had been on the other side with the same brush. The imagery previously applied to the dangerous classes now clung not only to the laboring classes but even to their defenders, like Blanqui. Furthermore, everyone knew where the barricades had been erected, what part of the city belonged to "the other." A barricade makes for a simple dividing line (fig. 14). The experience of 1848 lived on in simplified polarized representations of social and physical space.

Bourgeois representations of what existed "on the other side" were colored by the nature of their contacts. Most of the haute bourgeoisie, recall, were either economically inactive (in Paris) or in government service, while even the economically active tended to concentrate in high finance. Industrialists

Fig. 14.   *The distribution of barricades in Paris during the June uprising of 1848.*
(After L. Girard, 1981.)

who actually dealt with workers (like Poulot) were few and far between and in any case considered inferior. Yet Paris was a working-class city, increasingly organized so that the conspicuous consumers could, as Lazare (1870, 60) put it, "long savor the taste of the honey without being troubled by the buzzing of the bees." The imagery of what existed "on the other side" was not built out of human contact, save that of casual and usually unfortunate street encounters. The reports of bourgeois reformers (of no matter what political persuasion) on conditions in working-class Paris fueled rather than assuaged the imagery by dwelling upon the destitution and degradation. Living in such animal conditions, could the people be anything other than animals? That sort of racial reasoning was not far from the surface in influential circles and filtered with ease into literary representations. It was standard fare in response to the Commune. In all cities, wrote the poet Theophile Gautier, these are closed caverns for

wild animals, stinking beasts, venomous beasts, all the refractory perversities that civilization has been unable to tame, those who love blood, who are as amused by burning down as by fireworks, who delight in thievery, those for whom attacks against decency pass for gestures of love, all the monsters of the heart and the crippled of spirit; a population from another world, unused to daylight, crawling trapped in the depths of subterranean shadows. One day, when the animal tamer inadvertently leaves his keys in the gate of this zoo, these ferocious creatures go about a terrified city with savage cries. The cages open, the hyenas of '93 and the gorillas of the Commune pour forth. (cited in Lidsky 1970, 46)

The venomous violence of such sentiments was, as Lidsky (1970) documents *ad nauseam,* all too common. It is hard to read influential journals like the *Revue des Deux Mondes* during the 1860s without blanching. And the violence has a curious quality to it, rather as if there is an inner longing to exorcise a devil, burn out some excruciating sore on society, seek some ultimate denouement, a catharsis. "There are but three beings worthy of respect: the priest, the warrior and the poet," wrote Baudelaire (1983b, 65), "to know, to kill and to create." Flaubert (1979b, 49) confessed that the riot was the only thing he understood in politics: "I despise modern tyranny because it seems to me stupid, weak and without the courage of its convictions," adding, "I have a deep cult of ancient tyranny which I regard as mankind's finest manifestation." And he wrote such scenes of murderous violence toward conquered people into *Salammbô* that he was even accused of sadism. It was exactly such scenes that were to be acted out against the Commune, a brutal bloodletting justified by Goncourt as a bleeding white by killing off the combative reds. Fearfully recalling the Reign of Terror, it seems the bourgeoisie built images and representations to justify launching its own preemptive terror.

Revolutionaries, particularly those drawn from the ranks of students and *la bohème,* played the image in reverse. They saw the workers as skilled, self-reliant, intelligent, generous, and capable of leadership. The "other Paris" to the west was populated by speculators, stock-exchange wolves, rentiers, parasites, and vampires, who sucked the lifeblood of the workers and destroyed their dignity and self-respect. Crushed under the burden of the idle rich, working-class Paris had every right to rise up in revolution. The Blanquists took that idea even farther. They saw Paris as the revolutionary hearth from which liberation had to spread not only to the rest of France but to the rest of the world as it had in 1789. It was, furthermore, in the "other" Paris, more particularly in Belleville and the quarter of Père-Lachaise, that the revolution would have its origin (Hutton 1981, 66). It was into this quarter that those with Blanquist sympathies, like the influential Gustave Flourens (a professor of human anatomy, killed in the early days of the Commune), moved to cultivate their revolutionary base. And there is more than a hint of that same sense of violent revolutionary catharsis in the Blanquist rhetoric (drawing, as it did, so explicitly on the ideals of Hébertist revolutionary purity of 1793).

Not everyone was caught in such polarized imagery. Yet even those who sought to soften its edges often ended up reinforcing the general argument. Writers like Audiganne (1854, 1865), Corbon (1863), and Poulot (1980) at least had intimate contact with the Parisian workers and provide us with a composite character sketch. Writes Audiganne (1854, 154):

Paris workers are extremely sociable, open, with grand ideas and strong philanthropic concerns, expressed as mutual aid and reciprocal tolerance. On the other hand, they have an irresistible taste for dissipation and expenditure, an ardent thirst for pleasure, and a passionate love of change. . . . They participate in riots with the same enthusiasm as they do in fêtes, delighted to break the monotony of their daily life without concern for the consequences. The cult of *equality* and *nationality* is their hallmark.

The irresponsibility of Parisian workers was, of course, anathema to the rather puritanical radical bourgeoisie. But many commentators who knew them, like the socialist Vallès, who moved to working-class Paris out of sympathy for the oppressed, were amazed at the warmth and generosity they found there. All the more reason, therefore, to regret both the polarization of opinion and the weight of oppression which fell on working-class Paris. But in arguing for relief of the latter, reformers could not help but reinforce the former. Corbon (1863, 209) lamented the perpetuation and deepening of class divisions and argued that although the poor did not resent wealth as such, their own perilous condition, taken together with the increasing affluence of the rich, was certain to pose a threat to the security of the wealthy. That threat, moreover, had a geopolitical expression. "The transformation of Paris, having forcibly removed the working population from the center towards the extremities, has made two cities of the capital – one rich, one poor. . . . The deprived classes form an immense cordon around the well-off." Louis Lazare (1870, 1872) resorted to the same threatening imagery: "The flood of poverty rose in Belleville," he wrote, "while the river of luxury flowed at full crest in the new quarters of Paris."

The haute bourgeoisie suspected, with good reason, that the "reds" were submerging themselves in that flood of poverty in Belleville. To the degree that they could not and would not even set food in the place, such accounts could only exacerbate their fears. There dwell "the dregs of the people," editorialized newspapers like *Le Figaro* and *Le Moniteur*. There you find, wrote the journalist Sarcey, "the deepest depths of poverty and of hatred where ferments of envy, of sloth and anger, bubble without cease" (cited in Lepidis and Jacomin 1975, 285).

Baudelaire (1947, 52–53) captures the tragedy of such division in his prose poem "Eyes of the Poor." He explains why he hates his lover today. He recalls a magical day of closeness, intimacy, and sharing which ends with them sitting at dusk in a new café, dazzlingly lit, at the corner of a boulevard. Suddenly a "worthy man" in rags, with "tired face and greying beard" appears on the boulevard, leading two children. All three stare in wonder, though each in a special way, at the dazzling sight of the café. The poet feels deeply touched "by this family of eyes" and "even a little ashamed of our glasses and decanters, too big for our thirst." He turns to share the intimacy of his thoughts with his lover. "I plunged my eyes into your eyes, so beautiful and curiously soft." She breaks the spell. "Those people are insufferable with their great saucer eyes," she says. "Can't you tell the proprietor to send them away?" "So you would like to know why I hate you today?" is the poet's response.

Communists, Capitalists, and the Dream of Association

Disillusioned with the 1830 revolution, a young and impetuous Blanqui took to the hustings to denounce the great betrayal of the people's interest by the bourgeoisie. Arrested, he proudly declared his occupation "proletarian" and entered a dramatic defense that enunciated the principle of a just class struggle:

> The wheels of this machine, so marvelously crafted, strike at the poor every instant of the day, pursue them with respect to the tiniest necessities of their humble lives, cut in half their slightest gain and the most trivial of their pleasures. And it is not enough that so much money finds its way from the pockets of the poor into those of the rich through the spoliations of the tax system; even larger sums are levied off their backs by the privileged, through the laws which regulate industrial and commercial transactions, laws which the privileged have the exclusive power to make. (Dommanget 1970, 41)

So began an extraordinary life, forty years of which were spent behind bars, dedicated to uncompromising defense of proletarian interests, to conspiracies and attempts at insurrection, to subversion and attempts to seize state power, and to militant rhetoric directed against the iniquities of the bourgeoisie, religion, and false ideologies (like romanticism).

Yet, feared though he was by the bourgeoisie, Blanqui never succeeded in establishing a mass base within the working class. Indeed, there were periods when he seemed totally without influence, except as a remote, uncompromising, and incarcerated symbol. Only in the 1860s did the Blanquist movement spring to life, and then mainly among militant, atheist intellectuals and students, drawn to the nobility of his suffering and the purity of his cause (Hutton 1981). During the active class struggles of 1868–71, the Blanquists, partly out of their dedicated concern for education and their willingness to swim in the "rivers of poverty" that flowed in the "other Paris," did acquire an important following.

Their lack of mass influence was partly a matter of choice. The experience of 1848 and the foundation of Empire through universal suffrage made them suspicious of mass democracy under conditions of ignorance and bourgeois domination of the instruments of mass communication. Their roots in the pure forms of the French revolutionary tradition (as represented by Babeuf, Hébert, and Buonarotti) also led them to an insurrectionary Jacobin politics. Under conditions of tight police surveillance, this meant the formation of closed cells, impenetrable to infiltration but also closed to mass participation. Dictatorship of the proletariat through insurrectionary violence was their aim.

Their influence was also checked by circumstances of class structure which did not fit easily with the message they sought to convey. While insurrection against a state apparatus controlled by the haute bourgeoisie made a great deal of sense, it could not address the question of the organization of work in a city where the small workshop and the putting-out system dominated and where the line between capital and labor in production was blurred. The Parisian workshops had, in fact, been fertile breeding grounds for all kinds of other socialist, communalist, and communist ideologies ever since the early 1830s (Bartier et al. 1981; Corcoran 1983).

The communist slogan "from each according to his capacity had to each according to his need" sounded seductive to the mass of the impoverished and had a powerful hold among craft workers faced with insecurity of employment and the ravages of technological change. But the communists were, as Corbon (1863, 110) notes, of two sorts. There were those who sought to impose their system on the whole of society through an increase in state power vis-à-vis private property. They looked in 1848 to the formation of National Workshops as a prelude to state ownership, a guaranteed right to work, and equality of distribution. From this standpoint socialists like Louis Blanc, Raspail, and Barbès could make common cause with Blanqui (interpersonal rivalries permitting) to seize state power in the abortive movements of April 16 and May 15, 1848. There were, however, many groups like the Cabetists (Icarians) and the Fourierists who sought mainly to live out their doctrines in their own daily lives, hoping by their example to persuade people of the virtues of collective organization and communism. After the frustration of 1848, such groups saw emigration, mostly to the United States, as their only hope.

Proudhon drew quite different conclusions from the experience of 1848 (Hyams 1979). He felt the insurrectionary movements offered nothing but the replacement of one regime of repression and domination by another. The problem of work could not be solved through political channels. The state was the enemy no matter who controlled it. This put him at odds not only with Blanquists and communists but also with all those who saw the political republic as a necessary prelude to social change. The struggle to liberate the worker was to begin in the workshop with the implementation of practical plans rather than utopian schemes. Cooperation and mutualism meant a new conception of workers' democracy in the labor process, and it was to be backed by mutual credit and banking, mutual insurance and benefit societies, cooperative housing schemes, and the like. The virtue of such a program (which was a codification of ideas that had long resonated with Parisian craft workers) was that it avoided state intervention and could lay a basis for the withering away of the state. Just as important, it could by-pass class confrontation in the workshops and provide a program around which small masters (threatened by competition, changing conditions of credit and marketing, etc.) and craft workers could jointly rally. Proudhon supported private property in housing, retailing, and so forth, provided it was open to all; objected to strikes and unions; and was suspicious of the idea of association, since by 1860 it was becoming part of an ideology of class struggle. His ideas were influential. We thus find Clement, the shoemakers' representative to the Workers' Commission of 1867 (28–33), defying and condemning those who looked to strikes, class struggle, and other forms of confrontation to advance the worker's cause. The power of private property could be undermined and class struggle avoided, he argued, by laborers "working in solidarity, coming together, learning to know each other, living in the family," building up their own capital and so eliminating the power of external ownership over their lives. He was here restating a dominant theme expressed in the workers' movement of 1848 (Sewell 1980, 283).

But within the debates that swirled around the organization of labor in Second Empire Paris, one concept exercised a peculiar power and fascination – association. It acquired its central position in part because of its deep roots in tradition but also by virtue of its ambiguity. It had been central to Saint-Simonian thought in the 1830s as well as to the Fourierism and workers' socialism that cut its teeth in the same period. Initially it was an idea that sought to overcome class conflict and the social anarchy, selfish greed, and social inequalities engendered out of private property capitalism. In the hands of the Saint-Simonians, it meant the association of all capitals, great and small, mobilized to such productive and socially desirable ends that the whole of civil society, including the workers themselves, would be embraced within the harmony of social progress (Charlety 1931). The Pereires were schooled in that ideology in the 1830s and put it to use in the 1850s to try to construct a kind of democratic state-monopoly capitalism. And even though the incessant search for profit perverted the aim, the threat posed to private property by the centralization of credit, the omnium share (sec. 2), was sufficient to spark hostility within many segments of the business community. Their appeal to the idea of association gave the concept a certain legitimacy. Workers could point to imperial support for the association of capitals and the contrasting repression of workers' right to associate. Even Marx, who mocked the idea that the association of capitals could do anything other than spark orgies of speculation, also conceded that it might constitute a "form of transition to a new mode of production," thus endowing the Pereires "with the pleasant character mixture of swindler and prophet" (1967, 3:441).

In the hands of the workers' movement, the idea also underwent a significant evolution. In its earliest manifestations in the 1830s it meant producer associations, mutual benefit societies, and other forms of which Proudhon was later to approve. But the repression of the workers' movement and the ravages of technological change and capitalist exploitation of a work force with an intense corporatist tradition also turned "association" into a code word for class and corporatist resistance. The first sense seems to have remained dominant in Paris at least until 1848–51. When, in February 1848, the provisional government drew up a decree that guaranteed the right to work, it also guaranteed the right of workers to associate "in order to enjoy the legitimate benefits of their labor." The phrase is ambiguous. Does it mean the right to form trade unions or the right to found producer cooperatives? In practice, as Sewell (1980, 243–76) shows, it rallied all those craft workers who, understanding that wealth was founded on labor, saw the free association of workers in production as the means to capture the benefits of their own labor and simultaneously to ensure the peaceful reorganization of society under the control of the direct producers.

The experience of 1848 cast doubt on the feasibility of such a project. The vicious repression of all forms of worker organization in 1851 (save the mutual benefit societies and those under strict imperial control) drove such hopes underground, from whence Proudhon strove to resurrect them in their voluntaristic rather than state-directed form. But Corbon (1863, 122–41), surveying the wreckage of attempts at worker association in 1848, thought the idea was losing ground, not as a noble vision of some socialist future, but as a practical matter. Given the reorganization of the labor process and the increasing schism between capital and labor in Parisian industry (sec. 5), collective means had to be found to resist the de-skilling of labor and sagging real incomes (sec. 6). Corbon thus noted the revival of corporatist sentiments during the 1860s and the mobilization of corporatist forms (abolished in the French Revolution) to defend working-class interests and to challenge the liberty of labor markets. "Association" then meant the right to form unions to negotiate collectively over wage rates and work conditions. The two meanings ran along side by side in the late 1860s. Liberty of association was one of the demands of all workers at the Workers' Commission meetings of

1867. But they either meant different things by it or consciously chose to straddle the ambiguity in order to make good political use of it.

Gender and Revolution

Shortly before the Commune, Edmond de Goncourt noted in his journal, "They speak of the nervous over-excitation of women . . . of the fear of having to suppress riots of women" (cited in Lidsky 1970, 45). After the Commune that fear became a legend of "sinister females," of "amazons and viragos," inspiring and inflaming men by their obscene and unashamed immodesty, "clothing undone, their bosoms almost bare," inciting and leading the torching of Paris (Thomas 1966, 182). Contemplating the bodies of women dragged from houses and barricades and summarily shot, Houssaye wrote: "Not one of these women had a human face; only the image of crime and vice. They were bodies without souls, deserving of a thousand deaths, even before having touched the petrol. There is only one word to portray them: hideous" (cited in Lidsky 1970, 115).

This imagery of the bestiality and barbarism of women in the midst of riot and revolution, of the role of "women incendiaries" in the Commune, lived powerfully on, even though the military tribunals could find hardly any evidence for it – and not for want of trying (Thomas 1966). Zola (1954a), drawing heavily upon Maxime du Camp's descriptions of the Commune, inserted a horrendous scene of lynching and castration of the village shopkeeper by enraged women into *Germinal*. Images of this sort were far from uncommon. They can be traced throughout the whole of the Second Empire. What, then, was this all about?

The connection between women, liberty, and the Republic (and hence with revolution) had long been in the making. Agulhon (1981) traces it back to the French Revolution when the portrayal of *la republique* as a woman as against *le royaume* of the king entered into official iconography. The image stuck. Delacroix, temporarily swept up in the revolutionary fervor of 1830, portrayed *Liberty Leading the People at the Barricades* as a powerfully formed, bare-breasted woman, wearing the red cap of liberty and carrying a banner, surging across a barricade of very dead soldiers, urging on a motley assortment of bourgeois, workers, students, and a very prominent street urchin waving a pair of pistols (fig. 15). The picture was one of many, but it was so stunning that it disappeared from view (the king bought it) and was not seen again until 1848 (and then only briefly). But the theme and form of allegory remained important. It was an image to which the critics of monarchy and the supporters of republicanism could rally. After 1830 it was "reinforced by another equally revolutionary and feminine myth: socialism. And while they did not altogether merge, these two myths sufficiently

Fig. 15. Eugène Delacroix, Liberty leading the people.
(Permission of the Musées Nationaux, Paris.)

resembled one another for their cultural effects to prove cumulative"
(Agulhon 1981, 59).

How myth and action feed on each other is a curious process. That they did
so in 1848 is undeniable. Flaubert (1964, 290) inserted the following
incident, based on fact, into *L'education sentimentale*: "In the entrance-hall [of
the Tuileries], standing on a pile of clothes, a prostitute was posing as a
statue of Liberty, motionless and terrifying, with her eyes wide open." In the
June Days, the London *Examiner* reported another incident:

One of the females, a young woman neatly dressed, picked up the flag, and leaping
over the barricade, rushed towards the national guards, uttering language of
provocation . . . a shot reached her and she was killed. The other female then
advanced, took the flag, and began to throw stones at the national guards . . . (who)
killed the second female.

Victor Hugo recorded the same incident. But he calls both the women
prostitutes "beautiful, dishevelled, terrifying," who, uttering obscenities,

pulled up their dresses to the waist, crying "Cowards! Fire, if you dare, at the belly of a woman." "That was how this war began," adds Hugo somberly (cited in Hertz 1983).

Events of this sort put the allegory into motion. And the symbolism was surely not lost: for had not the Republic shot down liberty on the barricades? The iconography thereafter split along lines exactly demarcated by the distinction between the social and the political republic. The "cautious Republic of order and reconciliation" needed a quite different representation from the "impetuous and rebellious" image of the people's Republic: "It began to look as if soon the camps of those clad in worker's clothes would have one Republic with a red cap and a gaping bodice while the camp of dark-suited gentlemen would have another, a ladylike Republic behatted with foliage and draped in robes from top to toe" (Agulhon 1981, 99).

How, then, was the Republic to be represented? The state had an artistic competition on that theme in March 1848. It was a disaster (though it did produce Daumier's extraordinary image of a half-naked, seated woman of powerful build giving suck to two lusty infants). Impetuosity and respectability proved hard to combine. Nobody knew which side to take; the instructions were vague (should it have the cap of liberty?), and it was not judged until October (Clark 1973b, 63–69). Thereafter the respectable republicans set out to domesticate the image (Bartholdi first discussed his plans for the Statue of Liberty that now stands in New York's harbor in the late 1860s). For their part, the workers clung to a more revolutionary image, one that now had a name – Marianne. They formed "Mariannist conspiracies" mainly in rural areas, although one was broken up in Paris in 1855. The emancipation of women; the nationalization of land and "all that lies therein"; and guarantees of adequate living, employment, and education for all were part of its program (Thomas n.d., 164). Such sentiments evidently died hard. When women observers came to the Workers' Commission of 1867 (100), a worker was moved to cry out: "Madame, on seeing you enter, I believed I saw liberty enter. Whenever women sit down with men at these meetings, there commences the reign of liberty and justice. *Vive la Femme! Vive la Liberté!*"

All of this would have been innocent enough if it had not become mixed up with questions of gender roles and the position of women, particularly within the bourgeoisie. The debate had a long history. There was a slender tradition of militant feminism which initially cut across class lines (George Sand and Flora Tristan stand out), while the woman question had split the Saint-Simonian movement in the 1830s along fairly predictable lines: how could a theory of liberty and equality be reconciled with the special responsibilities of women to the family? One wing formed a rather weak women's movement "to reform industry to combine women's productive, maternal and housekeeping roles." They founded a journal and women's cooperatives that expanded somewhat in working-class Paris during the heady days of 1848. By 1850 most had disappeared, victims of repression under the bourgeois Republic that saw them, like liberty on the barricades, as a threat to social order (Moon 1975; Moses 1984).

That women belonged exclusively in the home was a fiercely held belief among the bourgeoisie. Even radical republicans, like Michelet, and socialists espoused it. Proudhon's notes for *Pornocratie,* according to an otherwise sympathetic Hyams (1979, 274), contain "every cruelly reactionary notion ever used against female emancipation by the most extreme anti-feminist." Reinforced by a cult of domesticity (which broadly paralleled the taming of the image of liberty), its material underpinnings lay in a conception of marriage as a business enterprise, in the increasing separation of workplace from residence, and in the crucial importance of a well-managed domestic economy to bourgeois success (sec. 7). It also had much to do with a system of property and inheritance which made the habits and morals of the aristocracy impractical except under conditions of enormous wealth. The typical bourgeois republican was trapped between the specter of collapse into the dissolute ways of the working class and the *noblesse oblige* of the aristocracy. For them, control over women was deemed essential to the preservation of class position. What is more, most women seem to have accepted that equation. Even George Sand took to lauding the virtues of the family in the 1860s and felt free after the Commune to direct the most vitriolic barbs against the communards, even though she had never as much as stirred from her rural estate. Those like d'Hericourt (1860) who dissented were not paid much attention, and there was little sign of an independent feminist politics – the question of women's suffrage (much debated in England) did not come up (Green 1965, 95). Only toward the end of Empire did a group of women (Louise Michel, Paule Minck, André Léo, and Elizabeth Dmitrieff) – begin to speak out on women's rights and organize groups such as the *Union des Femmes* that played such an important role in the Commune (Thomas 1966, 70–87).

It is tempting to speculate on the sociopsychological meaning of all this. The image of liberty as a terrifying and uncontrollable woman of the sort Tocqueville encountered – worse still, a public whore – in a phallocratic society where the preservation of bourgeois private property and class position depended on the control of women must have shaken the bourgeois male psyche to the core. Manet's representations of women (in *Olympia* or *Déjeuner sur l'herbe*) seem to have provoked bourgeois wrath precisely because the women appeared to be common prostitutes with an insufficiently submissive gaze (Reff 1982). Hertz (1983), less restrained than Agulhon (1981, 185), thus suggests that castration fears (of the sort that Zola made so explicit) combined with class antagonism to produce "male hysteria under political pressure." It is hard to explain the extraordinary violence of male rhetoric against women who participated in revolutionary action any other way. It is hard, even, to grapple with conventional republican representations.

Michelet's (1981) *La femme,* first published in 1859, was a very influential tract by a celebrated republican historian. When the Workers' Commission of 1867 turned its attention to the woman question, a certain Dr. Dupas spelled out a crude version of Michelet's ideas at length. The woman, he argued, is not equal to the man in physical strength, intellect, moral concerns, or devotion to public affairs, but her love and devotion as wife and mother surpass a thousandfold anything that men are capable of. Men are representatives of civilization, and women are creatures of nature ("woman is *natural,* that is to say abominable," sputtered Baudelaire [1983b, 53], while Manet's *Déjeuner sur l'herbe* seems simultaneously to represent and to parody the opposition that Michelet made so much of). That opposition between men and women could have a creative or a destructive resolution. In the absence of male restraint, the unclean side of woman's nature (represented by menstruation) could dominate and erupt into violent hysteria (which is presumably what Hugo, Tocqueville, and the anticommunards thought they saw in the midst of revolution). Woman at work and outside the restraint of men, Dupas continued, put a moral blot on society; this unhappy situation exposed society to the degradation and hysteria produced in the workshop. The only positive resolution lay in the union of male and female under the domination of men (the man is "1" and the woman is "0," he explained, and the only way to multiply their social power was to put the "1" in front of the "0"; that way you got 10). But it was essential that the woman be given respect and sympathy. And here was the crux of Michelet's message. The woman was to be cast in the role of suffering madonna, whose natural burdens could be relieved and whose infinite capacity for love and devotion could be released only under conditions of respectful and paternalistic male control. It is significant, I think, that not a single worker spoke up in support of such a view, and most condemned it outright.

Jules Simon also appeared before the commission (213–17), but he took a quite different tack. He deplored the fact that women worked, since that tended to destroy the family, lead to the neglect of children, and deprive the man of a stable, caring, and loving home environment wherein he could replenish his body and his soul. Some way had to be found to preserve the family. Yet Simon knew that for most of the working class, women's work was a necessity. He also knew that industry needed women's labor power. He attacked the idea that women should be banned from the workplace on the grounds that this interfered with a precious liberty (that of the market) and that women needed employment. The problem was to find respectable and well-remunerated employment and so to prevent the slide into debauchery and prostitution. The answer lay in free education provided by the state. This would allow women to increase the value of their labor power (a human capital argument) at the same time as they would improve their skills as educators within the family. The educational reforms of the late 1860s did open up this possibility and were apparently appreciated by workers and even the more militant feminists. Simon was popular enough to draw a massive working-class vote for his election in 1869. But as several workers pointed out at the commission meetings, the improved education of women would increase the range of jobs for which women could compete and would push wages down. Simon did indeed have the support of the industrial interest who saw merit in his proposals from their own standpoint.

So what did workers think? Fribourg, a member of the International, spoke up (232) for what was probably the majority, echoing Proudhon. The latter had argued quite simply that women belonged at home under the authority of men. Though there was more than a touch of the misogynistic in Proudhon's writings, worker sentiment did not rest on the kinds of arguments that Michelet or Dupas advanced. It drew, in the first instance, on a tradition in which the male had the legal and moral right to dispose of the family labor power. It also drew upon the desire to protect the family and the authority of the male as the grand provider. But in Second Empire Paris it was also fueled by intense hostility within the craft tradition to competition from women's labor power, whether mobilized by the convents or directly in the workshops. The printers' strike of 1862 was, in this regard, a cause célèbre; the introduction of women at a third less pay to break the strike was exactly what the workers feared. The short-run solution was to raise male wages to cover family needs and to legislate women out of the workshops. The printers petitioned the emperor to do just that. And in so doing they were not loath to use the same sorts of arguments advanced by Michelet. They pointed to the hysteria generated by exposure to the workshop and argued, probably correctly, that the nature of the work and the toxic substances to which women were exposed induced a high rate of stillbirths and natural abortions among the women employed there. So strongly were such views held that the French delegation to the Geneva meetings of the International in 1866 forced passage of a resolution banning women from the workshops and confining them to the home.

Socialist feminists like Paule Minck militated against such attitudes within the Parisian branch of the International. We want to be treated neither as madonnas nor as slaves, she argued at a public meeting in 1868, but as ordinary human beings, different but equal, with the right to work at equal pay and to associate for our own economic emancipation (Dalotel 1981, 122). She had male allies like Varlin, who rebutted Fribourg before the Workers' Commission (233) with exactly those arguments. Women's right to work was "the only means to their true liberation," and those who refused it "simply wanted to keep them under the domination of men." Varlin, at least, was as good as his word and wrote the right of women to work at equal pay into the constitution of the bookbinders' union. The shoemakers, however, thought it sufficiently progressive to permit women into their union only if they asked no questions except in writing or through a male member.

Representations and rhetoric flew past each other at the Workers' Commission meetings without touching. The real tragedy of that was already etched into women's daily lives. The grisly aftermath of the Commune illustrates the violence and horror unleashed when class and gender antagonism reinforce each other. Many of the women dragged before the military tribunals had simply acted as ambulance or canteen helpers and were totally mystified by the rhetoric and charges of heinous crimes directed against them. They had lived by the nobility of one vision only to be judged by the hysterical rhetoric of another.

Centralization and Decentralization

The relations between a traditionally centralized state, civil society, and individual liberties had long been the fulcrum of French political debate. Monarchy and religion had made common cause around the idea of respect for authority within a hierarchically-ordered state and civil society. The Jacobins looked to a strong, centralized power but sought to root its legitimacy in the sovereign will of a people liberated from hierarchy in civil society. They attacked the workers' corporations that restrained the liberty of labor with the same vehemence they attacked religion. The Second Empire tried to have the best of both worlds, using universal suffrage to legitimize the emperor, from whom all authority then flowed. But there had also long been currents of resistance to such forms of centralization. The debate over its virtues became very heated as the enemies of Empire used the idea of decentralization as a stick to beat it with.

The problem was that everyone had a different idea of what decentralization meant. But when political options are represented in both attractive and ambiguous terms, that representation can enter into rhetoric and action in compelling ways. It is important to understand the ambiguities that, for example, led ardent supporters of centralization (the Blanquists) and equally ardent supporters of decentralization (the mutualists) to die on the same side of the barricades in 1871. To unravel the ambiguities I shall look at economic decentralization, political decentralization, and the centralization of power in Paris as separate but intertwined themes.

The Second Empire saw the state enhance direct economic control and indirect economic influence through the formation of strong institutions for the centralization of capital. The connection between the Pereires and Haussman was typical of an organizational form close to state-monopoly or finance capitalism. Because they controlled banking, transport, communications, the press, urban services, and property speculation, there were few arenas of economic life outside of the orbit of finance capital and the state. This sparked debate over the nature of capitalism and the relative virtues of competition and monopoly. The debate pitted what might loosely be called Saint-Simonian ideology and practice against the doctrines of the free-market economists. The importance of the former is hard to evaluate, since the Saint-Simonians never developed a coherent economic theory. They cultivated an attitude of mind which, being both pragmatic and broadly oriented to social questions, led many of them to adapt their ideas, albeit always around the general theme of production, in diverse ways. The emperor may have entered the Empire as "Saint-Simon on horseback" (to use Sainte-Beuve's famous phrase), but he left it as a liberal free trader. Chevalier, an original member of the sect and then professor of economics, negotiated the free-trade agreement with Britain in 1860 and shifted ground on all manner of issues. And the practices of the Pereires evolved in pragmatic and often self-interested ways. But the doctrine gave legitimacy to imperial economic policy and the centralization of capital. Free-market economists like Bastiat and Say, by contrast, advocated greater market liberty and competition (supposed virtues already forced on the working class in 1852). As private property rights were reasserted against state power in Paris in the late 1850s, and as fears of the Pereires' power mounted, so free-market ideology was mobilized as part of an attack upon imperial policy. In the hands of industrialists or bankers like Rothschild, the arguments appeared hypocritical and self-serving. But the 1860s saw a growing consensus, within both the bourgeoisie and the workers' movement, that the excessive centralization of economic power had to be checked. Though the solutions they might offer were very different, a powerful class alliance (joining Proudhonists like Duchène and Rothschild's protégé Say) could form around the theme of opposition to the further centralization of capital. The downfall of the Pereires and of Haussman, the transition to liberal Empire, and the increasing credibility of the "economists" testified to the growing power of that alliance.

The question of political decentralization stirred similar passions. The Second Empire produced a tightly controlled hierarchy of power from the emperor down to the prefects and subprefects, appointed mayors and local councils, appointed heads of mutual benefit societies, worker-employer commissions, and the like. Local democracy was negligible. But local autonomy outside of Paris was partly protected by inaccessibility. The new transport and communications system, often pushed hard by local elites, had the ironic effect of making central government control easier and so reducing local autonomy. Increasing spatial integration seems to have been accompanied by a rising clamor for some degree of local self-government. Legitimists, Orleanists, republicans, and socialists all took to championing the cause of local liberties during the 1860s, while historians debated the relative merits of the Jacobin Robespierre and the more democratically-minded Girondists, almost always coming down on the side of the latter. By the late 1860s, says Greenberg (1971, 24), "decentralization had assumed all the appearances of a national crusade." It certainly became the centerpiece of attack against Haussman. It is hard to differentiate, however, between purely opportunistic arguments of those out of power (the monarchist case is particularly suspect) and deeply held beliefs of someone like Proudhon, who looked to the withering away of the state through the federation of independent and autonomous communities as his ideal and who in any case saw political reorganization as irrelevant in the absence of a fundamental reorganization of production against the centralization of capital. But whatever the basis, the fight for political decentralization was real enough, and it put the question of self-government for Paris squarely on the agenda.

But that posed another problem. For was not Paris, as Haussman (1890, 2:202) put it, "centralization itself"? Fearful of the immense centralization of economic, political, administrative, and cultural power in Paris, many a provincial who supported decentralization demurred when it came to self-government for so influential a city, one that had also been prone to radical if not "red" political leanings. And there were many in the Parisian haute bourgeoisie, like Thiers, who shared those fears. This was the sort of coalition that behaved in such an inflammatory way toward the Paris Commune. Nonetheless, there were many Parisians who supported the cause of decentralization but who also proudly held that Paris was "the head, the brain, and the heart of Europe" – a view "which may explain," an English visitor wryly observed, "why Europe sometimes plays such strange antics" (St. John 1854, 14). Proudhon thus wanted Paris to "discard the crown of capital" but nevertheless to "take the lead as a free and independent commune in the crusade for a federated nation." Blanqui agreed that the revolution had to begin in Paris, but, Jacobin that he was, he thought of a revolutionary Paris conquering, ruling over, and bringing enlightenment to the backward provincials (Greenberg 1971, 86–90). That Blanquists and mutualists fought to create and defend the Commune was, therefore, nowhere near as odd as some have thought.

Clearly, there was a sense in which the Commune was a rising for municipal liberty. That it was exclusively so in the social democratic sense, as Greenberg (1971) argues, is beyond the bounds of credibility. But different factions saw the Commune very differently. For mutualists and communists, it was the shield behind which they could begin their more solid work of reorganizing production, distribution, and consumption, in alliance with other movements in other centers. For the Blanquists it was the first step in the political liberation of France, if not the world. For the republican mayors of the arrondissements, it was the first step in integrating Paris into a republican system of government and, if necessary, a defensive weapon to be used against monarchist reaction. For all of them it was easier to define what the Commune was against than what it was for. And the paradox, of course, was that the strong sentiment for decentralization in the provinces could so easily be mobilized to crush a movement of decentralization within a city where so much power was centralized.

The Geographical Imagination

The transformation of space relations shook perceptions of space and place to their very roots. The geographies of the mind had to adapt to a welter of new experiences. Increasing competition and dependence within the international division of labor liberated Paris from local constraints but rendered the city vulnerable to far-off events (the American Civil War, for example). The spreading tentacles of the rail net and the growing regularity and speed of maritime and telegraph connections indicated the growing power to dominate space. Information, commodities, money, and people moved around the world with much greater facility in 1870 than they did in 1850.

It was not necessary to leave Paris to experience the shock. The changing mix of commodities in the market (from basic foods to exotic luxuries) gave daily testimony to the shifts. A burgeoning press placed instant information on people's lunch tables about everything from foreign investment and profit opportunities through geopolitical confrontations to bizarre stories of foreign habits. With the photograph, space and time seemed to collapse into one simple image. And to cap it all, every conquest of space – the opening of rail links or of the Suez Canal – became an occasion for enormous celebration. The World Exhibitions, as Benjamin (1973, 165–67) put it, were "places of pilgrimage to the fetish Commodity," occasions on which "the phantasmagoria of capitalist culture attained its most radiant unfurling."

Then, as now, the problem was to penetrate the veil of fetishism, to identify the complex of social relations concealed by the market exchange of things. The speed of change evidently sparked curiosity, judging by the mass of travelogues and popular geographies that swamped the penny press (Copping 1858). But travel can as easily confirm preexisting prejudices as broaden the mind. It takes experience and imagination to get behind the fetishism, and imagination is as much a product of interior needs as it is a reflection of external realities.

The French geographical imagination was encumbered with heavy doses of environmentalism. Montesquieu and Rousseau had agreed that liberty was not the fruit of all climates and therefore not within the reach of all peoples. "Despotism is suited to hot climates, barbarism, to cold, and good government, to temperate regions" (cited in Glacken 1967, 592). Michelet rendered that passive image dynamic by depicting history as a struggle between man and nature. But he also introduced ancillary imagery in which "the struggle of reason, spirit, the West, the male to separate themselves and establish their authority over their origins in nature, matter, the East, the female" became the struggle for civilization itself (Gossman 1974). It was imagery of this sort, reinforced by painters like Delacroix and romantic writers like Hugo, that lay at the root of the extraordinary mental construction that Said (1979) calls "orientalism." The Orient was seen as the womb from which civilization had issued forth but also as the locus of irrational and erotic femininity. That imagery remained untouched by the increasing ease of human contact. When Flaubert journeyed up the Nile in 1849, he went, like many before him, with only one thing in mind, to "find another home" in the voluptuous sensuality of the Oriental woman. His subsequent writings were not alone in confirming rather than demystifying the image. It is tempting, of course, to follow Hitzman (1981) and see all this as "unconscious projections onto aspects of the ancient world of underlying anxieties about the *mère terrible*," or of deep fears (similar to those that erupted around the Commune) of "destructive, castrating female sexuality." It is hard to read *Salammbô* and Flaubert's letters to his mother without giving such interpretations some credence.

But it is too simple to let matters rest there. For as Said (1979, 167) points out, the Orient posed threats other than imagined licentious sex, disturbing though that may have been to the bourgeois sense of family and its accompanying cult of domesticity. A European and very capitalistic "rationality of time, space, and personal identity" confronted "unimaginable antiquity, inhuman beauty, boundless distance." Michelet and the Saint-Simonians used their imagery to justify the penetration of the Orient by railroads, canals, and commerce and the domination of an irrational Orient in the name of a superior Enlightenment rationality. The submission of East to West was as necessary to the progress of civilization as the submission of female to male authority and control. Flaubert, however, did not take such an imperialist tack. Unconvinced of the virtues of bourgeois values and culture, he used the myth of the Orient, as did the many avid readers of tales of harems, princes, and the Arabian Nights in the penny press, to explore the "other" in his own personality and the underside of bourgeois culture. Reflecting on his Egyptian journey, he wrote:

The thing we all lack is not style, nor the dexterity of finger and bow known as talent. We have a large orchestra, a rich palette, a variety of resources. We know more tricks and dodges, probably, than were ever known before. No, what we lack is the intrinsic principle, the soul of the thing, the very idea of the subject. We take notes, we make journeys; emptiness! emptiness! We become scholars, archaeologists, historians, doctors, cobblers, people of taste. What is the good of all that? Where is the heart, the verve, the sap? Where to start out from? Where to go? We're good at sucking, we play a lot of tongue games, we pet for hours: but – the real thing! To ejaculate, beget the child! (Flaubert 1979a, 198–99)

"Travelling makes one modest," he later observed. He did not seek to appropriate the Orient itself. He seems to have seen the myth as a peculiarly Western neurosis. Thus did *Salammbô* dramatically prophesy the searing rage of male mysteria (a sickness that Flaubert knew at first hand) toward the Commune.

The case of orientalism illustrates a general point. The same processes that increased the capacity to understand the world rendered its misrepresentation all the more imperative. And this tension, as we shall see, applied as strongly to the urban view of rurality and to bourgeois views of "the other Paris" as it did to the Orient. The problem is to unravel the tension in order not naïvely to replicate it.

The unification of the world through monetization and commodity exchange could produce its own peculiar fetishisms. Thus did Hugo, in his essay in the *Paris Guide of 1867*, produce a simplistic panegyric to a unified Europe, one free of national boundaries and expressive of a common culture, at the very moment when geopolitical tensions were on the rise. The phantasmagoria of capitalist culture that reached its apogee in the 1867 Paris Exhibition blinded even him.

Consider also the attempt of Elisée Reclus to construct a very different kind of geographical understanding of the world compared, for example, to Michelet's. Reclus believed in the potential harmony not only of "man" with "nature" but also of all the different cultures that populated the earth. Behind that there lay a utopian vision. "Humanity, until now divided into distinct currents, will be no more than a single river, and, reunited into a single flow, we will descend together toward the great sea where all life will lose itself and be renovated" (cited in Dunbar 1978, 52). Free of the psychodrama imposed by the "progressive" Michelet, this admirer of Proudhon, fellow conspirator with Bakunin, and future collaborator with Kropotkin produced a geographical vision that had all the flavor of the Parisian craft workers' optimistic mutualism. An active supporter of worker cooperation and association, his vision paralleled that of the International as it reached out to unite workers of the world in common struggle. The rude shock of the Franco-Prussian War (when workers of the world, not for the first time, fought each other at ruling class behest) and the Commune demonstrated the weakness in the vision. Reclus never truly grappled with the paradox that the very processes that were opening up the world to his scrutiny (the railroads, the commercial links, and the information flows) were also crushing the independence and autonomy of local cultures and communities with the same ruthlessness as they were driving the craft worker into an undifferentiated proletariat. While Michelet unconsciously justified that triumph, Reclus gave testimony to powerful sentiments of resistance.

Images of the city-country relation within a changing national economy of space were no less confused by class interests and prejudices. While it was fashionable to affect a certain disdain for rural and provincial life in bourgeois circles, there was a deeper recognition that the country was the secure base for all those unearned revenues. It also appeared as a peaceful haven of submission and reaction compared to the rebellious incoherence of Paris. That was where the threatened bourgeois (and even their artists and writers like Delacroix, Flaubert, and George Sand) fled to when matters got out of hand, and it was from there that the National Guards was mobilized to crush Parisian revolts in 1848. It appeared as the secure rock upon which Parisian life and French politics were founded. Bucolic images of rurality in the novels of George Sand reassured. Even the worker poets (many from the provinces) whom she encouraged appeared naïve enough in their socialism to be unthreatening. Despised for its parochialism, mocked for its ignorance, and occasionally patronized, the peasantry was the broad back upon which much of Parisian society stood. The extensive rural resistance to the coup d'état came, therefore, as a shock. It indicated class relations, discontent, and revolutionary sentiment in the countryside. And this was the sentiment that Courbet brought to the *Salon* of 1851. Clark (1973b) tells the story of the rising tide of criticism as Courbet took his paintings from his rural home to Dijon and then to Paris. The trouble was that the paintings not only explored work but they also rendered explicit the class relations that lay behind it. And they did so with the fierce realism that many dubbed "socialist" and that made him "the Proudhon of painting." Courbet helped explode a myth as to what the countryside was all about. And it was, of course, from exactly that countryside, rich with the ambiguities of its own class experience, that new workers poured into Paris, carrying with them from Creuse and Var, from Seine-et-Oise and Doubs, their own particular brands of revolutionary sentiment. Many a leader of the workers' movement of 1868–71 had, like Varlin, provincial and rural origins.

The interior transformation of Paris and the beginnings of suburbanization were likewise perceived and understood through lenses of class. Subsequent commentators have replicated the ambiguities without always understanding them. On the one hand, we find Berman (1982, 153) treating Baudelaire's "Eyes of the Poor" as an image of how Haussman's boulevards "inadvertently broke down the self-enclosed and hermetically sealed world of traditional urban poverty," so making a fact of "the misery that was once a mystery." On the other hand, there is also a long tradition of thinking which sees increasing spatial segregation due to Haussmanization as the crux of the problem. And there may be a sense in which both can be true.

Paris experienced a dramatic shift from the introverted, private, and personalized urbanism of the July Monarchy to an extroverted, public, and collectivized style of urbanism under the Second Empire. An English visitor thought the latter "a coarse form of communism" and wondered how his compatriots could so laud the practical application of a doctrine which, in its theoretical form, "smites them with so much horror" (St. John 1854, 11). It was, of course, capitalistic communism (to use Marx's phrase). Public investments were organized around private gain, and public spaces appropriated for private use; exteriors became interiors for the bourgeoisie, while panoramas, dioramas, and photography brought the exterior into the interior (Benjamin 1973; Vidler 1978). The boulevards, lit by gas lights, dazzling shop window displays, and cafés open to the street (an innovation of the Second Empire), became corridors of homage to the power of money and commodities, play spaces for the bourgeoisie. When Baudelaire's lover suggests the proprietor might send the ragged man and his children packing, it is the sense of proprietorship over public space that is really significant, rather than the all-too-familiar encounter with poverty.

The irony, of course, was that the new means of communication (boulevards, streets, omnibuses) and illumination opened up the city to scrutiny in a way that had not been possible before. The urban space was experienced, therefore, in a radically different way. Frédéric Moreau, the hero of *L'education sentimentale,* moves from space to space in Paris and its suburbs, collecting experiences of quite different qualities as he goes. The sensation of space is quite different from that in Balzac. The same disaggregations may be there, but what is special is the way that Frédéric moves so freely and easily, even into and out of the spaces of the 1848 revolution. He glides as easily from space to space and relationship to relationship as money and commodities change hands. And he does so with the same cynicism and lassitude. And by the end of the Second Empire even the popular classes could take excursions to that strange hybrid landscape of the suburb, a frontier region in which the commodification of access to nature as a consumption artifact (see Chap. 2) was becoming as important as the search for open land for new industrial and housing development.

How, then, to distinguish oneself in the midst of that restless crowd of purchasers that confronted the rising tide of commodities on the boulevards?

Benjamin's (1973) stunning analysis of Baudelaire's fascination with the man in the crowd, the *flâneur* and the dandy, swept along in the crowd, intoxicated by it, yet somehow apart from it, provides a reference point. The rising tide of commodity and money circulation cannot be held back. The anonymity of the crowd and of money circulation can hide all kinds of personal secrets. Chance encounters within the crowd help us penetrate the fetishism. These were the moments that Baudelaire relished. The prostitute, the ragpicker, the impoverished and obsolete old clown, a worthy old man in rags, all become vital characters in an urban drama. The poet is startled by an encounter in a public park: "It is impossible not to be gripped by the spectacle of this sickly population which swallows the dust of factories, breathes in particles of cotton, and lets its tissues be permeated by white lead, mercury and all the poisons needed for the production of masterpieces" (cited in Benjamin 1973, 74). Open to chance encounters, the poet can reconstruct the innumerable interrelations between the medley of hands that money touches.

Yet it was exactly such encounters that the bourgeoisie (like the lover in "Eyes of the Poor") could not stomach. Rising class fears impelled them to try to close off the public spaces that Haussman had opened up. And they had another fear: the crowd might hide subversive elements or suddenly become an unruly mob. The fears were well grounded. When Blanqui decided to review his secret army, the word went out, and two thousand troops, all unknown to each other and to him, paraded past him in the midst of a crowd on the Champ-de-Mars that did not even notice. Spaces and the crowd had to be controlled if the bourgeoisie was to maintain its class position and power. The dilemma in 1868–71, as in 1848, was that the republican bourgeoisie had to open its space in order to achieve its own bourgeois revolution. Weakened, it could not resist the rising pressure of the working-class and revolutionary movements. It was for this reason that the reoccupation of central Paris by the popular classes took on such symbolic importance. For it occurred in a context where the poor and the working class were being chased, in imagination as well as in fact, from the strategic spaces and even off the boulevards now viewed as bourgeois interiors. The more space was opened up physically, the more it had to be partitioned and closed off through social practice. Zola, writing in retrospect, presents as closed those same Parisian spaces that Flaubert had seen as open. Thus did the geographical imagination of the bourgeoisie impose sociospatial structuration on a Paris that Haussman's works had opened up to closer scrutiny.

When private representations enter into public rhetoric, they become means and motivations for both individual and collective action. It is always easier, of course, to reconstruct what people said, much harder to guess how they thought. And individual variation in this sphere is often so great that any general statement must appear misleading. Yet within the numerous conflicting eddies of ideas, Henry James's "restless analyst" can sometimes distill broad themes or at least make broad and venturesome judgments about major configurations of motivation. The final testing ground must lie, however, in action. For there is much that can be thought that never acquires the status of material force, since it stays forever locked in the realm of dreams. The themes we have here examined were not of that sort. The experience of the Commune saw all of them enter into social life, often with a vengeance. And there is enough evidence of the ordering of daily life in Second Empire Paris to make it at least reasonable to infer that the manner of the rhetoric and representation, as well as of the science and the sentiment, were more than just idle moments for the few. What ought, however, to be added is another category, that of silences – the silences of that multitude whose ideas we cannot trace and the strategic silences of those we can.

XII. THE GEOPOLITICS OF URBAN TRANSFORMATION

> Mankind . . . inevitably sets itself only such tasks as it is able to solve, since closer examination will always show that the problem itself arises only when the material conditions for its solution are already present or at least in the course of formation.
>
> – *Marx*

"When the imperial mantle finally falls on the shoulders of Louis Bonaparte," Marx predicted in 1852, "the bronze statue of Napoleon will crash from the top of the Vendôme Column." On May 16 1871, the hated symbol was collapsed before a huge communard crowd, temporarily diverted from the threatening gunfire of the forces of reaction encircling Paris. Between the prediction and the event lay eighteen years of "ferocious farce."

The ferocity had dual, sometimes complementary, but in the end conflictual, origins. The Empire, to protect both itself and the civil society over which it reigned, resorted to an arbitrariness of state power which touched everyone, from the street entertainers hounded off the boulevards to the bankers excluded from the lucrative city loan business. But the accelerating power of the circulation and accumulation of capital was also at work, transforming labor processes, spatial integrations, credit relations, living conditions, and class relations with the same ferocity as it assumed in the creative destruction of the Parisian built environment. In the aftermath of 1848, the arbitrariness of state power appeared a crucial prop to private property and capital. But the farther the Empire degenerated into open farce, the more evident it became that modernity could not be produced out of imperial tradition, that there was and could be no stable class basis of imperial power, and that the supposed omnipotence of government sat ill with the omniscience of market rationality. The schism between the Saint-Simonians and the liberal political economists therefore symbolized a deep antagonism between political and economic processes.

Napoleon III's strategy for maintaining power was simple: "Satisfy the interests of the most numerous classes and attach to oneself the upper classes" (Zeldin 1958, 10). Unfortunately, the explosive force of capital accumulation tended to undermine such a strategy. The growing gap between the rich (who supported the Empire precisely because it offered protection against social-istic demands) and the poor led to mounting antagonism between them. Every move the emperor made to attach the one simply alienated the other. Besides, the workers remembered as fact (adorned with growing fictions) that there had once been a Republic that they had helped produce and that had voiced their social concerns. The demand for liberty and equality in the market also tended to emphasize a republican political ideology within segments of the bourgeoisie. This was as much at odds with the authori-tarianism of Empire as it was antagonistic to plans for the social republic. The split between political and social conceptions of the Republic – so evident in 1848 – continued to be of great significance. It could be and was used to great effect to divide and rule. But that gave no secure class basis to political power. The Empire was, however, so caught up in the maelstrom of capitalistic progress that it could not satisfy the traditionalists and the conservatives who objected to the new materialism and the new class configurations that were in the course of formation. The consensus behind imperial authority was hard to sustain and threatened to evaporate entirely when problems of overaccumu-lation and devaluation once more arose. The contradictions of capitalist growth were therefore matched by unstable political lurchings from this or that side of the class spectrum or from this or that faction. When, in 1862, the emperor graced James Rothschild with a visit to his country house (to the immense chagrin of the Pereires), and when, in the same year, he granted two hundred thousand francs to workers to send their elected delegates to London (where Karl Marx so eagerly awaited them), then something was plainly amiss. Such shifting, far from alleviating matters, only added anxiety as to what was to replace the Empire if and when it should fall.

The monarchists, though extremely powerful, offered no real alternative. Divided amongst themselves, they gathered around them ultraconservative Catholics, traditionalists, and almost every rectionary sentiment antagonistic to capitalistic progress. With a strong base in rural France, their influence in Paris tended to shrink during the Second Empire and in the end was confined mainly to the very traditional salons of the aristocratic Left Bank. While the

Empire had its supporters, particularly among the finance capitalists, state functionaries, and the bourgeois property owners of western Paris who were well satisfied with Haussman's works, the centers of business, commerce, and professional services (like law) on the Right Bank became bastions of republicanism, usually tempered by pragmatic financial opportunism that gave the Empire many opportunities to coopt them. The Café de Madrid on the boulevard Montmartre was the geopolitical meeting point of this kind of republicanism with the more declassé and sometimes bohemian sentiments of writers drawn to that area as a center of press and communications power. The republicanism of the Left Bank was of a rather different order. The product of students and academics, it was less pragmatic and more revolutionary and utopian, capable of spinning off in all kinds of directions into alliances with workers and artisans or into its own forms of revolutionary and conspiratorial politics. Working-class Paris, sprawled in a vast semicircle from northwest to southwest with its thickest concentration in the northeast, was solidly republican, but with strong social concerns and not a few resentments at the betrayal suffered at the hands of bourgeois republicanism in 1848.

The struggle that unfolded in Paris during the 1860s and presaged the Commune was of epic proportions. It was a struggle to give political meaning to concepts of community and class; to identify the true bases of class alliances and antagonisms; to find political, economic, organizational, and physical spaces in which to mobilize and from which to press demands. It was, in all these senses, a geopolitical struggle for the transformation of the Parisian economy, as well as the city's politics and culture.

The parting of the ways between capital and Empire was not registered by dramatic confrontation but by the slow erosion of the organic links between them. The counterattack of Parisian property owners against the conditions of expropriation, the resistance of the Bank of France to the cheap credit that the Saint-Simonians sought, the growing resentment of industrialists at Haussman's harassment, the increasing domination of small owners and shopkeepers by finance capital, all signaled growing disaffection of this or that fragment of the bourgeoisie. Though some, like the property owners, partially returned to the imperial fold, others were more and more alienated. Ironically, the more successfully the Empire repressed the workers, the freer the bourgeois opposition felt to express itself. Yet the more that opposition grew, the greater the political space within which workers could operate. On the one hand, republican rhetoric shielded them, while on the other, the growth of bourgeois opposition forced the Empire to curry the workers' favor as part of its populist base.

The reconstruction of the republican party was one of the most signal achievements of the Second Empire. And while it depended upon the coming together of many different currents of opinion in many parts of the country, what happened in Paris was crucial. Powerfully but incoherently implanted within the liberal professions (which saw the Republic perhaps as a means to acquire an autonomous class power) and with strong potential support in business, industry, and commerce, bourgeois republicanism needed a much sharper definition than it had achieved in 1848. The rambunctious, explosive image of femininity on the barricades had to be corseted, tamed, and made thoroughly respectable. The declassé republicanism of students, intellectuals, writers, and artists had somehow to be confronted and controlled. But the bourgeois republicans also needed working-class support if they were to succeed. How to gain that support without making any but the mildest concessions to social conceptions of the Republic that typically threatened private property, money power, the circulation of capital, and even patriarchy and the family was the fledgling republican party's most pressing problem. On questions of political liberty, legality, freedom of expression, and representative government (locally as in the nation), it was possible to make common cause. Bourgeois republicans therefore tried to keep such issues at the center of political debate. Questions of freedom of association, workers' rights, and representation were touchier. And debate over the social republic had to be buried within a reformist rhetoric on relatively safe questions like improved education. Bourgeois republicanism tended to become violent in its defense of patriarchy and vicious in its attitudes toward socialism. But the terms of alliance with the working class always had to be open to negotiation at the same time as the battle between social and political conceptions of the Republic had to be fought out, unto death, as it turned out, in the bloody week of the Commune.

The revival of working-class politics in the early 1860s initially rested upon the reassertion of traditional institutional rights. The mutual benefit societies, in spite of imperial regulation, had early become the legal front for all kinds of covert worker organization. Their direct subversion into trade union forms (they were at the root of most strike activity) provoked innumerable prosecutions in the 1850s. But their indirect use for political purposes was quite uncontrollable. Herein lay, for example, the significance of funerals, since this was a key benefit and brought all members together to listen to a graveside discourse that often became a political speech. The Empire became less willing to attack the mutual benefit societies because it increasingly needed them as a means to canvass and to mobilize working-class support. There is considerable evidence, says Thomas (n.d. 192), that association and coalitions existed in practice without prosecution by the early 1860s. The mutual benefit societies became centers of consciousness formation and means for organizing the collective expression of demands. The corporatist forms hidden within them became more explicit as craft workers sought to protect themselves against the ravages of technological and organizational change and the flood of unskilled immigration. This use of the mutual benefit frame had important effects. It helped bridge the separation between working and living and preserved a unity of concern for production and consumption questions. In the context of Parisian industry, it also reinforced the search for alternatives down mutualist, cooperative paths. Both consciousness and political action were to draw much of their strength from that sense of unity.

The wave of institution building became most marked after 1862. The emperor, under increasing attack from upper-class royalists in alliance with conservative Catholics and threatened on the other flank by the revival of bourgeois republicanism, was forced to seek support from a working class that even his own prefects were telling him was in dire straits. But imperial initiatives to draw workers to the side of industrial progress and Empire sparked little grass roots response save a lengthy explanation from Tolain, which earned him an interview with the emperor and the right to form a worker commission made up of presidents of mutual benefit societies, thus recognizing the latter's de facto corporatist and professional role (Thomas n.d., 199). Ironically, the commission meetings began at the very moment of one of the first major strikes of Parisian craft workers, that of the printers in 1862. The printers' leaders were imprisoned for the crime of coalition, even though public sympathy (including that of many republicans) was with them. When the emperor pardoned them, he in effect rendered the laws against coalition and association moot. He did so as the workers he had helped send to the fateful London exposition were returning, telling tales of better working conditions and wages achieved in Britain through trade union forms of organization.

But, curiously, neither side was yet willing to recognize the realities of class struggle. The opening given to working-class politics in the early 1860s initially provoked a wave of mutualist sentiments. The mutual benefit societies flourished in numbers and membership, while schemes for mutual credit (such as the Crédit au Travail), consumer cooperatives (two founded in 1864), and cooperative housing burst out all over (some even drew the emperor's private support). The International's statutes were approved by the government in 1864. At the same time, the Empire engaged Emile Ollivier (later to head the liberal Empire of 1869) to rewrite the law on combinations. The law, designed to avoid organized class struggle, gave the working class the right to strike but not the right to organize or assemble. The bookbinders and bronze workers, followed by the stonecutters, promptly celebrated by striking for shorter hours and no wage reductions. But the labor movement's main focus was on organizing rights and conditions of labor rather than on wage levels in the early 1860s. Proudhon was, at this point, at the height of his influence, inveighing against strikes and unions (he almost seemed to approve of Ollivier's law) and pushing for mutualist worker democracy. The French delegates to the International's meetings of 1866 in Geneva, led by Tolain, carried with them a veritable charter for Proudhonism and mutualism, thus testifying to the deep hold of such ideas over craft worker consciousness.

The workers' movement had its setbacks too. Attempts to create an independent workers' press were quickly squashed, in part through bourgeois republican opposition. The attempt to define an independent political space likewise failed. The celebrated *Manifesto of the Sixty*, put out in 1864 by craft workers with radical republican support, raised the question of workers' rights as a general political issue. The effect was to raise the spectre of class struggle and to provoke the unfounded but not unreasonable suspicion that the workers' movement was being used by the Empire to frustrate bourgeois republican opposition. When Tolain, a signer of the Manifesto and a founder of the Parisian branch of the International, ran as an independent workers' candidate in 1863 to emphasize the distinctiveness of the workers' cause, he was vilified in the republican press and so squeezed by opposition from that quarter that he received fewer than five hundred votes in a parliamentary election that saw the bourgeois republicans sweep to power in much of Paris.

The recession of 1867–68 marked a radical realignment of class forces as well as a turning point in worker militancy and rhetoric. What became known as the "millionaires' strike" saw the massive accumulation of surplus capital in the coffers of the Bank of France, stagnation in public works and in the upper-class Parisian property market, and fiercer international competition and rising unemployment in the face of strongly rising prices. The downfall of the Pereires, a jittery stock market, and the growing likelihood of geopolitical conflict with Prussia undermined the sense of security which the authoritarianism of Empire had earlier been able to impart. The spectacle of the 1867 Exposition diverted attention at one level, though many noted the irony that it celebrated the commodity fetish and consumerism at a time of shrinking real incomes and that it brought competitive commodities as well as the king of Prussia into the very heart of Paris at a time of heightened international competition and geopolitical tension.

The workers' movement became much more militant and concerned with real wages rather than organization. Within the International this was marked by the eclipse of the mutualists like Tolain and Fribourg and their replacement by communists like Varlin and Malon whose attitudes, given their youth, were less affected by memories of 1848 and more forged out of the actualities of class conflict through the 1860s. The persecution of the International at that point only helped the process of transition by removing the original leaders, giving it greater and greater credibility among Parisian workers and forcing it into the underground where it encountered militant Blanquists – themselves turning to the organization of the working class as part of their revolutionary strategy. Yet even though Varlin, for one, moved rapidly to a more and more collectivist politics, striving to organize and federate unions into agents of mass working-class action, he still clung to certain mutualist principles of organization as the basis for the transition to socialism (Lejeune 1977; Rougerie 1968b). The craft workers straddled the ambiguity between class organization and mutualism without, apparently, being too aware of the tension between them.

1867 saw important strikes by bronze workers (supported for the first time by international funds), tailors, and construction workers oriented primarily toward higher wages. In that same year generalized discontent over living standards spilled over into street demonstrations that touched the unorganized and unskilled workers. For the first time since 1848, the unorganized of Belleville descended into the space of inner-city craft workers to express their discontent. The bourgeoisie was not beguiled, either, by the important concessions made to it. The return to quasi-parliamentary government (symbolized by the restoration of the speaker's tribune in the legislature) opened up a forum for complaint. And there was much to complain about. The free-speech movement of the early 1860s had already turned the Left Bank into a hotbed of student and intellectual unrest. Industrialists complained about Haussman, and workshop masters and shopkeepers complained fiercely about conditions of credit and the power of the grand monopolies that the state had done so much to support. The recession and the defeat of Austria at Sadowa by Prussia (to say nothing of the unhappy Mexican venture) shook the confidence of everyone in a government that had come to power on the promise of peace and prosperity and that now looked like it could not deliver on either. Those bourgeois like Thiers who had long felt excluded from the grand feast of state wealth and power stood ready to mobilize the agitation and unrest to their own advantage. Even the monarchists could find causes, like that of decentralization, around which they sought to rally popular discontent.

All of this was mere prelude to the awesome struggles of 1868–71. But it was an important prelude because it posed the question of what class alliance could emerge capable of replacing the Empire. Could the monarchists wean away enough support from the bourgeois center to stymie the republican thrust? Could the bourgeois republicans control the working-class movement to keep the political republic out of the clutches of the socialists? Could the radical free-thinkers and declassé republicans enter into alliance with a workers' movement that overcame its craft worker bias and reached out to encompass the unskilled and so create a revolutionary and socialist republic? Could the Empire divide and rule and manipulate each and every one of these factions through cooptation and its police and provocateur power? In practice, the Empire was forced into more and more concessions. It relaxed press censorship (May 1868) and permitted public meetings on "non-political" topics (June 1868). The right to form unions was conceded in 1869. But the state in no way relinquished its powers of provocation and repression.

The International's leaders looked to collaborate with the republican bourgeois opposition and were promptly arrested as early as the end of 1867. The respectable republicans let the call for a class alliance pass unheard, while the workers were equally critical of such a tactic, since they remembered only too well how the political republic had betrayed them in 1848. The second wave of the International's leaders sought an independent space within which they could build the strength of their own movement. Varlin led the bookbinders' mutual benefit society and transformed it into a vigorous and coherent union in 1869. He helped found an extensive system of consumer cooperatives (La Marmite) in 1867, bringing cheap food, politics, and consumption together in a more coherent way than the cabaret, which the mass of workers who lived in boardinghouses otherwise patronized. He headed the movement to federate the numerous Parisian unions (perhaps twenty thousand strong) in 1869 and played a leading role in the International's efforts to unify working-class action over national and international space. It was exactly such a broad geopolitical conception of the struggle that terrified the "honest bourgeois." The problem for Varlin was to integrate the restless mass of unorganized and unskilled workers into a movement that always had a craft-worker base. The scaffold he and others had erected by 1870 was by no means sufficient to that task. Recognizing that weakness, he sought tactical alliances with the radical and often revolutionary fringe of the bourgeoisie.

There had always been such a fringe within *la bohème* and within the student movement. The Blanquists had set about organizing such discontent around their own program. But the relaxation of press censorship revealed a much wider swathe of disaffection. Rochefort became the instant hero of the popular and disaffected classes with *La Lanterne,* a newspaper full of radical critique and revolutionary rhetoric (which earned Rochefort periodic spells in jail and which horrified the bourgeoisie). Recognizing the power of this movement, Varlin established a tactical alliance to try to ensure that social questions were properly integrated into any radical republican program. The radical republicans, for their part, had to erase the memory of betrayal in 1848. They made the attempt in 1868 by recalling the death of a republican representative, Baudin, on the barricades of 1851. They proposed a massive pilgrimage to his tomb on the Day of the Dead. The government tried to bar their way, and those who did get into the cemetery of Montmartre had a hard time finding the grave. Hence arose the idea of a public subscription. The government's prosecution of those engaged in the affair only drew more attention to the "crime" of the coup d'état while allowing a young lawyer, Gambetta, to become another instant hero of the radical cause. The symbolic resurrection of Baudin, the creation of tradition, was, in a way, a stroke of genius. It focused on the illegitimacy of Empire in such a way as to symbolize the bourgeois role in the heart of the space of worker struggle (this was the special virtue of the cemetery of Montmartre). It was by gestures of this sort that the radical bourgeoisie reached out to embrace the "other Paris" in symbolic unity.

The "nonpolitical" public meetings, which began on June 28, 1868, were extraordinary affairs. Heavily concentrated in the zones of disaffection, no amount of government surveillance could prevent them from turning into occasions for mass education and political consciousness raising. The manner of the battle for political consciousness is described in detail in Dalotel, Faure, and Freirmuth (1980). The geopolitics was highly predictive of the Commune. Not only were the meetings unevenly spread across the Parisian space (fig. 16), but specialization of audience, topic, and place was quickly established. The political economists and bourgeois reformers who looked to the meetings as opportunities for mass education about their cause were outgunned and often shouted down in the meeting halls of the "other Paris." An assortment of radicals, feminists, socialists, Blanquists, and other revolutionaries dominated what became regular political theater in many popular quarters of the city. The political economists and reformers were forced to withdraw to the relative safety of the Left Bank and Right Bank center, leaving the north and northeast of the city entirely to the radicals, socialists, and revolutionaries. It seemed that the "other Paris" was now the exclusive space for popular political agitation. That trend was reinforced by a sudden resurgence of popular street culture, revolutionary songs and ballads suddenly bursting from a murky underground where they had lain dormant for almost two decades.

This kind of agitation was as disturbing to the respectable bourgeois as it was to the supporters of Empire. Could the Empire rally the disaffected in the name of law and order? Only if it made strong concessions. 1869 therefore began with official disavowal of Haussman's slippery financing in the face of fiscally conservative bourgeois critics. The appearance of Jules Ferry's swingeing attack on the prefect in the *Comptes fantastiques d'Haussman* in 1868 charged him with all kinds of improprieties. The aftermath was curious. First, it forced Haussman to reduce public works activities and depressed the construction trade and Parisian industry even further thus exacerbating social discontent. Second, none of those who attacked him denied the utility of his works, and many of them pleaded for completion of this or that part of his

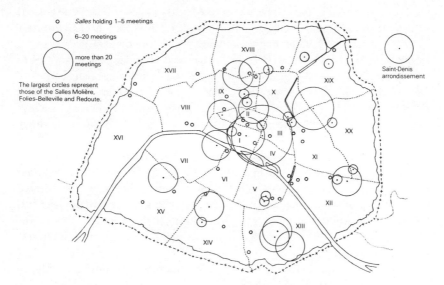

Fig. 16.   *The public meetings of Paris: Location and frequency, 1868–1870.*
(Reproduced, with permission, from A. Dalotel, A. Faure, and J-C. Freirmuth,
Aux Origines de la Commune: Le Mouvement des Réunions Publiques à Paris,
1868–1870, *Editions La Découverte, 1980.)*

project in 1869 or, like Rothschild, were only too happy to lend the city
money as it needed it. It increasingly appeared as if Haussman was a mere
surrogate target for the emperor and that the exclusivity of his seeming
patronage was what was at stake.

The subsequent election campaign of May 1869 was surrounded with
political agitation. A riot ensued when Ollivier tried to take the theme of
support for liberal Empire into the center of Paris. The crowd at Châtelet
moved noisily to the Faubourg Saint-Antoine, the traditional hearth of
revolution, before dispersing. The next day a crowd of twenty thousand
moved around the craft worker quarters; and the day after that a crowd of
fifteen thousand tried to move from the Sorbonne, where it had assembled, to
the Bastille, but found its way blocked. During this phase, Haussman's
boulevards were turned into a battleground. Hitherto appropriated by
bourgeois strollers and consumers, they were suddenly taken over by a
surging mass of discontented workers, students, shopkeepers, and street
people. On June 12 a crowd even penetrated as far as the Opera and set up the
first real barricade. The bourgeois response was to try and reassert their rights
to boulevard space by chasing off undesirables. Even the emperor saw the
symbolic value of passing along the contested terrain between the Opera and

the Port-Saint-Denis, though he was greeted with glacial silence as he passed. But the crowds upon the boulevards hid secrets. It was never clear, for example, whether the violent agitations and the "white blouses" were signs of secret police activity or not. Certainly, they had abundant opportunities to stir up threats to law and order and scare the respectable bourgeois back into the imperial fold. It was never clear, either, just how revolutionary in spirit the crowds were. Large crowds of twenty thousand or more frequently dispersed when asked to do so by law-abiding republicans. And the huge demonstration of over one hundred thousand people, which assembled after the emperor's nephew shot a radical journalist, Victor Noir, dispersed quietly at Rochefort's request rather than confront the forces of order that barred their way into central Paris, even though Rochefort himself had more than hinted that the day of revolution was near. On this occasion, the Blanquists had wanted to start the insurrection but found little support. Could the ambiguity and dispersal of opposition sentiment be overcome and transformed into revolution?

The elections of May and June 1869 indicated otherwise. Only in Belleville was a radical sympathizer elected, and Gambetta was a politician who could bridge moderate socialist and left bourgeois opinion with skill and authenticity. Elsewhere, the political republicans swept the board; it even took a very conservative Thiers to overcome narrowly the Empire's candidate in the bourgeois west. The plebiscite a year later was harder to interpret, but the abstentions (urged by the radical left) did not increase markedly, and although the no's prevailed, the Empire still received a surprising number of affirmative votes. It would take, it seemed, a much more thorough organization and education of the popular classes to bring the social republic into being. And it was exactly on such a task that the socialists spent their efforts. The public meetings provided a basis for neighborhood organizations, while the themes broached encouraged the formation of trade unions, consumer cooperatives, producers' cooperatives, feminist organizations, and the like. These were the organizational infrastructures that were to be used to such good effect in the Commune. And there is no question as to their revolutionary political orientation, though there was much room for disagreement, interpersonal feuds, and neighborhood conflicts. But this form of opposition had a different orientation from that on the streets. Strikes in commerce, tanning, and woodworking and the building of links between unions and neighborhoods proceeded at a different rhythm and had more definite targets at the same time as they were relatively more immune to police infiltration. Here was the grand dividing line between the socialists, who urged the patient building of a revolutionary movement, and the Blanquists, who looked to spontaneous violent insurrection. But by 1870 it was plain that the mass of the bourgeoisie was looking for a legal way out of the impasse of Empire, was shifting away from any coalition with the "reds." And it used its ownership and influence within the press to hammer home the message of law and order to workers and petite bourgeoisie alike. The discontent, however, daily became more threatening as living conditions deteriorated and the economy stagnated. Conflict in Belleville in February 1870 left several dead, many arrested, and considerable property damage (usually that of unpopular shopkeepers and landlords). The ferment of discontent seemed uncontainable as the Empire lost its nerve and the bourgeoisie held its ground. Though conditions were desperate, the International's leaders (unlike the Blanquists') thought the political conditions were not yet ripe for social revolution. They were, as the Commune was to show only too well, right in that judgment. What is extraordinary is how far, wide, and deep they had ranged in the construction of a revolutionary organization capable of uniting many disparate elements within the dispersed space of Paris (as well as France). The tragedy, in the end, was that conjunctural events forced them to put their efforts on the line so prematurely in defense of a losing cause. That conjuncture was less accidental, however, than might be supposed. For all the signs were there that the "honest bourgeois" were not only concerned to have done with Empire and seize the fruits of political power but that they were also determined to have done with the "reds" once and for all and to subject them to their own vile brand of "final solution." Thus was the final act of ferocious farce left until that bloody week in May.

Exactly what happened in the Commune is beyond our ken. But much of it had its roots in the processes and effects of the transformation of Paris in the Second Empire. The organization of municipal workshops for women; the encouragement given to producer and consumer cooperatives; the suspension of the nightwork in the bakeries; and the moratorium on rent payments, debt collections, and the sale of items from the municipal pawnshop at Mont-de-Piété reflected the sore points that had bothered working-class Paris for years. The assemblies of craft workers; the strengthening of unions; the vigor of the neighborhood clubs that grew out of the public meeting places of 1868–70 and that were to play a crucial role in the defense of *quartiers*; the setting up of the Union of Women; and the attempt to pull together working political organizations that bridged the tensions between centralization and decentralization, between hierarchy and democracy (the Committee of the Twenty Arrondissements, the Central Committee of the National Guard, and the Commune itself) all testified to the vigorous pursuit of new organizational forms generated from the nexus of the old. The creation of a Ministry of Labor and strong measures toward free and nonreligious primary and professional education testified to the depth of social concern.

But the Commune never challenged private property or money power in earnest. It requisitioned only abandoned workshops and dwellings and prostrated itself before the legitimacy of the Bank of France (an episode that Marx and Lenin noted well). The majority sought principled and mutually acceptable accommodation rather than confrontation (even some of the Blanquists in practice went in that direction). But then, too, much of the opposition to the Commune was also given. The schism between the "moderate" republican mayors of the arrondissements (who got short shrift in Versailles when they tried to mediate) and the Commune grew as tensions rose. The bourgeoisie, which had deigned to remain to brave the rigors of the siege, quickly showed its teeth in mobilizing the "Friends of Order" demonstration of March 21 and 22 and thereafter turned western Paris into an easy point of penetration for the forces of reaction. The map of voting patterns for the Commune was predictable enough. The difference this time was that hegemonic power now lay with a worker-based movement (fig. 17).

Thiers's decision to locate the National Assembly in Versailles and his withdrawal of all executive functions from Paris after his failure to disarm Paris on March 18, crystallized the forces of rural reaction in a way that the Commune's faint calls for urban and rural solidarity could not match. His mobilization of rural ignorance and fear, fed by vicious propaganda into an army prepared to give no quarter (were they not charged, after all, with chasing the red devils out of a sinful and atheistic Paris?), showed he meant to have a cathartic resolution, come what may. Once the possibility of a quick preemptive strike against Versailles was lost, there was little the Commune could do except await its fate. The stress of that brought out divisions and fed interior discontents and rivalries within the uneasy class and factional alliance that produced the Commune. Splits between radical bourgeois, each armed with his own splendid theory of revolution, between practical patriots and peddlers of rhetoric and dreams, between workers bewildered by events and leaders of craft unions trying to render consistent and compelling interpretations, between loyalties to *quartier*, city, and nation, between centralizers and decentralizers, all gave the Commune an air of incoherence and a political practice riddled with internal conflict. But such divisions had been long in the making; their roots lay deep in tradition, and their evolution had been confused by the turn to capitalist modernity and the clash between the politics of Empire and the economy of capital. Once more, as Marx had written in the *Eighteenth Brumaire*, "The tradition of all the dead generations weighs like a nightmare on the brain of the living," but this time it was the working-class movement that internalized the nightmare. The Commune was a high price to pay to discredit pure Proudhonism and the pure Jacobinism drawn from the reconstructed spirit of 1789.

The Commune was a singular, unique, and dramatic event, perhaps the most extraordinary of its kind in capitalist urban history. It took war, the

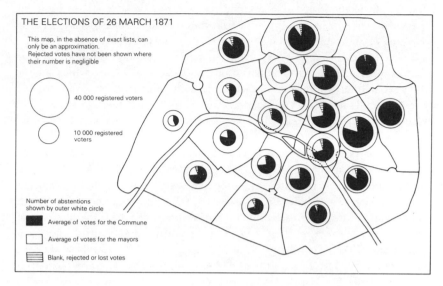

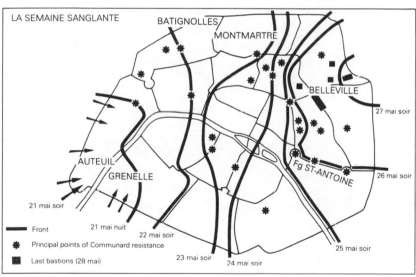

Fig. 17.   The elections of March 26, 1871, and the phases of reoccupation of Paris during the bloody week of May 1871. (Reproduced, with permission, from J. Rougerie, Paris Libre 1871, Editions du Seuil, 1971.)

desperation of the Prussian siege, and the humiliation of defeat to light the spark. But the raw materials for the Commune were put together by the slow rhythms of the capitalist transformation of its own historical geography. I have tried in this chapter to lay bare the complex modes of transformation in the economy and in social organization, politics, and culture which altered the visage of Paris in ineluctable ways. At each point along the way, we find people like Thiers and Varlin, like Paule Minck and Jules Michelet, like Haussman and Louis Lazare, like Louis Napoleon, Proudhon, and Blanqui, like the Pereires and the Rothschilds, swirling within the crowd of street singers and poets, ragpickers and craft workers, bankers and prostitutes, domestics and idle rich, students and grisettes, tourists, shopkeepers, and pawnbrokers, cabaret owners and property speculators, landlords, lawyers, and professors. Somehow all were contained with the same urban space, occasionally confronting each other on the boulevards or the barricades, and all of them struggling in their own ways to shape and control the social conditions of their own historical and geographical existence. That they did not do so under historical and geographical conditions of their own choosing is self-evident. The Commune was produced out of a search to transform the power and social relations within a particular class configuration constituted within a particular space of a capitalist world itself in the full flood of dramatic transition. We have much to learn from the study of such struggles. And there is much to admire, much that inspires there too.

4

Monument and Myth: The Building
of the Basilica of the Sacred Heart

Strategically placed atop a hill known as the butte Montmartre, the Basilica of Sacré-Coeur occupies a commanding position over Paris. Its five white marble domes and the campanile that rises beside them can be seen from every quarter of the city. Occasional glimpses of it can be caught from within the dense and cavernous network of streets which makes up old Paris. It stands out, spectacular and grand, to the young mothers parading their children in the Jardins de Luxembourg, to the tourists who painfully plod to the top of Notre Dame or who painlessly float up the escalators of the Centre Beaubourg, to the commuters crossing the Seine by metro at Grenelle or pouring into the Gare du Nord, to the Algerian immigrants who on Sunday afternoons wander to the top of the rock in the parc des Buttes Chaumont. It can be seen clearly by the old men playing "boule" in the place du Colonel Fabien, on the edge of the traditional working class quarters of Belleville and La Villette – places that have an important role to play in our story.

On cold winter days when the wind whips the fallen leaves among the aging tombstones of the Père Lachaise cemetery, the basilica can be seen from the steps of the tomb of Adolphe Thiers, first president of the Third Republic of France. Though now almost hidden by the modern office complex of La Défense, it can be seen from more than twenty kilometers away in the Pavillion Henry IV in St. Germain-en-Laye, where Adolphe Thiers died. But by a quirk of topography, it cannot be seen from the famous Mur des Fédérés in that same Père Lachaise cemetery where, on May 27, 1871, some of the last few remaining soldiers of the Commune were rounded up after a fierce fight among the tombstones and summarily shot. You cannot see Sacré-Coeur from that ivy-covered wall now shaded by an aging chestnut. That place of pilgrimage for socialists, workers, and their leaders is hidden from a place of pilgrimage for the Catholic faithful by the brow of the hill on which stands the grim tomb of Adolphe Thiers.

Few would argue that the Basilica of Sacré-Coeur is beautiful or elegant (fig. 18). But most would concede that it is striking and distinctive, that its

Fig. 18.   The Basilica of Sacré-Coeur

direct Byzantine style achieves a kind of haughty grandeur which demands respect from the city spread out at its feet. On sunny days it glistens from afar, and even on the gloomiest of days its domes seem to capture the smallest particles of light and radiate them outward in a white marble glow. Floodlit by night it appears suspended in space, sepulchral and ethereal. Thus does Sacré-Coeur project an image of saintly grandeur, of perpetual remembrance. But remembrance of what?

The visitor drawn to the basilica in search of an answer to that question must first ascend the steep hillside of Montmartre. Those who pause to catch their breath will see spread out before them a marvelous vista of rooftops, chimneys, domes, towers, monuments – a vista of old Paris that has not changed much since that dull and foggy October morning in 1872, when the archbishop of Paris climbed those steep slopes only to have the sun miraculously chase both fog and cloud away to reveal the splendid panorama of Paris spread out before him. The archbishop marveled for a moment before crying out loud: "It is here, it is here where the martyrs are, it is here that the Sacred Heart must reign so that it can beckon all to it!" (Jonquet n.d.). So who are the martyrs commemorated here in the grandeur of this basilica?

The visitor who enters into that hallowed place will most probably first be struck by the immense painting of Jesus which covers the dome of the apse. Portrayed with arms stretched wide, the figure of Christ wears an image of the Sacred Heart upon his breast. Beneath, two words stand out directly from the Latin motto – GALLIA POENITENS. And beneath that stands a large gold casket containing the image of the Sacred Heart of Jesus, burning with passion, suffused with blood and surrounded with thorns. Illuminated day and night, it is here that pilgrims come to pray.

Opposite a life-size statue of Saint Marguerite-Marie Alacoque, words from a letter written by that saintly person – date, 1689; place, Paray-le-Monial – tell us more about the cult of the Sacred Heart:

THE ETERNAL FATHER WISHING REPARATION FOR THE BITTERNESS AND ANGUISH THAT THE ADORABLE HEART OF HIS DIVINE SON HAD EXPERIENCED AMONGST THE HUMILIATIONS AND OUTRAGES OF HIS PASSION DESIRES AN EDIFICE WHERE THE IMAGE OF THIS DIVINE HEART CAN RECEIVE VENERATION AND HOMAGE.

Prayer to the Sacred Heart of Jesus, which, according to the scriptures, had been exposed when a centurion thrust a lance through Jesus' side during his suffering upon the cross, was not unknown before the seventeenth century. But Marguerite-Marie, beset by visions, transformed the worship of the Sacred Heart into a distinctive cult within the Catholic church. Although her life was full of trials and suffering, her manner severe and rigorous, the predominant image of Christ which the cult projected was warm and loving, full of repentance and suffused with a gentle kind of mysticism (Jonquet n.d.; Dansette 1965).

Marguerite-Marie and her disciples set about propagating the cult with great zeal. She wrote to Louis XIV, for example, claiming to bring a message from Christ in which the king was asked to repent, to save France by dedicating himself to the Sacred Heart, to place its image upon his standard and to build a chapel to its glorification. It is from that letter of 1689 that the words now etched in stone within the basilica are taken.

The cult diffused slowly. It was not exactly in tune with eighteenth-century French rationalism, which strongly influenced modes of belief among Catholics and stood in direct opposition to the hard, rigorous, and self-disciplined image of Jesus projected by the Jansenists. But by the end of the eighteenth century it had some important and potentially influential adherents. Louis XVI privately took devotion to the Sacred Heart for himself and his family. Imprisoned during the French Revolution, he vowed that within three months of his deliverance he would publicly dedicate himself to the Sacred Heart and thereby save France (from what, exactly, he did not say, nor did he need to). And he vowed to build a chapel to the worship of the Sacred Heart. The manner of Louis XVI's deliverance did not permit him to fulfill that vow. Marie-Antoinette did no better. The queen delivered up her last prayers to the Sacred Heart before keeping her appointment with the guillotine.

These incidents are of interest because they presage an association, important for our story, between the cult of the Sacred Heart and the reactionary monarchism of the *ancien régime*. This put adherents to the cult in firm opposition to the principles of the French Revolution. Believers in the principles of liberty, equality, and fraternity, who were in any case prone to awesome anticlerical sentiments and practices, were, in return, scarcely enamored of such a cult. Revolutionary France was no safe place to attempt to propagate it. Even the bones and other relics of Marguerite-Marie, now displayed in Paray-le-Monial, had to be carefully hidden during those years.

The restoration of the monarchy in 1815 changed all that. The Bourbon monarchs sought, under the watchful eye of the European powers, to restore whatever they could of the old social order. The theme of repentance for the excesses of the revolutionary era ran strong. Louis XVIII did not fulfill his dead brother's vow to the Sacred Heart, but he did built, with his own moneys, a Chapel of Expiation on the spot where his brother and his family had been so unceremoniously interred – GALLIA POENITENS. A society for the propagation of the cult of the Sacred Heart was founded, however, and proceedings for the glorification of Marguerite-Marie were transmitted to Rome in 1819. The link between conservative monarchism and the cult of the Sacred Heart was further consolidated.

The cult spread among conservative Catholics but was viewed with some suspicion by the liberal progressive wing of French Catholicism. But now another enemy was ravaging the land, disturbing the social order. France was undergoing the stress and tensions of capitalist industrialization. In fits and starts under the July Monarchy (installed in 1830 and just as summarily dispensed with in the revolution of 1848) and then in a great surge in the early years of the Second Empire of Napoleon III, France saw a radical transformation in certain sectors of its economy, in its institutional structures, and in its social order (Price 1975; Braudel and Labrousse 1976). This transformation threatened much that was sacred in French life, since it brought within its train a crass and heartless materialism, an ostentatious and morally decadent bourgeois culture, and a sharpening of class tensions. The cult of the Sacred Heart now assembled under its banner not only those devotees drawn by temperament or circumstance to the image of a gentle and forgiving Christ, not only those who dreamed of a restoration of the political order of yesteryear, but also all those who felt threatened by the materialist values of the new social order.

To these general conditions, French Catholics could also add some more specific complaints in the 1860s. Napoleon III had finally come down on the side of Italian unification and committed himself politically and militarily to the liberation of the central Italian states from the temporal power of the pope. The latter did not take kindly to such politics and under military pressure retired to the Vatican, refusing to come out until such time as his temporal power was restored. From that vantage point, the pope delivered searing condemnations of French policy and the moral decadence which, he felt, was sweeping over France. In this manner he hoped to rally French Catholics in the active pursuit of his cause. The moment was propitious. Marguerite-Marie was beatified by Pius IX in 1864. The era of grand pilgrimages to Paray-le-Monial began. The pilgrims came to express repentance for both public and private transgressions. They repented for the materialism and decadent opulence of France. They repented for the restrictions placed upon the temporal power of the pope. They repented for the passing of the traditional values embodied in an old and venerable social order. GALLIA POENITENS.

Just inside the main door of the Basilica of Sacré-Coeur in Paris, the visitor can read the following inscription:

THE YEAR OF OUR LORD 1875 THE 16TH JUNE IN THE REIGN OF HIS HOLINESS POPE PIUS IX IN ACCOMPLISHMENT OF A VOW FORMULATED DURING THE WAR OF 1870–71 BY ALEXANDER LEGENTIL AND HUBERT ROHAULT DE FLEURY RATIFIED BY HIS GRACE MSGR. GUIBERT ARCHBISHOP OF PARIS; IN EXECUTION OF THE VOTE OF THE NATIONAL ASSEMBLY OF THE 23D JULY 1873 ACCORDING TO THE DESIGN OF

THE ARCHITECT ABADIE; THE FIRST STONE OF THIS BASILICA ERECTED TO THE
SACRED HEART OF JESUS WAS SOLEMNLY PUT IN PLACE BY HIS EMINENCE CARDINAL
GUIBERT. . . .

Let us flesh out that capsule history and find out what lies behind it. As
Bismarck's battalions rolled to victory after victory over the French in the
summer of 1870, an impending sense of doom swept over France. Many
interpreted the defeats as righteous vengeance inflicted by divine will upon an
errant and morally decadent France. It was in this spirit that the empress
Eugene was urged to walk with her family and court, all dressed in
mourning, from the Palace of the Tuileries to Notre Dame, to publicly
dedicate themselves to the Sacred Heart. Though the empress received the
suggestion favorably, it was, once more, too late. On September 2, Napoleon
III was defeated and captured at Sedan; on September 4, the Republic was
proclaimed on the steps of the Hotel-de-Ville and a Government of National
Defense was formed. On that day also the empress Eugene took flight from
Paris having prudently, and at the emperor's urging, already packed her bags
and sent her more valuable possessions on to England.

The defeat at Sedan ended the Empire but not the war. The Prussian armies
rolled on, and by September 20 they had encircled Paris and put that city
under a siege that was to last until January 28 of the following year. Like
many other respectable bourgeois citizens, Alexander Legentil fled Paris at
the approach of the Prussian armies and took refuge in the provinces.
Languishing in Poitiers and agonizing over the fate of Paris, he vowed in early
December that "if God saved Paris and France and delivered the sovereign
pontiff, he would contribute according to his means to the construction in
Paris of a sanctuary dedicated to the Sacred Heart." He sought other
adherents to this vow and soon had the ardent support of Hubert Rohault de
Fleury (1903, 1905, 1907).

The terms of Legentil's vow did not, however, guarantee it a very warm
reception, for as he soon discovered, the provinces "were then possessed of
hateful sentiments towards Paris." Such a state of affairs was not unusual, and
we can usefully divert for a moment to consider its basis.

Under the *ancien régime,* the French state apparatus had acquired a strongly
centralized character which was consolidated under the French Revolution
and Empire. This centralization thereafter became the basis of French
political organization and gave Paris a peculiarly important role in relation to
the rest of France. The administrative, economic, and cultural predominance
of Paris was assured. But the events of 1789 also showed that Parisians had
the power to make and break governments. They proved adept at using that
power and were not loath, as a result, to regard themselves as privileged
beings with a right and duty to foist all that they deemed "progressive" upon

a supposedly backward, conservative, and predominantly rural France. The Parisian bourgeois despised the narrowness of provincial life and found the peasant disgusting and incomprehensible (Zeldin 1973, 1977).

From the other end of the telescope, Paris was generally seen as a center of power, domination, and opportunity. It was both envied and hated. To the antagonism generated by the excessive centralization of power and authority in Paris were added all of the vaguer small town and rural antagonisms toward any large city as a center of privilege, material success, moral decadence, vice, and social unrest. What was special in France was the way in which the tensions emanating from the "urban-rural contradiction" were so intensely focused upon the relation between Paris and the rest of France.

Under the Second Empire these tensions sharpened considerably (see Chap. 3). Paris experienced a vast economic boom as the railways made it the hub of a process of national spatial integration. At the same time, falling transport costs and the free trade policies signaled by the Anglo-French Treaties of Commerce in 1860 brought the city into a new relationship with an emerging global economy. Its share of an expanding French export trade increased dramatically, and its population grew rapidly, largely through a massive immigration of rural laborers (Gaillard 1977). Concentration of wealth and power proceeded apace as Paris became the center of financial, speculative, and commercial operations. The contrasts between affluence and poverty became ever more startling and were increasingly expressed in terms of a geographical segregation between the bourgeois quarters of the west and the working class quarters of the north, east, and south. Belleville became a foreign territory into which the bourgeois citizens of the west rarely dared to venture. The population of that place, which more than doubled between 1853 and 1870, was pictured in the bourgeois press as "the dregs of the people" caught in "the deepest depths of poverty and hatred" where "ferments of envy, sloth and anger bubble without cease" (Lepidis and Jacomin 1975). The signs of social breakdown were everywhere. As economic growth slowed in the 1860s and as the authority of Empire began to fail, Paris became a cauldron of social unrest, vulnerable to agitators of any stripe.

And to top it all, Haussman, at the emperor's urging, had set out to "embellish Paris" with spacious boulevards, parks, and gardens, monumental architecture of all sorts. The intent was to make Paris a truly imperial city, worthy not only of France but of Western civilization. Haussman had done this at immense cost and by the slipperiest of financial means, a feat which scarcely recommended itself to the frugal provincial mind. The image of public opulence which Haussman projected was only matched by the conspicuous consumption of a bourgeoisie, many of whom had grown rich speculating on the benefits of his improvements (Pinkney 1958).

Small wonder, then, that provincial and rural Catholics were in no frame of mind to dig into their pockets to embellish Paris with yet another monument, no matter how pious its purpose.

But there were even more specific objections which emerged in response to Legentil's proposal. The Parisians had with their customary presumptuousness proclaimed a republic when provincial and rural sentiment was heavily infused with monarchism. Furthermore, those who had remained behind to face the rigors of the siege were showing themselves remarkably intransigent and bellicose, declaring they would favor a fight to the bitter end, when provincial sentiment showed a strong disposition to end the conflict with Prussia.

And then the rumors and hints of a new materialist politics among the working class in Paris, spiced with a variety of manifestations of revolutionary fervor, gave the impression that the city had, in the absence of its more respectable bourgeois citizenry, fallen prey to radical and even socialist philosophy. Since the only means of communication between a besieged Paris and the nonoccupied territories was pigeon or balloon, abundant opportunities arose for misunderstanding, which the rural foes of republicanism and the urban foes of monarchism were not beyond exploiting.

Legentil therefore found it politic to drop any specific mention of Paris in his vow. But toward the end of February the pope endorsed it, and from then on the movement gathered some strength. And so on March 19, a pamphlet appeared which set out the arguments for the vow at some length (Rohault de Fleury 1903, 10–13). The spirit of the work had to be national, the authors urged, because the French people had to make national amends for what were national crimes. They confirmed their intention to build the monument in Paris. To the objection that the city should not be further embellished they replied, "Were Paris reduced to cinders, we would still want to avow our national faults and to proclaim the justice of God on its ruins."

The timing and phrasing of the pamphlet proved fortuitously prophetic. On March 18, Parisians had taken their first irrevocable steps toward establishing self-government under the Commune. The real or imagined sins of the communards were subsequently to shock and outrage bourgeois opinion. And as much of Paris was indeed reduced to cinders in the course of a civil war of incredible ferocity, the notion of building a basilica of expiation upon these ashes became more and more appealing. As Rohault de Fleury noted, with evident satisfaction, "In the months to come, the image of Paris reduced to cinders struck home many times" (1903, 10–13). Let us rehearse a little of that history.

The origins of the Paris Commune lie in a whole series of events which ran into each other in complex ways. Precisely because of its political importance within the country, Paris had long been denied any representative form of municipal government and had been directly administered by the national

government. For much of the nineteenth century, a predominantly republican Paris was chafing under the rule of monarchists (either Bourbon
"legitimists" or "Orleanists") or authoritarian Bonapartists. The demand for
a democratic form of municipal government was long-standing and com-
manded widespread support within the city.

The Government of National Defense set up on September 4, 1870, was
neither radical nor revolutionary (Guillemin 1956), but it was republican. It
also turned out to be timid and inept. It labored under certain difficulties, of
course, but these were hardly sufficient to excuse its weak performance. It did
not, for example, command the respect of the monarchists and lived in
perpetual fear of the reactionaries of the right. When the Army of the East,
under General Bazaine, capitulated to the Prussians at Metz on October 27,
the general left the impression that he did so because, being monarchist, he
could not bring himself to fight for a republican government. Some of his
officers who resisted the capitulation saw Bazaine putting his political
preferences above the honor of France. This was a matter which was to dog
French politics for several years. Rossel, who was later to command the armed
forces of the Commune for a while, was one of the officers shocked to the core
by Bazaine's evident lack of patriotism (Thomas 1967).

But the tensions between the different factions of the ruling class were
nothing compared to the real or imagined antagonisms between a traditional
and remarkably obdurate bourgeoisie and a working class that was beginning
to find its feet and assert itself. Rightly or wrongly, the bourgeoisie was
greatly alarmed during the 1860s by the emergence of working-class
organization and political clubs, by the activities of the Paris branch of the
International Working Men's Association, by the effervescence of thought
within the working class and the spread of anarchist and socialist philos-
ophies. And the working class – although by no means as well organized or as
unified as their opponents feared – was certainly displaying abundant signs of
an emergent class consciousness (see Chap. 3).

The Government of National Defense could not stem the tide of Prussian
victories or break the siege of Paris without widespread working-class
support. And the leaders of the left were only too willing to give it in spite of
their initial opposition to the emperor's war. Blanqui promised the government "energetic and absolute support," and even the International's leaders,
having dutifully appealed to the German workers not to participate in a
fratricidal struggle, plunged into organizing for the defense of Paris.
Belleville, the center of working-class agitation, rallied spectacularly to the
national cause, all in the name of the Republic (Lissagaray 1976).

The bourgeoisie sensed a trap. They saw themselves, wrote a contemporary
commentator drawn from their ranks, caught between the Prussians and
those whom they called "the reds." "I do not know," he went on, "which of

these two evils terrified them most; they hated the foreigner but they feared the Bellevillois much more" (Bruhat, Dautry, and Tersen 1971, 75). No matter how much they wanted to defeat the foreigner, they could not bring themselves to do so with the battalions of the working class in the vanguard. For what was not to be the last time in French history, the bourgeoisie chose to capitulate to the Germans, leaving the left as the dominant force within a patriotic front. In 1871, fear of the "enemy within" was to prevail over national pride.

The failure of the French to break the siege of Paris was first interpreted as the product of Prussian superiority and French military ineptitude. But as sortie after sortie promised victory only to be turned into disaster, honest patriots began to wonder if the powers that be were not playing tricks which bordered on betrayal and treason. The government was increasingly viewed as a "Government of National Defection."[1]

The government was equally reluctant to respond to the Parisian demand for municipal democracy. Since many of the respectable bourgeois had fled, it looked as if elections would deliver municipal power into the hands of the left. Given the suspicions of the monarchists of the right, the Government of National Defense felt it could not afford to concede what had long been demanded. And so it procrastinated endlessly.

As early as October 31, these various threads came together to generate an insurrectionary movement in Paris. Shortly after Bazaine's ignominious surrender, word got out that the government was negotiating the terms of an armistice with the Prussians. The population of Paris took to the streets and, as the feared Bellevillois descended en masse, took several members of the government prisoner, agreeing to release them only on the verbal assurance that there would be municipal elections and no capitulation. This incident was guaranteed to raise the hackles of the right. It was the immediate cause of the "hateful sentiments towards Paris" which Legentil encountered in December. The government lived to fight another day. But, as events turned out, they were to fight much more effectively against the Bellevillois than they ever fought against the Prussians.

So the siege of Paris dragged on. Worsening conditions in the city now added their uncertain effects to a socially unstable situation. The government proved inept and insensitive to the needs of the population and thereby added fuel to the smoldering fires of discontent (Lazare 1872; Becker 1969). The people lived off cats or dogs, while the more privileged partook of pieces of Pollux, the young elephant from the zoo (forty francs a pound for the trunk). The price of rats – the "taste is a cross between pork and partridge" – rose

---

[1] Marx (1968) uses this phrase to telling effect in his passionate defense of the Commune. The idea was widespread throughout Paris at that time; see Marcel Cerf (1971).

from sixty centimes to four francs apiece. The government failed to take the elementary precaution of rationing bread until January when it was much too late. Supplies dwindled, and the adulteration of bread with bone meal became a chronic problem which was made even less palatable by the fact that it was human bones from the catacombs which were being dredged up for the occasion. While the common people were thus consuming their ancestors without knowing it, the luxuries of café life were kept going, supplied by hoarding merchants at exorbitant prices. The rich that stayed behind continued to indulge their pleasures according to their custom, although they paid dearly for it. The government did nothing to curb profiteering or the continuation of conspicuous consumption by the rich in callous disregard for the feelings of the less privileged.

By the end of December, radical opposition to the Government of National Defense was growing. It led to the publication of the celebrated *Affiche Rouge* of January 7. Signed by the central committee of the twenty Parisian arrondissements, it accused the government of leading the country to the edge of an abyss by its indecision, inertia, and foot-dragging; suggested that the government knew not how to administer or to fight; and insisted that the perpetuation of such a regime could end only in capitulation to the Prussians. It proclaimed a program for a general requisition of resources, rationing, and mass attack. It closed with the celebrated appeal "Make way for the people! Make way for the Commune!" (Bruhat, Dautry, and Tersen 1971; Edwards 1971).

Placarded all over Paris, the appeal had its effect. The military responded decisively and organized one last mass sortie, which was spectacular for its military ineptitude and the carnage left behind. "Everyone understood," wrote Lissagaray, "that they had been sent out to be sacrificed" (1976, 75). The evidence of treason and betrayal was by now overwhelming for those close to the action. It pushed many an honest patriot from the bourgeoisie, who put love of country above class interest, into an alliance with the dissident radicals and the working class.

Parisians accepted the inevitable armistice at the end of January with sullen passivity. It provided for national elections to a constituent assembly which would negotiate and ratify a peace agreement. It specified that the French army lay down its arms but permitted the National Guard of Paris, which could not easily be disarmed, to remain a fighting force. Supplies came into a starving city under the watchful eye of the Prussian troops.

In the February elections, the city returned its quota of radical republicans. But rural and provincial France voted solidly for peace. Since the left was antagonistic to capitulation, the republicans from the Government of National Defense seriously compromised by their management of the war, and the Bonapartists discredited, the peace vote went to the monarchists.

republican Paris was appalled to find itself faced with a monarchist majority in the National Assembly. Thiers, by then seventy-three years old, was elected president in part because of his long experience in politics and in part because the monarchists did not want to be responsible for signing what was bound to be an ignoble peace agreement.

Thiers ceded Alsace and Lorraine to Germany and agreed to a huge war indemnity. He was enough of a patriot to resist Bismarck's suggestion that Prussian bankers float the loan required. Thiers reserved that privilege for the French and turned this year of troubles into one of the most profitable ones ever for the gentlemen of French high finance (Guillemin 1971; Bruhat, Dautry, and Tersen 1971, 104–5; Dreyfus 1928, 266). The latter informed Thiers that if he was to raise the money, he must first deal with "those rascals in Paris." This he was uniquely equipped to do. As minister of the interior under Louis Philippe, he had, in 1834, been responsible for the savage repression of one of the first genuine working-class movements in French history. Ever contemptuous of "the vile multitude," he had long had a plan for dealing with them – a plan which he had proposed to Louis Philippe in 1848 and which he was now finally in a position to put into effect (Allison 1932; Guillemin 1971). The plan was simple. He would use the conservatism of the country to smash the radicalism of the city.

On the morning of March 18, the population of Paris awoke to find that the remains of the French army had been sent to Paris to relieve that city of its cannons in which was obviously a first step toward the disarmament of a populace which had, since September 4, joined the National Guard in massive numbers (fig. 19). The populace of working-class Paris set out spontaneously to reclaim the cannons as their own. On the hill on Montmartre, weary French soldiers stood guard over the powerful battery of cannons assembled there, facing an increasingly restive and angry crowd. General Lecomte ordered his troops to fire. He ordered once twice, thrice. The soldiers had not the heart to do it, raised their rifle butts in the air, and fraternized joyfully with the crowd. An infuriated mob took General Lecomte prisoner. They stumbled across General Thomas, remembered and hated for his role in the savage killings of the June Days of 1848. The two generals were taken to the garden of No. 6, rue des Rosiers and, amid considerable confusion and angry argument, put up against a wall and shot.

This incident is of crucial importance to our story. The conservatives now had their martyrs. Thiers could brand the insubordinate population of Paris as murderers and assassins. But the hilltop of Montmartre had been a place of martyrdom for Christian saints long before. To these could now be added the names of Lecomte and Clément Thomas. In the months and years to come, as the struggle to build the Basilica of Sacré-Coeur unfolded, frequent appeal was to be made to the need to commemorate these "martyrs of yesterday who

Fig. 19.   The hillside of Montmartre on the eve of March 18, 1871

died in order to defend and save Christian society."[2] On that sixteenth day of June in 1875 when the foundation stone was laid, Rohault de Fleury rejoiced that the basilica was to be built on a site which, "after having been such a saintly place had become, it would seem, the place chosen by Satan and where was accomplished the first act of that horrible saturnalia which caused so much ruination and which gave the church two such glorious martyrs." "Yes," he continued, "it is here where Sacré-Coeur will be raised up that the Commune began, here where generals Clément Thomas and Lecomte were assassinated." He rejoiced in the "multitude of good Christians who now stood adoring a God who knows only too well how to confound the evil-minded, cast down their designs and to place a cradle where they thought to dig a grave." He contrasted this multitude of the faithful with a "hillside, lined with intoxicated demons, inhabited by a population apparently hostile to all religious ideas and animated, above all, by a hatred of the Church" (Rohault de Fleury 1903, 264). GALLIA POENITENS.

Thiers's response to the events of March 18 was to order a complete withdrawal of military and government personnel from Paris. From the safe distance of Versailles, he prepared methodically for the invasion and reduction of Paris. Bismarck proved not at all reluctant to allow the

[2] This phrase was actually used by the Committee of the National Assembly appointed to report on the proposed law that would make the Basilica a work of public utility. See Rohault de Fleury (1903, 88).

Fig. 20.   Executions at the Mur des Fédérés in Père Lachaise cemetery, May 1871;
gouache by Alfred Darjon. (Musée Carnavelet.)

reconstitution of a French army sufficient to the task of putting down the
radicals in Paris and released prisoners and material for that purpose.

Left to their own devices, and somewhat surprised by the turn of events,
the Parisians, under the leadership of the Central Committee of the National
Guard, arranged for elections on March 26. The Commune was declared a
political fact on March 28. It was a day of joyous celebration for the common
people of Paris and a day of consternation for the bourgeoisie.

The politics of the Commune were hardly coherent. While a substantial
number of workers took their place as elected representatives of the people for
the first time in French history, the Commune was still dominated by radical
elements from the bourgeoisie. Composed as it was of diverse political
currents shading from middle-of-the-road republican through the Jacobins,
the Proudhonists, the socialists of the International, and the Blanquist
revolutionaries, there was a good deal of factionalism and plenty of contentious argumentation as to what radical or socialist path to take. Much of this
proved moot, however, since Thiers attacked in early April and the second
siege of Paris began. Rural France was being put to work to destroy working-
class Paris.

What followed was disastrous for the Commune. When the Versailles
forces finally broke through the outer defense of Paris – which Thiers had had

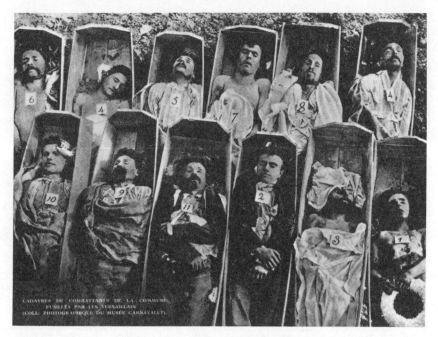

Fig. 21.   Bodies of communards shot by Versaillese troops, May 1871. (Musée Carnavelet.)

constructed in the 1840s – they swept quickly through the bourgeois sections of western Paris and cut slowly and ruthlessly down the grand boulevards that Haussman had constructed into the working-class quarters of the city. So began one of the most vicious bloodlettings in an often bloody French history. The Versailles forces gave no quarter. To the deaths in the street fighting, which were not, by most accounts, too extensive, were added an incredible number of arbitrary executions without judgment. The Luxemburg Gardens, the barracks at Lobau, the celebrated and still venerated wall in the cemetery of Père Lachaise, echoed ceaselessly to the sound of gunfire as the executioners went to work. Between twenty and thirty thousand communards died thus. GALLIA POENITENS – with vengeance (figs. 20 and 21).

Out of this sad history there is one incident which commands our attention. On the morning of May 28, an exhausted Eugène Varlin – bookbinder, union and food cooperative organizer under the Second Empire, member of the national guard, intelligent, respected, and scrupulously honest, committed socialist, and brave soldier – was recognized and arrested. He was taken to that same house on rue des Rosiers where Lecomte and Clément Thomas died. Varlin's fate was worse. Paraded around the hillside of

Fig. 22.　The toppling of the Vendôme Column during the Commune.
(Illustrated London News.)

Montmartre, some say for ten minutes and others for hours, abused, beaten, and humiliated by a fickle mob, he was finally propped up against a wall and shot. He was just thirty-two years old. They had to shoot twice to kill him. In between fusillades he cried, evidently unrepentant, "Vive la Commune!" His biographer called it "the Calvary of Eugène Varlin." The left can have its martyrs too. And it is on that spot that Sacré-Coeur is built (Foulon 1934).

The "bloody week," as it was called, also involved an enormous destruction of property. Paris burned. To the buildings set afire in the course of the bombardment were added those deliberately fired for strategic reasons by the retreating communards. From this arose the myth of the "incendiaries" of the Commune who recklessly took revenge, it was said, by burning everything they could. The communards, to be sure, were not enamored of the privileges of private property and were not averse to destroying hated symbols. The Vendôme Column – which Napoleon III had doted upon – was, after all, toppled in a grand ceremony to symbolize the end of authoritarian rule (fig. 22). The painter Courbet was later held responsible for this act and condemned to pay for the construction of the monument out of his own pocket. The communards also decreed, but never carried out, the destruction of the Chapel of Expiation by which Louis XVIII had sought to impress upon Parisians their guilt in executing his brother. And when Thiers had shown his true colors, the communards took a certain delight in dismantling his Parisian residence, stone by stone, in a symbolic gesture which de Goncourt felt had an "excellent bad effect" (Becker 1969, 288). But the wholesale burning of Paris was another matter entirely (fig. 23).

Fig. 23.   View of Paris burning from Père Lachaise cemetery. (Musée Carnavelet.)

No matter what the truth of the matter the myth of the incendiaries was strong. Within a year, the pope himself was describing the communards as "devils risen up from hell bringing the fires of the inferno to the streets of Paris."

The ashes of the city became a symbol of the Commune's crimes against the Church and were to fertilize the soil from which the energy to build Sacré-Coeur was to spring. No wonder that Rohault de Fleury congratulated himself upon that felicitous choice of words – "were Paris to be reduced to cinders." That phrase could strike home with redoubled force, he noted, "as the incendiaries of the Commune came to terrorize the world" (1903, 13).

The aftermath of the Commune was anything but pleasant. The blood-letting began to turn the stomachs of the bourgeoisie until all but the most sadistic of them had to cry "stop!" The celebrated diarist Edmond de Goncourt tried to convince himself of the justice of it all when he wrote:

It is good that there was neither conciliation nor bargain. The solution was brutal. It was by pure force. The solution has held people back from cowardly compromises . . . the bloodletting was a bleeding white; such a purge, by killing off the combative part of the population defers the next revolution by a whole generation. The old society has twenty years of quiet ahead of it, if the powers that be dare all that they may dare at this time. (Becker 1969, 312)

These sentiments were exactly those of Thiers. But when de Goncourt passed through Belleville and saw the "faces of ugly silence," he could not help but feel that here was a "vanquished but unsubjugated district." Was there no other way to purge the threat of revolution?

The experiences of 1870–71, when taken together with the confrontation between Napoleon III and the pope and the decadent "festive materialism" of the Second Empire, plunged Catholics into a phase of widespread soul-searching. The majority of them accepted the notion that France had sinned, and this gave rise to manifestations of expiation and a movement of piety that was both mystical and spectacular (Dansette 1965, 340–45). The intransigent and ultramontane Catholics unquestionably favored a return to law and order and a political solution founded on respect for authority. And it was the monarchists, generally themselves intransigent Catholics, who held out the promise for that law and order. Liberal Catholics found all of this disturbing and distasteful, but they were in no position to mobilize their forces – even the pope described them as the "veritable scourge" of France. There was little to stop the consolidation of the bond between monarchism and intransigent Catholicism. And it was such a powerful alliance that was to guarantee the building of Sacré-Coeur.

The immediate problem for the progenitors of the vow was, however, to operationalize a pious wish. This required official action. Legentil and Rohault de Fleury sought the support of the newly appointed archbishop of Paris.

Monseigneur Guibert, a compatriot of Thiers from Tours, had required some persuading to take the position in Paris. The three previous archbishops had suffered violent deaths: the first during the insurrection of 1848, the second by the hand of an assassin in 1863, and the third during the Commune. The communards had early decided to take hostages in response to the butchery promised by Versailles. The archbishop was held as a prime hostage for whom the communards sought the exchange of Blanqui. Thiers refused that negotiation, apparently having decided that a dead and martyred archbishop (who was a liberal Catholic in any case) was more valuable to him than a live one exchanged against a dynamic and aggressive Blanqui. During the "bloody week," the communards took whatever vengeance they could. On May 24, the archbishop was shot. In that final week, seventy-four hostages were shot, of whom twenty-four were priests. That awesome anticlericalism was as alive under the Commune as it had been in 1789. But with the massive purge which left more than twenty thousand communards dead, nearly forty thousand imprisoned, and countless others in flight, Thiers could write reassuringly on June 14 to Monseigneur Guibert: "The 'reds,' totally vanquished, will not recommence their activities tomorrow; one does not engage twice in fifty years in such an immense fight as they have just lost" (Guillemin 1971, 295–96; Rohault de Fleury 1905, 365). Reassured, Monseigneur Guibert came to Paris.

The new archbishop was much impressed with the movement to build a monument to the Sacred Heart. On January 18, 1872, he formally accepted responsibility for the undertaking. He wrote to Legentil and Rohault de Fleury thus:

You have considered from their true perspective the ills of our country. . . . The conspiracy against God and Christ has prevailed in a multitude of hearts and in punishment for an almost universal apostasy, society has been subjected to all the horrors of war with a victorious foreigner and an even more horrible war amongst the children of the same country. Having become, by our prevarication, rebels against heaven, we have fallen during our troubles into the abyss of anarchy. The land of France presents the terrifying image of a place where no order prevails, while the future offers still more terrors to come. . . . This temple, erected as a public act of contrition and reparation . . . will stand amongst us as a protest against other monuments and works of art erected for the glorification of vice and impiety. (Rohault de Fleury 1903, 27)

By July 1872, an ultraconservative Pope Pius IX, still awaiting his deliverance from captivity in the Vatican, formally endorsed the vow. An immense propaganda campaign unfolded, and the movement gathered momentum. By the end of the year, more than a million francs were promised, and all that remained was to translate the vow into its material, physical representation.

The first step was to choose a site. Legentil wanted to use the foundations of the still-to-be-completed Opera House, which he considered "a scandalous monument of extravagance, indecency and bad taste" (Jonquet n.d., 85–87). Rohault de Fleury's initial design of that building had, in 1860, been dropped at the insistence of Count Walewski ("who had the dubious distinction of being the illegitimate son of Napoleon I and the husband of Napoleon III's current favorite") (Pinkney 1958, 85–87). The design that replaced it (which exists today) most definitely qualified in the eyes of Legentil as a "monument to vice and impiety," and nothing could be more appropriate than to efface the memory of Empire by constructing the basilica on that spot. It probably escaped Legentil's attention that the communards had, in the same spirit, toppled the Vendôme Column.

By late October 1872, however, the archbishop had taken matters into his own hands and selected the heights of Montmartre because it was only from there that the symbolic domination of Paris could be assured. Since the land on that site was in part public property, the consent or active support of the government was necessary if it was to be acquired. The government was considering the construction of a military fortress on that spot. The archbishop pointed out, however, that a military fortress could well be very unpopular, while a fortification of the sort he was proposing might be less offensive and more sure. Thiers and his ministers, apparently persuaded that ideological protection might be preferable to military, encouraged the archbishop to pursue the matter formally. This the latter did in a letter of March 5, 1873 (Rohault de Fleury 1903, 75). He requested that the government pass a special law declaring the construction of the basilica a work of public utility. This would permit the laws of expropriation to be used to procure the site.

Such a law ran counter to a long-standing sentiment in favor of the separation of church and state. Yet conservative Catholic sentiment for the project was very strong. Thiers procrastinated, but his indecision was shortly rendered moot. The monarchists had decided that their time had come. On May 24, they drove Thiers from power and replaced him with the archconservative royalist Marshal MacMahon who, just two years before, had led the armed forces of Versailles in the bloody repression of the Commune. France was plunged, once more, into political ferment; a monarchist restoration seemed imminent.

The MacMahon government quickly reported out the law which then became part of its program to establish the rule of moral order in which those of wealth and privilege – who therefore had an active stake in the preservation of society – would, under the leadership of the king and in alliance with the authority of the church, have both the right and the duty to protect France from the social perils to which it had recently been exposed and thereby prevent the country falling into the abyss of anarchy. Large-scale demonstrations were mobilized by the church as part of a campaign to reestablish some sense of moral order. The largest of these demonstrations took place on June 29, 1873, at Paray-le-Monial. Thirty thousand pilgrims, including fifty members of the National Assembly, journeyed there to dedicate themselves publicly to the Sacred Heart (Dansette 1965, 340–45).

It was in this atmosphere that the committee formed to report on the law presented its findings on July 11 to the National Assembly, a quarter of whose members were adherents to the vow. The committee found that the proposal to build a basilica of expiation was unquestionably a work of public utility. It was right and proper to build such a monument on the heights of Montmartre for all to see, because it was there that the blood of martyrs – including those of yesterday – had flowed. It was necessary "to efface by this work of expiation, the crimes which have crowned our sorrows," and France, "which has suffered so much," must "call upon the protection and grace of Him who gives according to His will, defeat or victory" (Rohault de Fleury 1903, 88).

The debate which followed on July 22 and 23 in part revolved around technical-legal questions and the implications of the legislation for state-church relations. The intransigent Catholics recklessly proposed to go much further. They wanted the assembly to commit itself formally to a national undertaking which "was not solely a protestation against taking up of arms by the Commune, but a sign of appeasement and concord." That amendment was rejected. But the law passed with a handsome majority of 244 votes.

A lone dissenting voice in the debate came from a radical republican deputy from Paris:

When you think to establish on the commanding heights of Paris – the fount of free thought and revolution – a Catholic monument, what is in your thoughts? To make of it the triumph of the Church over revolution. Yes, that is what you want to extinguish – what you call the pestilence of revolution. What you want to revive is the Catholic faith, for you are at war with the spirit of modern times. . . . Well, I who know the sentiments of the population of Paris, I who am tainted by the revolutionary pestilence like them, I tell you that the population will be more scandalized than edified by the ostentation of your faith. . . . Far from edifying us, you push us towards free thought, towards revolution. When people see these manifestations of the partisans of monarchy, of the enemies of the Revolution, they will say to themselves that Catholicism and monarchy are unified, and in rejecting one they will reject the other. (Rohault de Fleury 1903, 88)

Armed with a law which yielded powers of expropriation, the committee formed to push the project through to fruition acquired the site atop the butte Montmartre. They collected the moneys promised and set about soliciting more so that the building could be as grand as the thought that lay behind it. A competition for the design of the basilica was set and judged. The building had to be imposing, consistent with Christian tradition, yet quite distinct from the "monuments to vice and impiety" built in the course of the Second Empire. Out of the seventy-eight designs submitted and exhibited to the public, that of the architect Abadie was selected. The grandeur of its domes, the purity of the white marble, and the unadorned simplicity of its detail impressed the committee – what, after all, could be more different from the flamboyance of that awful Opera House?

By the spring of 1875, all was ready for putting the first stone in place. But radical and republican Paris was not, apparently, repentant enough even yet. The archbishop complained that the building of Sacré-Coeur was being treated as a provocative act, as an attempt to inter the principles of 1789. And while, he said, he would not pray to revive those principles if they happened to become dead and buried, this view of things was giving rise to a deplorable polemic in which the archbishop found himself forced to participate. He issued a circular in which he expressed his astonishment at the hostility expressed toward the project on the part of "the enemies of religion." He found it intolerable that people dared to put a political interpretation upon thoughts derived only out of faith and piety. Politics, he assured his readers, "had been far, far from our inspirations; the work had been inspired, on the contrary, by a profound conviction that politics was powerless to deal with the ills of the country. The causes of these ills are moral and religious and the remedies must be of the same order." Besides, he went on, the work could not be construed as political because the aim of politics is to divide, "while our work has for its goal the union of all. . . . Social pacification is the end point of the work we are seeking to realize" (Rohault de Fleury 1903, 244).

The government, now clearly on the defensive, grew extremely nervous at the prospect of a grand opening ceremony which could be the occasion for an ugly confrontation. It counseled caution. The committee had to find a way to lay the first stone without being too provocative. The pope came to their aid and declared a day of dedication to the Sacred Heart for all Catholics everywhere. Behind that shelter, a much scaled-down ceremony to lay the first stone passed without incident. The construction was now under way. GALLIA POENITENS was taking shape in material symbolic form.

The forty years between the laying of the foundation stone and the final consecration of the basilica in 1919 were often troubled ones. Technical difficulties arose in the course of putting such a large structure on a hilltop rendered unstable by years of mining for gypsum. The cost of the structure increased dramatically, and, as enthusiasm for the cult of the Sacred Heart diminished somewhat, financial difficulties ensued. And the political controversy continued.

The committee in charge of the project had early decided upon a variety of stratagems to encourage the flow of contributions. Individuals and families could purchase a stone, and the visitor to Sacré-Coeur will see the names of many such inscribed upon the stones there. Different regions and organizations were encouraged to subscribe toward the construction of particular chapels. Members of the National Assembly, the army, the clergy, and the like all pooled their efforts in this way. Each particular chapel has its own significance.

Among the chapels in the crypt, for example, the visitor will find that of Jésus-Enseignant, which recalls, as Rohault de Fleury put it, "that one of the chief sins of France was the foolish invention of schooling without God" (Rohault de Fleury 1903, 269). Those who were on the losing side of the fierce battle to preserve the power of the church over education after 1871 put their money here. And next to that chapel, at the far end of the crypt, close to the line where the rue des Rosiers used to run, stands the Chapel to Jésus-Ouvrier.

That Catholic workers sought to contribute to the building of their own chapel was a matter for great rejoicing. It showed, wrote Legentil, the desire of workers "to protest against the fearsome impiety into which a large part of the working class is falling" as well as their determination to resist "the impious and truly infernal association which, in nearly all of Europe, makes of it its slave and victim" (Rohault de Fleury 1903, 165). The reference to the International Working Men's Association is unmistakable and understand-able, since it was customary in bourgeois circles at that time to attribute the Commune, quite erroneously, to the nefarious influence of that "infernal" association. Yet, by a strange quirk of fate, which so often gives an ironic twist to history, the chapel to Jésus-Ouvrier stands almost exactly at the spot where ran the course of the "Calvary of Eugène Varlin." Thus it is that the basilica, erected on high in part to commemorate the blood of two recent martyrs of the right, commemorates unwittingly in its subterranean depths a martyr of the left.

Legentil's interpretation of all this was in fact somewhat awry. In the closing stages of the Commune, a young Catholic named Albert de Munn watched in dismay as the communards were led away to slaughter. Shocked, he fell to wondering what "legally constituted society had done for these people" and concluded that their ills had in large measure been visited upon them through the indifference of the affluent classes. In the spring of 1872, he went into the heart of hated Belleville and set up the first of his *Cercles-Ouvriers* (Dansette 1965, 356–58; Lepidis and Jacomin 1975, 271–72). This signaled the beginnings of a new kind of Catholicism in France – one which sought through social action to attend to the material as well as the spiritual needs of the workers. It was through organizations such as this, a far cry from the intransigent ultramontane Catholicism that ruled at the center of the movement for the Sacred Heart, that a small trickle of worker contributions began to flow toward the construction of a basilica on the hilltop of Montmartre.

The political difficulties mounted, however. France, finally armed with a republican constitution (largely because of the intransigence of the monar-chists) was now in the grip of a modernization process fostered by easier communications, mass education, and industrial development. The country moved to accept the moderate form of republicanism and became bitterly disillusioned with the backward-looking monarchism that had dominated the National Assembly elected in 1871. In Paris the "unsubjugated" Bellevillois, and their neighbors in Montmartre and La Villette, began to reassert themselves rather more rapidly than Thiers had anticipated. As the demand

Fig. 24.   Sacré-Coeur as the enemy. (Reproduced, with permission, from the "Collection d'Affiches Politiques" of Alain Gesgon.)

for amnesty for the exiled communards became stronger in these quarters, so did the hatred of the basilica rising to their midst (fig. 24). The agitation against the project mounted.

On August 3, 1880, the matter came before the city council in the form of

Fig. 25. The Statue of Liberty in its Paris workshop

a proposal — a "colossal statue of *Liberty* will be placed on the summit of Montmartre, in front of the church of Sacré-Coeur, on land belonging to the city of Paris." The French republicans at that time had adopted the United States as a model society which functioned perfectly well without monarchism and other feudal trappings. As part of a campaign to drive home the point of this example, as well as to symbolize their own deep attachment to the principles of liberty, republicanism, and democracy, they were then raising funds to donate the Statue of Liberty that now stands in New York harbor (fig. 25). Why not, said the authors of this proposition, efface the sight of the hated Sacré-Coeur by a monument of similar order? (Ville de Paris, Conseil Municipal, *Procès Verbaux,* August 3, October 7 and December 2, 1880).

No matter what the claims to the contrary, they said, the basilica symbolized the intolerance and fanaticism of the right – it was an insult to civilization, antagonistic to the principles of modern times, an evocation of the past, and a stigma upon France as a whole. Parisians, seemingly bent on demonstrating their unrepentant attachment to the principles of 1789, were determined to efface what they felt was an expression of "Catholic fanaticism" by building exactly that kind of monument which the archbishop had previously characterized as a "glorification of vice and impiety."

By October 7 the city council had changed its tactics. Calling the basilica "an incessant provocation to civil war," the members decided by a majority of sixty-one to three to request the government to "rescind the law of public utility of 1873" and to use the land, which would revert to public ownership, for the construction of a work of truly national significance. Neatly sidestepping the problem of how those who had contributed to the construction of the basilica – which had hardly yet risen above its foundations – were to be indemnified, it passed along its proposal to the government. By the summer of 1882, the request was taken up in the Chamber of Deputies.

Archbishop Guibert had, once more, to take to the public defense of the work. He challenged what by now were familiar arguments against the basilica with familiar responses. He insisted that the work was not inspired by politics but by Christian and patriotic sentiments. To those who objected to the expiatory character of the work he simply replied that no one can ever afford to regard their country as infallible. As to the appropriateness of the cult of the Sacred Heart, he felt only those within the church had the right to judge. To those who portrayed the basilica as a provocation to civil war he replied: "Are civil wars and riots ever the product of our Christian temples? Are those who frequent our churches ever prone to excitations and revolts against the law? Do we find such people in the midst of disorders and violence which, from time to time, trouble the streets of our cities?" He went on to point out that while Napoleon I had sought to build a temple of peace at Montmartre, "it is we who are building, at last, the true temple of peace" (Rohault de Fleury 1905, 71–73).

He then considered the negative effects of stopping the construction. Such an action would profoundly wound Christian sentiment and prove divisive. It would surely be a bad precedent, he said (blithely ignoring the precedent set by the law of 1873 itself), if religious undertakings of this sort were to be subject to the political whims of the government of the day. And then there was the complex problem of compensation not only for the contributors but for the work already done. Finally, he appealed to the fact that the work was giving employment to six hundred families – to deprive "that part of Paris of such a major source of employment would be inhuman indeed."

The Parisian representatives in the Chamber of Deputies, which, by 1882, was dominated by reformist republicans such as Gambetta (from Belleville) and Clemenceau (from Montmartre), were not impressed by these arguments. The debate was heated and passionate. The government for its part declared itself unalterably opposed to the law of 1873 but was equally opposed to rescinding the law, since this would entail paying out more than twelve million francs in indemnities to the church. In an effort to defuse the evident anger from the left, the minister went on to remark that by rescinding the law, the archbishop would be relieved of the obligation to complete what was proving to be a most arduous undertaking at the same time as it would provide the church with millions of francs to pursue works of propaganda which might be "infinitely more efficacious than that to which the sponsors of the present motion are objecting."

The radical republicans were not about to regard Sacré-Coeur in the shape of a white elephant, however. Nor were they inclined to pay compensation. They were determined to do away with what they felt was an odious manifestation of pious clericalism and to put in its place a monument to liberty of thought. They put the blame for the civil war squarely on the shoulders of the monarchists and their intransigent Catholic allies.

Clemenceau rose to state the radical case. He declared the law of 1873 an insult, an act of a National Assembly which had sought to impose the cult of the Sacred Heart on France because "we fought and still continue to fight for human rights, for having made the French Revolution." The law was the product of clerical reaction, an attempt to stigmatize revolutionary France, "to condemn us to ask pardon of the Church for our ceaseless struggle to prevail over it in order to establish the principles of liberty, equality and fraternity." We must, he declared, respond to a political act by a political act. Not to do so would be to leave France under the intolerable invocation of the Sacred Heart (Rohault de Fleury 1905, 71 et seq.).

With impassioned oratory such as this, Clemenceau fanned the flames of anticlerical sentiment. The chamber voted to rescind the law of 1873 by a majority of 261 votes to 199. It appeared that the basilica, the walls of which were as yet hardly risen above their foundations, was to come tumbling down.

The basilica was saved by a technicality. The law was passed too late in the session to meet all the formal requirements for promulgation. The government, genuinely fearful of the costs and liabilities involved, quietly worked to prevent the reintroduction of the motion into a chamber which, in the next session, moved on to consider matters of much greater weight and moment. The Parisian republicans had gained a symbolic but Pyrrhic parliamentary victory. A relieved archbishop pressed on with the work.

Yet somehow the matter would not die. In February 1897, the motion was reintroduced (Lesourd 1973, 224–25). Anticlerical republicanism had by then made great progress, as had the working-class movement in the form of a vigorous and growing socialist party. But the construction atop the hill had likewise progressed. The interior of the basilica had been inaugurated and opened for worship in 1891, and the great dome was well on the way to completion (the cross which surmounts it was formally blessed in 1899). Although the basilica was still viewed as a "provocation to civil war," the prospect for dismantling such a vast work was by now quite daunting. And this time it was none other than Albert de Munn who defended the basilica in the name of a Catholicism that had, by then, seen the virtue of separating its fate from that of a fading monarchist cause. The church was beginning to learn a lesson, and the cult of the Sacred Heart began to acquire a new meaning in response to a changing social situation. By 1899, a more reform-minded pope dedicated the cult to the ideal of harmony among the races, social justice, and conciliation.

But the socialist deputies were not impressed by what they saw as maneuvers of cooptation. They pressed home their case to bring down the hated symbol, even though almost complete, and even though such an act would entail indemnifying eight million subscribers to the tune of thirty million francs. But the majority in the chamber blanched at such a prospect. The motion was rejected by 322 to 196.

This was to be the last time the building was threatened by official action. With the dome completed in 1899, attention switched to the building of the campanile, which was finally finished in 1912. By the spring of 1914, all was ready and the official consecration set for October 17. But war with Germany intervened. Only at the end of that bloody conflict was the basilica finally consecrated. A victorious France – led by the fiery oratory of Clemenceau – joyfully celebrated the consecration of a monument conceived of in the course of a losing war with Germany a generation before. GALLIA POENITENS at last brought its rewards.

Muted echoes of this tortured history can still be heard. In February 1971, for example, demonstrators pursued by police took refuge in the basilica. Firmly entrenched there, they called upon their radical comrades to join them in occupying a church "built upon the bodies of communards in order to efface the memory of that red flag that had for too long floated over Paris." The myth of the incendiaries immediately broke loose from its ancient moorings, and an evidently panicked rector summoned the police into the basilica to prevent the conflagration. The "reds" were chased from the church amid scenes of great brutality. Thus was the centennial of the Paris Commune celebrated on that spot.

And as a coda to that incident, a bomb exploded in the basilica in 1976, causing quite extensive damage to one of the domes. On that day, it was said, the visitor to the cemetery of Père Lachaise would have seen a single red rose on August Blanqui's grave.

Rohault de Fleury had desperately wanted to "place a cradle where [others] had thought to dig a grave." But the visitor who looks at the mausoleum-like structure that is Sacré-Coeur might well wonder what it is that is interred there. The spirit of 1789? The sins of France? The alliance between intransigent Catholicism and reactionary monarchism? The blood of martyrs like Lecomte and Clément Thomas? Or that of Eugène Varlin and the twenty thousand or so communards mercilessly slaughtered along with him?

The building hides its secrets in sepulchral silence. Only the living, cognizant of this history, who understand the principles of those who struggled for and against the embellishment of that spot, can truly disinter the mysteries that lie entombed there and thereby rescue that rich experience from the deathly silence of the tomb and transform it into the noisy beginnings of the cradle.

5

The Urbanization of Consciousness

Capitalist urbanization occurs within the confines of the community of money, is framed by the concrete abstractions of space and time, and internalizes all the vigor and turbulence of the circulation of capital under the ambiguous and often shaky surveillance of the state. A city is an agglomeration of productive forces built by labor employed within a temporal process of circulation of capital. It is nourished out of the metabolism of capitalist production for exchange on the world market and supported out of a highly sophisticated system of production and distribution organized within its confines. It is populated by individuals who reproduce themselves using money incomes earned off the circulation of capital (wages and profits) or its derivative revenues (rents, taxes, interest, merchants' profits, payments for services). The city is ruled by a particular coalition of class forces, segmented into distinctive communities of social reproduction, and organized as a discontinuous but spatially contiguous labor market within which daily substitutions of job opportunities against labor power are possible and within which certain distinctive quantities and qualities of labor power may be found.

The city is the high point of human achievement, objectifying the most sophisticated knowledge in a physical landscape of extraordinary complexity, power, and splendor at the same time as it brings together social forces capable of the most amazing sociotechnical and political innovation. But it is also the site of squalid human failure, the lightning rod of the profoundest human discontents, and the arena of often savage social and political conflict. It is a place of mystery, the site of the unexpected, full of agitations and ferments, of multiple liberties, opportunities, and alienations; of passions and repressions; of cosmopolitanism and extreme parochialisms; of violence, innovation, and reaction. The capitalist city is the arena of the most intense social and political confusions at the same time as it is a monumental testimony to and a moving force within the dialectics of capitalism's uneven development.

How to penetrate the mystery, unravel the confusions, and grasp the contradictions? The question is important for two reasons. Firstly, we know, as Lefebvre puts it, that capitalism has survived into the twentieth century through the production of space and that it has been an increasingly urbanized space that has been produced. A study of the urban process tells us much, therefore, about the mechanisms of capitalism's successful self-reproduction. That is the focus of *The Urbanization of Capital,* the companion volume to this. Secondly, increasing urbanization makes the urban the primary level at which individuals now experience, live out, and react to the totality of social transformations and structures in the world around them. To dissect the urban process in all of its fullness is to lay bare the roots of consciousness formation in the material realities of daily life. It is out of the complexities and perplexities of this experience that we build an elementary consciousness of the meanings of space and time; of social power and its legitimations; of forms of domination and social interaction; of the relation to nature through production and consumption; and of human nature, civil society, and political life.

Curious kinds of consciousness arise out of the confusions of that experience. The modes of thinking and acting cannot be captured directly by appeal to polarized or even complex class structures. With a real material basis in daily urban life, the modes of consciousness cannot be dismissed as false, although I shall insist that they are necessarily fetishistic. The replication in thought of the intricate material patternings of surface experience obscures the inner meanings, but the surface appearance is real enough. If it appears that decaying housing produces crime and that the automobile produces the suburb, then we have to recognize the material relations between such things, even though they hide the social forces they jointly represent and contain. And for purposes of daily life it is often sufficient and even necessary to stick to such surface appearances as the basis for action. To live in the suburbs without a car is as foolish as strolling in a slum oblivious of the higher probability of criminal behavior. But exclusive attachment to such surface appearances produces misinterpretations that make seemingly rational courses of action moot or even contradictory in relation to deeper social objectives. The consciousness produced by a fetishistic reading of daily urban life is not, therefore, bourgeois or capital-istic. It exists on a quite different plane. Failure to penetrate and demystify the purely fetishistic readings, however, can generate behaviors and actions fraught with all manner of unintended consequences. Avid defenders of capitalism can undermine what they most desire to defend, while socialists can end up supporting that which they decry.

Within that confusion, all kinds of other sentiments, illusions, and distortions can flourish. The ferment of discontent and opposition, of understandable and entirely reasonable misrepresentations, of unintended consequences, is always part of the urban brew. Therein lies an extraordinary though often latent energy for social transformation that has no easily predicted direction. Capitalist urbanization gives rise to forces that, once put in place and set in motion, can just as easily threaten as support the perpetuation of capitalism itself. Those who seek to preserve capitalism as well as those struggling to displace it have, in short, to confront the *urbanization of consciousness* as a key political problem.

The most signal virtue of thinkers like Simmel, Wirth, and Sennett is that they address that problem directly rather than leaving it, as do Marx, Weber, and Durkheim, for example, on the periphery of their thought. The defect of such writers is that they get so enmeshed in the complexities of surface appearances that either they fail to penetrate the fetishisms or they produce partial rather than integrated interpretations. Simmel (1971), in his famous essay, "The Metropolis and Mental Life," could not get much further than the alienated individualism and limited freedoms produced by the necessity for money integrations and rational coordinations of action in space and time. Wirth (1964), though more complex, could not free himself from some of the curious biological and ecological presuppositions of the Chicago school. Compared to that, the peripheral vision of a Marx or a Weber appears as a model of clarity in the sense that it at least provides a grounding for interpretation in some overall conception of civil society and its mode of production or organization. The problem as I construe it, therefore, is to build into the Marxian perspective the kinds of detailed sophistication that writers like Simmel and Wirth achieved. The urbanization of consciousness has to be understood in relation to the urbanization of capital.

The strategy I propose for attacking that question is simple enough – perhaps overly so. I conceive of five primary loci of consciousness formation. Individualism attaches to money uses in freely functioning markets. Class under capitalism reflects the buying and selling of labor power and the social relations embodied in the sociotechnical conditions of production under conditions of surplus value extraction. Community, as we shall see, is a highly ambiguous notion that nevertheless plays a fundamental role in terms of the reproduction of labor power, the circulation of revenues, and the geography of capital accumulation. The state also impinges on consciousness as a center of authority and as an apparatus through which political-economic power is exercised in a territory with some degree of popular legitimacy. The family, finally, has a profound effect upon ways of thought and action simply by virtue of its function as the primary site of social reproduction through child-rearing.

I now want to modify this conception in two very important ways. First of all, no one locus of consciousness formation can be understood independently of its relation to the others. It is the total patterning of interrelations between them that counts. We are blessed, of course, with innumerable psychological, sociological, and historical studies of this or that element in isolation and some studies that explore certain links between, say, community and class, individualism and the state, or family and class. But rare indeed is the study that puts all of them together. And it is not hard to understand why. The complexity of interactions and of possible meanings quickly proliferates to replicate the confusions of consciousness without necessarily shedding light on its material base or penetrating the fetishisms. This brings me to my second point. Urbanization of the capitalist sort requires that the interrelations be structured in a certain way. The urban condition imprints its own qualities on consciousness. This was, I believe, what Simmel (1971) and Wirth (1964) were driving at in their seminal essays, "The Metropolis and Mental Life" and "Urbanism as a Way of Life." Wirth, for example, focused on the social implications of the huge size, high density, and extraordinary heterogeneity characteristic of contemporary cities and sought to identify the range of human responses and possible adaptations to that condition. On this score he is extremely perceptive. The problem is that by picking on size, density, and heterogeneity as indicators of the urban condition he obviates any particular necessity to explain how that urban condition came to be. Wirth thus postulates such phenomena as Simmel's "pecuniary nexus" and Adam Smith's concern for the division of labor as necessary to contemporary urban life without conceding that the rise of money and the division of labor necessarily had anything to do with the production of capitalist urbanization.

The urbanization of consciousness cannot, I conclude, be understood independently of the urbanization of capital; nor can the latter be understood without the former. The task for historical materialist interpretation of the urban process is, therefore, to examine how the consciousness produced through the particular patterning of relations between individualism, class, community, state, and family affects the paths and qualities of capitalist urbanization that in turn feed back to alter the patterning of relations that underlie the urbanization of consciousness. Only in that way can we understand the socioeconomic and geopolitical dynamic through which capitalism survives, in spite of all of its internal contradictions, as a viable mode of production and consumption.

How is an urbanized consciousness produced, and what are the political implications of that consciousness? Consider, firstly, the relation between money and capital, the communities of which intersect to define much of what the urbanization process and the urban experience are about. Money, I showed in Chapter 1, functions as a concrete abstraction, imposing external and homogeneous measures of value on all aspects of human life, reducing infinite diversity to a single comparable dimension, and masking subjective human relations by objective market exchanges. The achievement of urbanization, as Simmel so correctly observes, rests on an increasing domination of the cash nexus over other kinds of human interactions and as such promotes exactly that kind of alienated individualism that Marx and Engels highlight in the *Communist Manifesto*. Money used as capital, however, subsumes all production processes as well as labor and commodity markets under a single, class-bound, profit-seeking logic. Marx shows us that such a mode of production has to expand, that it must simultaneously engage in continuous revolutions in productive forces and in the social relations of production through reorganizations of the division of labor. Here lies much of the dynamic force that produces vast, high-density urbanization and heterogeneity of the sort that Wirth describes (cf. *The Urbanization of Capital*).

Money and capital therefore confront us as double alienations, the compounding of which should surely produce energy of revolt sufficient to dispose quickly of both. Yet the alienations can also confound and confuse each other so as to frustrate rather than facilitate coherent political action against the domination of either. Class-bound political movements against the power of capital hesitate or fail if they appear to threaten real and cherished, though necessarily limited, liberties given by possession of money in the marketplace. Even the poorest person can relish the kind of liberty that even the minutest amount of money power can give. Workers may even connive or accede to their own exploitation in production in return for increased money power that gives them greater market freedoms and greater ability to control a portion of their own space (through home or car ownership) and their own time — all of which has fundamental implications for the family.

The consciousness of class derived out of the experience of earning money runs up against the consciousness of limited but important individual freedom in the spending of that money. The alienations of money and of money used as capital split apart to generate political confusion. Capitalists caught in the throes of violent and often debilitating class struggle learned to use that confusion creatively. It was the genius of Fordism and of the New Deal (with its Keynesian strategies of state management and its support for trade union consciousness) to offer greater market freedoms in return for diminished class struggle in production. But the effect was to change the face of capitalist urbanization dramatically and to shift the patterning of relations between individualism, class, community, family, and the state.

Consider, secondly, the consciousness of community. The communities of money and capital are communities without propinquity in the broadest sense. The particular kinds of communities we call cities, towns, or even neighborhoods are, in contrast, definite places within which a definite patterning of socioeconomic and political processes — and hence of consciousness – occurs. From the standpoint of the communities of money and capital, such places are no more than relative spaces to be built up, torn down, or abandoned as profitability dictates. But from the standpoint of the people who live there, such places form an absolute space of particular qualities that can be the focus of particular place-bound loyalties. We see again conflicting material bases for consciousness formation and political action. Individuals can internalize both aspects simultaneously. A pensioner might want maximum return on pension fund investments but struggle against the abandonment of community that the crass logic of profit maximization might imply.

That tension can be resolved in ways advantageous to capital. In *The Urbanization of Capital* (chap. 6) I show in detail how the organization of local "growth machines" and ruling class alliances that engage in collective speculation to attract other forms of capitalist development or actively defend a local economy against devaluation defines much of what local politics is about. Interurban competition – a process in which place-bound loyalty to community and community boosterism has an important role – is vital to the formation of the world market and to the uneven geographical development of capitalism in ways conducive to overall accumulation. The efficient geographical articulation of capitalism depends on innumerable communities evolving corporatist strategies toward capitalist development.

Images of knowable and affective communities can also be marketed as commodities. That technique is often used in association with speculative housing development. Examples can be found as long ago as the seventeenth century and abound in the nineteenth century (cf. Warner's 1962 study of Boston and Dyos's 1961 study of Camberwell). But the phenomenon became even more generalized after 1945. The Keynesian style of urbanization depended upon the strong mobilization of the spirit of consumer sovereignty in an economy where purchasing power was broadly though unevenly distributed among households. The sovereignty, though fetishistic, was not illusory. It allowed individuals to mobilize all kinds of marks of distinction through differentiations in consumption as a response to the bland universalisms of money (cf. Simmel 1978; above, Chap. 1). New kinds of communities could be constructed, packaged, and sold in a society where who you were seemed to depend more and more on how money was spent rather than on how it was earned. Living spaces could be made to represent status, position, and prestige in ways that made Weberian concepts of consumption classes look legitimate. And the degraded relation to nature in production was increasingly supplanted by a relation to nature packaged as a consumption artifact (see Chap. 2). Suburbanization typically promised access both to nature and to community, each packaged as a commodity (Walker 1981).

None of this was necessarily antagonistic to monetized individualism or to the integrity of the family. The desire to enhance or preserve the value of personal property and access to life chances dictated rational forms of community participation for individuals and households (Olson 1965). But the outcome was a particular kind of community, totally subservient to monetized individualism and family ambitions. Nor was it antagonistic to that more traditional sense of community as a breeding ground for different types of labor power and hence the site of basic processes of class reproduction (see *The Urbanization of Capital*, chap. 5).

Community, it transpired, could be constructed in ways entirely consistent with capital accumulation. Demand-side urbanization meant a shift in relations. Much greater emphasis was put upon the spatial division of consumption relative to the spatial division of labor so as to generate the surface appearance of consumption classes and status groupings (identified by life-style or mere position in social space) as opposed to class definitions achieved in the realm of production. The social spaces of distraction and display became as vital to urban culture as the spaces of working and living. Social competition with respect to life-style and command over space, always important for upper segments of the bourgeoisie, became more and more important within the mass culture of urbanization, sometimes even masking the role of community in processes of class reproduction. It also meant new relations to the state, the individual, and the family in a society where consumer sovereignty was mobilized to ensure consumption for consumption's sake to match capitalism's incessant drive toward production for production's sake and accumulation for accumulation's sake. The qualities of the urban experience and the conditions for consciousness formation shifted accordingly, as did the whole dynamic of capitalist urbanization.

Yet it is also within these spaces that active community building can take place in ways deeply antagonistic to the individualism of money, to the profit-seeking and class-bound logic of capital circulation, and even to particular views of the family and the state. Utopian movements (anarchist, feminist, socialist, ecological) abound, as do religious attempts to define an alternative sense of community. Urban uprisings like the Paris Commune, the Watts and Detroit rebellions of the 1960s, and the vast swathe of urban social protest movements (Castells 1983) testify to the powerful urge to escape the dominations of money power, capital, and a repressive state. Such movements are not confined to the underprivileged either. As consumers, even upper echelons of the bourgeoisie can demand protection against the ravages of some greedy developer. Peculiar kinds of consumer socialism, using local government power to check growth machine politics and the destruction of the environment, can take root in even the most affluent of areas (like Santa Monica or Santa Cruz). Consumer sovereignty, if taken seriously, presupposes, after all, a certain popular empowerment to shape the qualities of life directly and to drive beyond the pathologies of urban anonymity, monetized individualism, a degraded relation to nature, and profit maximization. But that also means the creation or imposition of a culture of community solidarity and bonding that goes far beyond that tolerable to pure individualism or the pure logic of capital accumulation. The seeds of conflict then are scattered across the social landscape.

Alternative communities find it hard, if not impossible, to survive. They cannot seal themselves off from the rest of the world (though some try by moving to remote regions), and daily existence is now heavily dependent upon integration into an international division of labor – and that means money contacts. It is hard to keep the "dissolving effects" of monetization at bay. The community domination of an absolute space also often entails the imposition of a repressive rigidity in the functioning of social relations and moral codes. There is, therefore, much that is repressive about community (Sennett 1970). New England townships may have been models of community, but they were also bastions of intolerance. Compared to that, the dissolving effects of money and the anonymity of urban life may appear as welcome relief; and the incoherencies of entrepreneurial capitalism, positively stimulating.

The construction of community within the frame of capitalist urbanization contains a tension. Movements against the power of concrete abstractions like money, capital, space, and time may spiral into fierce struggles to create an alternative kind of community. But there are also processes of community construction and community empowerment that integrate only too well into the dynamics of capital accumulation through the production of space. How the tension between these two dimensions of community formation is resolved cannot be exactly predicted in advance, but the historical record indicates how frequently they intersect. The capitalist selling of community as an opportunity for self-realization sparks alternative movements, while the latter can all too easily be coopted and used for the selling of community and proximity to nature as consumption goods. All kinds of intermediate mixes are possible. A community may be organized as a sophisticated coping mechanism that wards off the worst aspects of class domination and alienated individualism but in so doing merely makes the domination of money and capital more acceptable. But capitalists, in seeking to promote community for exactly such reasons, can also help create centers of guerrilla warfare against their own interests. Community, therefore, has always to be interpreted as a specific resolution of this underlying tension worked out in the context of relations to the family, the individual, class, and the state, under specific conditions of the urbanization of capital.

The family is a very distinctive locus of consciousness formation. The intimacy and affectivity of social relations and the importance of gender and child-rearing make for very special qualities of daily experience. The problem has been to unravel its relations to the other loci of consciousness formation. Engels (1942) argued, for example, that the family as a reproductive unit (as well as its internal structure) could be understood only through its relation to a dominant mode of production as well as to forms of state power. Marx (1967, 490) even went so far as to predict the rise of less patriarchal and more egalitarian family forms through industrialization and the increasing participation of women in the labor force. Simmel more closely replicated the argument in the *Communist Manifesto* that the family disintegrated with monetization and became entirely subservient to the individualism of bourgeois interests. But such arguments are controversial and still not resolved.

The rise of the family as an economic unit independent of community predates the rise of capitalism though not of monetization or, probably, of private property relations. It was later characterized by increasing privatization and the insulation of individuals (particularly children) from external influences, making reliance on the protective powers of community even less pressing. The transition of "family production economies" into "family wage economies" occurred with capitalist industrialization and urbanization, but was nowhere near as disruptive of traditional relations as Marx or Engels thought (Tilly and Scott 1978, 227–32). Indeed, the family, with some internal adjustment, managed to preserve itself as an institution at the same time as it played a vital role in the adaptation of individuals to conditions of wage labor and the money calculus of urban life (Tilly and Scott 1978; Hareven 1982; Sennett 1970; Handlin 1951). But it has been subject to considerable external pressure. While it may protect individuals against the alienations of money, it is perpetually threatened by the individualism that money power promotes (arguments over money still being a primary cause of family break-up). It becomes an object of bourgeois and state surveillance (see Chap. 2; Donzelot 1977) precisely because its insulated environment can become a breeding ground for all kinds of social relations antagonistic to money and to capital. Paradoxically, the family through its protections helps mollify such antagonisms, making for a most interesting intersection with the functions of community. To the degree that the latter provides a framework for coping, adaptation, and control, so the emphasis upon the family may diminish. But the more the capitalist form of community prevails (consistent with accumulation and monetized individualism), the more important the family may become as a protective milieu outside of the cold calculus of profit and the class alienations of wage labor. The family can also substitute for community as a primary agent for the reproduction of differentiated labor power and hence of basic class relations. Family authority structures may also be imported into and replicted within the organization of the labor process, thus making family relations a vehicle for class domination. But, again, it is by no means necessarily a passive agent in this regard. Family ambition helps shape social space at the same time as it can be an agent of transformation of class and employment structures.

Though the family may persist as a vital institution, its meanings and functions shift in relation to changing currents within the urbanization of capital. Tilly and Scott (1978), for example, discern a further shift, most pronounced since World War II, toward a "family consumer economy" specializing in reproduction and consumption. Pahl (1984) shows, however, that families have increasingly used that consumption power not only to protect and command space (through home and car ownership) but also to create new forms of household production, using capital equipment and raw materials purchased from the market but arranged according to their own personal tastes, divisions of labor, and temporal rhythms of production. The same phenomenon – the resurgence of household production systems – can be observed at the lower end of the social scale where it has, however, a quite different meaning; households lacking market power are forced to household production as a pure strategy for survival (Redclift and Mingione 1985).

The family therefore exists as an island of relative autonomy within a sea of objective bondage, perpetually adapting to the shifting currents of capitalist urbanization through its relations to individualism, community, class, and the state. It provides a haven to which individuals can withdraw from the complexities and dangers of urban life or from which they can selectively sample its pleasures and opportunities. But it is a haven perpetually buffeted by external forces – the loss of earning power through unemployment, squabbles over money rights, the sheer attractions of monetized individualism compared to patterns of familial repression, and the need to orient child-rearing practices to labor market ends are major sources of disruption in family life. The consciousness created behind bolted and barred doors tends, of course, to be inward looking and often indifferent to a wider world. It may encourage withdrawal from struggles to control money, space, and time as sources of social power through community or class action. From this standpoint the family appears to pose no threat to capitalism. But the consciousness forged out of affective family relations can be dangerous if it spills outward as a basis for moral judgment of all aspects of civil society. How to square the values and virtues of family life with the destructive force of money and capital is ever an interesting conundrum for bourgeois ideology.

Consider, finally, the state as a locus of consciousness formation. In the context of the communities of money and capital, the legitimacy of the state has to rest on its ability to define a public interest over and above privatism (individualistic or familial), class struggle, and conflictual community interests. It has to provide a basic framework of institutions backed by sufficient authority to resolve conflicts, impose collective judgments, pursue collective courses of action, and defend civil society as a whole from external assault and internal disintegration. The gains from its interventions are real enough – all the way from mundane matters of sewage disposal and the regulation of traffic flow to more general procedures for countering market failure, articulating collective class interests, protecting against abuses (community intolerance, excessive exploitation, the abuse of family authority), and arbitrating between warring factions. The gains provide a material basis for legitimate pride in and loyalty to the local or national state and to its symbols and representatives. The state loses legitimacy when it becomes or is seen to become captive to some particular individual, community, or class interest, or so totally inefficient as to yield no effective gains to anyone. I say "seen to become" because that state has at its disposal all manner of means for promoting and sustaining its legitimacy through control over information flow and outright propaganda, none of which is innocent in relation to consciousness formation. Furthermore, particular interests form within the state apparatus. The bearers of the scientific, technical, and managerial expertise that the state relies upon may use the state apparatus as a vehicle to express their power and so project a bureaucratic-managerial and technocratic consciousness onto the whole of civil society in the name of the public interest. The techniques, ideologies, and practices of "urban managerialism" are, many rightly argue, fundamental to understanding the contemporary urban process (Pahl 1977; Saunders 1981). The state, therefore, is not only a fulcrum for the articulation of place-bound loyalties and consciousness but also an apparatus that both internalizes and projects its own specific forms of consciousness.

But the state ought not to be viewed too statically, as a perpetual and unchanging locus of authority independent of the elements of individualism, class, family, and community. It adapts in terms of shifting relations with these other loci and also in relation to the changing dynamic of capitalist development and the urbanization of capital. The class alliances that form around issues of urban governance, for example, are fluid in their composition and by no means confine their field of action to formal channels. Indeed, the latter are often institutionalizations of long-established practices of collective decision making on the part of some ruling-class alliance (see *The Urbanization of Capital,* chap. 6). The history of local government reform movements, of annexations and interjurisdictional coordinations, wonderfully illustrates how capitalism's urban dynamic is matched by transformations in political and administrative structures. Even the rise of professionalism (political and administrative) and of managerial and technocratic modes of thought can be seen as both a response to and a moving force in the drive to find rational coordinations for the uses of money, space, time, and capital under increasingly chaotic conditions of capitalist urbanization. When the paths of capital circulation are dominated by the pure individualism of money and the traditional solidarity of communities almost totally dissolved, then a powerful state apparatus becomes essential to the proper management of capitalist urbanization. But even then, the political processes of class alliance formation within the urban region take precedence over the particular forms of state power through which that alliance may exercise its influence. When the urban community functions, for example, as a competitive unit within the uneven geographical development of capitalism, it necessarily deploys a mix of informal mechanisms (coordinated by such groups as a local chamber of commerce or a businessmen's round table) and local state powers (tax breaks and infrastructural investment). The celebrated public-private partnership, rather than pure urban managerialism, is a basic guiding force in the urbanization of capital.

But state action can also be antagonistic to individualism, the family, community, and capital. The dominant rationality embodied in the state apparatus conflicts with the typical modes of behavior and action emanating from other loci. It was, after all, in the name of the public interest that Haussman reorganized the interior space of Paris only to stir up a hornet's nest of privatistic responses (see Chap. 3). It was in the name of that same rationality that Robert Moses took the "meat-axe" to Brooklyn, stirring up, as did many a highway planner, severe community opposition. Rational urban planning, even of the socialist variety, often amounts to the same authoritarianism wielded more insidiously. A too closed coalition between the technocratic rationalism of a managerial elite and the authoritarianism of state power can undermine the legitimacy of both. Whether or not the state can continue to impose its will depends on the strength of the class alliance behind it and the relative power of opposing forces. The state is itself vulnerable to the power of money and capital, as well as to movements of revulsion and revolt centered in the family, the community, or the under-privileged classes. Struggles for control over the state apparatus are therefore paralleled by struggles over what kind of rational action the state is supposed to pursue and what kind of consciousness the state is supposed to represent and project. Policies with respect to the family, monetized individualism, and capital circulation, as well as to the processes of community formation and dissolution, must be continuously adjusted to new circumstances. The state is both the hope and the despair not only of revolutionary movements (which view it either as the pinnacle of power to be scaled or as the fount of all evil to be destroyed) but of all segments of society, no matter of what political persuasion.

Individuals draw their sense of identity and shape their consciousness out of the material bases given by the individualism of money, the class relations of capital, the limited coherence of community, the contested legitimacy of the state, and the protected but vulnerable domain of family life. But they also do so in the context of how these material bases intersect within a produced urban milieu that institutionalizes and reifies the social and physical patterning of all such human relations in space and time. The urbanization of capital – so vital to capitalism's survival as a dominant mode of production and consumption – entails a particular configuration of intersections of these different loci of consciousness formation. What is more, the dynamic of capitalism rests on innovative restructurings of these configurations in exactly the same way that it necessarily internalizes impulses toward perpetual revolutions in productive force and in dominant social relations. The urbanization of consciousness, like the urbanization of capital, is a process of continuous restructuring punctuated by periodic revolutions.

By the same token, the confusion of urban social and political movements under capitalism derives from the ways in which individuals internalize diverse conceptions and act upon them in a milieu that demands mixed conceptions rather than giving anyone a clear-cut identity. This helps explain the peculiar mix of satisfactions and disappointments; of fragmented ideologies and states of consciousness; the kaleidoscope of diverse urban social and political movements; the curious cross-cutting of labor struggles, community struggles, and struggles around the state apparatus or the family; and the seeming withdrawal of individuals and families from matters of broader social concern. It helps put in perspective also the active moments of sudden participation and revolutionary fervor and of equally sudden fading and collapse of political movements that seemed to have such a broad and solid base. It also helps in understanding the often extraordinary dissonance between opinions expressed and actions taken.

The Paris Commune, the background of which was detailed in Chapters 3 and 4, is a wonderful illustration of exactly such confusions. The egalitarian individualism of the radical petite bourgeoisie (with its money concerns) was certainly in evidence, but then so was the quest for community outside of the rule of money and capital. A powerful wing of the workers' movement looked to the free association of producers and consumers through mutual cooperation and federalism as the path to social progress, and many within the women's movement concurred because they sought ways fundamentally to modify the family economy. A different kind of class consciousness, internationalist and seeking to combat the community of capital by building a class movement with a universal perspective, was particularly evident within the new leadership of the Paris branch of the International. Republican revolutionaries, Jacobin by tradition, looked to a strong centralized state as the prime lever of social and political liberty, while the Blanquists viewed Paris as the revolutionary hearth from which a national revolution of the greatest purity would diffuse and liberate France from its capitalist chains and go on to build a national community totally outside of bourgeois valuations. Moderate republicans, in contrast, simply wanted self-governance for Paris, the right to command a local state apparatus that had so much command over them. Many women (and some men) saw the Commune as an occasion to build new kinds of family relationships based on free union and cooperative forms of household production and mutualist forms of exchange. And traditional family loyalties brought men and women together on the same barricades.

The alliance of forces ran the gamut from the rank individualism of money, self-government, household autonomy under conditions of equality between the sexes, the self-management of production and consumption in relation to human need rather than profit, and decentralized and centralized versions of revolutionary socialism, to the purest statism possible. Under such conditions the political confusions of the Commune are understandable. Should the Commune respect the spaces of private property in both production and consumption as well as money power (the Bank of France) as counterweights to the absolutism of state power? Should it use arbitrary police power to ensure discipline and counter subversion? Should it centralize or decentralize authority – and if so, how? That all died on the same barricades can be explained only by the ways in which different identities and states of consciousness fused in a given historical moment into a political movement to defend a particular space against those who represented the power of money and the power of capital unalloyed. Yet, in the iconography of the Commune, it is all too frequently forgotten that this was a distinctively urban event. Its multidimensionality can be comprehended only in terms of the urbanized consciousness that it expressed.

Academics, though not prone to die on barricades, exhibit similar confusions. Neoclassical economists privilege entrepreneurial and consumer sovereignties based on the individualism of money; Marxists, the productive forces and class relations necessary to the extraction of surplus value; Weberians, class relations constructed out of market behaviors, urban managerialism, and the organization of the local state; feminists, patriarchy, family, and women at work; representatives of the Chicago school, the ecology of communities in space; and so on. Each particular perspective tells its own particular truth. Yet they scarcely touch each other and they come together on the intellectual barricades with about the same frequency as urban uprisings like the Paris Commune. The intellectual fragmentations of academia appear as tragic reflections of the confusions of an urbanized consciousness; they reflect surface appearances, do little to elucidate inner meanings and connections, and do much to sustain the confusions by replicating them in learned terms.

Does this mean that we have to abandon Marx for some eclectic mix of theoretical perspectives? Not at all. If capitalism persists as the dominant mode of production, then it is with the analysis of that mode of production that we have to start. The circulation of capital is so fundamental to the ways we gain and use our collective and individual social power that we have no option except to put its class relations at the center of our analysis. There is a sense in which class relations invade and dominate all other loci of consciousness formation. This does not mean, however, that everything can be reduced to an analysis of class relations. To do so is to lose any capacity to understand the role of urbanization under capitalism. The problem is to build upon the Marxian themes so as to integrate the urban process into an understanding of the capitalist mode of production. Let me illustrate, schematically, how that might be done.

Marx represented the standard form of circulation of capital as:

$$M \rightarrow C \begin{cases} LP \\ MP \end{cases} \dots P \dots C' \rightarrow M + \triangle \, m \rightarrow \text{etc.}$$

Capital there passes through various metamorphoses; money is used to buy commodities (labor power and means of production), and these are combined in production to create a new commodity that is sold on the market for the original money plus a profit. Most of the basic goods that support daily life under capitalism are produced through such a mode of circulation. And the class relation between capital and labor is fundamental to its *modus operandi*. The capitalist economy in aggregate is made up of innumerable and intersecting circulation processes of this type. Some sort of balance has then to prevail between total production and consumption, between the creation of surplus value in production and its realization as profit in the market (Harvey 1982, chap. 3). Each transition in this circulation process is also spatially constrained; the buying and selling of commodities occurs over space, and the buying and selling of labor power on a daily basis is particularly constrained by the possibilities of daily labor movement to and from work. The circulation processes of capital have therefore to be considered as a geographical configuration of interactions (see *The Urbanization of Capital*, chaps. 2 and 6). We also know that this system is necessarily expansionary, technologically dynamic, and unstable (crisis prone).

Consider, now, how the various material bases we have identified for consciousness formation under urbanization integrate into this general conception. We know that the individualism of money is embedded within the circulation of capital at each and every moment of exchange. The alienations and freedoms that attach thereto are real enough and deserve examination in their own right, no matter whether we are dealing with laborers expending their wages or entrepreneurs making investment decisions.

What we cannot do, and this was Simmel's most glaring error, is to abstract the money moment of exchange from its context of capital circulation and its class relations. We also know that the circulation of revenues is essential to the circulation of capital — the goods capitalists produce have to be consumed either by the bourgeoisie or the working class expending their revenues or by capitalists seeking intermediate products and investment goods. The circulation of revenues, given the alienations of money, provides abundant opportunities for different structures of distribution to assert themselves, for the creation of new centers of economic power (finance capital, property capital, and the like), and for the construction of marks of distinction, status, and even consumption classes and communities (perhaps opposed, perhaps integrated into the powers of money and of capital). The reproduction of labor power within spatially structured labor markets depends on family actions and the social infrastructures of community, both supported out of the circulation of capital and revenues. The quantities, qualities, and value of labor power depend crucially on the nature of family economies and community structures. This is not to gainsay the fundamental Marxian thesis that capital creates an industrial reserve army and modifies fundamental class relations through control of the sociotechnical conditions of production. But it does say that a relative surplus population is relative to processes of reproduction of labor power mediated through family and community activities. The state, finally, has to be omnipresent within (and not external to, as many theories of the state seem to propose) all facets of this circulation process, compensating for market failure; creating long-term investments, regulating the family as well as the uses of money, time, space, and capital in key ways. Through the formation of local class alliances it also becomes a primary agent in the uneven geographical development of capitalism, thereby integrating the construction and evolution of absolute spaces into the evolving relative space of global capitalism. To the degree that capitalism survives through the production of space, the corporatist (sometimes bordering on mercantilist) behavior of urban class alliances is a key to understanding the self-perpetuation of capitalism.

All the elements I have described can be built into an expansion of Marx's representation of a capitalist mode of production and given an explicit spatial dimension. It is my primary thesis that urbanization can be understood in the first instance as the intersection of such particular processes in space and time to produce unique geographical configurations of physical and social relations. Once institutionalized and reified, however, these relations are transformed into complex codes of urban living that have their own significations and rigidities. The semiotic of the city reinforces the structurations of physical and social space and so enters directly into the urbanization of consciousness. We have to learn to read the social and physical signs and codes of the urban milieu – to understand the signals of status and power as written into physical landscapes, for example – in order to survive. The structures of physical and social space form a created context of significations in which the processes of community and state formation, class conflict, and the pursuit of personal or family ambition take place. The urban milieu, considered as a physical and social artifact, mediates the production of consciousness in important ways, thus giving urban life and consciousness many of their distinctive qualities.

The tendency to produce a structured coherence in urban politics and economy (see *The Urbanization of Capital,* chap. 6) is consequently paralleled by a tendency to produce unique configurations of consciousness in each urban context. This typically gives rise to distinctive urban traditions, an urban folklore and an urban folk culture, and even produces mythologies representing the qualities of life, thought, and character of particular places in symbolic form. Cultural distinctiveness can become as important as and even more striking than distinctions of political economy. Yet here, too, relatively autonomous processes of cultural development are constrained by spatial and interurban competition, the formation of hierarchies of cultural domination, and the ravages of cultural imperialism. Consciousness formation and the lived culture through which much of that consciousness finds expression are also qualities of created absolute place in the evolving relative space of global capitalism.

But all of this poses an immense political dilemma. How can an urbanized consciousness, with all its multiple, conflictual, and fragmented identities, confront and tame the monstrous power of creative destruction embodied in a capitalist mode of production? How can political movements be mobilized that can confront the deep structure of class relations that powers a capitalist mode of production?

Consider how that dilemma has arisen and pervaded politics in the advanced capitalist countries over the past few decades. After 1945 we were treated to a generation or so of what may be called "demand-side" urbanization. Keynesian policies sought to stabilize capitalism through the maintenance of effective demand. They emphasized the circulation of revenues and distribution, consumer sovereignty (a form of monetized individualism), and growth politics within powerfully organized state controls. Urban class alliances dedicated themselves to growth-machine politics and the rapid construction of totally new physical and social spaces (suburbanization and new settlement formation) as a means of guaranteeing continuously expanding markets for the circulation of capital within a shrinking relative space. Rising personal incomes emphasized the role of the family as a consumer economy and were met by multiple strategies to sell community and access to nature as commodities. Access to life chances and social reproduction possibilities (the reproduction of labor power) became submerged in social competition over life-style and struggles to command social space as a mark of status and prestige. Family, community, class, individualism, and the state came together into a particular configuration within the Keynesian frame of capitalist urbanization.

Look, now, at the kinds of oppositional movements that then arose. Primary struggles focused on questions of distribution (over access to decent housing, health care, social services, education), while struggles over production tended to fade into the background. The urban crises of the 1960s were crises of distribution exacerbated by particular movements of revulsion and revolt. The latter focused on the alienations of pure market valuations; the perversion of community and the degradation of nature (as a consumption good) for profit; the narrowness of growth machine politics; the insensitivity of managerial and technocratic rationality in the state management of space, time, and money uses; and the frustration of promises of self-fulfillment for those with weak money power. Questions about work and employment were but part of these far broader issues. The task of Marxist theory at that time was to show how all of these surface issues related to the underlying and often obscure requirements of capital accumulation and the perpetuation of the dominant structure of class relations in production that facilitated the continued production and appropriation of surplus value.

The Keynesian consensus broke down in the face of a global capitalist crisis of stagflation during the early 1970s. The paths of capitalist development and urbanization changed and the matrix of interrelations between family, class, community, state, and individual also underwent a transformation. Objective material conditions (rising unemployment, falling real wages, industrial restructuring, escalating competition, erosion of workers' rights, privatization, and deregulation) pointed to class polarization and heightened class conflict. But political consciousness was slow to respond, and popular opinion seemed to support rather than oppose the transformation. Urban political movements declined in intensity from their high points in the 1960s, though the 1970s and early 1980s were punctuated with occasional outbursts (Miami, Brixton, Toxteth). The same pattern, quiescence punctuated by occasional revolt, such as the air controllers in the United States and the miners in Britain (both of whom were crushed by state intransigence), prevailed in the arena of labor relations. And, curiously, many abandoned the Marxist perspective at the very moment when the underlying problems to which Marxian theory always points – the search for absolute and relative surplus value through revolutions in productive forces and social relations – were rising to the surface, plain for all to see. Why this response?

Old divisions and fragmentations inherited from the fierce struggles over distribution and consumption opportunities characteristic of the Keynesian era died hard. The social issues promoted by the New Right, directed primarily at the interrelations between individual, family, and state, helped divert attention from the restructuring of production and of class relations at the same time as they helped divide and rule in the social sphere many who should have made common cause in the economic sphere. But there is more to the story than this. Free-market liberalism and antistatism were immediately compatible with powerful ideologies of money-based individualism. They also built upon the ideology of family consumer sovereignty given so much emphasis in demand-side urbanization. Deeply held ideals of freedom could revert to their origins in the money form and at best accelerate the political swing to privatization, at worst degenerate into broad-based acceptance that freedom meant the freedom to exploit others. The family, at least those blessed with one wage earner in relatively secure employment, also became much more appreciated as an economic support system (the youth rebellion faded perhaps entirely in the face of sheer economic pressure – certainly the restoration of patriarchal power became much easier in situations where families had increasingly to rely on the male wage earner to provide for all). And the collapse of systematic planning that went with the return to free-market liberalism also had the positive effect of relieving individuals from an oppressive sense of an imposed bureaucratic-technocratic rationality in the use of money, space, time, and capital.

Fiercer competition also provoked a great deal of social transformation, as much among workers as among entrepreneurs, corporations, urban regions, and nations. The effects, to be sure, were destabilizing and entailed strong though sporadic devaluations – rising bankruptcies, bank failures, fore-closures, uncollectable debt, personal financial difficulty, fiscal difficulties of many governments, collapsing social welfare supports, and family break-ups (often consequent upon unemployment of the principal wage earner). But this war of all against all produced winners as well as losers – profitable commercial and office space development, accelerating gentrification, the quick fortune of some high-tech wizard or financial entrepreneur, the increasing purchasing power of those workers who did retain the jobs, the small business with the new product that made it, the entertainers and sports stars who captured popular imagination, the multinational that combined financial and production maneuvers in exactly the right way. The instability and insecurity created opportunities in which those with ambition and imagination could make their way. Losers, and those could be whole cities and nations as well as families and firms, seemed to have no one to blame but themselves. And winners were not loath to rub that message in. Under such conditions, the ideological traditions of rugged individualism, family self-sufficiency, entrepreneurial drive, and aggressive class-based government could more easily prevail over any class-conscious movements to confront the underlying crisis of capitalism.

The balance between individualism, class, community, the family, and the state has shifted radically since 1970. The failure of mass movements to respond to a crisis of capitalism in a class-conscious way has much to do with the shifting interrelations between the various loci of consciousness formation. But I have also argued that these interrelations cannot be understood independently of the particular configuration they achieve within the urban process. The latter also changed dramatically in the 1970s, creating new dilemmas for the urbanization of capital and an entirely new context for the urbanization of consciousness.

Ruling class alliances within urban regions, for example, have been forced to consider themselves less as growth machines for unproblematic capital accumulation coupled with perhaps problematic redistribution and more as competitive corporations fighting for survival in a capitalistic system of uneven geographical development that visits devaluation and abandonment on the hindmost. The geopolitical and economic options open to them are limited as each struggles to defend or enhance its interests in the face of radical restructuring and fiercer international and interurban competition. The options may be broadly divided into four types, roughly emphasizing the contrasts between cities as workshops for production; cities as consumption artifacts; cities as centers of information, finance capital, and administration; and cities as redistributive centers (see *The Urbanization of Capital*, chap. 8).

1. The active creation of the conditions for absolute or relative surplus value appropriation through production can improve the competitive position of the urban region in relation to the international division of labor. There are various paths to that end, such as investment in the physical and social infrastructures that support technological innovation, tax subsidies and support of business reorganization, and control of the local labor force – its quality, militancy, and cost – through some combination of state and private action.

2. The urban region can also seek to improve its competitive position with respect to the spatial division of consumption and the circulation of revenues. There is more to this than tourism and retirement attractions. The Keynesian style of urbanization promoted an ever-broader basis for participation in consumerism through focusing on life-style, the construction of community, and the organization of social space in terms of the symbols of status, prestige, and power. While recession, unemployment, and the high cost of credit have rendered participation in that game moot for important layers of the population, the possibility continues for the rest. Competition for their consumer dollars becomes more frenetic, while they, in turn, have the opportunity to be more discriminating. Investments to attract the consumption dollar focus on the quality of life (gentrification, cultural innovation, and physical upgrading), consumer attractions (sports stadia, convention and shopping centers, marinas, and exotic eating places), and entertainment (of

which Disney World is but a prototype). Above all, the city has to appear as an innovative, exciting, creative, and safe place to live. Spectacle and display become the symbols of dynamic community, much as they did in Haussman's Paris. That way, an urban region can survive as a locus of expanding consumption in the midst of spreading recession.

3. An urban region can also better survive to the degree that it captures those command functions in communications, finance, and government that permit surplus value to be skimmed off the world, national, or regional economy through the monopoly power that always goes with such command. To compete requires investment in a wide range of physical and social infrastructures (office space, communications facilities, an educated labor force). Competition is stiff, but the increasing importance of such functions and changing space relations creates all kinds of opportunities for potentially high payoffs.

4. The urban region can also improve its position through the direct or indirect redistribution of surpluses from other regions. This means the direct or indirect levying of tributes or the granting of subsidies, or redistribution through higher-order government mechanisms. The latter depends on geopolitical power or downright blackmail through the threat or actual occurrence of social unrest and violence.

These four options are not mutually exclusive. Happy the urban region that is attractive to control functions because it is an interesting place to live and that can thereby so expand the circulation of revenues and attract redistributions that local industry becomes both locally viable and inter-nationally competitive, thus attracting a strong inflow of low wage labor. This was the sort of mix that kept the Parisian economy going during the best years of the Second Empire (see Chap. 3). Los Angeles also did relatively well on all four options in the difficult years after 1973, while cities like Baltimore, Lille, and Liverpool had a much harder time of it.

The pursuit of some mix of these four options has important implications. There is nothing here that directly addresses the global problems of capitalist accumulation. Indeed, like any heightened form of intercapitalist compe-tition, there is much here to exacerbate the inherent instability of capitalism and so push it deeper into the mire of crisis. I take up this problem in *The Urbanization of Capital.* Pursuit of such strategies also carries profound implications for the political air we breathe and so transforms the atmosphere of consciousness formation. There is as much here to obscure the conscious-ness of class relations as there is to exacerbate global problems of overaccumu-lation.

To the degree that people see their fate tied in the immediate future to the health of the particular urban economy from which they draw their sustenance, so they tend to rally to the cause of any dominant class alliance that seems to offer even temporary or partial relief from the threat of devaluation. To the degree that the options for urban survival become more starkly posed, so the notion of making the urban economy competitive has to take precedence over all else. The concern for efficiency in interurban competition dominates that for social justice in distribution, for example. There will, of course, be considerable dispute over the paths to take, and those disputes will inevitably take on a class coloration. Blue collar workers and industries struggling to preserve jobs will push in a different direction from those seeking to expand control functions and white collar employment. Disciplining labor power (through unemployment, increasing pressure on the industrial reserve army, and state-led retrenchment on wages) sits ill with the promotion of conspicuous consumption in order to tap into the circulation of revenues. But even when the class effects may be obvious, the class options, given the urban focus of strategies for survival, are not.

For example, most strategies to keep jobs in town entail substantial regressive redistributions of income and economic power. Industries stay in town only if they are extensively subsidized either by wage cuts or by redistributions (tax breaks and infrastructural investments) out of the social wage. Interurban competition within the spatial division of consumption entails public subsidy of conspicuous consumption for the rich at the expense of the social wage of the poor. Privileged command functions are captured only with the help of vast investments in physical and social infrastructures, tax breaks, and other forms of subsidy. The net effect is to create a kind of corporate and affluent welfarism at the expense of social welfare for the underprivileged. Yet this seems the only way to preserve any kind of job prospects or tax base to support the latter. These sorts of urban perspectives on the crisis mean that the lower classes either have to sit by and hope, Micawber-like, that something will turn up (which it sometimes does), or else seek out a ruling-class alliance that articulates their interests, only then to see (as they did under the Kucinich administration in Cleveland or the labor council of Liverpool) the dismal headlines of job loss, abandonment, and fiscal crisis of the local state. The pressure of interurban competition, coupled with strong place-bound loyalties, can only lead to such no-exit situations, guaranteed at some point to lead to explosions of uncontrollable frustration on the part of a swelling urban under-class.

The interior reorganization of the urban process complicates matters even further. State power has increasingly to compromise with privatism and particularly with industrial and finance capital. The terms of that compromise are, quite simply, to bring the local state to heel as an agent of capitalist class domination. The reality and the threat of unemployment and reductions in welfare provision put a much greater burden upon the resources of family and community, both of which either crack or flourish under the strain. Communities and families endowed with adequate economic resources tend to survive better than those without, though similar patterns of adjustment – toward greater reliance upon the household economy and tightening community self-help and control – can be observed at different ends of the class and status spectrum with, however, rather different orientations. Fiercer struggles for control over turf within a decaying urban slum (like Toxteth or Brixton) contrast with increasing concern for defensible social spaces of privilege for the affluent in the same way that the revival of household production systems also means something quite different at opposite ends of the social scale (Pahl 1984; Redclift and Mingione 1985). Intercommunity and even interfamilial competition picks up, heightening and fragmenting tensions with respect to control over social space and access to life chances. Images of territoriality and of some Darwinian struggle for survival in the "jungle of urban life" take over with telling and often tragic effects. Since images of this sort fit so snugly into the logic of free-market competition, it seems that the communities of money and capital then dominate any alternative sense of community or the state, leaving individuals no recourse except withdrawal into narcissistic and self-seeking individualism or the pursuit of narrow, family-based satisfactions.

Yet such configurations of the individual, family, community, class, and state within the urban process are not particularly consistent with capital accumulation either. They generate even sharper discontinuities in the supply of labor power of different qualities, limit mass consumption markets, and often impose high costs of social control. They check that kind of open communication, experimentation, and tense tolerance for difference that promotes those cultural, technical, political, and life-style innovations that give the urban dynamic much of its luster and vigor and that make the urban process so integral to the dynamics of uneven but progressive capitalist development. Under such circumstances, the dialectics of urban living take odd shapes and forms, as the bourgeoisie struggles to undo with one hand what it creates with the other.

Tensions of this sort compound within the urban milieu into powerful configurations of personal and political consciousness that conceal underlying social relations of class within a miasma of material fetishisms. It is all very well to insist, as Marxists and even sensible bourgeois are wont to do, that the system has to be understood as a totality, that revenues and redistributions have their origin in value created in production, that monopoly powers in the realms of government and finance crumble to nothing without conjoining capital and labor power in production, that community solidarities and family economies cannot be abstracted from a political-economic context in which the circulation of capital, with its dominant class relations, reigns supreme. For the plain fact is that most economic agents have neither the opportunity nor the luxury (even if they had the predisposition and the education) to penetrate the fetishisms of daily life. And even if they did, their reflections (as many a radical thinker finds) are hard to translate into actions that do much more than address immediate needs and hence support the fetishisms rather than dissolve them.

Where, then, does this leave those of us who, for whatever reason, look to the transformation of capitalism into some saner, less life-threatening mode of production and consumption? We know that capitalism has survived into the twentieth century in part through the production of an increasingly urbanized space. The result has been a particular kind of urban experience, radically different quantitatively and qualitatively from anything that preceded it in world history. Capitalism has produced a "second nature" through urbanization and the creation of built environments of extraordinary breadth and intricacy. It has also produced a new kind of human nature through the urbanization of consciousness and the production of social spaces and a particular structure of interrelations between the different loci of consciousness formation. But these second natures, though produced out of the capitalist mode of production and circulation, are not necessarily consistent with the easy perpetuation of capital accumulation and its dominant class relations. Indeed, with time they often become key barriers. The urban process then appears as both fundamental to the perpetuation of capitalism and a primary expression of its inner contradictions now expressed as produced external constraints. Capitalism has to confront the consequences of its urban structurations at each moment in its history. The produced second natures become the raw materials out of which new configurations of capitalist activity, new productive forces, and new social relations must be wrought. The capitalist dynamic is forced to tear down much of what it has built in order to survive. The axe of creative destruction falls not only on capital made obsolescent before its time but on the skills of the worker and on the roles of family, individualism, community, and state.

The search for alternatives has to confront exactly that situation and be prepared to transform, not only that vast constructed second nature of a built environment shaped to accommodate capitalist modes and spatial divisions of both production and consumption, but also an urbanized consciousness. Failure to do so has, I suspect, lain at the root of many of the errors of socialist attempts to transform capitalism. For socialism is more than simply showing that the creative destruction unleashed in the course of socialist revolution is in the long run more creative and less destructive than that inherent in capitalism. It also means charting a path toward a radically different kind of urban experience – one that confronts the multiple sources of alienation and disaffection while preserving the minimal liberties and securities achieved. A study of the urbanization of capital and of consciousness helps identify the multiple traps into which proposals for social transformation can all too easily fall. It can also help, perhaps, to chart a path through the multilayered fetishisms that attach to the daily experience of urban living into a political movement that can confront the core of our prolems with the underlying class relations of the capitalist mode of production itself.

Can a coordinated attack against the power of capital be mounted out of the individualism of money, the more radical conceptions of community, the progressive elements of new family structures and gender relations, and the contested but potentially fruitful legitimacy of state power, all in alliance with the class resentments that derive from the conditions of labor and the buying and selling of labor power? The analysis of the conditions that define the urbanization of consciousness suggests that it will take the power of some such alliance to mount a real challenge to the power of capital. But there is no natural basis of such an alliance and much to divide the potential partici-pants. And its conceptualization says something about the kinds of politics to which it must adhere.

Consider, for example, the distinction between money and money used as capital. Failure to make that distinction has led many Marxists to view the abolition of price-fixing markets and of price signals as a precondition for the abolition of class relations in production. It has taken the experience of totally centralized planning, with its highly rationalized, disciplined, and repressive coordinations of production and consumption in a universalized space and time, to suggest that perhaps the equation of money and capital was an error and that blind control of money uses amounted to the abolition of the modicum of admittedly constrained individual freedom that bourgeois society has achieved. The bourgeoisie has pioneered a path toward greater individual liberty. The problem is to liberate that individual liberty from its purely capitalist basis. The price system is the most decentralized of all decision-making mechanisms for coordinating the social and geographical division of labor with a degree of individual liberty unrealizable in centralized planning or collective community control. Individuals plainly value the limited freedoms given by money uses, and price coordinations yield a more open kind of urban society than that which might otherwise arise. The problem, therefore, is to get beyond the pure money basis of bourgeois individualism, to curb the use of money power to procure privileged access to life chances, without falling prey to the repressions of community or the authoritarian state. The argument that private property offers one of the few protections against the arbitrariness of the state or the repressive intolerance of community must also be accorded a certain weight. But social democracy, which has shown itself sensitive at least to certain of these issues, has never been able to contain the forms of domination that arise when private property and money power are combined as capital. Nor has it ever dealt with the alienated individualism that pure money coordinations produce except through an equally alien welfare statism. The path to socialism has to run the gauntlet of such complicated oppositions.

Nor can the present spatial division of labor and of consumption be totally abandoned without almost total destruction of the material bases of contemporary life. The locational principles of the evolution of production can, however, shift away from the singular and roving calculus of profit toward some balance between respect for the integrity of the working community, with its history, tradition, and accumulated skills, and innovative probing for new techniques and more efficient spatial configurations. Abundant sentiment can be mobilized behind that idea. The search for less oppressive sociotechnical conditions and social relations of production is, after all, what class struggle in the workplace is all about. Yet it is hard to articulate the exact meaning of such a project in a world of such intricate interdependence that money power cannot help but dominate as a concrete abstraction that rules our lives. One first step, perhaps, is to curb interurban competition and search out more federated structures of interurban cooperation. Beyond that lies the problem of determining without over-rigid institutionalization some acceptable and dynamic balance between centralization and decentralization of economic decision making. That means that the power of finance capital and the state with respect to production has to be redefined and controlled in ways that fit strategies of codevelopment rather than competitive profit seeking.

On the surface, the spatial division of consumption appears an easier issue to address. The direct reorganization of the urban landscape to redistribute access to social power and life chances so as to rebuild a more equitable basis for an adequate social wage is essential. And certainly those forms of interurban competition that end up generating subsidies for the consumption of the rich at the expense of the social wage of the poor deserve instant attack. But this is, I suspect, a more dangerous arena than most socialists are wont to admit. The experience of demand-side urbanization bit deep into political consciousness. It played upon the fuzzy boundary between the selling of community and the genuine striving for real community, real cultural and personal freedoms exercised collectively. The mass merging of consumerist narcissism and inner longings for self-realization has been one of the most tragic aspects of the urbanization of consciousness. And it is a volatile mix, dangerous to provoke and hard to confront. Yet it increasingly appears as one of the key problems and opportunities for political mobilization. Here exists a major base for political agitation, a guerrilla base from which to mount a broader war, but one which is in perpetual danger of degenerating into mild forms of localized consumer socialism that feed rather than heal dissension. The problem is to sever the tight connection between self-realization and pure consumerism. That battle has to be fought if socialism is ever to stand a chance in the advanced capitalist world.

Failure to win battles of this sort leaves us at the mercy of an urban process that internalizes capitalist principles of production for production's sake, accumulation for accumulation's sake, consumption for consumption's sake, and innovation for innovation's sake. It also presages a future of accelerating creative destruction and abandonment that will implicate more and more people and places.

Zola closes *La bête humaine* with a terrifying image. Engineer and fireman, locked in mortal combat out of their own petty jealousies, tumble from the train to be severed limb from limb beneath its juggernaut wheels. The train, driverless and ever accelerating, rushes toward Paris, while the soldiers it carries, intoxicated and drunk with excitement at the prospect of the grand war with Prussia to come, bellow the loudest and bawdiest of songs with all their energy and might. It was, of course, the Second Empire careening toward war with Prussia and the tragedy of the Commune that Zola sought to symbolize. But the image has perhaps a broader application. The urbanization of capital on a global scale charts a path toward a total but also violently unstable urbanization of civil society. The urbanization of consciousness intoxicates and befuddles us with fetishisms, rendering us powerless to understand let alone intervene coherently in that trajectory. The urbanization of capital and of consciousness threatens a transition to barbarism in the midst of a rhetoric of self-realization.

If the urbanization of capital and of consciousness is so central to the perpetuation and experience of capitalism, and if it is through these channels that the inner contradictions of capitalism are now primarily expressed, then we have no option but to put the urbanization of revolution at the center of our political strategies. There is enough supporting evidence for that. Any political movement that does not embed itself in the heart of the urban process is doomed to fail in advanced capitalist society. Any political movement that does not secure its power within the urban process cannot long survive. Any political movement that cannot offer ways out of the multiple alienations of contemporary urban life cannot command mass support for the revolutionary transformation of capitalism. A genuinely humanizing urban experience, long dreamed of and frequently sought, is worth struggling for. Socialism has therefore to address the problem of the simultaneous transformation of capitalism and its distinctive form of urbanization. That conception is, of course, ambiguous. But I prefer to leave it so. Unraveling its meaning is what contemporary political-economic life has to be about.

References

Agulhon, M. [1979] 1981. *Marianne into battle: Republican imagery and symbolism in France, 1789–1880*. Trans. J. Lloyd. London.

———. [1973] 1983. *The republican experiment, 1848–1852*. Trans. J. Lloyd. London.

Allison, J. 1932. *Monsieur Thiers*. New York.

Alonso, W. 1964. *Location and land use*. Cambridge, Mass.

Anderson, R. 1970. The conflict in education. In *Conflicts in French society*, ed. T. Zeldin. London.

———. 1975. *Education in France, 1848–1870*. Oxford.

Audiganne, A. 1854. *Les populations ouvrières et les industries de la France dans le mouvement social du XIXe siècle*. Paris.

———. 1865. *Les ouvriers d'à présent et la nouvelle économie du travail*. Paris.

Auspitz, K. 1982. *The radical bourgeoisie: The Ligue de l'Enseignement and the origins of the Third Republic*. London.

Autin, J. 1984. *Les frères Pereire*. Paris.

Bartier, J., et al. 1981. *1848: Les utopismes sociaux*. Paris.

Baudelaire, C. [1869] 1947. *Paris spleen*. Ed. and trans. L. Varèse. New York.

———. [1845–64] 1981. *Selected writings on art and artists*. 2d ed., reprint, trans. P. E. Charvet. London.

———. [1857] 1983a. *Les fleurs du mal*. Trans. R. Howard. Boston.

———. [n.d.] 1983b. *Intimate journals*. Rev. ed., reprint, trans. C. Isherwood. San Francisco.

Becker, G., ed. 1969. *Paris under siege, 1970–71: From the Goncourt journal*. Ithaca.

Bellet, R. 1967. *Presse et journalisme sous le Second Empire*. Paris.

Bender, T. 1975. *Toward an urban vision: Ideas and institutions in nineteenth-century America*. Lexington, Ky.

Benjamin, W. [1969] 1973. *Charles Baudelaire: A lyric poet in the era of high capitalism*. Trans. H. Zohn. London.

Berlanstein, L. 1979–80. Growing up as workers in nineteenth-century Paris: The case of orphans of the Prince Imperial. *French Historical Studies* 11:551–76.

Berman, M. 1982. *All that is solid melts into air*. New York.

Bouvier, J. 1967. *Les Rothschild*. Paris.

Braudel, F., and E. Labrousse, eds. 1976. *Histoire économique et sociale de la France*, vol. 3. Paris.

Braverman, H. 1974. *Labor and monopoly capital.* New York.

Bruhat, J., J. Dautry, and E. Tersen. 1971. *La Commune de 1871.* Paris.

Buder, S. 1967. *Pullman.* New York.

Canfora-Argandona, E., and R. H. Guerrand. 1976. *La répartition de la population, les conditions de logement des classes ouvrières à Paris au XIXe siècle.* Paris.

Castells, M. 1975. Collective consumption and urban contradictions in advanced capitalist societies. In *Patterns of advanced societies,* ed. L. Linberg. New York.

———. 1983. *The city and the grassroots.* Berkeley and Los Angeles.

Cerf, M. 1971. *Edouard Moreau.* Paris.

Charlety, S. 1931. *Histoire du Saint-Simonisme.* Paris.

Charlton, D. 1959. *Positivist thought in France during the Second Empire, 1852–1870.* Oxford.

Chevalier, L. 1950. *La formation de la population parisienne au XIXe siècle.* Paris.

———. [1958] 1973. *Laboring classes and dangerous classes.* Trans. F. Jellinek. Princeton.

Clark, T. J. 1973a. *The absolute bourgeois: Artists and politics in France, 1848–1851.* London.

———. 1973b. *Image of the people: Gustave Courbet and the 1848 revolution.* London.

Cobb, R. 1975. *A sense of place.* London.

Cochin, A. 1864. *Paris, sa population, son industrie.* Paris.

Commission des Logements Insalubres de Paris. 1866. *Rapport générale sur les travaux de la commission pendant les années 1862–1865.* Paris.

Copping, E. 1858. *Aspects of Paris.* London.

Corbin, A. 1978. *Les filles de noce: Misère sexuelle et prostitution aux 19e et 20e siècles.* Paris.

Corbon, A. 1863. *La sécret du peuple de Paris.* Paris.

Corcoran, P. 1983. *Before Marx: Socialism and communism in France, 1830–1848.* London.

Cottereau, A. 1980. Etude préalable. In D. Poulot, *Le sublime.* Paris.

Counter Information Services. 1973. *Anti-report on the property developers.* London.

Dalotel, A. 1981. *Paule Minck: Communarde et feministe.* Paris.

Dalotel, A., A. Faure, and J. C. Freirmuth. 1980. *Aux origines de la Commune: Le mouvement des réunions publiques à Paris, 1868–1870.* Paris.

Dansette, A. 1965. *Histoire religieuse de la France contemporaine.* Paris.

Daumard, A. 1965. *Maisons de Paris et propriétaires parisiens au XIXe siècle.* Paris.

———. ed. 1973. *Les fortunes françaises au XIXe siècle.* Paris.

Daumas, M., and J. Payen, eds. 1976. *Evolution de la géographie industrielle de Paris et sa proche banlieue au XIXe siècle.* 2 vols. Paris.

Dautry, J. 1977. *1848 et la IIe République.* Paris.

Delacroix, E. [1926] 1980. *The journal of Eugene Delacroix.* Trans. L. Norton, ed. H. Wellington. Ithaca.

D'Hericourt, J. 1860. *La femme affranchi.* Paris.

Dickens, C. [1846–48] 1970. *Dombey and son.* Reprint. Harmondsworth, Middlesex.

Dommanget, M. [1926] 1970. *Blanqui.* Reprint. Paris.

Donzelot, J. 1977. La police des familles. Paris.

Dreyfus, R. 1928. *Monsieur Thiers contre l'Empire, la guerre et la Commune.* Paris.

Du Camp, M. 1875. *Paris, ses organes, ses functions et sa vie dans la seconde moitié du XIX* siècle*. 6 vols. Paris.

Duchêne, G. 1869. *L'empire industriel*. Paris.

Duclos, D. 1981. The capitalist state and the management of time. In *City, class, and capital*, ed. M. Harloe and E. Lebas. London.

Dunbar, G. 1978. *Elisée Reclus*. Hamden, Conn.

Dupont-Ferrier, P. 1925. *Le marché financier de Paris sous le Second Empire*. Paris.

Durkheim, E. 1965. *The elementary forms of religious life*. New York.

Duveau, G. 1946. *La vie ouvrière en France sous le Second Empire*. Paris.

Dyos, H. J. 1961. *Victorian suburb: A study of the growth of Camberwell*. Leicester.

Edwards, S. 1971. *The Paris Commune*. Chicago.

Engels, F. [1872] 1935. *The housing question*. International Publishers, New York.

Engels, F. [1884] 1942. *The origin of the family, private property, and the state*. New York.

Engels, F. [1845] 1971. *The condition of the working class in England in 1844*. 2d ed., trans. and ed. W. O. Henderson and W. H. Challoner. London.

Fay-Sallois, F. 1980. *Les nourrices à Paris au XIX* siècle*. Paris.

Ferry, J. 1868. *Comptes fantastiques d'Haussman*. Paris.

Fischer, C. (1982). *To dwell among friends: Personal networks in town and city*. Chicago.

Flaubert, G. [1869] 1964. *Sentimental education*. Trans. R. Baldick. Harmondsworth, Middlesex.

———. [1881] 1976. *Bouvard and Pécuchet*. Trans. A. J. Kailsheimer. Harmondsworth, Middlesex.

———. 1979a. *Flaubert in Egypt*. Trans. and ed. F. Steegmuller. Chicago.

———. 1979b. *Letters, 1830–1857*. Trans. and ed. F. Steegmuller. London.

———. 1982. *Letters, 1857–1880*. Trans. and ed. F. Steegmuller. London.

Flaus, L. 1949. Les fluctuations de la construction d'habitations urbaines. *Journal de la Société de Statistique de Paris* (May–June).

Flink, J. 1975. *The car culture*. Cambridge, Mass.

Fortescue, W. 1983. *Alphonse de Lamartine: A political biography*. London.

Foucault, M. [1961] 1965. *Madness and civilization*. Trans. R. Howard. New York.

Foulon, M. 1934. *Eugène Varlin*. Clermont Ferrand.

Fox, R., and Weisz, G. 1980. *The organization of science and technology in France, 1808–1914*. London.

Fribourg, A. 1872. *Le pauperisme parisien*. Paris.

Fried, M. 1963. Grieving for a lost home. In *The urban condition*, ed. L. Duhl. New York.

Fried, M., and P. Gleicher. 1961. Some sources of residential satisfaction in an urban slum. *Journal of the American Institute of Planners* 27:305–15.

Fried, Michael. 1969. Manet's sources: Aspects of his art, 1859–65. *Artforum* 7, no. 7:1–82.

Gaillard, J. 1977. *Paris, la ville, 1852–1870*. Paris.

Gans, H. 1962. *The urban villagers*. New York.

Giddens, A. 1973. *The class structure of the advanced societies*. London.

———. 1981. *A contemporary critique of historical meterialism*. London.

Giedion, S. 1941. *Space, time, architecture*. Cambridge, Mass.

Gildea, R. 1983. *Education in provincial France, 1800–1914.* Oxford.

Girard, L. 1952. *Les politiques des travaux publics sous le Second Empire.* Paris.

———. 1981. *Nouvelle histoire de Paris: La Deuxieme République et le Second Empire.* Paris.

Glacken, C. 1967. *Traces on the Rhodian Shore.* Berkeley and Los Angeles.

Godelier, M. [1966] 1972. *Rationality and irrationality in economics.* Trans. Pearce, London.

Goode, J. 1978. *George Gissing: Ideology and fiction.* London.

Gossez, R. 1967. *Les ouvriers de Paris: L'organisation, 1848–1851.* La Roche-sur-Yon.

Gossman, L. 1974. The go-between: Jules Michelet, 1798–1874. *MLN,* 89:503–41.

Gramsci, A. 1971. *Selections from the prison notebooks.* Trans. and ed. Q. Hoare and G. N. Smith. London.

Green, F. C. 1965. *A comparative view of French and British civilization, 1850–1870.* London.

Greenberg, L. 1971. *Sisters of liberty: Marseilles, Lyon, Paris, and the relation to a centralized state, 1868–1871.* Cambridge, Mass.

Guerrand, R-H. 1966. *Les origines du logement social en France.* Paris.

Guillemin, H. 1956. *Cette curieuse guerre de 1870.* Paris.

———. 1971. *L'avènement de M. Thiers et réflexions sur la Commune.* Paris.

Halbwachs, M. 1909. *Les expropriations et le prix de terrains, 1860–1900.* Paris.

———. 1928. *La population et les traces des voies à Paris depuis un siècle.* Paris.

Hanagan, M. P. 1980. *The logic of solidarity.* Urbana.

———. 1982. Urbanization, worker settlement patterns, and social protest in nineteenth-century France. In *French cities in the nineteenth century,* ed. J. Merriman. London.

Handlin, O. 1951. *The uprooted.* New York.

Hareven, T. 1982. *Family time and industrial time.* London.

Harvey, D. 1973. *Social justice and the city.* London.

———. 1975. The political economy of urbanization in the advanced capitalist societies – the case of the United States. In *The social economy of cities,* ed. G. Gappert and H. Rose, Annual Review of Urban Affairs no. 9. Beverly Hills.

———. 1982. *The limits to capital.* Oxford.

———. 1985. The geopolitics of capitalism. In *Social relations and spatial structures,* ed. D. Gregory and J. Urry. London.

Haussman, G-E. 1890. *Memoires du Baron Haussman.* 2 vols. Paris.

Hayden, D. 1981. *The grand domestic revolution: A history of feminist designs for American homes, neighborhoods, and cities.* Cambridge, Mass.

Hellerstein, E. 1976. French women and the orderly household. *Western Society for French History* 3:378–89.

Hershberg, T. 1981. *Philadelphia: Work, space, family, and the group experience in the nineteenth century.* New York.

Hertz, N. 1983. Medusa's head: Male hysteria under political pressure. *Representations* 4:27–54.

Hitzman, A. 1981. Rome is to Carthage as male is to female: Michelet, Berlioz, Flaubert, and the myths of the Second Empire. *Western Society for French History* 8:378–80.

Hobsbawm, E. 1964. *Laboring men.* London.

Howard, E. 1955. *Garden cities of tomorrow.* London.

Hugo, V. [1862] 1976. *Les misérables.* Trans. N. Denny. Harmondsworth, Middlesex.

Hutton, P. 1981. *The cult of the revolutionary tradition: The Blanquists in French politics, 1864–1893.* Berkeley and Los Angeles.

Hyams, E. 1979. *Pierre-Joseph Proudhon: His revolutionary life, mind, and works.* London.

Jackson, J. B. 1972. *American space.* New York.

Jacobs, J. 1984. *Cities and the wealth of nations.* New York.

James, H. [1907] 1946. *The American scene.* Reprint. New York.

Jonquet, R. P. (n.d.) *Montmartre, autrefois et aujourd'hui.* Paris.

Kellet, J. 1969. *The impact of railways on Victorian cities.* London.

Kelso, M. 1936. The French labor movement during the last years of the Second Empire. In *Essays in the history of modern Europe,* ed. D. McKay. New York.

Kern, S. 1983. *The culture of time and space, 1880–1918.* London.

Kerouac, J. 1955. *On the road.* New York.

Klein, R. 1967. Some notes on Baudelaire and revolution. *Yale French Studies* 39:85–97.

Kropotkin, P. [1898] 1968. *Fields, factories, and workshops.* New and rev. ed. New York.

Kulstein, D. 1969. *Napolean III and the working class.* San Jose.

Kuznets, S. 1961. *Capital in the American economy: Its formation and financing.* Princeton.

Lameyre, G-N. 1958. *Haussman, préfet de Paris.* Paris.

Landes, D. 1983. *Revolution in time: Clocks and the making of the modern world.* Cambridge, Mass.

Lasch, C. 1977. *Haven in a heartless world.* New York.

Lavedan, P. 1975. *Histoire de l'urbanisme a Paris.* Paris.

Lazare, L. 1869. *Les quartiers pauvres de Paris.* Paris.

———. 1870. *Les quartiers pauvres de Paris: Le XXe arrondissement.* Paris.

———. 1872. *La France et Paris.* Paris.

Leavitt, H. 1970. *Superhighway – super hoax.* Garden City, N.Y.

Lefebvre, H. 1974. *La production de l'espace.* Paris.

———. [1973] 1976. *The survival of capitalism.* Trans. F. Bryant. London.

Le Goff, J. [1977] 1980. *Time, work, and culture in the Middle Ages.* Trans. A. Goldhammer. Chicago.

Lejeune, P. 1977. *Eugène Varlin: Pratique militante et écrits d'un ouvrier communard.* Paris.

Leon, P. 1976. La conquest de l'espace nationale. In *Histoire économique et social de la France,* ed. E. Braudel and E. Labrousse, vol. 3. Paris.

Lepidis, C., and E. Jacomin. 1975. *Belleville.* Paris.

Le Play, F. 1983. *Ouvriers de deux mondes.* Abridged ed. Paris.

———. 1878. *Les ouvriers Européens.* 6 vols. Paris.

Leroy-Beaulieu, P. 1868. *De l'état moral et intellectuel des populations ouvrières et son influence sur le taux de salaires.* Paris.

Lescure, M. 1980. *Les sociétés immobilières en France au XIXe siècle*. Paris.

Lesourd, P. 1973. *Montmartre*. Paris.

Levy-Leboyer, M. 1976. Le crédit et la monnaie: L'évolution institutionelle. In *Histoire économique et sociale de la France*, ed. F. Braudel and E. Labrousse, vol. 3. Paris.

Lidsky, P. 1970. *Les écrivains contre la Commune*. Paris.

Lissagaray, P-O. 1976. *Histoire de la Commune*. Paris.

McBride, T. 1976. *The domestic revolution*. New York.

―――. 1977–78. A woman's world: Department stores and the evolution of women's employment, 1870–1920. *French Historical Studies* 10:664–83.

McKay, D. C. 1933. *The national workshops: A study in the French Revolution of 1848*. Cambridge, Mass.

McLaren, A. 1978. Abortion in France: Women and the regulation of family size. *French Historical Studies* 10:461–85.

McPherson, C. B. 1962. *The political theory of possessive individualism*. London.

Malthus, T. [1836] 1951. *The principles of political economy*. Reprint. New York.

Margadant, T. 1982. Proto-urban development and political mobilization during the Second Republic. In *French cities in the nineteenth century*, ed. J. Merriman. London.

Marx, K. [1852] 1963. *The eighteenth brumaire of Louis Bonaparte*. International Publishers, New York.

―――. 1964a. *Class struggles in France, 1848–1850*. International Publishers, New York.

―――. 1964b. *The economic and philosophic manuscripts of 1844*. International Publishers, New York.

―――. 1967. *Capital*. 3 vols. International Publishers, New York.

―――. 1972. *Theories of surplus value*, vol. 3. Lawrence and Wishart, London.

―――. 1973. *Grundrisse*. Penguin Publishers, Harmondsworth, Middlesex.

―――. 1976. The results of the immediate process of production. Appendix to *Capital*, vol. 1. Penguin Publishers, Harmondsworth, Middlesex.

Marx, K., and F. Engels [1848] 1952. *Manifesto of the Communist Party*. Progress Publishers, Moscow.

Marx, K., and V. I. Lenin. 1968. *The civil war in France: The Paris Commune*. International Publishers, New York.

Marx, L. 1964. *The machine in the garden*. London.

Massa-Gille, G. 1973. *Histoire des emprunts de la ville de Paris, 1814–1875*. Paris.

Michel, L. [1886] 1981. *The red virgin*. Trans. and ed. B. Lowry and E. Gunter. University, Ala.

Michelet, J. 1981. *La femme*. Paris.

Miller, M. 1981. *The Bon Marché: Bourgeois culture and the department store, 1869–1920*. London.

Mills, E. 1972. *Studies in the structure of the urban economy*. Baltimore.

Molotch, H. 1976. The city as a growth machine: Toward a political economy of place. *American Journal of Sociology* 82:309–32.

Moon, S. J. 1975. The Saint-Simonian association of working class women, 1830–1850. *Western Society for French History* 5:274–80.

Moses, C. 1984. *French feminism in the nineteenth century*. Albany.

Nadaud, M. 1895. *Mémoires de Léonard, ancien garçon maçon.* Bourganeuf.

Norris, F. [1903] 1981. *The octopus.* Reprint. New York.

Olson, M. 1965. *The logic of collective action.* Cambridge, Mass.

Pahl, R. 1977. Managers, technical experts, and the state: Forms of mediation, manipulation, and dominance in urban and regional development. In *Captive cities,* ed. M. Harloe. New York.

———. 1984. *Divisions of labour.* Oxford.

Paris Guide. [1867] 1983. Ed. Verdet. Paris.

Payne, H. C. 1966. *The police state of Louis Napoleon Bonaparte.* Seattle.

Pinkney, D. 1953. Migrations to Paris during the Second Empire. *Journal of Modern History* 25:1–12.

———. 1958. *Napoleon III and the rebuilding of Paris.* Princeton.

Plesis, A. 1973. *De la fête impériale au mur des fédérés, 1852–1871.* Paris.

———. 1982. *La banque de France et ses deux cents actionnaires sous le Second Empire.* Paris.

Pollard, S. 1965. *The genesis of modern management.* Cambridge, Mass.

Poulot, D. [1870] 1980. *Le sublime.* Ed. A. Cottereau. Paris.

Pred, A. 1973. *Urban growth and the circulation of information in the United States system of cities, 1790–1840.* Cambridge. Mass.

Preteceille, E. 1975. *Equipements collectifs, structures urbaines, et consommation sociale.* Paris.

Price, R. 1975. *The economic modernization of France.* London.

———. 1983. *The modernization of rural France.* London.

Redclift, N., and E. Mingione, eds. 1985. *Beyond employment: Household, gender, and subsistence.* Oxford.

Reff, T. 1982. *Manet and modern Paris.* Washington. D.C.

Retel, J. O. 1977. *Eléments pour une histoire du peuple de Paris au 19ᵉ siècle.* Paris.

Rex, J., and R. Moore. [1967] 1975. *Race, community, and conflict.* Reprint, 2d ed. London.

Reybaud, L. 1869. Les agitations ouvrières et l'Association Internationale. *Revue des Deux Mondes* 81:871–902.

Rifkin, A. 1979. Cultural movement and the Paris Commune. *Art History* 2:210–22.

Rohault de Fleury, H. 1903–7. *Historique de la basilique du Sacré-Coeur.* 3 vols. Unpublished. Bibliothèque Nationale. Paris.

Rothman, D. 1971. *The discovery of the asylum.* Boston.

Rougerie, J. 1965. *Procès des Communards.* Paris.

———. 1968a. Remarques sur l'histoire des salaires à Paris au dix-neuvième siècle. *Le Mouvement Sociale* 63:71–108.

———. 1968b. Les sections françaises de l'Association Internationale de Travailleurs. *Colloques Internationales du CNRS* (La Première Internationale, l'Institution, l'Implantation, le Rayonnement). Paris.

———. 1971. *Paris libre.* Paris.

Rubin, J. 1980. *Realism and social vision in Courbet and Proudhon.* Princeton.

Said, E. 1979. *Orientalism.* New York.

St. John, B. 1854. *Purple tints of Paris.* New York.

Saunders, P. 1981. *Social theory and the urban question.* New York.

Sennett, R. 1970. *The uses of disorder: Personal identity and city life.* New York.

Sewell, W. H. 1980. *Work and revolution in France*. New York.

Sharp, C. 1981. *The economics of time*. Oxford.

Simmel, G. 1971. The metropolis and mental life. In *On individuality and social forms*, ed. D. Levine. Chicago.

———. [1920] 1978. *The philosophy of money*. Trans. T. Bottomore and D. Frisby. London.

Simon, J. 1861. *L'ouvrière*. Paris.

Stein, G. 1974. *Gertrude Stein's America*. New York.

Stilgoe, J. 1983. *Metropolitan corridor: Railroads and the American scene*. New Haven.

Stone, M. 1975. Housing crisis, mortgage lending and class struggle. *Antipode* 7, no. 2:22–37.

Sutcliffe, A. 1970. *The autumn of central Paris*. London.

Tarbell, I. M. 1904. *The history of the Standard Oil Company*, vol. 1, New York.

Tarr, J. 1973. From city to suburb: The "moral" influence of transportation technology. In *American Urban History*, ed. A. Callow. New York.

Taylor, G. R. 1966. The beginnings of mass transportation in urban America. *Smithsonian Journal of History* 1, no. 2:35–50; no. 3:31–54.

Tchernoff, I. 1906. *Le Parti Républicain*. Paris.

Thomas, A. (n.d.) *Le Second Empire, 1852–1870*. Paris.

Thomas, E. [1963] 1966. *The women incendiaries*. Trans. J. Atkinson and S. Atkinson. New York.

———. 1967. *Rossell (1844–1871)*. Paris.

Thompson, E. P. 1967. Time, work-discipline, and industrial capitalism. *Past and Present* 38:56–97.

———. 1968. *The making of the English working class*. Harmondsworth, Middlesex.

Thrift, N. 1981. Owner's time and own time: The making of a capitalist time consciousness, 1300–1850. In *Space and time in geography*, ed. A. Pred. Lund.

Tilly, L. A., and J. A. Scott. 1978. *Women, work, and family*. New York.

Tryon, R. 1917. *Household manufactures in the United States, 1640–1860*. Chicago.

Tudesq, A-J. 1956. La crise de 1847, vue par les millieux d'affaires parisiens. *Etudes de la société d'histoire de la Révolution de 1848* 19:4–36.

Vance, J. 1966. Housing the worker: The employment linkage as a force in urban structure. *Economic Geography* 42:294–325.

Vanier, H. 1960. *La mode et ses métiers*. Paris.

Vidler, A. 1978. The scenes of the street: Transformations in ideal and reality, 1750–1871. In *On Streets . . .*, ed. S. Anderson. Cambridge, Mass.

Ville de Paris, Conseil Municipal. 1880. *Procès verbaux*.

Walker, R. A. 1976. The suburban solution. Ph.D. diss., Department of Geography and Environmental Engineering, the Johns Hopkins University, Baltimore.

———. 1981. A theory of suburbanization. In *Urbanization and planning in capitalist society*, ed. M. Dear and A. Scott. New York.

Ward, D. 1971. *Cities and immigrants*. New York.

Warner, S. B. 1962. *Streetcar suburbs*. Cambridge, Mass.

Webber, M. 1963. Order in diversity: Community without propinquity. In *Cities and space: The future use of urban land*, ed. L. Wingo. Baltimore.

———. 1964. Culture, territoriality, and the elastic mile. *Papers, Regional Science Association* 11:59–69.

Weber, E. 1976. *Peasants into Frenchmen.* Stanford.

Weisz, G. 1983. *The emergence of modern universities in France.* Princeton.

Williams, R. 1960. Introduction to C. Dickens, *Dombey and son.* Harmondsworth, Middlesex.

———. 1973. *The country and the city.* London.

Williams, R. L. 1965. *The world of Napoleon III, 1851–1870.* New York.

Wirth, L. 1964. *On cities and social life.* Ed. A. J. Reiss, Jr. Chicago.

Wohlfarth, I. 1970. Perte d'auréole and the emergence of the dandy. *MLN* 85:530–71.

Workers' Commission of 1867. 1868. *Commission ouvrière de 1867: Recueil des procès verbaux,* vol. 1. Paris.

Zeldin, T. 1958. *The political system of Napoleon III,* London.

———. 1963. *Emile Ollivier and the liberal empire of Napoleon III.* Oxford.

———. 1973, 1977. *France, 1848–1945.* 2 vols. London.

Zola, E. [1885] 1954a. *Germinal.* Trans. L. Tancock. Harmondsworth, Middlesex.

———. [1871] 1954b. *The kill (La curée).* Trans. A. Texeira de Mattos; intro. Angus Wilson. New York.

———. [1885] 1967. *L'argent.* Pléiade, Paris.

———. [1876] 1970. *L'assommoir.* Trans. L. Tancock. Harmondsworth, Middlesex.

———. [1877] 1980. *The earth.* Trans. D. Parmée. Harmondsworth, Middlesex.

Index of Names

286

Index of Subjects